Postcolonial Language Varieties in the Americas

Koloniale und Postkoloniale Linguistik
Colonial and Postcolonial Linguistics

Edited by Stefan Engelberg, Peter Mühlhäusler,
Doris Stolberg, Thomas Stolz and Ingo H. Warnke

Volume 18

Postcolonial Language Varieties in the Americas

Edited by
Danae Maria Perez and Eeva Sippola

DE GRUYTER

ISBN 978-3-11-112076-8
e-ISBN (PDF) 978-3-11-072397-7
e-ISBN (EPUB) 978-3-11-072403-5

Library of Congress Control Number: 2021935841

Bibliographic information published by the Deutsche Nationalbibliothek
The Deutsche Nationalbibliothek lists this publication in the Deutsche Nationalbibliografie;
detailed bibliographic data are available on the internet at http://dnb.dnb.de.

© 2022 Walter de Gruyter GmbH, Berlin/Boston
This volume is text- and page-identical with the hardback published in 2021.
Printing and binding: CPI books GmbH, Leck

www.degruyter.com

Contents

Preface —— VII

Eeva Sippola and Danae Maria Perez
Colonialism and new language varieties in the Americas: An introduction —— 1

Thomas Stolz, Deborah Arbes and Christel Stolz
Pero – Champion of Hispanization? On the challenges of documenting function word borrowing in Mesoamerican languages —— 17

Maja Robbers
A Mesoamerican perspective on contact-induced change in numeral classification —— 55

Maria Mazzoli
Secondary derivation in the Michif verb: Beyond the traditional Algonquian template —— 81

Danae Maria Perez
Social conditioning for the transmission of adstrate features in contact varieties of Spanish in the Central Andes —— 181

Ana Paulla Braga Mattos
The Afro-Brazilian community Kalunga: Linguistic and sociohistorical perspectives —— 207

Iwan Wyn Rees
Hispanicization in the Welsh settlement of Chubut Province, Argentina. Some current linguistic developments —— 237

Danae Maria Perez and Mirjam Schmalz
Complex patterns of variety perception in the Eastern Caribbean. New insights from St. Kitts —— 269

Britta Schneider
The contested role of colonial language ideologies in multilingual Belize —— 291

Index of Authors —— 317

Index of Languages —— 322

Index of Subjects —— 324

Preface

This volume originates from two linguistic colloquiums held at the University of Bremen in 2016 and 2017. In December 2016, the colloquium *New varieties in the Americas* organized by Danae Perez and Eeva Sippola brought together scholars and students interested in contact processes in the Americas. Half a year later, Carolin Patzelt, Eeva Sippola and Deborah Arbes organized a colloquium on Hispanization, i.e. the reshaping of languages due to their contact with Spanish, in the Americas and beyond. These meetings were celebrated as part of the activities of the research team Postcolonial Language Studies, a field of specialization of the University of Bremen, with the generous support of the university's Linguistic Colloquium series, and the Departments of Linguistics and Romance Linguistics. A selection of the papers of the colloquiums constitute this volume. They showcase the diversity of approaches to tackle fundamental questions regarding the processes triggered by language contact as well as the wide range of outcomes contact has had in postcolonial settings, especially in the Americas. We would like to extend our gratitude to the participants in the colloquiums, the members of the Postcolonial Language Studies team, Carolin Patzelt, and in particular Thomas Stolz, for his encouragement and support throughout the process.

Helsinki and Zurich, November 2020
Eeva Sippola & Danae Maria Perez

Eeva Sippola and Danae Maria Perez
Colonialism and new language varieties in the Americas: An introduction

1 Introduction

Social history and language development are profoundly entangled. Europe's colonial expansion and exploitation of territories and speakers caused a major reconfiguration of linguistic ecologies and had devastating consequences for generations of speakers around the world. In the Americas, both indigenous as well as postcolonial languages today bear witness of massive changes that have been taking place since the colonial era. The present volume centers around postcolonial language varieties on the American continent that attest to these processes. The language varieties presented here emerged due to changing linguistic and sociolinguistic conditions in different settings across the Americas as a result of Europeans bringing their languages into contact with indigenous and other non-indigenous languages, often involving unequal power relations and complex social dynamics. The volume adds to the documentation of the linguistic properties of these varieties in a socio-historically informed framework. It explores the complex dynamics of extra-linguistic factors that brought about the processes of language change in these varieties, and contributes to a better understanding of the determinant factors that lead to the emergence and evolution of such varieties.

The contributions in this volume cover diverse colonial and postcolonial contexts ranging from Argentina, Brazil, Bolivia, and Mexico to Canada and Belize and St. Kitts in the Caribbean, and they discuss the outcomes of language contact between colonial languages of power such as Portuguese, Spanish, English and French with a diverse set of other languages. It offers showcase scenarios of many typologically different varieties, i.e. indigenous languages in contact with colonial languages, mixed languages, creole languages, and new dialects of European languages, whose birth is tightly connected to the colonial

---

Eeva Sippola, University of Helsinki, Department of Languages, Unioninkatu 40, 00014 University of Helsinki, Finland. E-mail: eeva.sippola@helsinki.fi
Danae Maria Perez, Zurich University of Applied Sciences, Department of Applied Linguistics, Theaterstr. 15c, P.O Box, 8401 Winterthur, Switzerland. E-mail: peze@zhaw.ch

era. Many of these are spoken in multilingual and multiethnic settings where marginal or traditional cultures and speech forms are facing endangerment. The studies shed light on the current vitality and status of many underdescribed varieties and the social and linguistic factors that condition varieties in contact. In addition, this diversity of situations is intended to show that studies from different language fields benefit from a joint approach, by highlighting selected key processes and outcomes, as well as by reflecting on the methodological choices in their study.

America's linguistic uniformity in the official settings, due to the prestige and power situation of the colonial languages, and the linguistic diversity of its populations, both indigenous and migrant, make it a fascinating continent to explore the contact processes in a postcolonial framework. Due to its diversity and its history of competing colonial powers, the continent is rarely treated as one unit. However, the contributions of this volume show how similar processes at work are across the continent, and how speakers and linguists alike face related challenges irrespective of the colonial language or the specific area in question (Mufwene 2014b). Despite the typological diversity and distance between them, the varieties presented here show many parallel developments regardless of their lexifier. For example, all the varieties involved are experiencing change due to contact, most prominently on the level of phonology and the lexicon, but also on structural categories and functional domains. Correspondingly, the varieties represent different stages of language vitality due to the contact situation with a colonial language. While some are highly endangered and nearly extinct, others are vital and persist alongside other varieties, and some of them are in fact even supported institutionally.

This volume builds upon a promising line of recent research on historical and linguistic aspects of varieties in colonial and postcolonial contexts (Perez 2019; Weber 2019; Heggarty and Pearce 2011; Stolz et al. 2008a, 2008b; Schmidt-Brücken et al. 2017), including contact languages, such as creoles and mixed languages (e.g. Cardoso et al. 2012; Mazzoli and Sippola in press), and restructured varieties, such as varieties of Spanish, Portuguese, and English spoken by populations of African descent (Ornelas de Avelar and Álvarez López 2015; Sessarego 2015; Seoane and Suárez-Gómez 2016).

Before exploring the issues further, a note on terminologies is in order. Although we are using *variety* as a prominent term in this volume, we understand varieties and languages as ways of speaking, tightly connected to, if not as one with, their speakers, places and histories (see e.g. Lüpke and Storch 2013: 345). In situations of contact and change and the complex power dynamics involved in them, it is important to keep in mind that we are dealing with the representation of postcolonial realities that is of importance to us as linguists. This representation might coincide or not with the interests and concerns of the speakers. The contributions in this volume range from highly structure-oriented comparisons to vantage points of repertoires and ideologies. In our view, this methodologically and conceptually diverse approach is fruitful and a reflection of the multiple ways language is approached in the field of postcolonial linguistics as a whole (Levisen and Sippola 2019: 6).

2 Language and colonialism in the Americas

The complex precolonial history has made America home to a significant variety of languages from different language families with a range of typological differences. However, the disappearance of many languages in the colonial and postcolonial era make the estimations of the exact numbers and distribution of the languages in precolonial times difficult (Muysken and Crevels 2020). The continent has faced differing periods of intense communication between peoples and isolation and fragmentation due to both social and geographical motivations. Contact between speakers of indigenous languages is known, for example, in Mesoamerica (Campbell et al. 1986) or between speakers of a dominant indigenous language and speakers of other indigenous languages of a region, e.g. the Andes (Adelaar and Muysken 2004: 165). From the colonial period onwards, the role and prestige of the European colonial languages has been significant, causing shift of large populations to the dominant languages and situations of language endangerment and death of the autochthonous and other migrant languages (Grinevald 1998; Campbell 2000: 16–17). Actually, America can be seen as the most extreme case of cultural colonization by European cultures due to the extermination of the indigenous peoples and the destruction of their cultures and knowledge systems (as stated about Latin America by Quijano 2007: 170; for Canada, cf. Brody 2001).

America was particularly interesting for the colonial aspirations of European powers as it was comparatively easy to reach, only scarcely inhabited, and of an abundance of natural resources of various sorts. At the time of the Spanish conquest, most of the indigenous population lived in smaller communities, many of them as hunter-gatherers, while also few major and complex empires existed, i.e. the Aztec and the Incan Empires. The conquest and colonization of the continent was relatively fast, as imported diseases and the use of iron weapons quickly decimated the indigenous population (for an overview of the Spanish conquest, see e.g. Eakin 2007; Clements 2021). The spread of European settlers and their languages in America happened within a fairly short period of time, although the scope and permeability of the colonial language and a possible related language shift of an indigenous community has to be contextualized in each setting.

Some American territories changed administration several times until one colonial language was ultimately installed in the era of the American emancipation. The European colonization of the Americas created a specific colonial structure of power that produced and continues to reproduce the framework of social discriminations and inequalities, codified as 'racial', 'ethnic', 'anthropological' or 'national' according to the specific time and context (Quijano 2007), also visible in the languages and linguistic practices and policies. The most prominent languages on the continent today are English in North America, Spanish in Central and Western South America, and Portuguese in Brazil. In the Caribbean, English, Spanish and French have a prominent, regional status. In addition, it is interesting to observe how English has been established and replaced Spanish on the Northern continent, while it has hardly had any impact in South America (Perez 2019). In both settings, however, many new varieties of colonial languages have developed, and today, they represent the largest proportion of native speakers of world languages. Veronelli (2015) connects the monolingual linguistic ideology, seen in the prominent status of and ideologies about the colonial languages, to the colonial power structure and the reduction of the colonized to the status of non-humans without a language and knowledge system worth using and preserving. Although these colonial ideologies are still evident in many linguistic realities across America in the marginalization, endangerment, and oppression of other ways of speaking and knowing, they are also renegotiated and transformed in multiple and sometimes contradicting social discourses and practices (e.g. Schneider, this volume).

After European colonizers and settlers reached the continent and spread, their ways of speaking came in contact with others. In consequence, contact was triggered between different dialects of the same and other colonizer languages, indigenous American languages, as well as languages of forced migration. Intense dialect and language contact then produced a plethora of new contact situations and varieties across the continent. Indigenous languages, for example, have evolved in ecologies profoundly transformed by the colonial expansion, with differing degrees of influence of the colonial languages as well as maintenance of the traditional language or a shift away from it. In addition, forced and voluntary migration has brought about varieties that bare traces of diverse contact scenarios. Languages spoken by African-descendant populations, for instance, include varieties ranging from creoles to new dialectal varieties of the European colonial languages. Their study is of particular relevance to contact linguistics as their evolution from an African, an American, and a European root is unique to the American continent. Their varying degrees of restructuring in comparison to the lexifier pose particular challenges to linguistics as these ways of speaking are rarely considered distinct languages in their own right by linguists and speakers alike, yet they usually diverge typologically from their lexifier. The creole and creolized varieties discussed in this volume add to these debates. Finally, also other European, Asian and Middle-Eastern languages continue be spoken in migrant communities in the Americas as minority and/or heritage languages and often in isolated communities. Their peculiarities, especially in South American contexts, are also explored in this volume. In a nutshell, this diverse and relatively new cultural and linguistic setup of the American continent is fascinating.

3 Language vitality, attitudes and change

The dynamics of language vitality are in constant change and renegotiation. As shown by the chapters in this volume, there are many factors that influence language vitality and the course of a language, but it is clear that many changes can be connected to the changes brought by the colonial power structures. Today, the situation of many varieties is dire. Highly endangered and nearly extinct varieties are suffering the consequences of language shift due to cultural and linguistic pressure of the colonial languages that have been prominent at least since colonization and even more so in the postcolonial era. Their documentation, however, is of pivotal importance as these varieties allow insights into the history of their community as well as into the cognitive and cultural processes that triggered language change. Many contributions in this volume offer case studies of such varieties. Afro-Yungueño Spanish in Bolivia, for instance, is a clear example of a postcolonial variety that is no longer acquired or used by the community due to changes in the social and economic conditions of the speakers (Perez, this volume). The changing vitality of varieties may also reduce the number of functional domains in a language as speakers move away from the traditional communities or significant numbers of speakers of a dominant language move into the community; the latter scenario is the case of Welsh in Patagonia (Rees, this volume). When varieties are relatively close to their lexifiers, such as postcolonial dialects and certain creoles, their vitality may be particularly endangered, because some speakers shift gradually from their variety toward standard-nearer forms of the dominant lexifier or standard as they avoid the most stigmatized forms (Siegel 2010).

With only a couple of hundreds of speakers and its considerable variation of forms and functions, the story of Michif is an excellent case in point of an extraordinary yet highly endangered postcolonial variety whose speech community actively engages in countering language endangerment (Mazzoli, this volume). Similarly, also many Mesoamerican languages studied in this volume are facing endangerment due to growing pressure of the dominant Spanish-speaking society, but some have been and continue to be maintained with relatively little influence of the colonial language, mostly limited to the lexical level (Stolz et al., this volume). One of the key factors here is certainly geographical and socio-economical segregation from Europeans, because rural communities typically show less influence of the colonial language than those more closely connected to the standard language and culture (Mufwene 2014a; for different ways of resistance, see Hidalgo 2006: 120). For example, the social and geographical isolation and marginalization of the Afro-Brazilian community of Kalunga have contributed to the maintenance of more traditional ways of speaking (Mattos, this volume).

However, contact does not always lead to endangerment. Many varieties continue to be spoken alongside other languages, such as Kittitian and Belizean Creole Englishes in the Caribbean. Perez and Schmalz (this volume) show that languages spoken in today's centers of power, such as the US and UK, enjoy a higher prestige among Kittians as positive attitudes are attached to them, even if also the local standard varieties are appreciated. This might have an influence on the local variety's vitality in the long term. In other settings, by contrast, language attitudes and ideologies might also work against the prestige of a colonial language, as is the case of Spanish in Belize, where despite its demographic dominance, attitudes favor Kriol and English (Schneider, this volume).

All these cases fall well in line with what we know about the social predictors for vitality and change. Giles et al. (1977: 308) proposed the first descriptive framework to better understand linguistic vitality that is universally applicable also to the varieties presented here. The factors they fleshed out as determinant of language vitality are 1) demography, i.e. absolute and relative speaker numbers, 2) language institutionalization, i.e. the level of standardization and domains of use, and 3) language status, i.e. the prestige, attitudes, and ideologies attached to a language variety. These factors influence language vitality in different ways, and it is clear that in today's times, the relevance and relative weight of each of these factors has changed. For example, certain creole varieties have become more widespread as their online use has increased in numerically powerful diasporic communities that use their creole online, such as Jamaicans (Mair 2013). The intensity of contact and the degree of bilingualism and cultural pressure increase the contact effects (Thomason and Kaufman 1988: 75–76; for South American indigenous communities, see Sakel 2010). And while most of the varieties described here are demographically in a rather precarious situation, such as Afro-Yungueño Spanish, the degree of institutionalization as well as the status of others is changing and reinforcing their use.

Welsh classes in Patagonia and Michif revitalization efforts in Canada, for example, showcase different ways of language vitality being determined by the speakers themselves by strategically institutionalizing the language. The Welsh language in Patagonia is receiving institutional support from the Welsh Government, though it seems that the classes are reinterpreted as part of Welsh cultural activities in the region, instead of reversing language shift (Birt 2005). Michif is acquiring new speakers through the master-apprentice program, but its future as a community language remains unclear, as intergenerational transmission was interrupted and these efforts may come too late. However, they also highlight the importance of local identities for the resistance to language loss and the possible revitalization of the language. These examples illustrate that language vitality is not a static situation nor a unidirectional process, but rather highly dynamic and determined by relatively predictable linguistic and extralinguistic factors, and speakers often take actions and influence the direction of change themselves.

4 Colonial and postcolonial contact in the Americas

Postcolonial varieties are 'new' in the sense of being historically young. These languages have evolved over the past couple of centuries either out of older varieties that evolved into a new direction or out of the contact between different languages, from which new languages have emerged. As the contributions in this volume show, migration, contact, and the adaptation to new social conditions and extralinguistic environments have been among the most central factors driving language change. Language contact occurs between speakers of different dialects or languages after groups of people migrate from one place to another and start to interact with new groups. In these settings, languages change as soon as their speakers start to interact, and structures of social and political power quickly become reflected in changing linguistic behavior. For example, the vitality of an indigenous language can be affected by the arrival of an exogenous language to the degree of leading to its extinction, or the indigenous language can acquire new speakers and increase in speaker numbers, thus becoming socially powerful (for language endangerment in South America, see Crevels 2012; for Spanish and Portuguese sociohistorical evolution in America, see Mufwene 2014b).

As people move, their languages move with them. Mesthrie (2017) argues that different patterns of migration produce two main types of language varieties depending on the incentive to migrate. Communities in which most speakers migrate voluntarily for reasons of indented work or family ties usually come from a similar linguistic background and quickly build a new network in the new place. Such settler communities usually merge their language varieties and produce new leveled dialects, i.e. koinés. Forced migration entailing slavery, by contrast, usually produces communities that are more heterogeneous and not closely knit; rather, these communities are often based on unequal power structures and include slavery and other forms of exploitation. They usually become highly stratified with limited interaction between the groups, and this linguistic and social heterogeneity of the speakers brings about the emergence of pidgin and creole languages. Larger World Languages are particularly prone to develop a large number of new varieties as they are spoken in a myriad of different settings. The study of this fragmentation of World Languages has proven to be highly insightful; our knowledge, however, is mostly limited to English as the most prolific world language (e.g. Schreier et al. 2010; Williams et al. 2015). Studies on other languages with a global reach are urgently needed to test if insights gained from English can be generalized to other languages, such as Spanish (Perez et al. 2021).

At the same time, also endemic languages experience change due to their contact with the incoming language. This is particularly true when the incoming language is socially or politically powerful and more speakers become competent in it. Contact with speakers of another language can affect the social uses and language structures to varying degrees, from lexical borrowing to language mixing, depending on the social conditions of a specific contact situation and the typological nature of the languages involved (see Sippola 2020a; Sippola 2020b for Spanish). What becomes borrowed is thus conditioned by both language internal and external factors. Situations where borrowing happens continuously and to a prominent degree can lead to more conventionalized mixing at the lexical and structural level, as shown by many case studies in this volume. Lexical items and function words are borrowed, and even subsystems of grammar can be reorganized and restructured due to contact influence (cf. Matras and Sakel 2007).

In some communities, varieties coexist and speakers switch between them in their daily communication. The Belizean population, for example, is highly multilingual, and code-switching as well as language mixing is common. In certain cases, an entire community may be bilingual, and when the two languages are related, as in St. Kitts (Perez and Schmalz, this volume), speakers define their varieties along a continuum of variants that are either closer to, or more distant from, the standard. When speakers switch between two languages, they may even share patterns of code switching and language change (e.g. Spanish and English in the US, Torres Cacoullos and Travis 2018). In communities in which bilingualism and code-mixing persists, mixed languages may emerge, often connected to an expression of identity, reflecting either a new social category or an ancestral group membership, as a deliberate linguistic operation. Their double cultural and linguistic heritage is perpetuated and grammaticalized to the degree of constituting a new language that combines parts from different language families or branches, showing unique splits that challenge theories of genetic classification and contact-induced change (Mazzoli and Sippola in press). An example for such a mixed language is Michif in the US and Canada (Bakker 1997; Mazzoli this volume). These varieties, however, are relatively rare, and many of them face the threat of disappearing as new generations become competent in a more dominant language. Overall, these varieties show that migration and contact does not only change the language that moves to a new location, but also the languages present in the environment before their arrival. It is a reciprocal, though often imbalanced, process.

5 A note on the methodologies

In the present volume, several chapters discuss methodological challenges when dealing with such new varieties that emerged out of colonial-era contacts. These challenges concern the description of structural aspects, functional domains, as well as contact processes. In principle, postcolonial varieties should be studied using the same methods as any other natural language. However, their social history is tightly connected to colonialism and dynamics of unequal power relations. Many of these varieties and their speakers have further suffered a long history of stigmatization and marginalization, which requires special attention to methodological approaches (for an overview of methodological choices in fieldwork with creole speakers, see Sippola 2018).

Many of the present volume's contributions highlight the relevance of ethnographically informed descriptions and the importance of cooperation between the linguist and community members when working with language data in marginalized communities. Complex power relations between the linguistic repertoires present in the community, as well as between the linguist and the speakers involved in data collection, can best be approached by a combination of anthropological and sociolinguistic field methods, as shown by Perez (this volume) for Afro-Yungueño Spanish, and Mattos (this volume) for the Afro-Brazilian community of Kalunga. Mazzoli (this volume), by contrast, integrates her grammatical description and analysis within the Michif revitalization program. The linguistic work done in cooperation with the speakers in this case is also meant to serve as data for pedagogical materials that can be used by Michif learners and heritage speakers. The description thus additionally serves an applied purpose in this case.

With their study of Hispanization, Stolz et al. (this volume) address an old problem in contact studies. How can the outcomes of contact processes be measured? The balance between the material for analysis and the complexity of many localized contact situations is delicate and should be approached with caution, in contrast to large-scale typological and comparative studies that offer tools to explain global patterns. Higher-level abstractions have to be contrasted with detailed studies of text types and context-bound variation in order to better understand processes of change and prestige on the local level. Similarly, the need for including both inter- and intra-speaker variation into explanatory models is acknowledged by Robbers (this volume) in her study on loan integration of numeral classifiers on several Mesoamerican languages and Rees (this volume) on the phonetics and loanword integration of Patagonian Welsh. Furthermore, Perez and Schmalz (this volume) study of Kittian language repertoires and attitudes and Schneider's (this volume) study on language ideologies in Belize make evident that fluid ways of de- and reconstructing language varieties and ideologies open vantage points to multilingual realities, and the possibility of analysis with changing concepts should therefore be reflected on data collection procedures.

It is clear that postcolonial situations are characterized by language contact and asymmetrical power relations. They are reflected in many speech communities and central to methodological concerns, thus providing more support for a sociohistorically-informed approach to the descriptive, structural, and cultural analysis of language. The contributions to this volume are based on fieldwork data that allowed for the collection of authentic data not only for linguistic, but also for ethnographic purposes. This is relevant for an in-depth understanding of processes that shape linguistic and extralinguistic realities on the local level.

6 The chapters in this volume

The present volume presents postcolonial American varieties of different lexifiers of European and American origin that emerged in the course of the past 500 years. They experience change due to the migration of colonizers and settlers to new territories where the arrival of a new language triggered changes in all the varieties involved. The first chapters cover indigenous languages that are undergoing lexical and grammatical change due to the presence of French, Spanish, and English. The following chapters look at settings in which European languages, i.e. English, Portuguese, Spanish, and Welsh, experience the emergence of new dialects and creoles due to contact with either indigenous, African, or other colonial languages.

Stolz, Arbes, and Stolz's chapter addresses the Spanish adversative connector *pero* 'but' that is very frequently borrowed by indigenous languages of Mesoamerica (and beyond). The authors first review the extant literature on the topic of function word borrowing and grammatical Hispanization in indigenous languages before focusing on instances of variation in the documentation of borrowed *pero* 'but' in two parallel corpora of written language data from 46 languages. They also raise methodological issues regarding corpus selection and data collection methods that are in order when addressing the challenge of determining the degree of Hispanization of replica languages adequately.

Robbers' chapter discusses phenomena that result from ongoing contact of classificatory numeral systems of Mesoamerican languages with the non-classifying Spanish numeral system. Robbers tests to what extent indigenous numeral classifier systems are open to contact-induced change and shows that early borrowings in numeral classifier constructions are provided by mensuratives which restructure the system if a different base number underlies. She also shows that in addition to the changes in the numeral system, a great deal of morphology, lexicon, and syntax is affected in the language shift situations studied and ponders on the issue of to what degree numeral systems reflect the overall vitality of the language.

Mazzoli's chapter focuses on Michif, a Plains Cree-French mixed language spoken in Canada, and analyzes the difference between primary and secondary derivation in the Michif verb phrase. She documents the current status of the Michif varieties and their speakers and proposes a verb template for Michif that is independent from the ones created for Plains Cree, since it is based on Michif occurrences only. Based on the analysis of the text of *La pchit Sandrieuz*, reproduced and glossed in the appendices, Mazzoli also lists 20 secondary derivatives in Michif, their semantic functions, and their linguistic behavior.

Perez outlines the complex situation in the Bolivian Andes with the example of Afro-Yungueño Spanish and its adstrates. In this region, Aymara and Quechua used to be dominant until well into the 20th century, and due to prolonged contact and ongoing bilingualism, Spanish has experienced substantial changes, such as the explicit marking of evidentiality. At the same time, also a small African-descendant enclave community exists here, which shows relatively few features from Aymara and Quechua but its own grammatical system that does not correspond to any of the languages spoken in this ecology. On the basis of these observations, Perez argues that the limited interaction of African-Bolivians with the surrounding communities has hindered linguistic contact and the transmission of areal features in Afro-Yungueño Spanish.

Mattos describes non-canonical features in the grammar of Kalunga Portuguese. This community descends from enslaved Africans who had escaped into a remote rural area in Goiás, Brazil, and who have been living in isolation there until today. Their postcolonial variety of Portuguese shows clear traits of contact-induced change, and the data show that Kalunga Portuguese shares many linguistic and sociohistorical features with other Afro-Brazilian varieties, such as the limited use of gender and number agreement. This adds to the picture on Afro-Brazilian Portuguese as well as to the debates on contact-induced language change triggering morphological reduction.

Rees describes Patagonian Welsh, which has been in contact with Spanish to various degrees for over 150 years in the Chubut Province of Argentina. This study constitutes the first attempt to analyze several linguistic features of this isolated variety of Welsh mainly from a contact perspective, and the results establish a number of differences as well as similarities between various speaker types, namely heritage speakers, heritage learners, and L2 learners. Rees also discusses the implications of the data for pedagogical practices in Chubut and for heritage languages in general.

Perez and Schmalz provide insights into the current situation of the small Caribbean island of St. Kitts about whose sociolinguistic situation little is known today. They describe the coexistence of Kittitian English, a relatively standard-near Caribbean variety of English, together with an underanalyzed English-based creole, and how Kittitians themselves define the value and status of these two varieties, as well as of other international varieties of English. The results are based on first-hand data collected during sociolinguistic interviews and attitudinal questionnaires and show that Caribbean varieties have lower prestige than international ones.

Schneider's chapter discusses and deconstructs the idea of languages corresponding to distinct ethnic and national categories as an effect of colonial knowledge production. On the basis of the example of Belize, Schneider analyzes language ideologies as part of postcolonial language activism and shows how they are interwoven with discourses of power and the desire to differentiate from an 'other' in a colonial frame. Schneider also shows the limits of European-based approaches in analyzing complex, multilingual language contact situations.

References

Adelaar, Willem & Pieter Muysken. 2004. *The languages of the Andes*. Cambridge: Cambridge University Press.
Bakker, Peter. 1997. *A language of our own: The genesis of Michif, the mixed Cree-French language of the Canadian Métis*. Oxford: Oxford University Press.
Birt, Paul. 2005. The Welsh language in Chubut Province, Argentina. In Diarmuid Ó Néill (ed.), *Rebuilding the Celtic languages: Reversing language shift in the Celtic countries*, 115–151. Talybont: Y Lolfa.
Brody, Hugh. 2001. *The other side of Eden. Hunters, farmers, and the shaping of the world*. New York: North Point Press.
Campbell, Lyle. 2000. *American Indian languages: The historical linguistics of native America*. Oxford: Oxford University Press.
Campbell, Lyle, Terrence Kaufman & Thomas Smith-Stark. 1986. Meso-America as a linguistic area. *Language* 62(3). 530–570.
Cardoso, Hugo, Alan Baxter & Mario Pinharanda Nunes (eds.). 2012. *Ibero-Asian Creoles. Comparative perspectives*. Amsterdam & Philadelphia: John Benjamins.
Clements, J. Clancy. 2021. Some (unintended) consequences of colonization: The rise of Spanish as a global language. In Danae Perez, Daniel Schreier, Marianne Hundt & Johannes Kabatek (eds.), *English and Spanish: World languages in interaction*. Cambridge: Cambridge University Press.
Crevels, Mily. 2012, Language endangerment in South America: The clock is ticking. In Lyle Campbell & Verónica Grondona (eds.), *The indigenous languages of South America: A comprehensive guide*, 167–233. Berlin & Boston: De Gruyter Mouton.
Eakin, Marshall C. 2007. *The history of Latin America: Collision of hultures*. New York: Palgrave McMillan.
Giles, Howard, Richard Y. Bourhis & Douglas M. Taylor. 1977. Towards a theory of language in ethnic group relations. In Howard Giles (ed.), *Language, ethnicity, and intergroup relations*, 307–348. London: Academic Press.
Grinevald, Colette. 1998. Language endangerment in South America: A programmatic approach. In Leonor Grenoble & Lindsay Whaley (eds.), *Endangered languages: Language loss and community response*, 124–160. Cambridge: Cambridge University Press. doi:10.1017/CBO9781139166959.007.
Heggarty, Paul & Adrian J. Pearce (eds.). 2011. *History and language in the Andes*. New York: Palgrave MacMillan.
Hidalgo, Margarita G. 2006. *Mexican indigenous languages at the dawn of the twenty-first century*. Berlin & New York: De Gruyter.

Levisen, Carsten & Eeva Sippola. 2019. Postcolonial linguistics: The editor's guide to a new interdiscipline. *Journal of Postcolonial Linguistics* 1. 1–15.

Lüpke, Friederike & Anne Storch. 2013. *Repertoires and choices in African languages*. Berlin & Boston: De Gruyter Mouton.

Matras, Yaron & Jeanette Sakel. 2007. *Grammatical borrowing in cross-linguistic perspective*. Berlin & New York: De Gruyter.

Mair, Christian. 2013. The World System of Englishes. Accounting for the transnational importance of mobile and mediated vernaculars. *English World-Wide* 34(3). 253–278.

Mazzoli, Maria & Eeva Sippola (eds.). in press. *New perspectives on mixed languages: From core to fringe*. Berlin & Boston: De Gruyter Mouton.

Mesthrie, Rajend. 2017. Slavery, indentured work, and language. In Suresh Canagarajah (ed.), *The Routledge handbook of migration and language*, 228–242. London: Routledge.

Mufwene, Salikoko S. 2014a. Latin America. A linguistic curiosity from the point of view of colonization and the ensuing language contacts. In Salikoko S. Mufwene (ed.), *Iberian imperialism and language evolution in Latin America*, 1–37. Chicago: The University of Chicago Press.

Mufwene, Salikoko S. (ed.). 2014b. *Iberian imperialism and language evolution in Latin America*. Chicago: The University of Chicago Press.

Muysken, Pieter & Mily Crevels. 2020. Patterns of dispersal and diversification in South America. In Mily Crevels & Pieter Muysken (eds.), *Language dispersal, diversification, and contact*, 253–274. Oxford: Oxford University Press.

Ornelas de Avelar, Juanito & Laura Álvarez López (eds.). 2015. *Dinâmicas Afro-Latinas*. Bern: Peter Lang.

Perez, Danae. 2019. *Language competition and shift in New Australia, Paraguay*. London: Palgrave Macmillan.

Perez, Danae, Marianne Hundt, Johannes Kabatek & Daniel Schreier (eds.). 2021. *English and Spanish. World languages in interaction*. Cambridge: Cambridge University Press.

Quijano, Aníbal. 2007. Coloniality and modernity/rationality. *Cultural Studies* 21(2/3). 168–178.

Sakel, Jeanette. 2010. Grammatical borrowing from Spanish/Portuguese in some native languages of Latin America. *STUF/Language Typology and Universals* 36(1). 65–78.

Schmidt-Brücken, Daniel, Susanne Schuster & Marina Wienberg (eds.). 2017. *Aspects of (Post)Colonial Linguistics. Current perspectives and new approaches*. Berlin & Boston: De Gruyter Mouton.

Schreier, Daniel, Peter Trudgill, Edgar W. Schneider & Jeffrey P. Williams (eds.). 2010. *The lesser-known varieties of English. An introduction*. Cambridge: Cambridge University Press.

Seoane, Elena & Cristina Suárez-Gómez. 2016. *World Englishes. New theoretical and methodological considerations*. Amsterdam & Philadelphia: John Benjamins.

Sessarego, Sandro. 2015. *Afro-Peruvian Spanish: Spanish slavery and the legacy of Spanish Creoles*. Amsterdam & Philadelphia: John Benjamins.

Siegel, Jason. 2010. Decreolization. A critical review. In J. Clancy Clements, Megan E. Solon, Jason F. Siegel & B. Devan Steiner (eds.), *Decreolization: A critical review*, 83–98. Bloomington, IN: IULC Publications.

Sippola, Eeva. 2018. Collecting and analysing creole data. In Wendy Ayres-Bennett & Janice Carruthers (eds.), *Manual of Romance sociolinguistics*, 91–113. Berlin & Boston: De Gruyter Mouton.

Sippola, Eeva. 2020a. Multilingualism and the structure of code-mixing. In Miriam Meyerhoff & Umberto Ansaldo (eds.), *The Routledge handbook of Pidgins and Creoles*. London: Routledge.

Sippola, Eeva. 2020b. Contact and Spanish in the Pacific. In Raymond Hickey (ed.), *The handbook of language contact*. London: Wiley.

Stolz, Thomas, Dik Bakker & Rosa Salas Palomo (eds.). 2008a. *Aspects of language contact. New theoretical, methodological and empirical findings with special focus on Romancisation processes*. Berlin & New York: De Gruyter.

Stolz, Thomas, Dik Bakker & Rosa Salas Palomo (eds.). 2008b. *Hispanisation. The impact of Spanish on the lexicon and grammar of the indigenous languages of Austronesia and the Americas*. Berlin & New York: De Gruyter.

Thomason, Sarah G. & Terrence Kaufman. 1988. *Language contact, creolization, and genetic linguistics*. Berkeley: University of California Press.

Torres Cacoullos, Rena & Catherine Travis. 2018. *Bilingualism in the community. Code-switching and grammar in contact*. Cambridge: Cambridge University Press.

Veronelli, Gabriela A. 2016. Sobre la colonialidad del lenguaje. *Universitas Humanística* 81. 33–58. http://dx.doi.org/10.11144/Javeriana.uh81.scdl.

Weber, Birgitte. 2019. *The linguistic heritage of colonial practice*. Berlin & Boston: De Gruyter Mouton.

Williams, Jeffrey, Edgar Schneider, Peter Trudgill & Daniel Schreier (eds.). 2015. *Further studies in the lesser-known varieties of English*. Cambridge: Cambridge University Press.

Thomas Stolz, Deborah Arbes and Christel Stolz
Pero – Champion of Hispanization?
On the challenges of documenting function word borrowing in Mesoamerican languages

Abstract: The paper addresses the particularly frequent case of the Spanish adversative connector *pero* 'but' being borrowed by indigenous languages of Mesoamerica (and beyond). After reviewing the extant literature on the topic of function word borrowing and grammatical Hispanization, the authors focus on instances of variation in the documentation of borrowed *pero* in two (written) parallel corpora. Data from 46 languages are discussed. Furthermore, methodological issues are raised in order to address the challenge of determining the degree of Hispanization of replica languages adequately.

Keywords: borrowing, function words, variation, documentation, Mesoamerica

1 Introduction

This study raises the issue of what it means when we say that languages X and Y have borrowed the same element from language Z. Does our knowledge of the parallel borrowing imply that we can predict how the borrowed item behaves in one of the replica languages if we have an idea of how it behaves in the other? Is the behavior of the borrowed item predictable on the basis of what we know about the grammar and lexicon of the donor language? We attempt to show that these are very interesting but difficult-to-answer questions by way of discussing (mainly) Mesoamerican evidence of linguistic Hispanization in the domain of function word borrowing with special focus on the success of *pero* 'but'. Since our database consists exclusively of written material which has gone through the process of editing, we stipulate that the instances of *pero* in these texts fall

---

Thomas Stolz, University of Bremen, FB 10: Linguistics/Language Sciences, Universitäts-Boulevard 13, 28359 Bremen, Germany. E-Mail: stolz@uni-bremen.de
Deborah Arbes, University of Bremen, FB 10: Linguistics/Language Sciences, Universitäts-Boulevard 13, 28359 Bremen, Germany. E-Mail: d.arbes@uni-bremen.de
Christel Stolz, University of Bremen, FB 10: Linguistics/Language Sciences, Universitäts-Boulevard 13, 28359 Bremen, Germany. E-Mail: cstolz@uni-bremen.de

https://doi.org/10.1515/9783110723977-003

under the rubric of borrowings because code-switches would most probably have been eliminated from the documentation (Brody 1998: 71–73).

Our inspiration stems from prior work of Zimmermann's (1987) on grammatical Hispanisms in Otomí. The foundations of our project have been laid in Stolz and Stolz (1996). It is situated within the wider framework of the research program which investigates cases of Romancization processes world-wide (Stolz 2008). Methodologically we are indebted to the approach sketched in Bakker et al. (2008: 167–181). This means that, for the purposes of this study, we make use of very simple ("explorative") quantitative methods, i.e. we exclusively determine absolute frequencies.

Data from 46 languages are discussed in this paper. If a given language is represented by several varieties, these varieties are identified but subsumed under the umbrella of one language. More generally, this study also contributes to the comparative study of language contact phenomena. To identify language-independent patterns which allow for generalizations about the behavior of languages in language contact situations, the comparative approach promises the best results. However, if we want to determine the extent to which replica languages have undergone Hispanization, for instance, it is hardly sufficient to confirm or disconfirm that, according to our database, function words like *pero* are attested at least once in a given language. The parallel attestation of *pero* in several replica languages does not tell us much about how similar they are in terms of their grammatical Hispanization.

We expose our ideas in three steps. Section 2 is dedicated to the exposition of the general backdrop against which this study has been conducted. In Section 3 we zoom in on the situation in Mesoamerica. In this part of the paper we check the occurrence of *pero* in and its absence from the documentation of indigenous Mesoamerican languages within the series *Archivo de lenguas indígenas de México* (= ALIM). We then look beyond Mesoamerica in Section 4 which focuses on the employment of *pero* in translations of *Le Petit Prince* (= LPP) in indigenous languages of the Philippines, South America, and Mesoamerica. The conclusions are drawn in Section 5. The sample composition is spelled out in Appendix I. Those sentences of the ALIM-questionnaire which involve the connector *pero* both in the Spanish and the Mesoamerican Indian versions are presented in Appendix II unless a sentence has been previously employed for the purpose of illustrating a given phenomenon already in the main body of the text.

2 The big picture

From the point of view of Romance donor languages, it is surprising to see that the *Loanword typology meaning list* (Haspelmath and Tadmor 2009: 22–34) does not include an entry for BUT whereas there are entries for AND, OR, BECAUSE, and IF.[1] The absence of BUT is striking because adversative connectors are known to rank very high on the extant borrowability hierarchies (e.g. Muysken 1981; Matras 1998; Sakel 2007). Functional equivalents of the English conjunction *but* are reported as borrowings in numerous language contact situations independent of the genetic affiliation of the donor language and the replica language (Matras 2007: 54–55). Romance BUT has made it into the grammatical systems of a wide variety of languages. In (1)–(2), we present two examples which illustrate the borrowing of French *mais* and Italian *però* into Luxembourgish as *mä* 'but' and Maltese as *però* 'but', respectively.[2]

(1) Luxembourgish [LPP Luxembourgish, 48][3]
 Mä ech sinn e seriöse Mënsch.
 but 1SG be.1SG ART.INDEF serious human_being
 '**But** I am a serious person.'

(2) Maltese [Aquilina 1990: 1050][4]
 Però ma sibtux marid
 but NEG find:1SG.PERF:O.3SG.M:NEG ill
 '**However**, I did not find him ill [...]'

In the wider framework of Romancization studies, MAT-borrowing, i.e. the borrowing of phonologically expressed matter (Sakel 2007) of an expression of BUT into replica languages is a commonality – and it is especially frequent in lan-

---

1 Small caps are used for language-independent concepts.
2 In the sentential examples, the adversative connectors are printed in bold (including the morpheme gloss and the translation). In case further elements of a given example are of interest for the ensuing discussion, those are marked by single underlining. Except otherwise stated, the English translations are ours. We respect the graphic representation of the object languages as given in the sources from which we draw the examples. Wherever our sources provide morpheme glosses we tried to preserve them. We do not claim that all inconsistencies have been eliminated. Especially with the older sources, it has proved extremely difficult to determine the internal morphological structure of the syntacic words. For reasons of space, we do not indicate specifically which part of a given morpheme gloss is original and which is ours.
3 Morpheme glosses added.
4 Morpheme glosses added. We have dropped the second half of the sentence since the first half is already a fully grammatical sentence on its own.

guage contact situations with Spanish as donor language as shown for cases of Russian and Arabic language contats (Stolz accepted).

Spanish *pero* belongs to a small set of function words (*antes* 'before', *porque* 'because', *para* 'for', etc.) from which literally dozens of replica languages have taken their pick (Sakel 2010: 70–71). There is ample evidence of borrowed *pero* in indigenous languages of the Philippines, South America, and Mesoamerica so that this conjunction can be considered to be the prime candidate for function word borrowing in processes of Hispanization (Stolz 1996: 152). In 33 of his 41 (~ 80 %) sample languages from the above-mentioned geographical regions, borrowed *pero* is attested. As to borrowability, no other function word can compete with *pero* (Stolz 1996: 148–149). For languages as genetically, structurally, and areally different as Guaraní (3), Quechua (4), Yucatec (5), Otomí (S) (6), Cebuano (7), and Rapanui (8) the presence of *pero* has been reported.

(3) (Paraguayan) Guaraní [Gómez Rendón 2008: 365][5]
  oĩ heta aranduka castellano-pe jai-poru ara **pero**
  3.be many book Spanish-LOC 1PL-use need **but**
  mba'éicha jai-porú-ta la aranduka castellano-pe?
  how 1PL-use-FUT PRO.DEM book Spanish-LOC
  '[...] there are many books in Spanish that we need to use, **but** how are we going to use the books in Spanish?'

(4) (Bolivian) Quechua [Muysken 2001: 64][6]
  ka-chun aycha-qa **pero** mana ranti-nki-chu
  be-EXH meat-TOP **but** NEG buy-2SG-NEG
  'There may be meat **but** you do not buy it'

(5) Yucatec [Pool Balam and Le Guen 2015: 361]
  le ka' ok-s-a'ab-en-o' **pero** le k'i'ik' ten-o' po
  DET CONJ enter-CAUS-PAS-B1-DT **but** DET blood 1SG-DT then
  hach tun-chooh ts'o'ok tun ts'-u-p'áat-a
  very PRG.A3-drip TERM CONJ TERM-A3-remain-PAS
  pero sak-pil-e'en-en
  but white-clear-INT-B1
  'However, when they made me enter [the car] my blood was dripping and in the end I stopped bleeding **but** I remained pale!'

---

[5] Original English translation whose initial part we have omitted because it lacks a correlate in the Guaraní version.
[6] Original English translation.

(6) Otomí (S) [Hekking 1995: 174]
Nugi hindi he ya 'bitu nu'u̱ hewa
1SG NEG:PRS.1SG dress ART.PL clothes DEM:LOC.DIS.3 dress:LOC.PROX
jar hnini, **pero** *num meni hä he*
LOC.ART village **but** DEM.POSS.1 relative AFF dress
'I do not wear the clothes they use here in the village **but** my relatives do wear them'

(7) Cebuano [Steinkrüger 2008: 212]
gústo ko nímo, **pero** *póbre man ka*
like 1SG 2SG.O **but** poor PART 2SG
'I like you, **but** you are poor'

(8) Rapanui [Pagel 2010: 247]
he ngaro'a, **pero** *me'e ra'e era eko ngaro'a*
ACT listen **but** thing first DEM NEG listen
'They (will) listen (eventually) **but** at first they do not listen'

There can be no doubt that *pero* displays a particularly wide distribution across the languages of the former Spanish colonial empire and the officially Hispanophone independent successor states in the Americas and Austronesia. Its remarkably wide distribution notwithstanding, *pero* has not yet been the subject of a dedicated in-depth study in the domain of language contact research. This paper is meant to show that from a linguistic perspective it makes sense to closely look at borrowed *pero* in as many replica languages as possible.

The presence of *pero* among the function words of Mesoamerican languages has been signaled time and again as e.g. in Bright and Thiel (1965) for Nahuatl, Fernández de Miranda (1965) for Zapotec, Brody (1995: 137) for Tojolab'al, Verbeeck (1998: 144) for Mopan, Stolz (1998: 169–170) for Yucatec, Chamoreau (2007: 470–471) for Purépecha, etc. References to *pero* are also recurrent in those studies which adopt a comparative or contrastive perspective such as e.g. Suárez (1983: 136) for ten genetically diverse Mesoamerican languages, Brody (1987) on function word borrowing in twenty Mayan languages, Hekking and Muysken (1995) on grammatical Hispanization of Quechua and Otomí, Gómez Rendón (2008) on the Spanish grammatical impact on Quechua, Otomí, and Guaraní as well as Stolz (1996) and Stolz and Stolz (1996, 1997) who gather evidence of function-word borrowing from several dozens of indigenous languages including those of Austronesia. To determine the degree of Hispanization we need to describe in full the functional domain and text frequency of *pero* for each of the replica languages. How this goal can be reached and what pitfalls are to be expected is discussed in the subsequent Sections 3–4.

3 Creating a common ground for comparing Mesoamerican languages

3.1 Just like Spanish but not entirely

Hill and Hill (1986: 179–180) discuss the use of *pero* in Mexicano. They conclude that "[a]ll of these functions of *pero* are shared with local Spanish" (Hill and Hill 1986: 180). Similarly, Flores Farfán (1999: 135) observes that "[d]e los nexos españoles *pero* y *para* son los que más han llegado a integrarse al repertorio náhuatl."[7] These and equivalent statements might give rise – unintentionally – to the idea that borrowed *pero* in the replica languages behaves always the same as in the donor language so that it is unnecessary to describe the grammar of *pero* for each language individually. This impression can be shown to be too simplistic.

First of all, the Spanish adversative connector *pero* can take a strikingly different phonological shape in the replica language so that

> it is difficult to determine if it is an indigenous marker of that phonological form, or whether it is a consistently reduced form of the Spanish word[...] **pero** []. (Brody 1998: 72, original boldface)

Another case in point is Cora *haru* 'but' (< Spanish *pero*) as in (9).

(9) Cora [Casad 1985: 386]
haru kúmu rá-mwa'aree tikín pu-'urí vástakìra'i
but since DISTR.SG-know QUOT S-now old_man
'**But** it was because he knew that he was already an old man'

The sound changes which affect the borrowed function word do not only make it difficult sometimes to identify it as a grammatical Hispanism, but they are also suggestive of a relatively high degree of (in this case phonological) nativization which, in turn, may mean that cases like Cora *haru* are largely dissociated from the grammar of *pero* in (Mexican) Spanish. As Brody (1998: 73) states

> [i]t should not be assumed that the Spanish discourse markers borrowed into Mayan languages retain their precise Spanish meaning through the course of borrowing.

---

7 Our translation [among the Spanish connectors, *pero* and *para* are those which have been integrated the most into the Nahuatl system].

This caveat is not limited to the case of Hispanisms in Mayan languages.

Differences between the rules of the donor language and the replica language come to the fore also in the domain of grammar. In her description of Mazatec, Jamieson (1988: 158, original boldface and italics) states that

> [l]as conjunciones **o** y **peru** del mazateco son préstamos del español [...]. Generalmente, funcionan de la misma manera en las dos lenguas. Pero cuando una oración mazateca comienza con **handasa** *aunque*, la segunda parte comienza con **peru** *pero*.

This means that the morphosyntactic behavior of Mazatec *peru* cannot be predicted to a 100 % on the basis of our knowledge of the morphosyntactic behavior of Spanish *pero*. Mazatec *peru* is used systematically in a context from which Spanish *pero* is barred as shown in (10).[8]

(10) Mazatec [Jamieson 1988: 158]
Handasa   *mijí*   *ná*   **peru**   *cjué*
although   NEG:want.3SG   O.1SG   **but**   go.1SG
'Although I do not want to go, I go **nevertheless**'
(Spanish *Voy aunque no quiero*)

Like in the Mazatec case, there is an affinity to concessive constructions also with *pɛ* in Otomí de la Sierra (Voigtlander and Echegoyen 1985: 318). Not only has the function word undergone phonetic reduction via the loss of the final syllable but it also displays properties which are alien to its Spanish etymon. Among other things and like several other connectors it frequently combines with *gue* (< Spanish *que* [Voigtlander and Echegoyen 1985: 312] to yield *pɛgue* without any discernible change in meaning as can be seen in (11)).[9]

(11) Otomí de la Sierra [Voigtlander and Echegoyen 1985: 317]
Pɛ-gue   *hin*   *dadí*   *ungä*   *ma*   *t'ʉhni*
but-that   NEG   PRS:1SG   give:1SG   POR.1SG   son
'**But** I do not give [anything] to my son [...]'

Spanish *pero* and Mazatec *peru*, thus, display different distributive characteristics which may also be responsible for differences in the text frequency of the

---

8 The RAE (2009: 2459) mentions that formerly *aunque* 'although' also had adversative meanings like *pero* but the combinability of both conjunctions in a concessive construction is admissible only clause-initially (RAE 2009: 3603) whereas the distribution of *aunque* and *pero* over protasis and apodosis as in Mazatec is counted out for Spanish.

9 What comes superficially close to the Otomí case in Spanish is the combination *pero (que) muy [+ adjective]* with emphasizing function (RAE 2009: 2458). However, we do not consider this Spanish construction to be at the origin of Otomí *pɛgue*.

two function words. García (1995) argues that, (not only) in language contact situations, relative frequency of use can be understood as an indicator of ethnopragmatic diversity (cf. also Hill and Hill 1986: 222–232). Hill and Hill (1986: 183) also report cases of speakers of Mexicano who make use of borrowed function words "in ways that are unclear" simply to give their "speech a more 'Hispanic' flavor". This social prestige-based motivation can also have an impact on the frequency statistics. We claim that differences in the frequency of use of borrowed function words such as *pero* might also serve as a measurement for the degree of (grammatical) Hispanization of different replica languages.

3.2 Exploiting the ALIM-questionnaire

To guarantee comparability of the empirical findings, it is helpful to collect data which have originated under very similar (ideally even identical) circumstances. In this sense, the ALIM-series provides an excellent point of departure because it constitutes a database for 32 languages of Mexico and Guatemala for which one and the same questionnaire has been employed. The syntax part of the questionnaire comprises 594 subsections many of which consist of a single Spanish sentential stimulus and its morpheme-glossed rendering in a given Mesoamerican language. There are altogether seven Spanish sentences which involve the adversative connector *pero* in all of the 32 volumes of the ALIM-series. These sentences are given and translated in (12). In addition, we also provide the number under which the sentence is registered in the ALIM-questionnaire.

(12) Spanish – sentences from the ALIM-questionnaire

#272 *Sé   escribir   **pero** no   puedo   porque*
       know.1SG write:INF   **but**   NEG   can:1SG   because
       no   tengo   lápiz.
       NEG   have:1SG   pencil
       'I know how to write, **but** I cannot do it because I have no pencil.'

#273 *Quiero   subirme   a   ese   árbol   **pero** no   puedo.*
       want:1SG climb:INF:REFL.1SG   on   this tree   **but**   NEG   can:1SG
       'I want to climb this tree **but** I cannot [do it].'

#274 *Puedo   subirme   a   ese   árbol   **pero** no   quiero.*
       can:1SG climb:INF:REFL.1SG   on   this tree   **but**   NEG   want:1SG
       'I can climb this tree **but** I do not want to [do it].'

#312 *Estaba   por   ir   al   mercado*
     be:IMPF:1SG for   go.INF to:ART   market
     ***pero* *me*   *quedé*   *en*   *casa.*[10]
     but   REFL.1SG   remain:1SG.PRET in   house
     'I was about to go to the market-place, **but** I stayed at home.'

#368 *Este   niño   ahora   es   malo   **pero** se*
     this   child   now   be.3SG   bad   **but**   REFL.3SG
     va   a   hacer   bueno.[11]
     go.3SG to   make:INF good
     'This child is naughty/bad now, **but** s/he will become good.'

#576 *Juan   va   a   sembrar   chile, **pero** yo   no.*
     Juan   go.3SG to   sow:INF   chili   **but**   I   NEG
     'Juan is going to sow chili **but** I am not.'

#577 *Juan   no   va   a   sembrar, **pero** yo   sí.*
     Juan   NEG   go.3SG to   sow:INF   **but**   I   yes
     'Juan is not going to sow **but** I will.'

If we assume for the sake of the argument that borrowed *pero* behaves like Spanish *pero*, one expects to find that *pero* pops up in each and every translation of these stimuli in the sample languages. For a variety of reasons, Brody (1998: 71–73) is sceptical however as to the possibility of finding evidence of discourse markers in elicited sentences, in the first place. We are thus confronted with an implicit alternative hypothesis according to which the turnout for *pero* in the ALIM-questionnaire should equal nil. However, neither of the expectations is met by the empirical data.

Table 1 is the synopsis of the occurrences of *pero* and its indigenous functional equivalents in the responses to the above seven Spanish sentences in the ALIM-volumes. Attested *pero* (or a phonologically modified version thereof) is highlighted in bold. The cells which host an instance of *pero* are additionally shaded grey. The symbol Ø is indicative of the absence of any dedicated marker of the adversative relation. The languages are ordered top-down according to the decreasing number of attestations of *pero*. Table 1 is divided in two. In the upper part, those languages are listed in which *pero* is attested at least once, whereas the lower part of the table is reserved for the languages which lack evidence of *pero* in the seven sentences under scrutiny. Upper case numbers indicate tone.

---

[10] In some versions of the questionnaire, the noun *mercado* 'market-place' has been replaced with *tienda* 'shop'.
[11] Some native-speaker respondents have interpreted Spanish *malo* 'bad' as meaning 'ill'.

Table 1: *pero* and its equivalents in seven sentences of the ALIM-questionnaire

Language	#272	#273	#274	#312	#368	#576	#577	Sum
Mazatec	pe⁴ro⁴	pe⁴ro⁴	pe⁴ro⁴	pe⁴ro⁴	pe⁴ro⁴	pe⁴ro⁴	pe⁴ro⁴	7
Mexicanero	pero	pero	pero	pero	pero	pero	pero	7
Popoluca	pero	pe	pe	pe	pero	pe	pe	7
Zoque	pero	pero	pero	pero	pero	pero	pero	7
Chuj	pero ~ palta	pero ~ palta	pero ~ palta	pero	pero	Ø	pero	6
Otomí	Ø	pe	pe	pe	pe	pe	pe	6
Pima Bajo	pero	Ø	pero	pero	pero	per	pero	6
Purépecha	'peru	'pero	'pero	'pero	'peru	'ka	'peru	6
Totonac (P)	pero	pero	pero	pero	pero	pero	Ø	6
Zapotec	peru	peru	peru	peru	peru	Ø	peru	6
Chontal	pero	pero	le'a	pero	Ø	pero	pero	5
Huave	pere	pere	pere	pere	pero	mbič	mbič	5
Mazahua	pe	pe	pe	pero	pe	ñe	ñe	5
Nahuatl (A)	pero	pero	pero	pero	pero	wan	Ø	5
Matlatzinca	xamu	xamu	Ø	pero	pero	Ø	Ø	2
Acatec	tol	tol	tol	b'el	pero	xal	xal	1
Huichol	xeikɨa	xeikɨa	xeikɨa	mɨ	peru	Ø	Ø	1
Tlapanec	Ø	Ø	Ø	Ø	pe²ro³	Ø	Ø	1
Yucatec	chen ba'le'	chen ba'le'	chen ba'le'	chen ba'le'	chen ba'le'	péeroh	Ø	1
Chatino	lo'o²³	lo'o²³	lo'o²³	lo'o²³	lo'o²³	lo'o²	lo'o²	0
Chinantec	hó⁻⁴	hó⁻⁴	hó⁻⁴	hó⁻⁴	hó⁻⁴	hó⁻⁴	hó⁻⁴	0
Chocho	Ø	Ø	Ø	Ø	Ø	Ø	Ø	0
Guarijío	nahpé	naa	naa	nahpé	Ø	Ø	Ø	0
Kiliwa	Ø	Ø	Ø	Ø	Ø	Ø	Ø	0
Mayo	te	te	te	te	te	te	te	0
Mixe	Ø	Ø	Ø	Ø	Ø	myatoy	Ø	0
Mixtec	diko	diko	diko	Ø	diko	diko	diko	0
Seri	χo	χo	χo	χo	χo	χo	χo	0
Tepehua	x'amán'	x'amán'	x'amán'	x'amán'	x'amán'	x'amán'	x'amán'	0
Totonac (M)	naa	naa	naa	naa	naa	naa	naa	0
Trique	ɛah⁴	ɛah⁴	ɛah⁴	ɛah⁴	ɛah⁴	ɛah⁴	ɛah⁴	0
Yaqui	bweta	bweta	bweta	bweta	bweta	bweta	bweta	0
Total	13	13	13	15	17	9	10	90

Of the 32 languages surveyed in Table 1, 19 (~ 60 %) give evidence of the use of *pero*, whereas 13 (~ 40 %) do not employ *pero* in the sample sentences. The maximum number of languages which use *pero* in a given sentence is 17. Only four languages make use of *pero* in all of the seven sample sentences. The number of sentences which involve *pero* ranges from maximally seven to a single occurrence. There is thus a wide margin for variation. For each of the sentences, there are at least nine languages which employ *pero* in their renderings of the Spanish stimulus. If the frequency of *pero* were the only indicator of Hispanization, we could dare to claim that
– languages without evidence of borrowed *pero* are exempt from Hispanization,
– Mazatec, Mexicanero, Popoluca, and Zoque display the highest degree of Hispanization whereas
– Acatec, Huichol, Tlapanec, and Yucatec are the least Hispanized of those languages which give evidence of *pero*
– the space in-between the highest and the lowest rate of Hispanization is occupied by three groups of languages, namely in decreasing order (a) Chuj, Otomí, Pima Bajo, Purépecha, Totonac (P), and Zapotec, (b) Chontal, Huave, Mazahua, and Nahuatl (A), and (c) Matlatzinca, with a noticeable gap separating (b) and (c).

As will become clear below, the situation is more intricate and requires a more sophisticated approach to be adequately captured.

According to Table 1, the vast majority of the Mesoamerican languages (29 of 32 = 90 %) do not (fully) conform to the Spanish patterns as to the employment of *pero*. Either the function word is absent from the sample sentences or it is used only in a subset thereof. Of the (32 x 7 =) 224 cases covered by Table 1, only 89 (= 40 %) involve *pero*, i.e. it is a minority option albeit a relatively frequent one. These quantitative facts cast doubt on two assumptions which we have tacitly taken for granted, namely that
(a) *pero* is (almost) ubiquitous in Mesoamerica and
(b) its distribution over sentences is more or less the same as in Spanish.

For obvious reasons we cannot dwell on those languages which lack any evidence of *pero* according to Table 1. The investigation of the structures these languages have on offer has to be relegated to a follow-up study. In the context of this paper however, it suffices to take note of the following.[12] Of the 13 lan-

---

12 For Yaqui, for instance, Estrada Fernández and Guerrero (2007: 430) mention *pero* only as part of extended chunks of Spanish text in Yaqui–Spanish code-switching.

guages which do not employ *pero* at all in the above sentences, only three give evidence of variation, i.e. in Guarijío, Mixe (cf. below), and Mixtec several strategies are used to represent the adversative relation. Thus, in these cases, there is no one-to-one correspondence of Spanish *pero* and a given strategy of the replica languages. Furthermore, the three languages have in common that one of the strategies they apply is that of asyndetic yuxtaposition which means that there is no phonologically realized equivalent of Spanish *pero*. For Chocho and Kiliwa, the sample sentences exclusively trigger the zero-strategy. In the remaining eight languages, we find indigenous free morphemes which function as connectors. With reference to these eight languages, what strikes the eye is the consistency with which one and the same strategy is made use of every time a Spanish stimulus of those in (12) has to be translated. Since 18 of the above-mentioned Mesoamerican languages attest to variation as to the expression of the adversative relation, it cannot be ruled out that (except the zero-cases) those languages which have the same filler for each of the cells in Table 1 are cases of covert Hispanization in the sense that the indigenous connectors share their functional domain with that of Spanish *pero*. Covert Hispanization is however beyond the scope of this paper.

Two implications can be deduced on the basis of the patterns in Table 1. These implications can be understood as means to predict the behavior of replica languages on the basis of the knowledge about other replica languages.

– First of all, if *pero* is attested in one of the sentences #272, #273, #274, #312 or #577, it is always also attested in at least another of the sample sentences.
– More specifically, *pero* is involved in the replica language's version of #312 if it is also attested in one of the sentences #272, #273, #274 or #577.

Since the stimuli in (12) form small sub-sets of semantically and/or syntactically similar sentences, these implications do not come as a surprise. In the case of the triplet #272, #273, #274 we are dealing with an adversative negated modal predicate. For #312 and #368 a full-blown verbal predicate plays a role in the adversative clause, whereas the pair of sentences represented by #576 and #577 involves an adversative predicative pronoun. For each of the three sub-sets, Table 1 gives evidence of variation. We illustrate the variation with data from two languages for each of the three sub-sets of sample sentences. In each pair of languages, one is representative of the zero-strategy whereas the other provides an example of the use of an indigenous connector. The absence of the connector is marked by the symbol Ø (in the position that we consider most suitable for *pero*), and the indigenous connector is underlined. For the English translations, the reader is referred to (12) above.

(13) Variation with #272, #273, #274
    a. Pima Bajo   [Estrada Fernández 1998: 91][13]

#272   aan   maat   o'os,   **pero** an im apod,
        1SG   know:IMPF write   **but**   1SG NEG be_able:IRR
        ani im   nukad   laapis
        1SG NEG have:IMPF pencil

#273   uus am tisadia   taadam,   Ø   an im   apod
        tree LOC climb:PROB wish:CONT Ø   1SG NEG be_able:IRR

#274   uus am tisadia   taadam, **pero** an im higa
        tree LOC climb:PROB wish:CONT **but** 1SG NEG want:IRR

    b. Chontal   [Waterhouse 1980: 114]

#272   ayšina'   kiniłma   **pero** aymi'iya   porke
        1SG:know 1SG:write **but** NEG:possible because
        aykai'weka'   kaylapiz
        1SG:NEG:have   POR.1SG:pencil

#273   ła   aypik'a   kaf'ahla'   el   'ek   **pero**
        frustration POR.1SG:pleasure 1SG:climb.IRR ART trunk **but**
        aymi'i
        NEG:possible

#274   ti'i   kaf'aki ła   el   'ek   ma   *le'a*   aykakwa
        possible 1SG:climb DEM ART trunk already *only* 1SG:NEG:say:want

(14) Variation with #312, #368
    a. Tlapanec   [Suárez 1988: 103, 109]

#312   e³no³   ma'³ga¹   šwa:¹   Ø
        already_only go.1SG market_place:LOC Ø
        ni³gwa³nu¹   go'²o'¹²
        remain.1SG   house:POR.1SG

#368   a²da³ci¹ge'³   ška³we'³   a³kwĩ:³   pe²ro³
        childDEM   bad   feeling:POR.3 **but**
        ma'³ne²   ma¹hã¹   a³kwĩ:³
        make:3SG good   feeling

    b. Huichol   [Gómez 1999: 139, 145]

#312   mɨ-r-a-tui-ya   ne-pɨ-ye-mie-xime-kai
        ASS-GNR-LOC-sell-PAS 1SG.S-ASS-LOC-go-IMM-IMPF

---

13 In the Pima Bajo version of #274 the modal verb of the initial clause does not correspond to that of the Spanish stimulus which is probably an error of the cut-and-paste kind. As it is now, the Pima Bajo translation sounds awkward semantically.

	mɨ	*ne-ti-i-ku-nua*					
	but	1SG.S-GNR-VIS-LOC-arrive					
#368	*'ikɨ*	*nunuei*	*'axa*	*pɨ-ti-u-ka-'iyari*			
	DEM	child	bad	ASS-INT-VIS-LOC-heart			
	peru	*'aixɨ*	*ti-u-ka-'iyari-tɨ*		*p-a-ya-ni*		
	but	well	INT-VIS-LOC-heart-S		ASS-CISLOC-go-FUT		

(15) Variation with #576, #577

    a. Chuj   [Buenrostro 2009: 230]

#576	*ol-Ø-b'at*	*winhaj*	*Xun*	*aw-oj*	*ich*	*Ø*	*a*	*in*	*tik*	*ma'ay*
	FUT-3B-go	CM	Juan	sow-INF	chili	Ø	TOP	1B	DEM	NEG
#577	*man*	*ol-Ø-b'at*	*laj*	*winhaj*	*Xun*	*aw-oj*	*ich*			
	NEG	FUT-3B-go	NEG	CM	Juan	sow-INF	chili			
	pero	*a*	*in*	*ol-in-b'at-ok*						
	but	TOP	1B	FUT-1B-go-IRR						

    b. Purépecha   [Chamoreau 2003: 141]

#576	*'Xwanu*	*'ni-a-ti*	*'xukskani*	*ka'waši*	*'ka*	*'xi*	*'no*
	Juan	go-FUT-ASS.3	sow	chili	and	1E	NEG
#577	*'Xwanu*	*'no*	*'xukska-a-ti*	**'peru**	*'xi*	*'xo*	
	Juan	NEG	sow-FUT-ASS.3	**but**	1E	yes	

The above examples show that in these replica languages, the use of *pero* is by no means compulsory. There are alternative ways of expressing the adversative or leaving it unexpressed. On the other hand, nothing bars the possibility that *pero* might have been an option also for those sentences from which it is missing or where it is expressed with something else. What factors have induced the native speakers to opt for or against the use of *pero* is still largely unclear to us. At the same time, the identification of implicational relations in Table 1 is indicative of a certain degree of systematicity which determines the distribution of *pero*. Put differently the presence/absence of *pero* is neither arbitrary nor random.

One might argue that the turnout of our search for evidence of *pero* in Mesoamerican languages is biased insofar as the Spanish stimuli already contain *pero*. The presence of *pero* in the stimulus probably has a priming effect so that the respondents are subconsciously induced to use the same function word also in their answers, meaning *pero* could be artificially overrepresented. However, Table 2 (cf. below) shows that *pero* is sometimes also used for the translation of other sentences of the ALIM-questionnaire. Sentence #61 is special in the sense that the attestations of borrowed *pero* can be attributed to a wrong reading of the instructions for the fieldworker. In some of the older versions of the questionnaire, the Spanish stimulus was #61 *Tenía un caballo* 'I used to have a horse' to which the bracketed clause (*pero lo vendí*) '(but I sold it)' was added. We assume that the bracketed part was never intended to be translated in the first place. It only served as an explanatory contextualization of the main clause. Therefore, translations of the bracketed part are found only for some of the sample languages four of which give evidence of the employment of borrowed *pero* like Zapotec in (16).

(16) Zapotec [Pickett and Embrey 1974: 58]
Gupa ta mani' (**peru** bituaa laa)
have:1SG.IMPF one horse **but** sell:1SG.PAST 3SG.O
'I used to have a horse (**but** I sold it)'

Cases like this one do not alter the picture much since it can still not be ruled out that the presence of *pero* in the Spanish original is solely responsible for the use of the same element in the replica language. Note that with Guarijío *nahpé*, Tepehua *x'amán'*, Trique *ɛah⁴*, and Yaqui *bwéta* we find exactly those indigenous function words as equivalents of *pero* in #61 which the same languages are reported to use in Table 1.

In the seven other questionnaire sentences in Table 2, however, the Spanish stimulus does not involve the function word *pero*. Those languages which are reported to use *pero* in Table 2 are also among the languages which attest to the employment of *pero* in Table 1.

Table 2: Additional evidence of the use of *pero* from the ALIM-questionnaire

Language	#61	#400	#402	#409	#412	#527	#557	#558	Sum
Zoque	*pero*						*pero*	*pero*	3
Huave	*pere*			*pere*					2
Otomí				*pe*	*pe*				2
Pima Bajo	*per*								1
Zapotec	*peru*								1
Mazatec		*pe⁴ru⁴*							1
Nahuatl (A)			*pero*						1
Purépecha				*pero*					1
Chontal						*pero*			1
Total	4	1	1	3	1	1	1	1	13

Thus, we can predict that if a language is associated with the use of *pero* in Table 2, it will also be among the *pero*-users in Table 1. A further possible claim could be that languages which give evidence of *pero* in both Table 1 and Table 2 are more Hispanized than those which are featured only in one of the tables. Given that this is a feasible way of determining the degree of Hispanization, Zoque would occupy the topmost position alone followed by Mazatec.

We illustrate the unpredictable occurrences of *pero* with examples from Huave (17), Nahuatl (A) (18), and Zoque (19).

(17) Huave [Stairs and Stairs 1983: 96]
#409 *taoel* **pere** *naeel*
tie.3SG **but** difficult
'S/he tied it **but** it was difficult' (Spanish *Lo amarró con dificultad*)

(18) Nahuatl (A) [Lastra 1980: 103]
#402 *o-wecka-k* **pero** *asta* *o-wec*
ANT-laugh-PRET **but** until ANT-fall
'He laughed until he fell down' (Spanish *Se rió hasta caerse*)

(19) Zoque
#557 *'aunke* *tuhi* *nimpa* **pero** *'in* *nikspa*
although rain fall.PRG **but** 1SG 1SG:go
'Although it is raining I will go' (Spanish *Voy a ir aunque está lloviendo*)

The use of *pero* in (19) from Zoque is in line with the use of *pero* in concessive constructions in Mazatec (10) and Otomí de la Sierra (cf. above). As to *pero* in the Nahuatl example (18), we assume that its use is motivated pragmatically, i.e. *pero* has no genuinely adversative function but rather adds emphasis to the utterance. The emphatic character of borrowed *pero* is also mentioned for Otomí de la Sierra (Voigtlander and Echegoyen 1985: 317) and Yucatec (Pool Balam and Le Guen 2015: 361). It needs to be studied further whether some of the cases of variation discussed in the foregoing paragraphs can be explained adequately with reference to the concept of pragmatic emphasis and focus.

The idea that there is no need for a Spanish stimulus which involves *pero* to trigger the use of *pero* in a given replica language receives further support from a look at the stories and dialogues which are included in the volumes of the ALIM-series. These additional texts are originals in the Mesoamerican languages, i.e. no Spanish stimulus was used. In Figure 1 we specify the absolute frequency of *pero* for each of the languages which give evidence of using this function word. Note, however, that the texts differ hugely in terms of their size. The absolute frequencies therefore are not directly comparable to each other.

Different colors identify the different parts of the ALIM-volume from which the evidence is taken: dark grey marks the instances of *pero* which stem from the sentences used for Table 1 (= questionnaire tout court), black indicates occurrences of *pero* according to Table 2 (= surplus), and light grey is used for the evidence of *pero* in the additional original monologues and dialogues (= texts).

Figure 1 is suggestive of yet another two implications, namely
– each language which employs *pero* in the surplus sentences also makes use of *pero* in the questionnaire tout court, and
– with a probability of 95 %, a language which uses *pero* in the texts will also use *pero* in the questionnaire tout court.

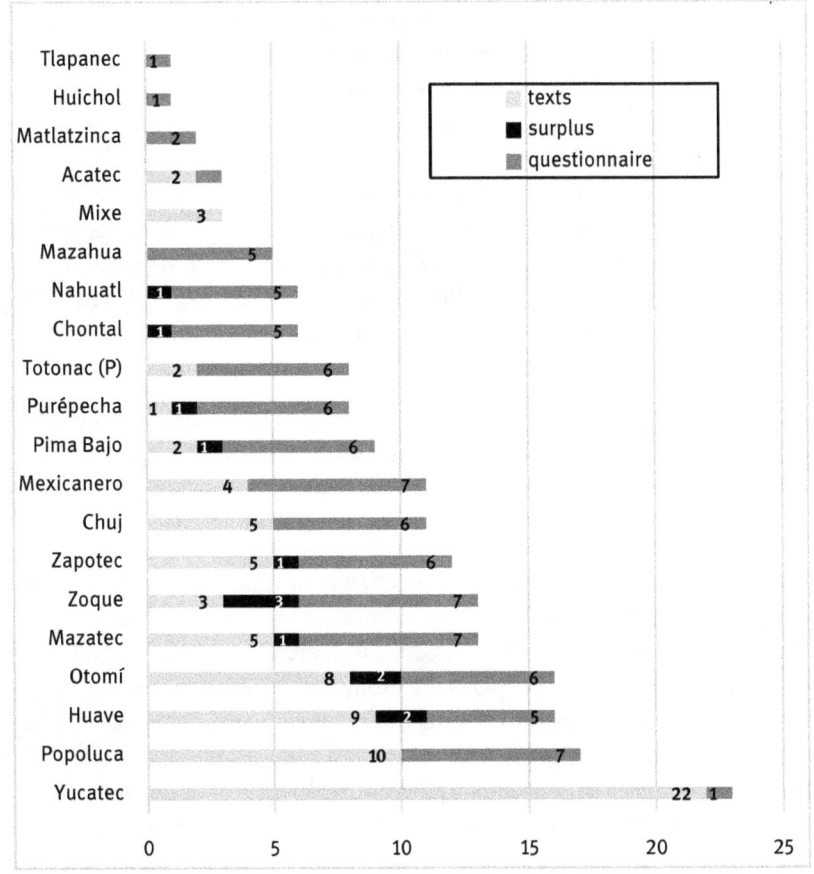

Figure 1: Absolute frequency of *pero* in the ALIM-volumes.

There are 19 languages which employ *pero* in the questionnaire tout court, nine languages which also have evidence of *pero* in the surplus, whereas 14 languages use the borrowed adversative connector also in the texts-section of the ALIM-volume. If we take as a criterion of particularly strong Hispanization the employment of *pero* in each of the three parts of the ALIM-volumes, seven languages can be classified as especially Hispanized. Huave and Otomí outrank all other contenders followed by Zoque and Mazatec, Zapotec and, with much smaller turnouts, Pima Bajo and Purépecha. At the opposite extreme, Chontal, Mazahua, Matlatzinca, Huichol, and Tlapanec give evidence of *pero* exclusively in the questionnaire proper. There is a striking difference to the situation depicted in Section 3.2 because the ranking order of Hispanization is not exactly the same. None of those languages which were classified as strongly Hispanized in Section 3.2 occupies the top-rank positions according to Figure 1. At the same time neither Huave nor Otomí figure among the most strongly Hispanized languages in the hierarchy exposed in Section 3.2, whereas they are prominent cases of Hispanization in Figure 1.

Mixe is the only language which attests to *pero* only in the text section of the ALIM-volume. The number of sample languages which give evidence of *pero* thus increases by one to 20 of 32 equaling a share of 62.5 % whereas that of languages without evidence of *pero* diminishes accordingly to 37.5 %. The Mixe example in (20) is representative of the majority of the instances of *pero* found the text sections of the ALIM-series.

(20) Mixe [Lyon 1980: 45][14]
pero yʌ'ʌkʌšp ku ʌte'n tkahɔttʌ suco tne'eptʌt
but ART:reason when thus NEG:know.PL how sow
'**But** the reason is that they do not know how to sow it [...]'

The borrowed function word occupies the leftmost i.e. utterance-initial position because it connects the sentence to the immediately preceding discourse. Of the 22 instances of *pero* in the Yucatec texts, for instance, 19 (= 86 %) fill the slot on the left margin of the sentence. This is, as Brody (1998: 72) observes, "[b]ecause discourse markers are optional discourse level phenomena, sentences elicited in isolation do not include them."

Thus, the at times striking quantitative discrepancy between the attestations of *pero* in the three different parts of the ALIM-volumes is probably caused by the lack of textual coherence in the questionnaire part. This means that the

---

[14] We have omitted the following causal clause because the first part of the complex sentence is already grammatically self-sufficient.

data from the questionnaire alone do not provide a reliable basis for generalizations about the role *pero* plays in a given replica language. It is therefore necessary to enlarge the corpus by way of including sizable prose texts. How this might look is shown very briefly in Section 4.

4 Going beyond

If we discount Bible translations, it is very difficult to come by a parallel literary corpus of Mesoamerican languages to facilitate the comparative study of borrowed *pero*. The sole mundane candidate for this purpose is Antoine de Saint-Exupéry's *Le Petit Prince* (= LPP) which has been translated into a dozen indigenous languages of the Americas half of which are located in Mesoamerica. Except Yucatec, however, the varieties represented by the translations of the French modern classic are not identical with those covered by the ALIM-series. What we say in the subsequent paragraphs thus has to be taken with a grain of salt. Moreover, we also take account of the fate of *pero* in the LPP-translations into other languages which have experienced Hispanization.

Figure 2 shows that the Spanish translation[15] yields the highest frequency values for *pero* relatively closely followed by those of the Austronesian language Tagalog. Otomí (V) comes in third place but already with a significantly smaller turnout as compared to Spanish and Tagalog. The other Austronesian language of our sample, Bikol, cannot compete with Otomí but has slightly more instances of *pero* than we have counted for Huastec.

What is most striking however is the fact that only four languages which have been subject to Hispanization display evidence of borrowed *pero* at all. It is also worth noting that two of these languages are spoken in the Philippines where Spanish has long since lost its formerly dominant social role. In contrast, there is a group X of ten languages from Mesoamerica and South America for which not a single occurrence of *pero* has been confirmed. This group X includes Aymara, Guaraní, Kaqchikel, Nahuatl (H), Quechua (C), Quechua (E), Toba, Totonac (S), Wayuu-Guajiro, and Yucatec. All of these languages are still in contact with dominant Spanish.

---

15 There is a plethora of translations of the reference text into Spanish, be they legal or clandestine. We have chosen one of many translations made in Spain which is representative of European Spanish. Whether or not a translation into Latin American (especially Mexican) Spanish would have made a difference cannot be clarified in this paper.

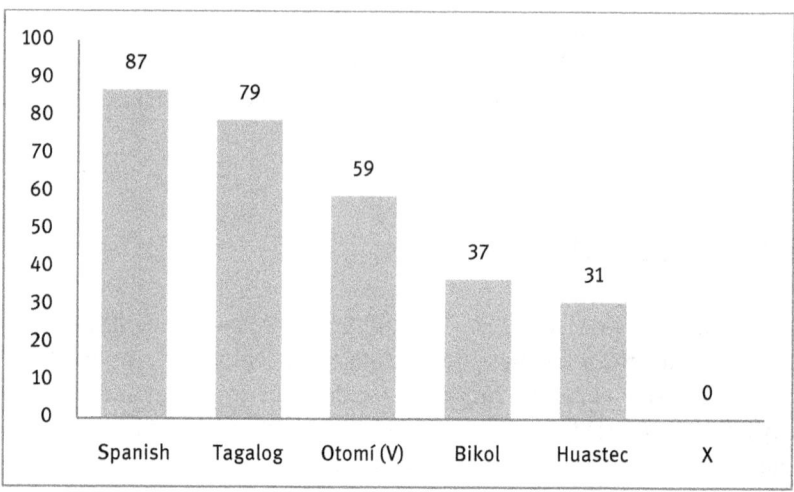

Figure 2: Absolute frequency of *pero* in translations of *Le Petit Prince*.

It is tempting to attribute the absence of *pero* from the LPP-translations to the conscious decision of the translators to purify their texts as much as possible by way of avoiding (grammatical) Hispanisms (Flores Farfán 2009: 117–120). The frequent use of *pero* in the (spoken) Yucatec texts in the ALIM-volume (as shown in Figure 1) is in stark contrast to the failure of *pero* to show up in the written Yucatec of the LPP-translation. To our mind it is very likely that we are facing the emergence of more or less rigid registers or style differences with the deliberate avoidance of (grammatical) Hispanisms developing into a distinctive trait of the belles-lettres no matter how socially prestigious the Hispanization of one's spoken discourse might be. This situation is in line with Brody's (1995: 134) statement according to which speakers of Mesoamerican languages show ambivalence to their speech so that it makes sense

> to posit a scale of syncretism, with each language, speech community, or individual located somewhere between purism and mixing, between affiliation with Spanish and affinity for the native language. (Brody 1995: 135)

We fully agree with the gist of this quote. Students of language contact with Spanish in Mesoamerica should seize the opportunity of their empirically rich database to develop the master-version of the scale of syncretism as envisaged by Brody. This is a demanding task which requires time and energy but will prove to be worth the effort because the scale will be to the benefit of language contact studies in general.

5 Conclusions

The discussion of the Mesoamerican facts in Sections 3–4 answers the research questions we have posed in the introduction. The predictability of the behavior of *pero* in one replica language on the basis of our knowledge about the behavior of *pero* in another language is limited, yet without being absolutely impossible. Moreover, the degree of Hispanization can be determined quantitatively only for a corpus – but not for an entire diatopic system, at least not with the very simple tools we have used for this study.

First of all, there is more than enough evidence of variation as to the use of *pero* in the replica languages. On the basis of our database, it seems that a not negligible number of Mesoamerican languages avoid *pero* strictly. Taken at face value this sizable group of *pero*-avoiders pays a serious blow to the wide-spread assumption that *pero* is borrowed by each and every indigenous language of Mesoamerica. The group of Mesoamerican *pero*-avoiders is perhaps even bigger since studies like that by Veerman-Leichsenring (1984) on Popoloca describe the object-languages without mentioning *pero*.[16] However, the absence of references to borrowed *pero* in descriptive grammars of Mesoamerican languages does not necessarily exclude the possibility of this conjunction forming part of the indigenous system of connectors and discourse markers. Among those Mesoamerican languages which give evidence of borrowed *pero* there is no homogeneity as to the uses *pero* is put to. The languages differ considerably regarding the range of contexts in which the employment of *pero* is considered appropriate. The picture is relatively variegated but at the same time not entirely chaotic. We have shown that it is possible to identify systematic correlations between sentences and languages which can be represented in the format of (probabilistic) implications. The variation is such that it is not feasible to describe the grammar of *pero* in the replica languages by way of applying the rules which have been established for *pero* in Spanish. It is therefore necessary to determine the functional domain of *pero* for each replica language separately. In connection to determining the functional domain, those contexts have to be identified in which the employment of *pero* is mandatory. For the time being, we can only hypothesize that this is the case for concessive constructions as those reported for e.g. Mazatec in (10) which are at odds with the rules of European Spanish.

---

[16] The anonymous reviewer argues that the absence of *pero* in this case may have to do with the fact that evidence of Spanish influence on this language is generally ignored in the descriptive grammars dedicated to it. It is possible that *pero* is attested in actual texts. However, the publication contains no separate text section.

Our study additionally corroborates what scholars like Brody (1998) have claimed, viz. that the form in which the language is documented has a very strong impact on the representation of given linguistic phenomena. In our case this means that *pero* might be absent from the answers to the questionnaire because the sequence of sample sentences does not constitute a genuine text. Moreover, *pero* might also fall victim to the puristic leanings of native speakers. Yet, some instances of *pero* are probably triggered by the presence of *pero* in the Spanish stimulus. The differences between the three parts of the ALIM-volumes are indicative of the necessity to enlarge and diversify the database. The inclusion of many more original discourse data is urgently called for (Adamou 2016). Moreover, the ALIM-questionnaire as well as the LPP-translations more often than not reflects the idiolect of an individual native speaker. To create a really representative documentation, the speech habits of several native speakers have to be recorded if one aspires to generalize over function word borrowing in a given language.

To put it succinctly, we have only scratched the surface of the phenomenon under review. If we want to understand better how far the Hispanization of the grammars of replica languages can go, it is paramount to conduct in-depth studies of *pero* in Mesoamerican languages and sundry Hispanized languages. Subsequently, similar inquiries have to be conducted ideally for each of the more widely borrowed function words. Only then will it be possible to put flesh to the bones of Brody's above "scale of syncretism".

Acknowledgments: We are grateful to Eeva Sippola and Danae Perez not only for inviting us to contribute to this edited volume but also for commenting on the draft version of this paper. We gratefully acknowledge the kind assistance which José Antonio Flores Farfán, Paulette Levy and Pedro Pérez Luna offered to help us getting our hands on those volumes of the *Archivo de Lenguas Indígenas de México* and translations of *Le Petit Prince* which were still missing from our collection when we started to work on this project. Yolanda Lastra has provided additional reading matter. Nataliya Levkovych deserves a word of thanks too for running additional searches for instances of *pero* in a variety of texts. We like to thank Maike Vorholt for her help with technical matters. Maja Robbers kindly gave her opinion as to the contents of the first version of this paper. We are also grateful to the anonymous reviewer who helped us to revise our original ideas and concepts. The responsibility for the content and form of this paper is exclusively ours.

Abbreviations

1, 2, 3	first, second, third person
A	A-set marker
ABS	absolutive
ACT	action
ADJ	adjective marker
ADV	adverbial
AFF	affirmative
ANT	anterior
AOR	aorist
ART	article
ASS	assertive
B	B-set marker
C	classifier
CAUS	causative
CISLOC	cislocative
COMPL	completive
COND	conditional
CONJ	conjunction
CONT	continuator/continuative
COP	copula
DEM	demonstrative
DEP	dependent
DES	desiderative
DET	determiner
DIM	diminutive
DIR	directional
DIS	distal
DISTR	distributive
E	emphatic
EPEN	epenthesis
ERG	ergative
EXH	exhortative
EXI	existential
F	feminine
FUT	future
GNR	generalized patient
HAB	habitual
HYP	hypothetical
IMM	imminent
IMPF	imperfective
INAN	inanimate
INCP	incompletive
INDEF	indefinite
INF	infinitive

INGR	ingressive
INST	instrumental
INT	intensive
INTRO	introductory
IRR	irrealis
LOC	locative
M	masculine/male
NEG	negation
NR	nominalizer
O	object
OBL	obligation
PART	particle
PAS	passive
PERF	perfective
PL	plural
POR	possessor
POSS	possessive
POST	postposition
PRET	preterit
PRG	progressive
PRO	pronoun
PROB	probability
PROX	proximal
PRS	present
QUOT	quotative
REFL	reflexive
REL	relator
REM	remote
RES	resultative
S	subject
SBJ	subjunctive
SG	singular
STAT	stative
SUB	subordination
TERM	terminative
TOP	topic
TR	transitive
TVI	thematic vowel of intransitive verbs
VIS	visible

References

Primary Sources

(a) *ALIM and* Archivo de lenguas indígenas del estado de Oaxaca *(= ALIEO)*

Buenrostro, Cristina. 2009. *Chuj de San Mateo Ixtatán* (= ALIM 28). México, DF: El Colegio de México.
Canger, Una. 2001. *Mexicanero de la Sierra Madre Occidental* (= ALIM 24). México, DF: El Colegio de México.
Cárdenas Martínez, Celestino & Yolanda Lastra. 2011. *Mazahua de San Pedro de Alto, Temascalcingo, Estado de México* (= ALIM 31). México, DF: El Colegio de México.
Chamoreau, Claudine. 2003. *Purépecha de Jarácuaro, Michoacán* (= ALIM 25). México, DF: El Colegio de México.
Daly, John & Margarita Holland de Daly. 1977. *Mixteco de Santa María Peñoles* (= ALIM 3). México, DF: El Colegio de México.
Escalante Hernández, Roberto & Marciano Hernández. 1999. *Matlatzinca de San Francisco Oxtotilpan, Estado de México* (= ALIM 23). México, DF: El Colegio de México.
Estrada Fernández, Zarina. 1998. *Pima Bajo de Yepachi, Chihuahua* (= ALIM 21). México, DF: El Colegio de México.
Estrada Fernández, Zarina. 2009. *Yaqui de Sonora* (= ALIM 29). México, DF: El Colegio de México.
Freeze, Ray A. 1989. *Mayo de los Capomos, Sinaloa* (= ALIM 14). México, DF: El Colegio de México.
Gómez, Paula. 1999. *Huichol de San Andrés Cohamiata, Jalisco* (= ALIM 22). México, DF: El Colegio de México.
Hollenbach, Fernando & Elena E. de Hollenbach. 1975. *Trique de San Juan Copala* (= ALIEO 2). México, DF: El Colegio de México.
Jamieson, Allan & Ernesto Tejeda. 1978. *Mazateco Chiquihuitlán, Oaxaca* (= ALIM 5). México, DF: El Colegio de México.
Knudson, L. 1980. *Zoque de Chimalapa, Oaxaca* (= ALIM 6). México, DF: El Colegio de México.
Lastra, Yolanda. 1980. *Náhuatl de Acaxochitlán, Hidalgo* (= ALIM 10). México, DF: El Colegio de México.
Lastra, Yolanda. 1989. *Otomí de San Andrés Cuexcontitlán, Estado de México* (= ALIM 13). México, DF: El Colegio de México.
Levy, Paulette. 1990. *Totonaco de Papantla, Veracruz* (= ALIM 15). México, DF: El Colegio de México.
Lyon, Don D. 1980. *Mixe de Tlahuitoltepec, Oaxaca* (= ALIM 8). México, DF: El Colegio de México.
Mackay, Carolyn J. & Frank R. Trechsel. 2005. *Totonaco de Misantla, Veracruz* (= ALIM 26). México, DF: El Colegio de México.
Mackay, Carolyn J. & Frank R. Trechsel. 2010. *Tepehua de Pisaflores, Veracruz* (= ALIM 30). México, DF: El Colegio de México.
Miller, Wick R. 1993. *Guarijío de Arechuyvo, Chihuahua* (= ALIM 16). México, DF: El Colegio de México.

Mixco, Mauricio J. 1996. *Kiliwa del arroyo León, Baja California* (= ALIM 18). México, DF: El Colegio de México.

Mock, Carol. 1977. *Choco de Santa Catarina Ocotlán, Oaxaca* (= ALIM 4). México, DF: El Colegio de México.

Moser, Mary Beck. 1996. *Seri de Sonora* (= ALIM 19). México, DF: El Colegio de México.

Pickett, Velma & Virginia Embrey. 1974. *Zapoteco del Istmo. Juchitán, Oaxaca* (= ALIEO 1). México, DF: El Colegio de México.

Pride, Leslie & Kitty Pride. 1997. *Chatino de la Zona Alta, Oaxaca* (= ALIM 20). México, DF: El Colegio de México.

Rupp, John. 1980. *Chinanteco de San Juan Lealao, Oaxaca* (= ALIM 9). México, DF: El Colegio de México.

Stairs, Glem A. & Emily F. de Stairs. 1983. *Huave de San Mateo del Mar, Oaxaca* (= ALIM 8). México, DF: El Colegio de México.

Stolz, Christel, Thomas Stolz & Elisabeth Verhoeven. 2012. *Maya yucateco de X-Hazil Sur, Quintana Roo* (= ALIM 32). México, DF: El Colegio de México.

Suárez, Jorge A. 1988. *Tlapaneco de Malinaltepec* (= ALIM 12). México, DF: El Colegio de México.

Waterhouse, Viola. 1980. *Chontal de la Sierra, Oaxaca* (= ALIM 7). México, DF: El Colegio de México.

Wichmann, Søren. 2007. *Popoluca de Texistepec* (= ALIM 27). México, DF: El Colegio de México.

Zavala Maldonado, Roberto. 1992. *Acateco de la frontera sur* (= ALIM 17). México, DF: El Colegio de México.

(b) Le Petit Prince

Aymara	Segura, Roger Gonzalo. 2015. *Prinsipi wawa*. Buenos Aires: Javier Merás.
Bikol	Tria, Wilmer Joseph S. 2016. *An Sadit na Prinsipe*. Philippines: Ina nin Bikol Foundation.
Filipino	Ching, Desiderio. 1991. *Ang munting prinsipe*. Quezon City: Claretian.
Guaraní	Las Nieves, Domínguez de & Enrique Chamorro. 2005. *Mitãmi*. Asunción: Espectrograf.
Huastec	Kondic, Ana. 2015. *An Chikam Príncipe*. Mexico: Instituto Nacional de Lenguas Indígenas.
Kaqchikel	Matzar, Lolmay Pedro Oscar García. 2011. *Ri ch'uti'ajpop*. Neckarsteinach: Edition Tintenfaß.
Luxembourgish	Braun, Josy. 2009. *De Klenge Prënz*. Differdange: Editions Phi.
Nahuatl	Miranda San Román, Refugio & Rodolfo Ávila. 1946. *In piltlajtoanpili*. Itsminkilpa, Hidalgo, México: Instituto Humboldt de Investigaciones Interdiciplinarias en Humanidades & Centro de Estudios Mexicanos y Centroamericanos.
Otomí	Alavez, Raymundo Isidro. 2012. *Ra zi ts'unt'u dängandä*. Ixmiquilpan: CEMCA & Hmunts'a Hem'i.

Quechua (Cuzco)	Cornejo Endara, Lydia & César Itier. 2002. *Quyllur llaqtayuq wawamanta*. Cuzco: Asociación Pukllasunchis.
Quechua (Ecuador)	Gallegos, Teodoro & León Coloma. 1989. *Auquicu*. Quito: CEDIME (EBI).
Spanish	del Carril, Bonifacio. 1995. *El principito*. Madrid: El Libro de Bolsillo.
Toba	Moreno, Valentín et al. 2005. *So shiỹaxauolec nta'a*. Asnières sur Seine: Association pour l'échange artistique et culturel.
Totonac	Pérez Luna, Pedro. 2012. *Wa xa' aktsú' púxku*. Puebla: COECULTA.
Wayuu-Guajiro	Álvarez, José, José Ángel Fernández, Edixa Montiel & Alicia Dorado. 2016. *Pürinsipechonkai*. Maracaibo: Milagros Rosales.
Yucatec (Maya)	Colli Colli, Amedée. 2010. *Chan Ajau*. Neckarsteinach: Edition Tintenfaß.

Linguistic Studies

Adamou, Evangelia. 2016. *A corpus-driven approach to language contact. Endangered languages in a comparative perspective*. Berlin & Boston: De Gruyter Mouton.

Aquilina, Joseph. 1990. *Maltese-English dictionary*. Vol. 2: M–Z and addenda. Malta: Midsea.

Bakker, Dik, Jorge Gómez Rendón & Ewald Hekking. 2008. Spanish meets Guaraní, Otomí and Quichua: A multilingual confrontation. In Thomas Stolz, Dik Bakker & Rosa Salas Palomo (eds.), *Aspects of language contact. New theoretical, methodological and empirical findings with special focus on Romancisation processes*, 165–238. Berlin & New York: De Gruyter.

Bright, William & Robert A. Thiel. 1965. Hispanisms in a modern Aztec dialect. *Romance Philology* 18. 444–452.

Brody, Jill. 1987. Particles borrowed from Spanish as discourse markers in the Mayan languages. *Anthropological Linguistics* 29. 507–521.

Brody, Jill. 1995. Lending the 'Unborrowable': Spanish discourse markers in indigenous American languages. In Carmen Silva-Corvalán (ed.), Spanish in four continents. *Studies in language contact and bilingualism*, 132–147. Washington, DC: Georgetown University Press.

Brody, Jill. 1998. On hispanisms in elicitation. In Andreas Koechert & Thomas Stolz (eds.), *Convergencia e Individualidad. Las lenguas mayas entre hispanización e indigenismo*, 61–84. Hannover: Verlag für Ethnologie.

Casad, Eugene H. 1985. *Cora grammar sketch*. México, DF: Summer Institute of Linguistics.

Chamoreau, Claudine. 2007. Grammatical borrowing in Purépecha. In Yaron Matras & Jeanette Sakel (eds.), *Grammatical borrowing in cross-linguistic perspective*, 465–480. Berlin & New York: De Gruyter.

Estrada Fernández, Zarina & Lilián Guerrero. 2007. Grammatical borrowing in Yaqui. In Yaron Matras & Jeanette Sakel (eds.), *Grammatical borrowing in cross-inguistic perspective*, 419–434. Berlin & New York: De Gruyter.

Fernández de Miranda, María Teresa. 1965. Los préstamos españoles en el zapoteco de Mitla. *Anales del Instituto Nacional de Antropología e Historia (México)* 20. 259–273.

Flores Farfán, José Antonio. 1999. *Cuatreros somos y toindioma hablamos. Contactos y conflictos entre el náhuatl y el español en el sur de México*. México: CIESAS.

Flores Farfán, José Antonio. 2009. *Variación, ideologías y purismo lingüístico. El caso del mexicano o náhuatl*. México, DF: CIESAS.

García, Erica C. 1995. Frecuencia (relativa) de uso como síntoma de estrategias etnopragmáticas. In Klaus Zimmermann (ed.), *Lenguas en contacto en Hispanoamérica*, 51–72. Frankfurt am Main: Vervuert.

Gómez Rendón, Jorge. 2008. *Typological and social constraints on language contact: Amerindian languages in contact with Spanish*. Utrecht: LOT.

Haspelmath, Martin & Uri Tadmor. 2009. The loanword typology project and the world loanword database. In Martin Haspelmath & Uri Tadmor (eds.), *Loanwords in the world's languages. A comparative handbook*, 1–34. Berlin & New York: De Gruyter.

Hekking, Ewald. 1995. *El otomí de Santiago Mexquititlán: Desplazamiento lingüístico, préstamos y cambios gramaticales*. Amsterdam: IFOTT.

Hekking, Ewald & Pieter Muysken. 1995. Otomí y Quechua: una comparación de los elementos gramaticales prestados del español. In Klaus Zimmermann (ed.), *Lenguas en contacto en Hispanoamérica*, 101–118. Frankfurt am Main: Vervuert.

Hill, Jane H. & Kenneth C. Hill. 1986. *Speaking Mexicano: Dynamics of syncretic language in central Mexico*. Tucson: University of Arizona Press.

Jamieson, Carole Van den Hoeck. 1988. *Gramatica mazateca del municipio de Chiquihuitlan, Oaxaca*. México: El Colegio de México.

Matras, Yaron. 1998. Utterance modifiers and universals of grammatical borrowing. *Linguistics* 36(2). 281–331.

Matras, Yaron. 2007. The borrowability of structural categories. In Yaron Matras & Jeanette Sakel (eds.), *Grammatical borrowing in cross-linguistic perspective*, 31–74. Berlin & New York: De Gruyter.

Muysken, Pieter. 1981. Halfway between Quechua and Spanish: The case for relexification. In Arnold Highfield & Albert Valdman (eds.), *Historicity and variation in creole studies*, 52–78. Ann Arbor: Karoma.

Muysken, Pieter. 2001. Spanish grammatical elements in Bolivian Quechua: The Transcripciones Quechuas Corpus. In Klaus Zimmermann & Thomas Stolz (eds.), *Lo propio y lo ajeno en las lenguas austronésicas y amerindias. Procesos interculturales en el contacto de lenguas indígenas con el español en el Pacífico e Hispanoamérica*, 59–82. Frankfurt am Main: Vervuert.

Pagel, Steve. 2010. *Spanisch in Asien und Ozeanien*. Frankfurt am Main: Lang.

Pool Balam, Lorena I. & Olivier Le Guen. 2015. La integración de préstamos en maya yucateco. Una perspectiva interaccional acompañada de una reflexión sobre la ideología del lenguaje. *Amerindia* 37(2). 343–384.

RAE. 2009. Real Academia Española. Nueva gramática de la lengua española. Madrid: Asociación de Academias de la lengua española.

Sakel, Jeanette. 2007. Types of loan: matter and pattern. In Yaron Matras & Jeanette Sakel (eds.), *Grammatical borrowing in cross-linguistic perspective*, 15–30. Berlin & New York: De Gruyter.

Sakel, Jeanette. 2010. Grammatical borrowing from Spanish/Portuguese in some native languages of Latin America. STUF/*Language Typology and Universals* 63(1). 65–78.

Steinkrüger, Patrick O. 2008. Hispanisation processes in the Philippines. In Thomas Stolz, Dik Bakker & Rosa Salas Palomo (eds.), *Hispanisation. The impact of Spanish on the lexicon and grammar of the indigenous languages of Austronesia and the Americas*, 203–236. Berlin & New York: Mouton de Gruyter.

Stolz, Christel. 1998. Hispanicisation in modern Yucatec Maya: Grammatical borrowing. In Andreas Koechert & Thomas Stolz (eds.), *Convergencia e Individualidad. Las lenguas mayas entre hispanización e indigenismo*, 165–194. Hannover: Verlag für Ethnologie.

Stolz, Christel & Thomas Stolz. 1996. Funktionswortentlehnung in Mesoamerika. Spanisch-amerindischer Sprachkontakt. *STUF/Language Typology and Universals* 49(1). 86–123.

Stolz, Christel & Thomas Stolz. 1997. Universelle Hispanismen? Von Manila über Lima bis Mexiko und zurück: Muster bei der Entlehnung spanischer Funktionswörter in die indigenen Sprachen Amerikas und Austronesiens. *Orbis* 39. 1–77.

Stolz, Thomas. 1996. Grammatical Hispanisms in Amerindian and Austronesian languages. The other kind of Transpacific isogloss. *Amerindia* 21. 137–160.

Stolz, Thomas. 2008. Romancisation world-wide. In Thomas Stolz, Dik Bakker & Rosa Salas Palomo (eds.), *Aspects of language contact. New theoretical, methodological and empirical findings with special focus on Romancisation processes*, 1–42. Berlin & New York: De Gruyter.

Stolz, Thomas. accepted. Entlehntes ABER. Kontaktinduzierte Diffusion adversativer Konnektoren des konjunktionalen Typs. In Julia Nintemann und Cornelia Stroh (eds.), *Über Widersprüche sprechen – Linguistische Beiträge zu Contradictions Studies*. Wiesbaden: Springer VS.

Suárez, Jorge A. 1983. *The Mesoamerican Indian languages*. Cambridge: Cambridge University Press.

Veerman-Leichsenring, Annette. 1984. *El popoloca de Los Reyes Metzontla*. Paris: A.E.A.

Verbeeck, Lieve. 1998. Borrado de la memoria, grabado en la lengua: interferencias españolas e inglesas en el mopan de Belice. In Andreas Koechert & Thomas Stolz (eds.), *Convergencia e Individualidad. Las lenguas mayas entre hispanización e indigenismo*, 141–164. Hannover: Verlag für Ethnologie.

Voigtlander, Katherine & Artemisa Echegoyen. 1985. *Luces contemporáneas del otomí. Gramática del otomí de la Sierra*. México, DF: El Colegio de México.

Zimmermann, Klaus. 1987. Préstamos gramaticalmente relevantes del español al otomí. Una aportación a la teoría del contacto entre lenguas. *Anuario de Lingüística Hispánica* 3. 223–253.

Appendix I (Sample)

Acatec (Mayan, Guatemala), Aymara (Aymaran, Peru), Bikol (Austronesian, Philippines), Cebuano (Austronesian, Philippines), Chatino (Oto-Manguean, Mexico), Chinantec (Oto-Manguean, Mexico), Chocho (Oto-Manguean, Mexico), Chontal (Tequistlatecan, Mexico), Chuj (Mayan, Guatemala), Cora (Uto-Aztecan, Mexico), Guaraní (Tupian, Paraguay), Guarijío (Uto-Aztecan, Mexico), Huastec (Mayan, Mexico), Huave (Huavean, Mexico), Huichol (Uto-Aztecan, Mexico), Kaqchikel (Mayan, Guatemala), Kiliwa (Hokan, Mexico), Luxembourgish (Indo-European, Luxembourg), Maltese (Afro-Asiatic, Malta), Matlatzinca (Oto-Manguean, Mexico), Mayo (Uto-Aztecan, Mexico), Mazahua (Oto-Manguean, Mexico), Mazatec (Oto-Manguean, Mexico), Mexicanero (Uto-Aztecan, Mexico), Mixe (Mixe-Zoque, Mexico), Mixtec (Oto-Manguean, Mexico), Nahuatl [Acaxochitlan, Huasteca] (Uto-Aztecan, Mexico), Otomí [San Andrés de la Sierra, Valle Mezquitlán] (Oto-Manguean, Mexico), Pima Bajo (Uto-Aztecan, Mexico), Popoluca (Oto-Manguean, Mexico), Purépecha (Tarascan, Mexico), Quechua [Cuzco, Ecuador] (Quechuan, Peru + Ecuador), Rapanui (Austronesian, Chile), Seri (Hokan, Mexico), Spanish (Indo-European, Spain, etc.), Tagalog (Austronesian, Philippines), Tepehua (Totonacan, Mexico), Tlapanec (Tlapanecan, Mexico), Toba (Guaicuruan, Argentina), Totonac [Misantla, Papantla, Sierra de Puebla] (Totonacan, Mexico), Trique (Oto-Manguean, Mexico), Wayuu-Guajiro (Arawacan, Colombia + Venezuela), Yaqui (Uto-Aztecan, Mexico), Yucatec (Mayan, Mexico), Zapotec (Oto-Manguean, Mexico), Zoque (Mixe-Zoque, Mexico)

Appendix II (Sentences with *pero* according to Table 1 excluding those which are included in the main body of the text)

(a) #272, (b) #273, (c) #274, (d) #312, (e) #368, (f) #576, (g) #577

Acatec [Zavala Maldonado 1992: 201]

(e) kaw č'i:tax-Ø nax ʔunin ti? **pero**
very bad-B.3 person child DEM **but**
ox-Ø-wač'-ox=ʔel nax
IRR-B.3-good-IRR=DIR person

Chontal [Waterhouse 1980: 153]

(d) koła ay'wapa mane la plasa **pero**
go.IMPERF 1SG:go.PRET already ART market **but**
aypanenamma lahuł'
1SG:remain.PRET ART:house

(f) aWan tifata kaši **pero** iya' ay-ka'waya
Juan 3:FUT:sow chili **but** 1SG NEG-1:go

(g) aWan ay-mifaya **pero** iya' ka'waya'ma kafata
Juan neg-3:FUT:sow **but** 1SG 1:go:FUT 1:FUT:sow

Chuj [Buenrostro 2009: 159–160, 170, 181]

(a) Ø-w-ojtak tz-Ø-in-tz'ib'-an-i **pero** ma-x Ø-yal
3B-1A-know PRS-3B-1A-write-SUB-TVI **but** NEG-PRS 3B-be_able
laj w-u'uj yujto malaj in-lapis
NEG 1A-REL.N because NEG 1A-pencil

(b) in-nab'en tz-in-k'e t'a s-k'ab' jun te' te' tik
A.1-want PRS-B.1-climb LOC A.3-branch one C.wood tree DEM
pero ma-x Ø-yal laj w-uj
but NEG-PRS B.3-be_able NEG A.1-RN

(c) tz-Ø-yal in-k'e t'a s-k'ab' jun
PRS-B.3-be_able B.1-climb LOC A.3-branch one
te' te' tik **pero** ma-laj in-gana
C.wood tree DEM **but** NEG-NEG A.1-desire

(d) wan-xo in-b'at t'a merkado **pero**
PRG-ADV A.1-go LOC market **but**
in-kan-xi t'a in-pat
A.1-remain-ADV LOC A.1-house

(e) | a | jun | unin | tik | te | chuk, | **pero**
 | TOP | one | child | DEM | very | bad | **but**
 wach' ol-Ø-aj-ok
 good FUT-B.3-exist-IRR

Huave [Stairs and Stairs 1983: 81, 85, 91]

(a) alndom narang letre **pere** nganɨy ngo ndom
 1SG:be_able 1SG:do letter **but** now NEG 1SG:be_able
 kos ngo nahiɨ lapis
 because NEG 1SG:have pencil

(b) sandiɨ nahtep a šiɨl kiah **pere** ngo ndom
 1SG:want 1SG:climb DEM tree DEM **but** NEG 1SG:be_able

(c) alndom nahtep a šiɨl kiah **pere** ngo nandiɨm
 1SG:be_able 1SG:climb DEM tree DEM **but** NEG 1SG:want

(d) tahlɨy namb tiɨl plas **pere** taton ndoh
 1SG.IMPERF:be 1SG:go LOC market **but** NEG also
 takɨliɨsan tinden
 1SG.IMPERF:remain LOC:house

(e) aaga nine kam šomɨy memeeč **pero** apmarang nahneah
 DEM child DEM very bad **but** 3SG.FUT:make good

Matlatzinca [Escalante Hernández and Hernández 1999: 132–133, 140]

(d) pe-ka-ta-ru-n-pa be-tetáni **pero**
 almost-INTRO-1SG-FUT-EPEN-go LOC-market **but**
 ta-tó-yhempi be-báani
 1SG-TR-remain LOC-house

(e) ninhí we-to-wá'a ma-ki-n-máalo **pero**
 DEM person-DIM-child big-3SG-EPEN-bad **but**
 ka-ta-'iti
 INTRO-3SG-put_together

Mazahua [Cárdenas Martínez and Lastra 2011: 109–110, 114, 119][17]

(a) ri-fechi ra-ofʉ, **pe** dya ri-sɔɔ nangeje
 1-know 1FUT-write **but** NEG 1-be_able because
 dya ri-jʉʉ lapi
 NEG 1-have pencil

(b) ri-nee ra-tese-go a ngejenu zaa **pe**
 1-want 1FUT-climb-1E LOC DEM tree **but**

---

[17] In the (b)-sentence of the Mazahua version, the first modal verb was glossed incorrectly in the original.

(c) dya   ri-sɔɔ
    NEG   1-be_able
    ri-sɔɔ   ra-tese-go   a   ngejenu   zaa   **pe**
    1-be_able   1FUT-climb-1E   LOC   DEM   tree   **but**
    dya   ri-nee
    NEG   1-want

(d) ya   mero   mi-paa   kʔa   no   chomɨ,
    already   only   1IMPERF-go   LOC   ART   square
    pero   ro-kemĕ   kʔa   nu   ngumɨ
    but   1PRET-remain   LOC   ART   house

(e) ngenu   tʔii   nudya   ngeje   na   sʔoo   **pe**
    DEM   child   now   be   DET   bad   **but**
    ra-tsjaa   na   jo   tʔii
    3FUT-make   DET   good   child

Mazatec   [Jamieson and Tejeda 1978: 92, 96, 103, 131][18]

(a) mą³   ɕi³ʔi⁴ntu⁴   **pe⁴ru⁴**   ɕi⁴ʔi⁴ntų²¹⁴   ta⁴
    be_able   write.1SG   **but**   write.1SG:NEG   REL
    caeʔ¹⁴śi³   ɛąih⁴¹-ną⁴   la¹pi⁴
    because   NEG.EXI-1SG   pencil

(b) meh³¹   kųeh³¹⁴   ya²-bæ²⁴   **pe⁴ru⁴**   mąih⁴¹   kųeh³¹⁴
    want.3SG   climb.1SG   tree-DEM   **but**   NEG:be_able   climb.1SG

(c) ku⁴mą³   kųeh³¹⁴   ya²-bæ²⁴   **pe⁴ru⁴**   mih²¹   kųeh³¹⁴
    be_able.3SG   climb.1SG   tree-DEM   **but**   NEG:want.3SG   climb.1SG

(d) 'a⁴   tu⁴   'o³ra³⁴   sa⁴śi⁴   khuæ²   nte²⁴ɕį³⁴   **pe⁴ru⁴**
    already   only   time   for   go.1SG   market   **but**
    ka³bi⁴te¹hñą¹-nį¹   ntą¹⁴-nąʔ¹⁴
    sit.1SG.PRET-only   house-POR.1SG

(e) ća²   li²ʔnti¹⁴   biʔ³⁴   ne³⁴   he¹mų¹   ɛęʔ¹⁴   ća²   kiʔʔntæ⁴
    boy   small   DEM   TOP   very   bad   3SG   now
    pe⁴ru⁴   ku⁴mą⁴ntah³¹   khua²⁴   ta⁴kų¹⁴-ræ⁴   ća²
    but   make:REFL.3SG.FUT   good   thought-POR.3SG   3SG

(f) ća²   hųą¹   ne¹⁴   ɕi¹⁴thæ²⁴   ɛa²   ya²hñą²⁴   **pe⁴ru⁴**
    M   Juan   TOP   sow:FUT:3   3SG   chili   **but**
    nką'³   nę¹   ɕi¹⁴thį⁴¹
    1SG   TOP   sow:NEG:FUT:1SG

---

18 In the (b)-sentence, the Mazatec version involved the wrong verb in final position. We have replaced it with the appropriate verb.

(g) ća² huą¹ nę¹⁴ ɛi¹⁴thį⁴¹ ɛa² **pe⁴ru⁴** nką'³
    M   Juan TOP SOW:NEG:FUT:3   3SG **but** 1SG
    nę¹ ɛi¹⁴thæ¹
    TOP SOW:FUT:1SG

Mexicanero   [Canger 2001: 116, 121, 129, 161]
(a) ni-ki-mati   ni-eskribiro   **pero** amo   wel
    1SG-O.3SG-know   1SG-write   **but**   NEG   be_able
    porke   amo   ni-ki-piya   lapis
    because   NEG   1SG-O.3SG-have   pencil
(b) ni-ki-neki   ni-tehko-s   pa   yelin kwawi-t
    1SG-O.3SG-want   1SG-climb-FUT   LOC   DEM   tree-ABS
    pero amo   wel
    but   NEG   be_able
(c) wel   ni-tehko   pa   yelin   kwawi-t   **pero** amo
    be_able   1SG-climb   LOC   DEM   tree-abs   **but**   NEG
    ni-ki-neki
    1SG-O.3SG-want
(d) ni-katka   para   ni-ya-ha   pa   merkado   **pero**
    1SG-be.PRET   for   1SG-go-HYP   LOC   market   **but**
    ni-mo-kawa   pa   kal
    1SG-REFL-remain   LOC   house
(e) inin   piltonti   aška   yel   Ø-malo   **pero**
    DEM   boy   today   3SG   3SG-bad   **but**
    Ø-mo-čiwa-s   Ø-bweno
    3SG-REFL-make-FUT   3SG-good
(f) In   Xwan   Ø-ki-toka-s   čil   **pero** nel   no
    ART   Juan   S3-O3SG-sow-FUT   chili   **but**   1SG   NEG
(g) In   Xwan   amo   Ø-ta-toka-s   **pero** nel   si
    ART   Juan   NEG   S3-O.INAN-sow-FUT   **but**   1SG   yes

Nahuatl (A)   [Lastra 1980: 87, 92, 98]
(a) kʷali   ni-ʎa-kʷilowa   **pero**   a'wel   porke
    good   1SG-O.INDEF-write   **but**   NEG:be_able   because
    a'mo   pia   lapis
    NEG   have   pencil
(b) ni-k-neki   ni-paweci-s   iteč   in   kowi-ʎ   **pero**
    1SG-O.3SG-want   1SG-climb-FUT   LOC   ART   tree-ABS   **but**
    a'wel   ni-paweci
    NEG:be_able   1SG-climb

(c) kʷali   ni-paweci   iteč   in   kowi-ʎ   **pero** a'mo   neki
    good   1SG-climb   LOC   ART   tree-ABS   **but**   NEG   want
(d) yi   mero   n-ia-ya   in   tiankis-ko **pero**
    already only   1SG-go-IMPERF   ART   market-LOC **but**
    a'mo   n-ia   o-ni-mo-kaw   no-ča
    NEG   1SG-go   ANT-1SG-REFL-remain   POR.1SG-house
(e) inin   telpoka-to   ašan   a'mo   kwali   ʎaka-ʎ
    DEM   boy-DIM   now   NEG   good   person-ABS
    pero   yaw   mo-kwepa   kwali   ʎaka-ʎ
    but   go   REFL-turn   good   person-ABS

Otomí   [Lastra 1989: 101, 106, 112, 138]

(b) di-né   go-pɨ̌ci   kʔʌ   rʌ   šĭcʔŏ   **pe**   híngi   có
    1SG-want   1FUT-climb   DEM   ART   tree   **but** NEG   be_able
(c) da-zǒ   go-pɨ̌ci   kʔʌ   rʌ   šĭcʔŏ   **pe**   hín   di-né
    1SG-be_able   1FUT-climb   DEM   ART   tree   **but** NEG   1SG-want
(d) ndrʌ-mǎmá   a   tói   **pe**   dó-kŏhí
    1SG.CONT.IMPERF-go   LOC   market   **but**   1SG.PRET-remain
(e) ni   rʌ   bą̌hcį̌   rʌ-ndí-máhkó   **pe**
    DEM   ART   child   3SG.CONT-big-bad   **but**
    do-mą́-n-khá   čala   bą̌hcį̌
    3SG.FUT-DIST-RES-make   good   child
(f) rʌ   šúa   da-mą-tų́   yʌ   ʔí   **pe**   hína-gí-gó
    ART   Juan   3FUT-go-sow   ART.PL   chili   **but**   NEG-1O-1E
(g) rʌ   šúa   hín   da-tų́hų́   **pe**   nugó   hą̌
    ART   Juan   NEG   3FUT-sow   **but**   1SG   yes

Pima Bajo   [Estrada Fernández 1998: 95, 100, 125]

(d) aan   am   himia-tad-va   tieend-vui,   **pero**   an
    1SG   LOC   go:PROB-REM-COMPL   shop-DIR   **pero**   1SG
    am   ab   i'i   ki-tam
    LOC   DIR   here   house-POSTP
(e) li   oob   siv   im   kɨg,   **pero**   kɨg   a-dun-ia
    DIM   person   now   NEG   good   **but**   good   REFL-make:PROB
(f) huaan   ko'okol   ɨɨs-ia   **per**   aan   im
    Juan   chili   SOW-PROB   **but**   1SG   NEG
(g) huaan   im   ɨɨs-ia   **pero**   ani   pɨg   ɨɨs-ia
    Juan   NEG   SOW-PROB   **but**   1SG   also   SOW-PROB

Popoluca [Wichmann 2007: 189–190, 195, 202–203, 238]

(a) bus k-hay, **pero** ʔeñč wɨ: n-hay
know B.1-write.DEP **but** NEG be_able A.1-write
poko ʔeñdʸe n-ʔê:čaʔ la:pis
because NEG A.1-have pencil

(b) n-sun n-kêʔm-kaʔ-p hepeʔ kuy-ʔa:p, **pe**
A.1-want A.1-climb-INT-FUT DEM tree-F **but**
ʔeñč wɨ: n-keʔm
NEG be_able A.1-climb

(c) wɨ: n-kêʔm-kaʔ-p hepeʔ kuy-ʔa:p, **pe** ʔeñdʸe n-sun
be_able A.1-climb-INT-FUT DEM tree-F **but** NEG A.1-want

(d) ʔupa-am=chiʔk n-dɨk merka:ɖu **pe**
now-already=COND.PRET A.1-go market **but**
maʔ k-ɛiʔy n-tik-ɨ
PERF B.1-remain A.1-house-1

(e) yɨ:ʔpiʔ ba:n nhumbuʔ Ø-weʔyaʔ **pero** ke Ø-wɨ:
DEM child very B.3-naughty **but** ADJ B.3-good
Ø-se:t-p=esh y-ɛo:koʔ
B.3-turn-FUT=FUT A.3-heart

(f) hwaŋ y-dʸêp-p dʸe:w, **pe** ʔɨɛ-iʔ ʔeñdʸe:
Juan ERG3-sow-FUT chili **but** 1SG-E NEG

(g) hwaŋ ʔeñč y-dʸêp-p, **pe** ʔɨɛ n-dʸêp-p
Juan NEG ERG3-sow-FUT **but** 1SG ERG1-sow-FUT

Purépecha [Chamoreau 2003: 104, 108, 114]

(a) ‘mi-ti-šin-ka-ni ka‘rani **‘peru** ‘no
know-eye-HAB-ASS.1/2-1 write **but** NEG
‘u-šin-ka-ni xim’poka ‘no xa‘ɛi-š-ka la‘pišɨ
be_able-HAB-ASS.1/2-1 because NEG have-AOR-SBJ pencil

(b) ‘we-ka-šin-ka-ni ka‘ɽarani xi’mini in’te a’natapu-ɽu
want-STAT-HAB-ASS.1/2-1 climb:REFL there DEM tree-DIR
‘pero ‘no ‘u-šin-ka
but NEG be_able-HAB-ASS.1/2

(c) ‘u-šin-ka-ni ka‘ɽarani xi’mini in’te a’natapu-ɽu
be_able-HAB-ASS.1/2-1 climb:REFL there DEM tree-DIR
‘pero ‘no ‘we-ka-šin-ka
but NEG want-STAT-HAB-ASS.1/2

(d) ni’ra-šam-an-ka-ni mer’kadu-ɽu
go-CONT-PRET-ASS.1/2-1 market-DIR

	'pero	pa'ka-ra-š-ka-ni		xu'čini-o	
	but	remain-REFL-AOR-ASS.1/2-1		POR.1SG-residence	
(e)	'i	ta'taksa'piču	'yaši	'malu-i-š-ti	
	DEM	child	now	bad-COP-AOR-ASS.3	
	'peru	'sesi-i-a-ti			
	but	good-COP-FUT-ASS.3			

Totonac [Levy 1990: 97, 103, 109–110, 141]

(a) *ʎa:n   k-cu'q-nán   **pero**   chi   ni: la*
    well   1SG-write-O.INDEF   **but**   now   NEG   possible
    porque   ni: k-qa'lhí   li:-cu'q-ni
    because   NEG   1SG-have   INST-write-NR

(b) *k-ta-ak-xtu-pu'tún   namá: nak   ki'wi*
    1SG-INGR-head-outside-DES   DEM   LOC   tree
    ***pero*   ni: la**
    but   NEG   possible

(c) *ʎa:n   k-ta-ak-xtú   namá: nak   ki'wi*
    well   1SG-INGR-head-outside   DEM   LOC   tree
    ***pero*   ni: k-lakaskí'n**
    but   NEG   1SG-want

(d) *ix-k-an-ma-já   li:-tamá:w   **pero***
    PRET-1SG-go-PRG-already   INST-buy   **but**
    k-ta-maqxti-li   nak   kin-chik
    1SG-INTR-desist-COMP   LOC   POR.1SG-house

(e) *ja'í   cu-qa'wasa   chi   snu:n la-ní:t   **pero**   na-ka:x-lá*
    DEM   small-boy   now   very   turn-PERF   **but**   FUT-correct-turn

(f) *Juan   an-ma   cha'n   pi'n,   pero   akit   ni:*
    Juan   go-PRG   sow   chili   but   1SG   NEG
    k-an-ma   k-cha'n
    1SG-go-PRG   1SG-sow

Yucatec [Stolz et al. 2012: 155]

(f) *Pèedroh-e'   yan   u   pak'-ik   iik   **pèeroh***
    Pedro-CONT   OBL   A.3   sow-TR.INCP   chili   **but**
    tèen-e'   ma'
    E.1SG-CONT   NEG

Zapotec [Pickett and Embrey 1974: 87–88, 91, 97, 121]

(a) *nanna   gukaa   **peru**   ké   zanda   purti*
    1SG:know   1SG:write   **but**   NEG   1SG:be_able   because

	ké	gapa	lapis			
	NEG	1SG:have	lapis			

(b) *napa   gana   kiba   lu   yaga   ka*
    1SG:have   desire   1SG:climb   LOC   tree   DEM
    peru   *ké   ganda*
    but   NEG   1SG:be_able

(c) *zanda   kiba   lu   yaga   ka   **peru** ké   na'ya'*
    1SG:be_able   1SG:climb   LOC   tree   DEM **but**   NEG   1SG:want

(d) *uyuaa   de   ñaa   lugiaa,   **peru***
    1SG:IMPERF:be   of   1SG:PRET:go   market   **but**
    biaana   ra   yoo
    1SG:PRET:remain   LOC   house

(e) *nagasi   najaba   ba'du   ri'   **peru**   zaka   be   nača'wi'*
    now   bad   child   DEM   **but**   3SG.FUT:make 3SG   good

(g) *Ké   zujiiba   Juan   **peru**   naa   zujiiba'*
    NEG   FUT:sow   Juan   **but**   1SG   FUT:sow:1SG

Zoque   [Knudson 1980: 106, 110, 116, 141]

(a) *'ic   haymuspa   **pero**   ye'k   wan   haymusɨ*
    1SG   write:know   **but**   now   NEG   write:be_able
    porke   yamɨn   lapis
    because   NEG:have   pencil

(b) *'ic   ki'mɨ   ti'pa   te   kuymɨ'   **pero**   'ic   wat   ki'mmusɨ*
    1SG   climb   want   DEM   tree:LOC **but**   1SG   NEG   climb:be_able

(c) *'ic   ki'mmuspa   te   kuymɨ'   **pero**   'ic   wan   tihɨ'ɨ*
    1SG   climb:be_able   DEM   tree:LOC **but**   1SG   NEG   want

(d) *'ic   nɨkspa'ittɨ   ka   ma'icikɨ nɨmpahɨ   **pero***
    1SG   about_to_go   DEM   selling_place   **but**
    'ic   cagɨmmɨ   tɨkho'
    1SG   remain   at_home

(e) *yɨ'p   yɨ   'une   malu   **pero**   te'p   wɨhɨ'ahpa*
    DEM   DEM   child   bad   **but**   DEM   make_good:FUT

(f) *Pwa'nɨs   nɨwɨ   penpa,   **pero**   'icci's   wat   pena*
    Juan   chili   3FUT:sow   **but**   1SG   NEG   1FUT:sow

(g) *Pwa'nɨs   wat   pena,   **pero**   'icci'n   penpa*
    Juan   NEG   3FUT:sow   **but**   1SG   1FUT:sow

Maja Robbers
A Mesoamerican perspective on contact-induced change in numeral classification

Abstract: This study aims to provide a synopsis of phenomena that result from ongoing contact of classificatory numeral systems of Mesoamerican languages with the non-classifying Spanish numeral system. It is tested to what extent indigenous numeral classifier systems are open to contact-induced change. Comrie's (2005) claim concerning the substitutability of numeral systems as autarkical subsystems is put in relation to classifying numeral systems. It is shown that early borrowings in numeral classifier constructions are provided by mensuratives which re-structure the system if a different base number underlies.

Keywords: morphosyntax, language contact, numeral classifiers, Mesoamerican languages, Spanish

1 Introduction

In the course of increasing contact with colonial languages, many indigenous languages forfeit their traditional numeral systems to shift toward the model of the dominant language. The indigenous, often multifaceted numeral systems include parallel sets, numeral classification, varying bases, and various higher numeral formation strategies that may strike westerners as exotic. Due to language contact, however, these languages become more and more decimal (Comrie 2005; Harrison 2008: chapter 6). In Mesoamerica, vigesimal systems were dominant (Comrie 2005: 210) before the impact of European languages began in the course of colonization. Even before that, stages of gradual contact-induced change were often characterized by a pre-existing system being enriched by new items.[1]

---

[1] Languages that lack terms for higher numerical values such as HUNDRED and THOUSAND, for example, potentially borrow and thereby integrate such items into the native morphosyntactic structure. In (i), Mapuche integrates the loan *waranqa* 'thousand' from Quechua or Aymara:

Maja Robbers, Uppsala University, Department of Linguistics and Philology, mailbox 635, 75126 Uppsala, Sweden. E-Mail: maja.robbers@lingfil.uu.se

https://doi.org/10.1515/9783110723977-004

Matras (2009: 201) describes the replacement of an indigenous numeral system by a colonial one as "another one of those instances where participation in an activity context that is associated with a particular language leads to a generalization of the relevant word-form from that language." The idea that a numeral system can be replaced partly or completely without affecting the main corpus of the language has been discussed in-depth and summarized as follows by Comrie (2005: 204):

> Perhaps the main reason for the high level of endangerment of numeral systems is that numeral systems are particularly susceptible to the kinds of sociolinguistic changes that arise through language contact. [...] It is not unusual for the numeral system of that dominant language to replace the numeral systems of the other languages, starting with higher numerals, long before these languages as a whole become endangered, indeed in many instances, [...] without these languages becoming endangered.

In his pioneering study, Comrie (2005) discusses many languages the numeral systems of which have been replaced or changed significantly due to contact, yet without having had endangering effects on the language itself, such as Thai and Japanese. It is thus possible to regard numeral systems as independent subsystems of languages where contact phenomena do not have the same impact as they have outside the subsystem.[2] However, the effects of gradual borrowing on systems that are not limited to numerals in the mathematical sense alone, since their numeral classifiers also affect other domains of the language, has not yet been studied in detail. The partial or complete replacement of the indigenous number system by the colonial system due to trade relations is a known development (Comrie 2005). To explore the alternatives it must firstly be analyzed if, and if yes to what degree, a morphosyntactic category that is bound to numerals, i.e. numeral classification, may remain functional in contact with borrowed material. To this end, I will check to what extent a non-classifying language, such as Spanish, may enrich or restructure a pre-existing numeral classifier system of an indigenous language, as opposed to unidirectional change which leads to replacement.

(i)   Mapuche   [Smeets 2008: 410]
        Chile   petú   müle-wü-y-Ø   külá   warangka   chi,   meli   warangka   chi
        chile   still   be-PS-IND-3SUB   three   thousand   PART   four   thousand   PART
        mapuche   müle-wü-y-Ø.
        mapuche   be-PS-IND-3SUB
        'In Chile, there are still about 300,000 or 400,000 Mapuche left.'

2 Harrison (2008) has promoted the somewhat opposed opinion that with the loss of a culture-specific numeral system, manifold valuable and unrecoverable information concerning human history and cognition is lost.

In general linguistic research, much attention has been given to the formation and morphology of cardinal numerals. Here, attention is directed to the domain where numerals and members of a particular dependent category thereof, i.e. numeral classifiers (NC), are morphosyntactically integrated in phrases involving contact-induced change. The impact of a non-classifying language with a decimal base like Spanish on a language with base 20 and which obligatorily adds a NC to a numeral-noun construction in quantifier phrases (QP) potentially involves both types of borrowing, viz. of structure or pattern (= PAT) and of lexemes or matter (= MAT) (Matras 2009). The influx of new lexematic material into these constructions is genuine MAT replication; the potential omission of the NC-slot can be regarded as a kind of *negative* PAT replication. Furthermore, constructions like [NC-numeral noun]$_{QP}$ involve numerals, content words, and grammaticalized classifying morphemes. NCs in contact therefore constitute an interesting field of research for contact linguistics.

To start with, I outline the research topic by shortly elaborating on NCs in Section 2. The anticipated results of a comparison of contact-induced change in the realm of NCs are discussed in Section 3. Firstly, logically possible types of MAT borrowing are defined, which are subsequently tested on linguistic data obtained from grammatical descriptions of languages that obligatorily or frequently employ NCs. As a starting point, I will use experiences and results I gathered from my 2012 fieldwork in the Totonac speaking community of Filomeno Mata. In Section 4, four languages are discussed that provide disparate data as to the integration of loans in QPs. This initial and qualitative approach shall test the potentiality of the topic for further research. Results and outlooks are discussed in Section 5. References will be made also to languages spoken outside Mesoamerica.

2 On numeral classification

The areal distribution of NC languages is high especially in (South) East Asia and Mesoamerica (Aikhenvald 2000: 101). NCs appear next to numerals or quantifiers and classify the noun referent according to inherent properties. Underlying etymologies of NCs may reveal facts about culture-specific lifestyle and culturally relevant taxonomies and categories of objects and living beings. Especially in Mesoamerica, classifiers often grammaticalize from body part nouns (Levy 1994). Within language families, body-part related cognates can be found among spatial locatives and classifiers, often involving semantic bleaching, abstraction, and metaphorical extension (Aikhenvald 2000: 401). In Filomeno

Mata Totonac, among several body-part related classifiers, we find the face-related NC *laka-* for places and towns, cf. (1).

(1) Filomeno Mata Totonac [McFarland 2009: 107]
 laka-tutu n kaa-ciki-n k-lakapás
 NC-three EP LOC-house-PL 1SUB-recognize
 'I know three towns'

As shown in (1), the NC fulfills the function of categorizing the noun referent according to semantic fields, in this case *laka-* indicates a geographical place. Syntactically, NCs are essential to their host languages also outside of QPs. Greenberg (1972) states that NC languages usually (or tendentially) lack nominal number, and that anaphora is realized with NCs. Aikhenvald (2000: 300) discusses the anaphoric and deictic use of classifiers in general. In Filomeno Mata Totonac, youngsters tend to reduce the NC system, mostly by overusing the default classifier (cf. Section 2.1). However, the NC slot is filled obligatorily, as the deictic phrase uttered by a child from the language community in (2) exemplifies.

(2) Filomeno Mata Totonac [Santiago Francisco 2012: 63]
 A-waka **aq**-*tim (xanati)*
 PROX-up NC-one (flower)
 'here is one (flower)'

What we can infer from comparison of (1) and (2) is that the noun referent is optional when predefined or inferred from context. Truly obligatory is the binary structure of the NC and numeral. Since NCs can classify as well as quantify a countable or measurable noun, so-called sortal classifiers are usually distinguished from mensural classifiers, which, in turn, may in some cases be difficult to differentiate from measure terms (Aikhenvald 2000: 114–120). This will be discussed in more detail in Section 2.3.

2.1 Classifiers in contact

Aikhenvald (2000: 383–388) dedicates a section to classifiers in contact. As to Mesoamerica, NCs are widespread and have been distributed among certain language groups via PAT borrowing. For instance, the Lowland Mayan languages, which continuously borrowed from one another, had extensive and "somewhat open" classes of classifiers (Law 2014: 58). Berlin's 1968 monograph on Tzeltal NCs includes more than 500 items that are analyzed as such by the author, mensuratives included. A separation from genuine sortal and qualitative NCs would lead to a significant decrease of morphemes taken into consideration by the author. This indicates that different semantic criteria for the identification of NCs exist, which may strongly depend on the individual field researcher's ideas.

Classifiers are not separately mentioned in the borrowing scale of Thomason and Kaufman (1988: 74–76). Matras (2009: 218) emphasizes the high degree of compatibility of classifiers with loan nouns, so that noun classifiers occupy the second rank in his scale for likelihood of borrowing of nominal modifiers. As to the omission of NCs without contact-induced replacement of numerals, Greenberg (1972: 6) states that it is "particularly common for classifiers not to occur with higher units of the numerical system and their multiples, e.g. 12, 20, 60, 100, 300". This indicates a potential shift in word class of numerals like HUNDRED, TWENTY or THOUSAND that are even numbers with a high value. I will hence refer to such items as high and even numerals (HEN).

It should be emphasized that during the acquisition of a classifier repertoire by children the most general classifiers are learnt first. While children tend to overuse the more general NCs initially, they acquire more specialized ones at a later stage (Aikhenvald 2000: 418–423). In the case of Filomeno Mata Totonac, the acquisition of NCs is not completed by many young Totonac–Spanish bilinguals. In the community, a shift from a rich NC system to a reduced system is now observable, resulting from interrupted acquisition and semantic overextension of the DEFAULT classifier. This can have language-internal reasons, but is equally likely to be the result of strong contact-induced change that is observable due to increasing bilingualism and the gradual shift to Spanish by the younger generation (Robbers 2012). These observations are in line with those of Weinreich (1968: 76):

> [i]n the initial stage of bilingualism, the mother-tongue is, indeed, at the same time the language of greatest proficiency; but later on, many bilinguals exceed their mother-tongue proficiency in the second language under certain circumstances.

Consequently, bilingualism may well cause some categories to be omitted in the course of time. Also Aikhenvald (2012: 3) subsumes that "categories absent from the dominant language are particularly endangered." Similarly, Poplack and Levey (2010: 399) discuss hypotheses concerning the relationship between, and simplification or even loss of, categories:

> [The] individual level of bilingualism is **inversely correlated** with mastery of the minority-language grammar, such that the greater the proficiency in the other language, the more likely the possibility of simplification or loss of minority-language linguistic structure. [emphasis mine]

Due to its frequent use in school, Spanish is the primary language of counting for Totonac-speaking children, and much of the ongoing change is to be ascribed to the high prestige of Spanish as taught in school. Moreover, its use is promoted even by monolingual elders, since as in other postcolonial Mesoamerican settings, the indigenous Totonacs refer to more Hispanicized people as *gente de razón* 'people of reason' or 'reasonable people' (Santiago Francisco 2012: 95). However, contact-induced change outside the numeral system is not extensive. I will come back to the question of whether the avoidance of the own traditional system is the sole option, as well as to other possible outcomes of contact situations involving NCs, in Section 3.

2.2 Mensurals as a subtype of numeral classifiers

As mensurals quickly become obsolete, they are easily replaced by measure terms of another more dominant language (Aikhenvald 2000: 386). Mensurals will also gain special attention here, since their replacement or enrichment seems to happen most rapidly in contact situations. For the current approach, a very broad definition of NCs is adopted. I take the existence of a NC continuum that includes highly grammaticalized and qualitatively classifying items on the one end, and strictly quantifying or measuring items on the other, as the point of departure. Thus, in this initial study, the purely formal criterion of the obligatory filling of a pre-existing morphosyntactic slot for NCs by loan or native MAT is given priority before semantics.

A little support for the inclusion of mensuratives that occupy NC slots in this study is found in Greenberg (1972), who refers to NC languages as usually lacking grammatical distinctions between mass and count nouns and establishes UNIT-COUNTING as a subtype of numeral classification. Unit-counters behave very much like generic classifiers by attaching to unclassified, i.e. semantically underspecified, nouns and may consist of HENs as well as of nouns referring to exact indications of quantity (e.g. 'dozen'), therefore "[m]any analysts consider words for 'ten', 'hundred' etc. in these languages as a subtype of classifiers" (Greenberg 1972: 11). These items may occupy the same syntactic slot as genuine NCs while bearing numerical values within themselves. However, there is still uncertainty among linguists about the exact relationship of mensurals or unit-counters to those NCs denoting qualitative properties, such as shape, consistency, or animacy (Aikhenvald 2000: 115). To this end, a closer look at NC systems in contact may also be beneficial for a better understanding of mensurals in the light of a continuum of numeral classification strategies. Some cases where mensurative terms are reinterpreted as NCs will be shown in Section 3.3.

3 Setting the scene: possible contact-induced developments in NC constructions

In the following sections, two broad trends are introduced that can be inferred from linguistic descriptions of languages that employ NCs. These will form the basis for the comparison of the subsequent case studies. Since sociolinguistic comparisons are beyond the scope of this paper, this aspect is only touched upon.[3] The main body consists of a cursory discussion of possible formal outcomes of NCs in contact and tests the suitability of the data for future studies.

3.1 Reduction, simplification, overgeneralization

Contact phenomena, such as the collapse of an originally vigesimal system and its development into a mixed decimal-vigesimal system, affect the domain of numeral classification, too. Normally, the classifier system is reduced, and individual classifiers adopt a broader or more general meaning, as observed by various authors working on Mesoamerican languages (among them Stolz 2001: 107). There are two processes to be highlighted, viz. (1) OVERGENERALIZATION of the semantically most basic NC, which is normally the DEFAULT classifier, and (2) REDUCTION to the most frequent NCs. For instance, in Palikúr (Arawakan) ordinal formation, youngsters strongly generalize over referents; as Green (2001: 30) puts it: "It appears that the younger generation is not using the ordinal numerals with all the classifiers. Many prefer to use only the 'series' classifier, no matter what nouns the numerals occur with." Similar citations concerning various languages of the world can be found in Aikhenvald (2000: 379–382) and Robbers (2012: 5–7). Thus, NC systems may ultimately be reduced to the default NC, which often originally denotes round or spherical objects, e.g. in Malay, as stated by Aikhenvald 2000: 381, and in Filomeno Mata Totonac as discussed below.[4] One may refer to such a situation as NEGATIVE BORROWING (Aikhenvald 2012: 3). All types of outcomes that were found during my research will be discussed in what follows.

---

3 Likewise, due to space restrictions, the effects of the replacement of classificatory numeral systems in anaphoric contexts is only briefly mentioned here, which would constitute an interesting study not only for Mesoamerican languages.
4 The prominence of "roundness" as an essential concept for classification is also apparent in classificatory parallel numeral sets, e.g. in Yurok (Mithun 1999: 104–106), where animacy is another important factor.

3.2 Resistance towards lexical borrowing

In contrast to languages that borrow quickly, there are also languages where borrowing seems especially cumbersome. To illustrate such a case, an excursus to North America follows. Oneida (Iroquoian) is generally reluctant to integrate borrowed items into its system (Abbott 2016), counting being one of the domains where the language is structurally conservative. QPs regularly involve varied affixation of noun roots and eventually classificatory nouns that resemble numeral classifiers (cf. Abbott 2016: 172–173). Even with borrowings, Oneida uses native numerals, e.g. *tekni kwénis* 'two pennies, two cents' and *kayé sílu* 'four bits (= 50 cents)' (Abbott 2016: 173). Nevertheless, also in the case of Oneida it is stated that the domain of measurement and quantification, i.e. money, place, and time, is especially prone to replication. Subsequently, all types of "foreign measurements seemed to provide a haven for a few borrowings as whole words", such as *minit* 'minute' (Abbott 2016: 173). However, in many cases Oneida clearly favors innovations created by semantic shift instead of direct MAT borrowing, e.g. in (3), the stem *-hwist-*, which "originally may have meant *metal*", was extended to refer to the new concept of coins (Abbott 2016: 173).

(3) Oneida [Abbott 2016: 174]
 skahwístat
 s- ka- hwist- at
 REPET- 3SG.N money one
 'one dollar'

The creation of neologisms by semantic extension is thus one strategy to avoid the loss of native morphology and lexis; this type of contact-induced enrichment, however, is not the standard case.

3.3 Lexical borrowing and mixed QPs

NCs can connect both the clash of two numerical systems and of cultural items when new objects are introduced as noun referents in the language. This can well be tested in the broader Mesoamerican area which hosts various languages that obligatorily employ NCs, and where the colonial languages quickly introduced new numeral systems due to trade and education. For instance, Chontal Maya's system is reduced to the NCs *p'e* for inanimates and *tu* for animates due to the influx of Spanish lexemes. Spanish measure nouns are (additionally) integrated into QPs with classifiers, such as *'um p'e rasimo de ha'as* 'one bunch of bananas' (from Sp. *racimo* 'bunch') (Karttunen 2000: 396). A similar type of

MAT borrowing is also found in Jakaltec. Two constructions mentioned in Day (1973: 61) illustrate the integration of loans in NC position, cf. *ca pulato chib'e* 'two plates of meat' (from Sp. *plato* 'plate') and *cab' líbra panéla* 'two pounds of raw sugar' (from Sp. *libra* 'pound' and *panela* 'unrefined sugar'). This indicates that there are possibilities of enrichment, renovation, and restructuring of NC systems in contact.

On the basis of the previous illustrative examples, two broad trends of NC systems in contact are ponderable:

1. The traditional counting system remains intact; however, due to bilingualism (and eventual language shift), the NC repertoires are not fully acquired by younger speakers. The system is paralleled by the colonial counting system, and depending on extralinguistic factors, the traditional system persists in a reduced form and may ultimately be replaced by the dominant system.
2. The system persists as loans are integrated either in the numeral slot, in the NC slot, and/or in the noun referent position.

As this paper focuses on enrichment, innovation and restructuring via loan integration, possible outcomes of 2 including both native and borrowed material or structurally integrated loans are subsumed in Table 1.

Table 1: Possible combinations of native and loan items in NC constructions.

	NUMERAL CLASSIFIER	NUMERAL	NOUN
(a)	loan	native	native
(b)	loan	loan	loan
(c)	loan	loan	native
(d)	loan	native	loan
(e)	native	loan	loan
(f)	native	loan	native
(g)	native	native	loan
(h)	absent	loan	native
(i)	absent	native	loan
(j)	absent	loan	loan
(k)	absent	native	native

As to the predictability of the foregoing combinations, scenario (g) is especially common as nouns rank very high or highest in borrowing scales (cf. Thomason and Kaufman 1988: 74). Scenario (f) potentially applies in contexts where a high number loan enters a system, scenario (e) does not differ much from (f) and is likewise conceivable as shown by Chontal Maya. Scenarios (a) and (d) are strongly related, since the only difference is made by the choice of the noun, which is in turn largely irrelevant for the current aim. The commonality of (a)–(d) to occupy the NC slot with a loan term in combination with a native numeral will be tested for in what follows. As to the constructions lacking NCs altogether, scenario (h) is common as well and hints at the replacement of the numeral system while retaining native noun referents. Scenarios (h)–(k) are attested for languages with optional NCs, such as Classical Nahuatl as described by Stolz (2001; 2018), and are not primarily relevant here.

4 Case studies

In the following, two Totonacan, a Mayan and a Chibchan language are discussed as to their strategies to integrate loans into QPs. None of these cases can be regarded as showing merely either positive or negative influence of Spanish loans in the sense of supplying MAT or triggering the use of Spanish numerals completely. All sociolinguistic situations are characterized by gradual replacement of the numeral systems and the presence of Spanish as superstrate.

The selection of data is based on an examination of Mesoamerican grammars that include information on NC sets with evidence for MAT borrowing from Spanish. For this purpose, the identified cases that illustrate the possible outcomes of NCs in contact are discussed subsequently. To begin with, Filomeno Mata Totonac (= FMT) is compared with a genetically and regionally related language. In order to strongly contrast these cases to other possible outcomes of contact, a case of productive MAT influence on the NC system of a Southern Mesoamerican language is presented. Finally, syntactic factors are discussed with a Mayan language in Section 4.4.

4.1 Filomeno Mata Totonac

FMT is a Totonacan language spoken in Veracruz, Mexico, where it is still the local mother tongue even though youngsters acquire Spanish in school.[5] More

---

[5] The UNESCO Atlas of the World's Languages in Danger provides a count of 11,710 speakers of FMT according to the 2005 census (http://www.unesco.org/culture/languages-atlas/index.php, checked 18/05/2017).

or less permanent contact with Spanish speakers came quite abruptly to the Totonacos from Filomeno Mata after a small road and telephone connections were established during the 1980s. Nowadays, young speakers are normally bilingual, many with a strong favor for Spanish, while around a third of the elders is monolingual in FMT (McFarland 2009: 2).

FMT's vigesimal numeral system is particularly striking in numerals above 20 (McFarland 2009: 105).[6] There are more than 30 documented NCs, most of whom are shape-related. The size of the repertoire varies among speakers, yet FMT has a few more NCs in use than the related Upper Necaxa Totonac spoken in Patla and Chicontla (Beck 2004: 26). NCs are obligatorily prefixed to numerals up to 20 (McFarland 2009: 105), similar to the faster declining system in Upper Necaxa Totonac (Beck 2004: 27). When counting round or unclassified objects, or when counting without a specific reference object, the default classifier *aq-* is used.

During my field study, the picture was quite diverse as to the usage of NCs. In an experiment designed to elicit certain classifiers via visual stimuli, speakers performed quite differently. The overgeneralization of the default classifier was evident in 50.8 % of all cases, while in 36.5 % of them the more specific classifier was used. In 9.8 % of all instances, speakers confused specialized classifiers, plus there was 2.9 % omission due to long hesitation. Male speakers used more of the specific NCs than female speakers, the default NC was used by them in 34.7 % of all cases, and the specialized NC in 51.8%. Female speakers, on the other hand, scored 64 % usage of the default classifier (Robbers 2012). What may serve as an explanation for the prominence of some peculiar classifiers in contrast to others is usage frequency and the association of a specific classifier only with prominent reference subjects and without extending the meaning to the corresponding class of objects. For instance, many participants used the NC for flat objects to count tortillas but did not use it to count layers of paper.[7] This may be due to the connection of traditional food with the home language, as with usage of paper with Spanish as spoken in school.

FMT numerals can co-occur in a construction involving NCs and Spanish loans as shown in (3). Here the lower numeral serves as a multiplier and is classified by the default NC. Note that the NC is not directly attached to the higher

---

[6] For a detailed record of the numeral system and a list of numeral classifiers in FMT, the reader is referred to McFarland (2009: 105–107).

[7] The simplification and loss of NCs in FMT was again tested and documented in detail by Santiago Francisco and Figueroa Saavedra (2016), who also noted that their younger participants experienced difficulties counting in FMT from 'four' onwards (Santiago Francisco and Figueroa Saavedra 2016: 254–255).

loan number, the borrowed high numeral behaves rather as noun referent of the construction, which in turn is multiplied by the smaller, classified numeral. As in all examples, Spanish loans will be marked by single underlining and are contrasted with native parts of constructions in some examples via boldface, such as the default NC in (4).

(4) Filomeno Mata Totonac [Santiago Francisco 2012: 63]
Aq-chaxan-milh   a-**aq**-tsayan-cieto   a-tati-puxama-ku-kitsis
NC-six-thousand   and-NC-eight-hundred   and-four-twenty-ten-five
'six thousand eight hundred ninety-five'

FMT actually has an expression for 'hundred', which is *kitsispuxam* (multiplicational *kitsis*/five*puxam/twenty), yet more often in use is *aqtimsientu* (*aq-tímsientu* = NC-one*hundred) (Santiago Francisco and Figueroa Saavedra 2016: 244). FMT integrates Spanish loan numerals into higher numeral constructions but abstains from combining NCs with single lower numerals of Spanish origin. Note here that numerals are often seen as constituting a word class of their own, but in fact may belong to different word classes, e.g. lower numerals are rather affixal in NC languages, while higher numerals are rather nouny (cf. Lehmann 2010: 40).

Although in FMT counting from 100 onwards is often done completely in Spanish (Santiago Francisco 2012: 62), Example (4) demonstrates the ability of numeral constructions to integrate Spanish HENs with a native low numeral multiplier. Since not only higher numerals are loans, but also phrases that refer to or contain information about currencies and monetary values (in the Mexican currency *peso*), and other concepts introduced via Spanish, cf. (5) and (6), one is at least led to consider a triggering effect between loan nouns and loan numerals.

(5) Filomeno Mata Totonac [Santiago Francisco 2012: 60]
Dos   peso   xoqo-ma-ka   n-kilo
two   pesos pay-CAUS-S.INDEF EP-kilo
'two pesos are payed for the kilo'[8]

(6) Filomeno Mata Totonac [Santiago Francisco 2012: 61]
Once   alumno   k-taxtú-wa
eleven   students   1PL.EXC-go.out.PFV-1PL.S
'We left as eleven students'

---

8 The sentence is quite difficult to translate accurately since the indefinite subject marker -*ka(n)* marks agentless passivity, which is however unimportant for the aim of this paper.

There is no known case of loan integration in QPs involving NCs on low numerals in FMT. In constructions like ***aq-tím-<u>sientu</u>***, the higher numeral does in fact take the slot of the noun referent and can thus be regarded as such. Therefore, the patterns encountered in FMT are scenario (g), i.e. [[NC$_{native}$-numeral$_{native}$]-noun $_{Spanish}$]$_{QP}$, and scenario (j), which is rather unsurprising. Thus, NCs do not directly combine with loan numerals, the two systems are kept apart by speakers.

Santiago Francisco and Figueroa Saavedra (2016: 255) refer to the changes in counting in FMT as an indicator for the replacement of the language itself. This is in opposition to Comrie's (2005) general observations. The case of FMT can well be compared to those of its close relatives.[9] As Beck (2004: 28) states for Upper Necaxa Totonac:

> Although proficient speakers consistently agree on the correct classifier to use with a particular noun, there is a tendency to replace all of these with the generic *q?-* in casual speech, and many younger speakers are unable to produce the less frequent forms without prompting.

In the related language Huehuetla Tepehua, the reduction is also more advanced than in FMT:

> Huehuetla Tepehua has a rich system of numeral classifiers; however, today the numeral classification system is falling into disuse, with more and more HT speakers using only the two most common classifiers: the general classifier *laqa-* and the human classifier *puma-*. (Smythe Kung 2007: 489)

Overgeneralization and simplification are thus found among the family members, too. As to the intrusion of loans, the Tepehua examples differ from the abovementioned FMT examples mostly in terms of noun referents that occur with NCs, as will be discussed in the following section.

---

9 Similar to FMT, in the revised Papantla Totonac texts, a classified native 'one' functions as multiplier and precedes the borrowed item for 'hundred'. Further high numerals are Spanish loans and never classified, cf. (i).

(ii) Papantla Totonac (Matthew 13: 1–9, verse 8) [PA.BIB]
  Huí nimą lątą akstum ixtalhtzi chalh tahuácalh **aktum** <u>ciento</u> *ixtalhtzi, huí nimą* <u>sesenta</u>, *y huí nimą caj* <u>treinta</u> *mástąlh ixtahuácat.*
  'But another part fell onto good soil and borne fruit, some a **hundredfold**, some <u>sixtyfold</u>, some <u>thirtyfold</u> [of what was sown].'

4.2 Huehuetla Tepehua

Huehuetla Tepehuas lived in contact with Spanish ever since the colonization of their territory, and with many other indigenous languages even before that. As a close relative of Totonac, Tepehua as spoken in Huehuetla (HT) shares many cognates among the numeral classifiers, such as *laq-* for coins (cf. Smythe Kung 2007: 525–534). As Smythe Kung (2007: 5) states, "[a]lmost all HT-speakers are bilingual in Spanish", and similar to the situation in FMT, younger speakers tend to speak Spanish in most settings, even at home. Most parents or grandparents who speak HT address children and toddlers in Spanish (Smythe Kung 2007: 6). HT borrowed content words for new concepts from Spanish, and few grammatical words, such as the conjunctions *y* 'and' and *pero* 'but' (Smythe Kung 2007: 615). Spanish numerals are employed from 'five' onwards even by fluent speakers (Smythe Kung 2007: 479). The NC system is now dramatically reduced. However, Spanish noun loans do not trigger the use of Spanish numerals in phrases like (7)–(9).

(7) Huehuetla Tepehua [Smythe Kung 2007: 504]
 majʔata-*t'uy* *kapen*
 NC:branch-two coffee
 'two branches of (a) coffee (bush)'

(8) Huehuetla Tepehua [Smythe Kung 2007: 647]
 waa naa maa xtaq-ni-kan **laq**-*kiis* *peexuu*.
 FOC EMP RPT give-DAT-S.INDEF NC:money-five peso
 'Then they gave him five pesos.'

(9) Huehuetla Tepehua [Smythe Kung 2007: 667]
 juu **laqa**-*tam* *siglo dieciocho*.
 DET NC:general-one century eighteen
 'Another one from the eighteenth century.'

In the given examples, indigenous HT [NC-numeral] patterns appear next to Spanish loan nouns, for instance in partitive constructions such as (7) and (9) and in object position as in (8). Pattern (g) is thus met. However, according to Smythe Kung's (2007: 489) statement (cf. Section 4.1) concerning the use of NCs in HT, it can be assumed that the cited examples reflect older stages of HT or otherwise more purist usage as was stated for younger speakers. As in FMT, NCs solely attach to the indigenous numerals or as multipliers, or else the QP is characterized by loss of NCs and the sole use of Spanish numerals in all revised examples.

4.3 Kuna

The Chibchan language Kuna behaves differently from the previous cases. Contact between the Spanish and the indigenous Kuna began in the 1600s and took a largely antagonistic course in the centuries after, mostly with limited trade relations. After many Kunas settled in Panama fleeing from the Spaniards before gradual relocation to today's Colombia, a rebellion took place in 1925 which made quasi-autonomy possible for the Kunas. Nevertheless, bilingualism is common today and "Spanish numbers increasingly dominate" due to schooling (Howe 2009: 230). Contact-induced change in the entire numeral system along with integration of Spanish loans can be inferred from several studies of the Kuna language. Generally, Kuna borrows verbs, nouns and numerals especially for new concepts, while the presence of Spanish loans is "significant (but not particularly pervasive)" according to Giannelli and Zamponi (2008: 83).

In Holmer's (1946) description, a pure Kuna numeral system is listed. Table 2 shows the Kuna numeral system with indications for ordinal forms.

Table 2: San Blas Kuna numerals (Holmer 1946: 189).

CARDINAL		ORDINAL	
kwena	'one'	*kepe ~ kepet*[10]	'first'
po(o)	'two'	*po(o)*	'second'
pa(a)	'three'	*pa(a)*	[etc.]
pakke	'four'	...	...
attale	'five'		
nerkwa	'six'	*kukle*	'seven'
paapakka	'eight'	*pakkepakka*	'nine'
ampeki	'ten'		

The numeral system is basically vigesimal. Kuna NCs precede the numeral and follow the noun, as shown in (10).

---

[10] Note that the value for ONE has special status due to suppletive morphology for FIRST, i.e. both ordinals are morphologically unrelated to *kwena* 'one'. Items for FIRST are also often nouny and therefore prone to borrowing (cf. Stolz and Robbers 2016).

(10) San Blas Kuna [Holmer 1946: 190]
　　　tule　　war-kwena
　　　man　　NC:OBL-one
　　　'one man'

As a first hint for integrated loans, Holmer (1952: 49) mentions *mili* 'thousand', *mirkwen* 'one thousand' and *mir pokwa* 'two thousand'. Two decades later, Sherzer (1978) dedicates an article to San Blas Kuna NCs wherein he discusses types of classifiers he analyzed as such during his work with the Kuna. Sherzer (1978: 334) discusses in his section on closed-class mensurative classifiers two loans from Spanish: *mili(-)* 'thousand' and *sientu(-)* 'hundred' as opposed to *tul(a)-* 'twenty' which is, in the semantic domain of monetary values, the unit-counting NC for units of 'ten dollars'. I could neither find applied examples of *mili(-)* and *sientu(-)* in Sherzer (1978) nor in Sherzer (1986); however, in Kuna versions of the Bible (where each book differs somewhat in translation style), the following forms are found:

(11)　Spanish-Kuna unit-counters in translations of the New Testament
　　　mili(-)attar　　　　'five thousand'　　　　[John, 28]
　　　mili(-)pakke　　　　'four thousand'　　　　[Mat, 17]
　　　mili(-)pa　　　　　'three thousand'　　　　[Mat, 12]
　　　mili kuikle　　　　 'seven thousand'　　　 [Rom, 11]

but:

　　　tula(-)nerkwa (20*6)　'a hundred and twenty'　[Mat, 5]

Whereas *mili(-)* for 'thousand' is found continuously, *sientu(-)* for 'hundred' is not. Quite the contrary, at the time of translation it was still constructed via *tula-* 'twenty', as well as variation is found in construction of HUNDREDS, cf. *ila-pa* 'three hundred (denars)'[11] including the default NC *il(a)* for 'number of times' (Sherzer 1978: 334). Several Kuna NCs carry numerical values within themselves. The meanings assigned to the classifier *tula-*, which is both the NC for numerals denoting 'units of 20' and for 'units of 10 dollars', thereby show the friction between the vigesimal and the decimal system. It is used to create expressions for higher values via multiplication. Number words may enter a NC system in a noun-like fashion because of the perceived nouny-ness of HENs, and "Kuna numerals are derived for the most part from nouns currently in use in the language or in use at one time" (Sherzer 1978: 336).

---

11 The noun referent is omitted in anaphorical use.

Another type of impact of Spanish which productively contributes to the Kuna NC system is shown in the domain of NCs derived from verbs, for example *malale(-)* which originates from the native Kuna verb *mare* 'to split'. This domain is however very small. As the only instance of MAT borrowing from Spanish verbs, the form *talle(-)* classifies a load or unit of 'one hundred coconuts' and can be traced back to the Spanish exclamation *¡dale (uno, dos, ...)!* that was used by the Kuna in colonial trade situations according to Sherzer (1978: 336).

Giannelli and Zamponi (2008) take a closer look at Kuna NCs.[12] Similarly tentative about the exact status of borrowed mensurals, they state that "[s]ome Spanish loanwords denoting units of measurement are commonly used as nouns, which are also 'classifiers for themselves' (...)", and which function "analogous to native Kuna nouns with similar denotata" (Giannelli and Zamponi 2008: 88). To illustrate the formal semblance, I henceforth cite all examples provided by the authors that display a typical [noun [NC-numeral]]$_{QP}$ construction:

(12) Kuna [Giannelli and Zamponi 2008: 88]
    a.   san   *nibir*[13]   bo
         meat   NC:pound two
         'two pounds of meat'
    b.   mor   *yarda*   bo
         cloth   NC:yard   two
         'two yards of cloth'
    c.   gwebo *dosin*   bo
         egg   NC:dozen two
         'two dozen of eggs'

In the above examples, it becomes clear that Spanish measure terms are fit to occupy the classifier slot in a numeral-noun construction. If analyzed as NCs, pattern (a) is met by the Kuna examples in (12). However, another construction type is presented in (13), where the English loan *mani*, cited as 'five cents' classifier in Sherzer (1978: 334), contains both the unit, which implies the necessary multiplication, and the object to be measured, i.e. it also denotes the nominal meaning.[14]

---

12 The authors emphasize the hitherto rather unknown dialectology of Kuna. Their work is based on varieties spoken in Playon Chico/Ukupseni, Tupile/Dupir and Ustupu/Usdup.
13 From Spanish *libra* 'pound' (Giannelli and Zamponi 2008: 81).
14 In Holmer's (1952: 70) dictionary, *mani* is generally analyzed as indicating 'silver', 'silver money' or just 'money', without any numerical value within. Sherzer's (1978) description may

(13) Kuna [Giannelli and Zamponi 2008: 88]
    mani   bo
    NC:five-cents   two
    'ten cents (of balboa/dollar)'

By now, also the Kuna numeral system has been widely replaced by Spanish numerals. Due to the original vigesimal system, Giannelli and Zamponi (2008: 88) call the intrusion of numeral loans of decimal nature like *siendo* and *mili* "a violence on the Kuna numeral system". In examples of abstract counting without reference noun given by Giannelli and Zamponi (2008: 89), loans act as multipliers managing the newly introduced decimal system in the first place. All loans are lexically assimilated but cause a severe change in the mathematical operations applied to construct higher numerals. Note also the lack of a NC on the smaller multiplier, indicating the adequacy for loan nouns to shift to, and occupy, the classifier slot:

Table 3: Kuna merging of noun referent and NC (Giannelli and Zamponi 2008: 88).

HEN	NC	MULTIPLIER	OPERATION	NUMERAL
dula	wal-	atar	[400 x 5]	"2000"
	mili	bo	[1000 x 2]	"2000"

As shown in Table 3, the item *mili* acts as noun referent instead of the native *dula* '400' and placeholder for the NC simultaneously. This new development cannot be analyzed according to Table 1 above, since the function of two slots, viz. noun and NC, merges into one.

Whereas the traditional Kuna higher numeral formation is realized in a vigesimal fashion, following the two-layered pattern [numeral base$_{vigesimal}$*[NC-multiplier]]$_{HIGHER\ NUMERAL}$, the Hispanicized numeral construction is reduced or simplified and surfaces as [numeral base$_{decimal}$/NC*multiplier]$_{HIGHER\ NUMERAL}$. Alternatively, the data in Table 3 can be analyzed as attesting pattern (i) with loss of the NC and relocation of the noun referent.

The example of Kuna shows that Spanish loans may enter a classificatory system not only as noun denotata but also in the form of placeholders for classifiers, or combine both functions as reference noun and NC. A numeral system

---

thus display a later development and semantic specification to an exact value or worth of 'five cents', thus a 'nickel'.

that turns into a mixed system is thus assisted by a re-interpretation of the NC slot in abstract counting. However, it has to be emphasized that loan integration in NC position seems to be restricted to mensurals (or unit-counters) and does not take place without interfering with the original numeral system. Invoking formal and functional criteria, it heavily depends on the definition of NCs at hand whether to regard these mensurative items as such.

4.4 Yucatec

Speakers of Yucatec Mayan initially had sparse contact with Spaniards since the early 16th century because the former sprawled in urban areas whereas Mayan speakers inhabited the countryside and were superior in number until the count of Spanish speakers increased in the late 17th century and a permanent contact set in (Michnowicz 2015: 21–23). Today the Yucatecan situation is characterized by a high number of bilingual Mayans working in the urban areas of the peninsula. The language itself enjoys a significantly higher prestige compared to other indigenous languages of Mexico, and regarding borrowings from Spanish it can be stated that there were in fact some mutual influences. Nevertheless, speaker numbers decrease in favor of the dominant colonial language (Michnowicz 2015: 24, 33–35).

The Yucatec variety described by Stolz (1996) shows both the use of optional NCs along with Spanish numerals and the complete absence of NCs. Example (14) where the shift to the Spanish numeral occurs in the course of self-correction illustrates the general picture. Numerals up to the value THREE are expressed by a [[numeral-NC] noun]$_{QP}$ construction, whereas Spanish numerals are used for all higher numbers and do not directly take NCs.

(14)   Yucatec   [Stolz 1996: 388]
*kaxt-eh   túun   **hum-p'éel**   cham   ba'l   de*
search-IMP   then   one-NC:IA   little   thing   of
áasul,   chan...   chan   chichan,   de   kwàadradoh,
blue   little   little   small   of   square
*de   **óox- p'éel**   u   mehen, (...),   kwàatroh*
of   three-NC:IA   3   small   (...)   four
u   mehen   (...)   làadoh-s   bey-a'
3   small   (...)   side-PL   thus-D1
'look for **a (~one)** little blue thing, it is... it is small, it is square, there are **three** of its little, (...), four of its little sides like this'

The author emphasizes that in Yucatec "there seem to exist no productive strategies for shaping new numeral classifiers" (Stolz 1996: 68). Nevertheless, one option remains for Spanish numerals to co-occur with NCs in Yucatec, namely in predicate function as in (15) where the classifier serves as an anaphoric referent in subject or head position. Lehmann (2010) cites the same construction type, cf. (16), wherein NCs may function as dummy nouns, or as he puts it, as "nominalizers in the broadest sense" (Lehmann 2010: 444).

(15) Yucatec [Stolz 1996: 71, following Lucy 1992: 51]
dyes u **túul**-ul máak
ten POS.3 NC:ANIM-REL person
'ten people'

(16) Yucatec [Lehmann 2010: 440]
Hay-**túul**-o'b? – *Seis* u **túul**-ul.
how.many-NC:ANIM-PL six [POS.3 NC:ANIM-REL]$_{NP}$
'How many were they?' – 'There were six of them.' (lit. 'six (are) of them')

Spanish numerals are thus not integrated into QPs involving NCs in Yucatec, whereas a Spanish numeral can co-occur with a NC but only if detached from it and placed to the left of the construction, thus constituting a further additional type that can be depicted as [numeral$_{Spanish}$ [POR NC-REL noun]$_{POSS}$]$_{QP}$. Beyond that, only pattern (g) applies here and is restricted to values up to THREE, followed by pattern (j) (and potentially (h)) for FOUR onwards. Nevertheless, the anaphoric use in phrases (15) and (16) still calls for a separate study.

5 Conclusions

This peek into the realm of loan integration in NC constructions raises more questions than it gives answers, but even this limited data provides many interesting indications for research. Over and above, the present study shows that what is affected in language shift situations is not only the numeral system per se, but also a great deal of related morphology, lexicon, and syntax. This is interesting relating to Comrie (2005) who states that the replacement of a numeral system is not necessarily a sign of decreasing vitality of the language, but often one of the *symptoms* of gradual language replacement. Since particularly the anaphoric (or cataphoric) use of NCs occurs in contexts other than counting, it is conceivable that in classifying languages, application areas of the NCs are also affected when numerals are gradually replaced by Spanish numerals that do not take NCs. Additionally, it is possible that NCs persist longer in the realm of non-QPs, e.g. as anaphoric referents. The gradual replacement of numerals in NC languages therefore potentially has a more extensive influence on grammar than in languages without NCs. This, however, shall be tested on the basis of richer and more comparable data in future studies. As an interesting case in point, the Yucatec examples in (15) and (16) are not captured in the summarizing Table 4.

Table 4: Attested combinations of native and loan items in NC constructions.

	NUMERAL CLASSIFIER	NUMERAL	NOUN	LANGUAGE
(a)	loan	native	native	Kuna
(b)	loan	loan	loan	–
(c)	loan	loan	native	–
(d)	loan	native	loan	–
(e)	native	loan	loan	–
(f)	native	loan	native	–
(g)	native	native	loan	FMT, HT, Yucatec
(h)	absent	loan	native	–
(i)	absent	native	loan	Kuna
(j)	absent	loan	loan	FMT, HT, Yucatec
(k)	absent	native	native	–
	NUMERAL CLASSIFIER + NOUN REFERENT	NUMERAL		
(l)	loan	native		Kuna

It can be summarized that scenario (a) as exemplified by Chontal is attested in Kuna, and, importantly, only for mensurative items. The most frequently employed pattern is, unsurprisingly, pattern (g) as described for FMT, HT and Yucatec, and only for a defined range of small numerals in each case. Pattern (j) is attested in FMT, HT and Yucatec and is likely to be more common throughout Mesoamerica. Some more general remarks are added below.

– The discussed examples of loans in NC position are strictly mensural or quantifying and fail to meet the semantic criteria for genuine qualitative NCs.
– Mensurals are integrated well before items that refer to qualitative (e.g. culture-specific) properties.

- Newly introduced numerals that occupy NC slots potentially interfere with numeral systems of non-decimal bases and thus re-structure parts of the system.
- The NC slot as a 'multiplier-slot' is preconceived.

In addition, it is clear that Table 1 (Section 3.2.2) is far too rigid to take account of the constructions in question due to the Yucatec case as discussed above, and since a borrowed numeral may shift to noun position or combine both numerical value and noun reference as in Kuna. A new model would have to allow for syntactic variation, and potentially also for merging of noun reference and classifier. This will be done best on the basis of a larger dataset.

As to putative numerals it can be stated that the data discussed once again confirm that units like HUNDRED and THOUSAND act as nouns in particular instances. These items enter QPs in a classifier-like manner, but occupy a marginal position in the numeral classification continuum as they are mensuratives and unit-counters. The special role of HUNDRED and THOUSAND also in borrowing contexts is of course not new information. Among many others, Tohono O'odham's numeral system was enriched by *mi-yohn* 'million', *siant* 'hundred', and *mihl* 'thousand' (Saxton and Saxton 1969: 125). Similarly in Jakaltec, indigenous numerals are used when counting from 1–99, while the item for HUNDRED is the loan *syénto* and counting units of hundreds and thousands is realized via multiplication in the same operation as with indigenous numerals, e.g. *cab' syénto* 'two hundred' (Day 1973: 57–58). Also, in Berlin's survey of Tzeltal NCs, he states that *mil* is "the only classifier which is clearly Spanish in origin" (Berlin 1968: 22). HUNDRED and THOUSAND may actually be perceived as self-contained entities instead of dependent members of a coherent (numeral) system. The same applies to the precolonial base numbers such as TWENTY in Kuna.

Again I emphasize that much more research is needed to approach the many open questions concerning the permeability of NC systems in the realm of QPs and beyond. Based on Comrie's (2005) seminal work on endangered numerals in the world's languages, further to be considered is the question whether and how far the replacement of an indigenous numeral system shall be regarded as a factor of language endangerment or replacement, or whether a numeral system and its annexes show influence merely within themselves and thus truly qualify as autarkical subsystems. It is therefore hoped to inspire other linguists to keep these questions in mind when working with NC languages.

Acknowledgments: I am very grateful to Eeva Sippola for having invited me to the *New Varieties in the Americas Colloquium* which took place in Bremen, Germany, in December 2016, where I presented data from fieldwork that was realized back in the early years of my university studies. Since my former project, a test on the use of numeral classifiers in the speech of young Totonacs in Filomeno Mata, Mexico, has successfully been reworked by Santiago Francisco and Figueroa Saavedra (2016), I seized the opportunity to contribute here by revisiting the sphere of numeral classification in language contact situations and compare my results with other cases retrieved from the literature. I also sincerely thank Danae Perez for her valuable comments on a draft version of this paper, José Santiago Francisco for introducing me to his mother tongue, and Christel and Thomas Stolz for being great motivators and inspirers to work with indigenous languages of the Americas.

Abbreviations

1SUB	first person subject
3SUB	third person subject
ANIM	animate
CAUS	causative
D1	first person deixis
DAT	dative
DET	determiner
EMP	emphatic
EP	epenthetic segment
EXC	exclusive
FMT	Filomeno Mata Totonac
FOC	focus
HEN	high and even numeral
IA	inanimate
IMP	imperative
IND	indicative
INDEF	indefinite
LOC	locative
MAT	matter
N	neuter
NC	numeral classifier
NP	noun phrase
OBL	(ob)long
PAT	pattern
PART	particle
PFV	perfective

PL	plural
POR	possessor
POS	possessive
PROX	proximal
PS	persistence
QP	quantifier phrase
REL	relational
REPET	repetitive
RPT	reported speech/evidential
S	subject
SG	singular

Sources

[Mat, 17]	Sociedad Bíblica Americana Nueva York. 1951. *Pap Kaya Purpa Nuet San Markkos Soiksatti.* http://biblacy.org/pdfs/Kuna/02Mark-Kuna.pdf. (checked 18/05/2017)
[Mat, 12]; [Mat, 5]	Sociedad Bíblica Americana Nueva York. no year. *Tummat Ikar Par Soik Malat Kus Malatti.*http://biblacy.org/pdfs/Kuna/01Matt-Kuna.pdf. (checked 18/05/2017)
[John, 28]	Sociedad Bíblica Americana Cristóbal. 1960. *Pap Kaya Purpa Nuet San Wan Soiksatti* (El Evangelio segun San Juan). http://biblacy.org/pdfs/Kuna/04John-Kuna.pdf. (checked 18/05/2017)
[Rom, 11]	Sociedad Bíblica Americana Nueva York – Cristóbal. 1959. *Oroma Tule Mar Se Paplo Karta Narmaiksat* (La Epistola del Apostol San Pablo a los Romanos). http://biblacy.org/pdfs/Kuna/06Roman-Kuna.pdf. (checked 18/05/2017)
[PA.BIB]	Wycliffe Bible Translators, Inc. 1979. *Xasasti talaccaxlan* (New Testament in Totonac, Papantla). http://worldbibles.org/language_detail/eng/top/Papantla+ Totonac. (checked 18/05/2017)

References

Abbott, Clifford. 2016. Contact and change in Oneida. In Andrea L. Berez-Kroeker, Diane M. Hintz & Carmen Jany (eds.), *Language contact and change in the Americas: Studies in honor of Marianne Mithun,* 167–188. Amsterdam & Philadelphia: John Benjamins.

Aikhenvald, Alexandra Y. 2000. *Classifiers: A typology of noun categorization Devices.* Oxford: Oxford University Press.

Aikhenvald, Alexandra Y. 2012. Language contact in language obsolescence. In Claudine Chamoreau & Isabelle Léglise (eds.), *Dynamics of contact-induced language change,* 77–109. Berlin & Boston: De Gruyter Mouton.

Beck, David. 2004. *A grammatical sketch of Upper Necaxa Totonac.* Munich: LINCOM. Europa.

Berlin, Brent. 1968. *Tzeltal numeral classifiers: A study in ethnographic semantics*. The Hague: Mouton.
Comrie, Bernard. 2005. Endangered numeral systems. In Jan Wohlgemuth & Tyko Dirksmeyer (eds.), *Bedrohte Vielfalt: Aspekte des Sprach(en)tods*, 203–230. Berlin: Weißensee-Verlag.
Day, Christopher. 1973. *The Jacaltec language*. Bloomington: Indiana University Press.
Giannelli, Luciano & Raoul Zamponi. 2008. Hispanisms in Kuna. In Thomas Stolz, Dik Bakker & Rosa Salas Palomo (eds.), *Hispanisation. The impact of Spanish on the lexicon and grammar of the indigenous languages of Austronesia and the Americas*, 77–94. Berlin & New York: De Gruyter.
Green, Diana. 2001. Palikur numerals. *Summer Institute of Linguistics (Brazil)*. 1–44. www.sil.org/americas/brasil/PUBLCNS/LING/englplnb.pdf. (checked 18/05/2017)
Greenberg, Joseph H. 1972. Numeral classifiers and substantival number: Problems in the genesis of a linguistic type. *Working Papers on Language Universals* 9. 1–39.
Harrison, K. David. 2008. *When languages die: The extinction of the world's languages and the erosion of human knowledge*. Oxford: Oxford University Press.
Holmer, Nils Magnus. 1946. Outline of Kuna grammar. *International Journal of American Linguistics* 12(4). 185–97.
Holmer, Nils Magnus. 1952. *Ethno-linguistic Kuna dictionary, with indices and references to a critical and comparative Kuna grammar* (Etnologiska studier 14) and *The grammatical sketch in Kuna chrestomathy* (Etnologiska studier 18). Göteborg: Etnografiska Museet.
Howe, James. 2009. *Chiefs, scribes, and ethnographers: Kuna culture from inside and out*. Austin, TX: University of Texas Press.
Karttunen, Frances. 2000. Approaching the semimillenium: Language contact in Latin America. In Eugene H. Casad & Thomas L. Willet (eds.), *Uto-Aztecan structural, temporal, and geographic perspectives: Papers in Memory of Wick R. Miller by the Friends of Uto-Aztecan*, 387–409. Sonora: Universidad de Sonora.
Law, Danny. 2014. *Language contact, inherited similarity and social difference: The story of linguistic interaction in the Maya lowlands*. Amsterdam & Philadelphia: John Benjamins.
Lehmann, Christian. 2010. On the function of numeral classifiers. In Franck Floricic (ed.), *Essais de typologie et de linguistique générale. Mélanges offerts à Denis Creissels*, 435–445. Lyon: École Normale Supérieure.
Levy, Paulette. 1994. *How shape becomes grammar: On the semantics of part morphemes in Totonac*. Nijmegen: Max-Planck Institute for Psycholinguistics.
Lucy, John A. 1992. *Grammatical categories and cognition: A case study of the linguistic relativity hypothesis*. New York: Cambridge University Press.
Matras, Yaron. 2009. *Language contact*. Cambridge: Cambridge University Press.
McFarland, Teresa A. 2009. *The phonology and morphology of Filomeno Mata Totonac*. Berkeley: University of California doctoral dissertation.
Michnowicz, Jim. 2015. Maya-Spanish contact in Yucatan, Mexico: Context and sociolinguistic implications. In Sandro Sessarego & Melvin González-Rivera (eds.), *New perspectives on Hispanic contact linguistics in the Americas*, 21–42. Madrid: Iberoamericana/Vervuert.
Mithun, Marianne. 1999. *The languages of Native North America*. Cambridge: Cambridge University Press.
Poplack, Shana & Stephen Levey. 2010. Contact-induced grammatical change. In Peter Auer & Jürgen Erich Schmidt (eds.), *Language and space – An international handbook of linguistic variation:* Vol. 1 – *Theories and methods*, 391–419. Berlin & Boston: De Gruyter Mouton.

Robbers, Maja. 2012. *On the declining use of numeral classifiers in young people's Totonac.* Bremen: University of Bremen B.A. thesis.

Santiago Francisco, José. 2012. *Contacto lingüístico español-totonaco en Filomeno Mata, Veracruz.* Mexico City: Centro de Investigaciones y Estudios Superiores en Antropología Social MA thesis.

Santiago Francisco, José & Miguel Figueroa Saavedra. 2016. El desuso de los números y los clasificadores numerals en la lengua totonaca entre los jóvenes de Filomeno Mata, Veracruz (México). *UniverSOS* 13. 239–257.

Saxton, Dean & Lucille Saxton. 1969. *Dictionary Papago and Pima to English, English to Papago and Pima.* Tucson: The University of Arizona Press.

Sherzer, Joel F. 1978. Kuna numeral classifiers. *Kuna Collection of Joel Sherzer.* The Archive of the Indigenous Languages of Latin America. www.ailla.utexas.org Media: text. Access: public. Resource: CUK031R001. (checked 18/05/2017)

Sherzer, Joel F. 1986. The report of a Kuna curing specialist: the poetics and rhetoric of an oral performance. In Joel F. Sherzer & Greg Urban (eds.), *Native South American discourse*, 169–212. Berlin & New York: De Gruyter.

Smeets, Ineke. 2008. *A grammar of Mapuche.* Berlin & New York: De Gruyter.

Smythe Kung, Susan. 2007. *A descriptive grammar of Huehuetla Tepehua.* Austin: University of Texas PhD dissertation.

Stolz, Christel. 1996. *Spatial dimensions and orientation of objects in Yucatec Maya.* Bochum: Universitätsverlag Dr. N. Brockmeyer.

Stolz, Thomas. 2001. *Die Numeralklassifikation im klassischen Aztekischen.* München: Lincom Europa.

Stolz, Thomas. 2018. On classifiers and their absence in Classical and Colonial Nahuatl. *STUF/Language Typology and Universals* 71(3). 339–396.

Stolz, Thomas & Maja Robbers. 2016. Unorderly ordinals: On suppletion and related issues of ordinals in Europe and Mesoamerica. *STUF/Language Typology and Universals* 69(4). 565–594.

Thomason, Sarah G. & Terrence Kaufman. 1988. *Language contact, Creolization, and genetic linguistics.* Berkeley: University of California Press.

Weinreich, Uriel. 1968. *Languages in contact. Findings and problems.* The Hague: Mouton.

Maria Mazzoli
Secondary derivation in the Michif verb: Beyond the traditional Algonquian template

Abstract: Scholars use the terms primary and secondary derivation to describe stem formation in Plains Cree and other Algonquian languages, in a way that does not highlight the substantial difference between the two processes and does not create a distinction between final morphemes (involved in primary derivation) and derivatives of the stem (involved in secondary derivation). This approach is also generally used for Michif. In this paper, I focus on the difference between primary and secondary derivation in Michif, recognizing that: (1) so-called primary derivation is combination of categorizing items (finals) to lexical initials, it is mostly unavailable to speakers as a conscious process, and non-productive, while (2) so-called secondary derivation is canonical derivation of suffixes deriving autonomous stems, it is available to speakers and productive. Based on this, I propose a Michif verb template that originates in Michif occurrences only. I also provide the list of 20 secondary derivatives in Michif, their semantic functions and their linguistic behavior, based on the analysis of the text of *La pchit Sandrieuz* (Fleury and Bakker 2004) included as an Appendix.

Keywords: Michif, mixed language, Plains Cree, primary derivation, secondary derivation, verb template, word formation

1 Introduction

Michif combines Plains Cree verbs and Metis French nouns. It is a mixed language that, given the split in the source of lexical and grammatical items, is classified as a Noun-Verb mixed language (Bakker 2017; cf. also Mazzoli and Sippola in press). Michif formed in the first decades of the 19th century along with the emergence of the Metis (Bakker 1997) and is severely endangered (Mazzoli 2019, 2020).

Michif is under-described, especially in the verbal domain. Linguists generally consider Michif verb morphology to be equivalent to that of Plains Cree, although the complex history of contact among Cree, French, and other Algonquian languages suggests that some restructuring has taken place. Therefore, even where the Michif verb stem is etymologically Algonquian and its phonological shape is well preserved with respect to the Cree source, several issues remain to be assessed. For example, it is unclear whether the morphosyntactic structures postulated for the Cree source are transparent to Michif speakers synchronically or whether semantic drift has taken place. The rather unique social history of Michif and its rare mixed structural features call for a specific linguistic description and analysis tailored to this language variety. Notwithstanding the fact that numerous mixed languages (Michif included) show remarkable similarities to their source languages, recent work has challenged the idea that the phonological and grammatical features were transferred intact from each language into the emerging contact language. Rather, it suggests that the resulting structural features are a complex arrangement involving transfer, innovation, and mixing (for Michif, cf. Stewart and Meakins in press; Gillon and Rosen 2018; Sammons 2019).

In this paper, I propose a verb template that is the first to be designed to specifically account for Michif data, from a Michif-specific perspective. The analysis of the verb differs in several respects from those previously presented for either Michif or Plains Cree. First, in the description of the Michif verb, Rhodes (1977) and Bakker (2004) focused on the Michif verb inflectional paradigm and highlighted the differences between Plains Cree and Michif. Second, the morphological structure of the stem in Algonquian languages, and consequently in Michif, has been interpreted in terms of composition (prefixed preverbs), primary derivation (stem-internal combination of non-autonomous roots and suffixes), and secondary derivation (post-stem suffixes, derivation in a traditional sense) (Wolfart 1973; Goddard 1990; Bakker 2006). Since Bloomfield (1946), the morphemes that compose the lexical core of the Algonquian verb have been labeled in terms of their relative position in a template with three slots, *initials*, *medials*, and *finals* (Goddard 1990: 471, Valentine 2001b). While this conventional analysis in the Algonquian scholarship is partly adopted here, the taxonomy is employed critically. The terms initial and final, for instance, "reflect the templatic, lexical, and non-hierarchical nature of traditional accounts of Algonquian word formation" (Mathieu 2013: 100, note 9). Since I assume a hierarchical, typologically-oriented configuration for all Michif verb stems, I propose a revised use of the traditional templatic terms for Michif, where no medial slot is included in the template, and a distinction between the stem-internal final morphemes and a set of derivatives that are distinct from the stem-internal finals is added.

This analysis aims to provide Michif data that can be better integrated in cross-linguistic comparison. Moreover, it will contribute to developing accessible pedagogical materials grounded in the real occurrences of Michif data to the benefit of learners.

The paper is structured as follows. In Section 2, I outline the historical and sociolinguistic profile of Michif. In Section 3, I provide a template consisting of 12 slots for the Michif verb. In Section 4, I concentrate on secondary derivation, providing the exhaustive list of secondary derivatives in Michif and discussing their function and relative order. In Section 5, conclusions follow.

2 Michif historical and sociolinguistic profile

The Metis people are a distinct Aboriginal Nation sharing a common history and culture. Michif, including its various regional varieties, is identified by the Metis as a unique language that is symbolic of the Metis identity (cf. the Report of the Royal Commission on Aboriginal Peoples, volume 1, 1996: 138–145, 606). Michif was adopted as the official language of the Metis Nation in July 2000 (Barkwell 2004: 1).

The emergence of the Metis Nation is related to the fur trade and the dynamics of the European settlement in what today is Canada. In the second half of the eighteenth century, marriages between fur traders, or *voyageurs* (mostly of French origin), and Indigenous women became common in the Great Lakes region in Eastern Canada. Most of the marriages involved Saulteaux women (from a branch of the Ojibwa/Ojibwe/Chippewa, autoglossonym *Anishinaabe*). However, Plains Cree was commonly spoken as a lingua franca outside the immediate family in Saulteaux communities (Rhodes 1982). Although the early mixed communities probably developed in present-day southern Ontario, the origins of the Michif as a mixed language has been traced to the forks of the Assiniboine and Red rivers in the Red River settlement (present-day Winnipeg, Manitoba). The specific mixture of the Michif language stabilized between the 1820s and the 1870s, when the Metis gathered to participate in annual buffalo hunts and related camp activities, mainly based in the area of the Red River basin (Bakker 1997: 274ff.). The emergence of the Metis' identity is also related to the socio-political events leading to the Red River (1870) and the Northwestern (1885) resistances of Indigenous populations against the Euro-Canadian expansion. During this era, the Metis were forced to disperse towards the West, which has resulted today in pockets of Michif speakers located across a wide area, primarily in Manitoba, Saskatchewan, and North Dakota (with some as far west as Alberta, British Columbia, and Montana).

Speakers and scholars use the term "Michif" to refer to at least three distinct languages, identified by linguists as follows (Bakker 1997: 119–139; Rosen 2007: 3; Bakker 2013):

- **Michif** (southern Michif, or mixed Michif), the main object of this paper, is the mixed language stemming from Plains Cree and Metis French. It is mostly spoken in Manitoba, southern Saskatchewan, and northern North Dakota. It is indicated using the stars in Figure 1. Its speakers refer to it as *Michif* or *li Krii*.
- **Michif Cree** (northern Michif, marked with filled triangles in Figure 1) is basically Plains Cree with extensive French noun borrowing, including in the basic lexicon, but not as extended as in southern Michif. It is spoken mainly in northern Saskatchewan (e.g. Ile a la Crosse), and it was mostly called *nîhiyawîwin* or Cree (in English) by its speakers until the 1980s.
- **Michif French** (marked with empty triangles in Figure 1) is a variety of Canadian French with great Algonquian influence in the phonology, syntax, and lexicon. It is mainly spoken in southern Manitoba (e.g. Saint Laurent). Its speakers refer to it as *Michif*.

In this paper, the term Michif refers to southern mixed Michif.

Today, Michif in all its varieties is severely endangered. The mixed or southern variety of Michif has 100–150 speakers between Canada and the USA, all in their 70s or older, with no children learning the language (Golla 2007: 62). Most Michif speakers are today fluent in English, and a few have knowledge of Cree, Ojibwe, or French. Language loss is a direct result of colonial and postcolonial policies. The imposition of the English language (and French, to a lesser extent) had its most violent expression in the context of residential schools, which were government-sponsored religious institutions established to assimilate Indigenous children into Euro-Canadian culture. In about one century, about 150,000 First Nations, Inuit, and Metis children were taken away from their families and communities. At least three generations of people were affected: most of the children involved lost connection with their culture as well as their languages, and some of them lost their lives (cf. the final Report of the Truth and Reconciliation Commission of Canada released in 2015, and Mazzoli 2019: 108–110).

The map in Figure 1 shows the distribution of Michif-speaking communities in Ontario, Manitoba, Saskatchewan, Alberta, and North Dakota, relying on data from Statistics Canada 2016 (and the *Kitchitwa Ondwewe Nooding* report for

North Dakota 2011). The map gives the approximate location of communities where speakers identified themselves having Michif as a mother-tongue in the 2016 Canadian Census, as well as information on the Michif variety they speak. A similar map is published in Mazzoli (2019), with data from the previous census (Statistics Canada 2011).

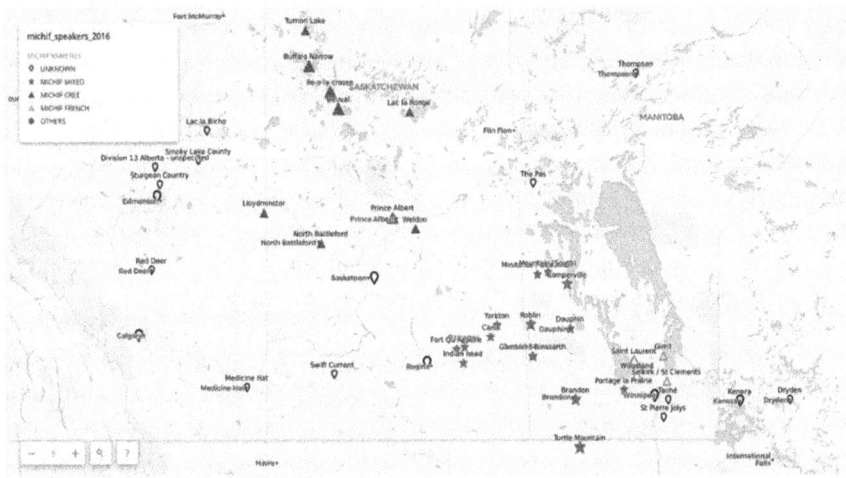

Figure 1: Michif-speaking communities in Ontario, Manitoba, Saskatchewan, Alberta, and North Dakota.

Metis community members and researchers are currently involved in different types of revitalization, documentation, and description activities. Some learners developed fluency in Michif as a second language thanks to the pedagogic resources available and programs of language immersion (i.e. several Mentor-Apprentice programs in Camperville between 2004 and 2010, the Brandon Mentor-Apprentice program in summer 2017; cf. Mazzoli 2019: 110–116; and the six Mentor-Apprentice programs concluded in 2019 in Brandon, Yorkton, and Dauphin, organized by the Prairies to Woodlands Indigenous Language Revitalization Circle).

3 Michif language: verb stem structure

Michif is classified as a Noun-Verb mixed language (Bakker 2017), which was considered highly exceptional before other languages with similar characteristics were also identified (e.g. Okrika Igbo-Ijo in Nigeria). Mixed languages are the result of a massive lexical manipulation and or the crystallization of practices of phrase insertion. This may result in languages that mix lexemes (content words) from one language and grammar (affixes, function words and word order) from another language, as is the case for Media Lengua and Angloromani. In contrast to those languages, however, Michif presents a rather sharp dichotomy in the source of its lexemes and grammar: the whole verb phrase (verb stems and affixes, adverbials, and personal pronouns) derives from Plains Cree, while most of the noun phrase (nouns, adjectives, and articles) derives from French. However, in the noun phrase, demonstratives and obviative markers are Cree-derived, and Gillon and Rosen (2018) argue that the noun phrase has a mainly Algonquian-derived syntax. As for the verb phrase, it is strikingly similar to Plains Cree, but it remains unknown to what extent language contact altered the morpho-syntactic structure of the Cree verbs at the time Michif was formed. Moreover, the integration of French-derived nominals, including nominalized verb infinitives as Michif stems, contributed specific functional elements, like the morpheme *-ii-*, derived from the French infinitive marker *-er* and reanalyzed as a FINAL assigning the features of animacy and intransitivity to the verb stem (Mazzoli et al. in press). Some influence from Ojibwe and other Algonquian languages have also been attested in Michif (Rhodes 2008), and recently from English as well.

Since the morpho-syntactic complexity of Michif is mainly derived from Plains Cree, it has been classified as an Algonquian language (Gillon et al. 2018). Its verbal complexity is described as "polysynthetic", which is a multifaceted theoretical notion (Mattissen 2017). In the case of Michif, it refers to (1) a high ratio of morphemes per word (up to 12 slots in the verb template), (2) polypersonal agreement within the transitive animate verb, (3) a tendency to non-root (bound) lexical affixation within the stem, (4) verb root serialization, and (5) denominal formations exclusively from French noun phrases (also called light verb noun incorporation, Mazzoli et al. in press). In Michif, as in other Algonquian languages, there are four main verb stem classes based on the intersection of transitivity and animacy features. Each class requires different inflectional markers: inanimate intransitive (II), animate intransitive (AI), transitive inanimate (TI), and transitive animate (TA). In addition, there are semitransitive verb stems (Dryer 2007), which are semantically (ambiguously) transitive verbs that are morphologically intransitive but can take objects (abbreviated here as AI+O).

In accordance with the tradition in the Algonquian literature to provide templates for Algonquian languages' morphological verb structure (Valentine 2001a; Bakker 2006; Harrigan et al. 2017), I will provide and discuss the template for Michif.

Table 1: A template for the Michif verb.

1	2	3	STEM (open = lexicon)		6	7	8	9	10	11	12
ORDER or PERS PRON	TENSE/MOOD (close set, rigid order)	PRE-VERB (open, free)	4	5	THEME TI	DERIVATIVES Voice Valency Animacy (full list in Fig. 3)	THEME TA (TI)	OBV AGR (POSS SBJ)	PERS AGR	PLURAL	SJ
			INITIAL	FINAL							
ee- kaa- chi- CNJ	kii- PST ka- FUT wii- VOL	kaahkwee- TRY noohte- WANT	open set	closed set	x	output VTA -aw TA -h CAUS -t TR	-aa -ee -i -iti -iko DIR/INV	-yi OBV	-w IND	-aan -ak -ik -a	-i SJ
		[...]		concrete -eeyiht TI -eeyim TA -payi INTR	*-am THE.TI	-shtaw BEN -m COM			[...]	[...]	
OR		miyo- GOOD mayi- BAD				-*(am)aw APP [...]			-aan -an CNJ		
ni- ki- IND		[...]		abstract -ee/aa AI -aa AI -i AI -oo AI -ee II	x	output VTI -t TR -sht BEN	-am THE.TI	x	[...]		
					x	output VAI -ikee GEN -ikaashoo MED -aakwa PRED -ito REC -*(am)aashoo AC.FOC [...]	x	-yi OBV	-n -w IND [...] -yaan -yen -t -k CNJ		
				[...]	*-am THE.TI						
					x	output VII -maka II		x			

3.1 Michif verb template

Until present, there has been no study on Michif verb structure and processes of stem formation, apart from brief mentions by Rhodes (1977: 8), Bakker (2004: 73–74), and Rosen (2007: 33–35). In order to sketch an outline of the general structure of the Michif verb and its stem-internal structure, linguists have relied on Cree descriptions (Wolfart 1973; Goddard 1990; Bakker 2006) and assumed that the same holds for Michif. Bakker and Papen (1997: 313) argued that "the Michif verb seems to have the full derivational and compositional possibilities of the Plains Cree verb, with preverbs, object incorporation, voice and valency marking suffixes, agreement morphemes, etc." Similarly, Souter's *Index of Verb Finals in Michif* (2010) is modeled after the Cree finals analyzed by Wolfart (1973) and listed in Cook and Muehlbauer's *Morpheme index of Plains Cree* (2010). The general assumption of the morphosyntactic similarity between Michif and Plains Cree remains unchallenged and is also stated as a given fact in more general textbooks (cf. Comrie 2010: 28).

In Table 1, I present a verb template designed specifically for Michif that differs from those presented in Bakker and Papen (1997: 314), Bakker (1997) for Michif, and Bakker (2006) for Plains Cree. In particular, I make a case for splitting the general category of finals for Michif between (1) stem-internal finals which *combine* (primary derivation) with bound lexical roots on their left (position 5 in the template), and (2) stem-external derivatives, that *derive* (secondary derivation) new stems from existing ones (position 7 in the template). The group of secondary derivatives consists of productive morphemes (mainly voice and valency suffixes) that differ substantially from the stem-internal finals. Therefore, I present a list of secondary derivatives that apply to full stems only, and that I suggest that they should not be labeled as finals. Moreover, I do not include a slot for medials in the Michif stem nor the slot for the possessed/ obviative object marker *-im* (before the TA direction sign slot). Finally, I identify a set of stem-ending (long) vowels as intransitive finals and create two separate slots for the TI theme signs (slot 6 and 8) and the TA theme signs (slot 8).

The data come from several sources. The main source is the text and the audio of the tale *La pchit Sandrieuz aañ Michif* (Cinderella), told in Michif by Norman Fleury (Fleury and Bakker 2004). The glossed text is annexed in the Appendix. The Cinderella story is part of the Metis oral tradition and was common throughout the Metis homeland (Bakker 2012: 171). Other data come from elicitations I conducted between February and July 2017 in Manitoba, Saskatchewan, and North Dakota, from the Michif online dictionary (Rosen 2019), and from Laverdure and Allard (1983). Additional data was obtained by consulting Cree examples from Wolfart (1973) and Bloomfield (1946) and then eliciting the correspondent Michif forms. In the following, examples come from Fleury and Bakker (2004) unless otherwise stated. In order to provide a homogeneous dataset, all examples have been adapted to the Michif spelling coventions proposed in Rosen and Souter (2009, 2015).

I will first describe what happens in the slots preceding the stem (1 to 3). Then, I will illustrate the slots traditionally called endings (9–12, conflating polyperson agreement, number and obviation) plus the so-called transitive themes in Algonquian (slots 6 and 8). Then, I will turn to the more lexical part of the verb and describe the stem internal structure (slots 4–5) and the voice and valency derivative slot (7). In Section 4, I will narrow the focus to list and describe the secondary derivatives in Michif.

3.2 Pre-stem: order, person prefixes and preverbs

The pre-stem includes slots number 1–2–3. Plains Cree and Michif, like other Algonquian languages, have two main orders, the independent and the conjunct. The independent order corresponds to main clauses and it is unmarked, but can be recognized by the use of personal pronoun prefixes (*ki-* 2nd, *ni-* 1st, and zero for the third person; slot 1). The prefixes match with the correspondent inflectional suffixes, which express person and number agreement (slots 10 and 11). The conjunct order is used in embedded clauses and WH-interrogatives; its use appears to be slightly different in Michif compared to Plains Cree. In Michif, the complementizers marking the conjunct are *ee-*, *chi/shi-*, and *kaa-* (slot 1).

After the person prefixes or the conjunct markers, slots 2 and 3 host the preverb positions. Preverbs are traditionally divided into two slots (Bloomfield 1962: 214; Edwards 1954, both cited in Bakker 2006). Tense is expressed through a limited set of morphemes that occur in slot 2 in a rigid order (present tense is unmarked). The second set of preverbs in slot 3 encompasses both modal auxiliaries (e.g. *kaahkwee-* 'try', *noohtee-* 'want') and adverbials (e.g. manner *miyo-* 'good', direction towards the speaker *pee(t)-*, aspectual forms *kana-*, and relative roots *ishi-*).[1] Native speakers recognize, single out, and translate preverbs rather easily, and are able to remove them from or add them to existing verb stems during elicitation. Russell (1999) argues that in Algonquian languages, the prefixed material (person, order and preverbs) should be considered to be a

---

[1] Many preverbs occur also as initials in similar shape. For instance, *shipwee-* ('away, off') occurs as a preverb in *kii-shipwee-pimoht-ee-w-ak* ('they left on foot'), and as an initial in *shipwee-payi-w-ak* ('they left by car or horse').

separate word on phonological and syntactic grounds with respect to the "stem plus suffixes" complex.

3.3 Post-stem positions

The post-stem positions treated here are slots 6 and 8–12. This includes markers of theme (or theme signs) for TI (e.g. *-am*) and TA verbs (the direction set), obviation (*-yi*, indicating a possessed subject), and polyperson agreement, including number. In the last position, a conditional marker can be added to the conjunct form in the protasis of hypothetical sentences (*-i*).

In the TA conjugation, the theme indicates the direction (inverse or direct with respect to the Algonquian person hierarchy, 2 > 1 > 3 > 4). Goddard (1990: 450) claims that the direction marker for TA verbs represents a "segment of the inflectional ending complex that gives information about the gender and person of the subject and the object." TA direction markers always appear only after the TA FINAL or the TA derivative and, crucially, they never appear before any derivatives that apply to TA (cf. ex. 19). Throughout the paper, I gloss TA theme signs as DIR (direct) or INV (inverse, not attested in the examples here).

Instead, TI theme signs are somehow more difficult to analyze; arguably, they sort the TI verb stems into three inflectional classes (Pentland 1999). Here, I place TI signs (slot 6 and 8) in a different position with respect to the TA signs (slot 8), depending on the position of the sign *-am*, and more work would be needed to confirm these positions for the other TI signs. In fact, the TI sign *-am* is placed *before* the applicative *-aw* and the actor focus *-aashoo* (slot 7), as illustrated in Sections 4.7 and 4.10, and is therefore represented in slot 6. However, the TI sign *-am* is also placed *after* the valency operators *-t* and *-sht* (slot 7), and therefore it is represented in slot 8 of the template. In the paper, I gloss TI themes as THE.TI ('theme transitive inanimate').

The obviation marker *-yi-* (slot 9) indicates a possessed or obviative subject. There is an additional possessed/obviated marker, *-im*, that is not included in Table 1 because it is not attested in my data and was not accepted by speakers during elicitation. It does appear in the Michif data provided by Sammons (2019: 89ff.). In general, this marker is exceedingly rare and virtually non-existent in many Algonquian languages (Muehlbauer 2008: 129). For Plains Cree, Bakker (2006), Russell (1999: 205), Wolfart (1973: 54f.), Muehlbauer (2008: 127f.) and Harrigan et al. (2017) place *-im* right before the TA theme signs (in a slot between

7 and 8 in the template in Table 1), although the different authors assign it diverse functions and distributions.[2]

In the examples, the gloss of the verb endings (inflectional suffixes, slots 10–11) will indicate the order (IND, CNJ), person (0, 1, 2, 3, 4), number (S, PL), and, in a few cases, the stem class (if deducted from the conjugation suffix only).

3.4 The stem

Slots number 4 and 5 compose the stem. Following Bloomfield (1946) and subsequent descriptive scholarship on different Algonquian languages, the stem is the lexical part of the verb stripped of all inflections and the optional specifications of manner, aspect, and direction. When one removes the prefixed preverbs (Section 3.2) and the suffixes (Section 3.3) from the Michif verb, the remaining portion is the stem, which expresses the semantics of the verb, can be divided into smaller units. It is obligatorily featured for transitivity and animacy, as shown in (1):

(1) prefixes- **stem** -suffixes
 ki- ***tip-eeyiht*** -eenaan
 2- rule-do.by.mind.FIN.TI -IND.non3PL.INCL
 'we (you too) rule it'

Several stem-internal components are visible in distributional terms, since they recur in different stems in the same positions. The morphological make-up of the lexical portion of an Algonquian verb is commonly analyzed in the templatic terms proposed by Bloomfield and replicated in the Algonquian scholarship today, using a schema consisting of three positions, initials, medials and finals. The three terms refer to the relative position of the elements within the stem, although Goddard (1990: 463) proposed an analysis that takes meaning into consideration.[3] Throughout this paper, the stem and its internal components will be in bold, so as to quickly differentiate them from personal prefixes, preverbs, secondary derivatives (which will be underlined), and inflectional

---

[2] Russell (1999) restricts -*im* for Plains Cree to indicate the possessed object of a non-third subject (1 or 2), Wolfart (1973: 54f.) gives a different account that includes occurrences with third person subjects, Muehlbauer (2008) contests the notion of -*im* as an obviative marker at all, and Harrigan et al. (2017) define -*im* as indicating "thematic disjoint", namely that the persons involved in the action are further removed from each other on the person hierarchy.

[3] According to Goddard (1990), initials denote a state or a configuration, while finals refer to the means by which this state or configuration has come about.

suffixes. The scholarship on Algonquian languages has generally presented stem-internal components as morphemic: recently, many theoretical accounts *de facto* adopted this assumption (e.g. Slavin 2012a; Tollan and Oxford 2018) and other approaches claim a cognitive reality for certain finals (cf. Junker 2003 on *eyi-* in East Cree). However, the synchronic morphemic status and parsability of Michif stem-internal components is dubious in some cases. Not only are speakers unable to single out components such as {tip} and {eeyiht} in (1) (which is to be expected), but the ability of the single components to combine with new linguistic material to create interpretable formations has not been tested (but cf. examples of mixed constructions with Cree finals in Michif in Mazzoli et al. in press). Moreover, any structural properties that instantiate their status as morphemes are generally lacking in the literature. I will now describe the stem-internal components in more detail.

Initials (slot 4) are an open class of morphemes covering a huge array of meanings, and they are sometimes referred to as "roots". Some scholars in the generative tradition describe initials as pre-categorical lexical heads that are underspecified semantically (Slavin 2012b for Oji-Cree; Tollan and Oxford 2018 for Plains Cree, etc.), although others, working in different theoretical frameworks, argue for them to be subcategorized for inherent (in)transitivity (Armoskaite 2010 for Blackfoot; Genee 2013).

Medials are always noun-like in traditional Algonquian descriptions (Goddard 1990: 463), although in Plains Cree there is not always an immediate similarity between medials and the corresponding separate nouns. Medials can be classificatory (e.g., they can denote items as belonging to one of a half dozen categories such as 'stone-like', 'metal-like', etc.), or they can be related to body parts (e.g., 'by swinging foot'). In Michif, there appear to be only a handful cases in which a medial could be synchronically analyzable within the stem structure, as, for examples, in the construction *ki-t-**ohpwee-shtikw-aa**-n-aan* (2-EPEN-up-head-AI-IND.non3-PL, 'your hair is disheveled'), given that *-stikw-* is a medial for 'head' in Plains Cree. However, the synchronic evidence for assigning to the Michif element *-shtikw-* the status of morpheme is scarce, and the complex formative *-shtikwaa-* could be analysed as a concrete AI final. This is similar to what is usually done for the formative *-eeyi-*, analyzed as part of the complex concrete finals *-eeyiht* (TI) and *-eeyim* (TA). Therefore, I do not use a medial slot to place the semantically heavier portion (*shtikw-* 'head', *-pay-* 'move', *-aap-* 'vision' or *-eeyi-* 'mind') to combine it with an abstract FINAL (*-aa*, *-i*, *-ishi*, *-ht*). Instead, I consider elements like *-shtikwaa-* (have.head.like.AI), *-payi* (move.INTR), *-aapishi* (BE.by.sight.AI) or *-eeyiht* (do.by.mind.TI) complex finals. For these reasons, I do not include a special position for medials in the Michif template. When more than two formatives appear to compose the stem, it is always possible to analyze the stem as having a concrete final (e.g., *-shtikwaa, -eeyiht, -naakoshi* or *-naakwa*) or individuate multiple secondary derivation at play (ex. 75).

Finals (slot 5) in Algonquian languages are unanimously analyzed as category-defining elements: they determine the features of transitivity and animacy of the entire stem, and therefore the paradigm in terms of the selected conjugation (endings). The list of verb finals in Michif is numerous but finite. It includes concrete and abstract finals. Concrete finals are bound lexical roots that add "palpable meaning" (Bloomfield 1946: 104), while abstract finals add no more information than transitivity and animacy (Bloomfield 1946; Wolfart 1996: 425–426; Frantz 2009: 97–107 for Blackfoot). The list of alleged final morphemes for Michif includes but is not limited to the TA *-h* and *-eeyim*, the TI *-ht, -in*, and *-eeyiht*, and the AI *-i, -payi, -inaakoshi, -ishi, -shtikwaa*. Also, I include in the list of finals stem-final long vowels of AI (*-ee/aa, -ee, -aa, -oo*) and II stems (*-ee, -aa*). For verb stems exhibiting the variant *-ee/aa* (e.g. *atoshk-aa-n/atoshk-ee-w*), some derivatives (position 7) choose the form *-ee* and some others the form *-aa* (e.g. **atosh-ee**-m-*ee-w Elvis*: 'Harvey worked with Elvis, vs. *kii-**atoshk-aa**-h-ee-w-ak*: 'they made her work'). The so-called concrete finals like *-shtikwaa, -inaakoshi, -eeyiht* or *-(i)hkaashoo* appear etymologically to be a combination of a lexical (incorporated) root and an abstract final, or a final and a derivative. Finals are glossed as FIN in Sections 3.5 and 3.6.

Some authors maintain that the Algonquian stem is composed at least of an initial and a final (Bloomfield 1946: 104–105), but some analyses claim that the Algonquian verb stem can be simple, thus composed of one initial only (cf. Zúñiga 2016: 210; Goddard 1990: 451 for the general Algonquian stem; Bloomfield 1962: 246 for Menominee). In this paper, I will assume that each stem includes a categorizing final (e.g. *-eeyiht* in 1), which defines the verb for features of transitivity and animacy, and assign it to one of the five verb stem classes: inanimate intransitive (II), animate intransitive (AI), transitive inanimate (TI), transitive animate (TA) or semitransitive (AI+O). This classification is fundamental when discussing secondary derivation, since derivatives apply to certain verb stems modifying these features (for instance, transforming TI stems into AI stems).

3.5 More on primary derivation

Although originally Goddard used the term *primary derivation* to define how the internal components of a stem are themselves derived from other lexemes, most of the Algonquian literature uses the term "primary derivation" to describe how bound initials, medials and finals combine (Wolfart 1973; Goddard 1990: 451).

The way these stem-internal components merge is quite similar in the different Algonquian languages, and, notwithstanding its name, the process is not "derivation" in the traditional sense (Spencer 2015). For instance, in Michif, the bound initial *ohpi-* 'raise' or 'up' combines with the bound intransitive concrete final *-payi* 'move.INTR' to produce the intransitive primary-derived stem *ohpi-payi-* 'raise' (AI or II) as in (2) and (3). Most initials generate a complex network of related stems, as in (2)–(5):

(2) li gaaz **ohpi-payi**-n
 DEF.M.S gas.M.INAN up-move.FIN.INTR-IND.II.OS
 'the gas raises, it goes up' (II) [Mazzoli, elicitation]

(3) li paeñ **ohpi-payi**-w
 DEF.M.S bread.M.AN up-move.FIN.INTR-IND.AI.3S
 'the bread rises' (AI) [Mazzoli, elicitation]

(4) **ohpiki-h**-ee-w laañfaañ
 up-FIN.TA-DIR-IND.3>4 child.AN
 's/he raises the child' (TA) [Mazzoli, elicitation]

(5) **ohpiki-ht**-<u>am-aashoo</u>-w li shyaeñ[4]
 up-FIN.TI-THE.TI-AC.FOC.AI-IND.3S DEF.M.S dog.M.AN
 's/he adopts the dog' (AI) [Mazzoli, elicitation]

A similarly complex network stems from a concrete final such as the intransitive (either animate or inanimate) *-payi* (6)–(10):

(6) naandaw **ish-payi**-yaan-i
 anything so-move.FIN.INTR-CNJ.AI.1S-SJ
 'if something happens to me' (AI)

---

[4] Note that in (4) and (5), the initial is *ohpiki-* and not *ohpi-*. Bloomfield (1946: 104) and Wolfart (1973: 63) observe that many immediate constituents (either initials, medials or finals) exhibit a ("lexomorphemic", in their terminology) alternation of shorter and longer forms. Both authors regard the shorter alternant as basic and call the longer alternant "extended" (although I tend to see it the other way around). The status of the "accretive" elements (post-radical, pre- and post-medial, and pre-final) is not commonly addressed in the literature, with the exception of Macaulay and Salmons (2017), who conceive of "postradical extensions" and "prefinal accretions" as diachronic formatives in Menominee that should not be taken as synchronically available to speakers. In (4)–(5), the accretive element *-ki-* is a post-radical that pertains to the extended form of the initial *ohpi-*.

(7) **ako-payi**-w
stick-move.FIN.INTR-IND.II.OS
'it sticks, it holds in place' (II) [Mazzoli, elicitation]

(8) **apwee-payi**-w
sweat-move.FIN.INTR-IND.AI.3S
's/he has a sudden hot flash, blushes' (AI) [Mazzoli, elicitation]

(9) **kishii-payi**-w
intense-move.FIN.INTR-IND.AI.3S
'he is driving fast' (AI) [Mazzoli, elicitation]

(10) kii-**shipwee-payi**-w-ak
PST-away-move.FIN.INTR-IND.AI.3S.3-PL
'they drove away, took off (on a car or horse)' (AI) [Mazzoli, elicitation]

The components of primary-derived stems in bold do not stand on their own: *shipwee-* (10) or *-payi* (6)–(10) are not forms to which endings, preverbs, or derivatives can attach, but they are bound to other components. Their meaning in composition is idiosyncratic, and their individual semantics are underspecified outside the combination. Also, stem-internal components are subject to internal sandhi. For instance, the stem *miyo-eeyiht-* 'to think positively about something' is pronounced /mjøht/, with the fusion of the final and initial vowels of adjacent morphemes. Stem-internal combinations differ from other mechanisms such as prototypical derivational processes (like those examined in the Section 3.6) or preverbal composition (cf. example 40).

3.6 Secondary derivation

When one of the constituents of a complex stem is a fully formed self-standing stem, we are dealing with secondary derivation (Wolfart 1973: 63; Goddard 1990). Henceforth, I use the term "derivation" to indicate secondary derivation only. Morphemes that derive secondary verb stems include a limited set of elements in Michif, such as the medio-passive *-(i)kaashoo* (Section 4.15), the animacy converter *-aw* (Section 4.1), or the causative *-h* (Section 4.5). Michif derivative mophemes are underlined throughout the text of this paper. Virtually all Algonquian scholars recognize substantial differences between processes of primary (internal stem formation) and secondary derivation (cf. Goddard 1990: 471; Frantz 1991; Valentine 2001b; Brittain and Acton 2014). However, secondary derivative morphemes are included in the category of the finals in virtually all Algonquian language descriptions (e.g., Wolfart 1973; Pentland 1999; Rhodes

2016; Tollan and Oxford 2018). This has to do with the templatic nature of traditional terms, which do not capture the structural roles of the morphemes but just identify their relative position in between the endings and the preverbs. However, a descriptive taxonomy conforming to a more typologically-oriented approach will be able to capture the differences between stem-internal morphemes and derivatives, which diverge in several respects:

(1) Derivatives apply to existing stems that are defined for transitivity and animacy and are recognized by speakers to have a specific meaning. For instance, when the middle attributive predicative suffix -*aakoshi* (Section 4.17) is removed, its TI base, *kishkeeyiht*- 's/he to know it', is self-standing and can be inflected (11–12):

(11) **kishk-eeyiht-*aakoshi*-w**
      knowledge-do.by.mind.FIN.TI-PRED.AI-IND.3S
      's/he is well known' (AI)   [Mazzoli, elicitation]

(12) **kishk-eeyiht-am**
      knowledge-do.by.mind.FIN.TI-THE.TI
      's/he knows something' (TI)   [Mazzoli, elicitation]

This self-standing nature does not apply to stem-internal components. The concrete final -*payi* cannot be removed from (13), since the initial *apwee*- is bound and needs another final to build a well-formed stem, as in (14):

(13) **apwee-payi-w**
      sweat-move.FIN.INTR-IND.AI.3S
      's/he has a sudden hot flash, blushes' (AI)   [Mazzoli, elicitation]

(14) **apwee-ishoo-w**
      sweat-FIN.AI-IND.3S
      's/he sweats' (AI)   [Mazzoli, elicitation]

(2) On semantic grounds, Michif derivatives are relatively abstract and have a clear function, since they intervene to change the stem category with regard to its valency features and/or the animacy of its arguments. For instance, derivatives can modify the verb voice (passive, middle) or add event participants (applicative, causative, valency increaser). Instead, stem-internal finals apply their categories onto roots, which are not previously specified (cf. 2–10).

(3) Derivatives in Michif behave predictably, in the sense that they attach to certain types of bases only, and their semantic and syntactic outcome is expected. For example, the comitative derivative -*m* attaches to AI bases and output TA stems (Section 4.3). In contrast, combinatory finals behave idiomatically in combination with a variety of initials.

For these reasons, in the template in Table 1, derivatives and stem-internal finals occupy two different positions, slot 7 and 5, respectively. A distinct position for finals and derivatives is also suggested for Plains Cree by Harrigan et al. (2017: 18) based on the position of the comitative derivative -*m* alone.

In the following sections, stem-internal components (initials and finals) will not be indicated in the glosses.

4 Voice, valency, and animacy (plus one valutative): secondary derivation in Michif

In this section, I will survey the derivatives in Michif, which are the morphemes that modify the transitivity, voice, and valency of a verb stem and its arguments' animacy-based gender. The derivative slot is placed right before the TA theme signs for Michif (and also for Plains Cree, Harrigan et al. 2017), as in the template in Table 1, summed up in 15.[5] This portion of the template differs from Bakker (2006), who places the derivative slot (valency and voice) *after* the TA theme signs and before the obviative subject marker -*yi*, as exemplified in (16):

(15)   STEM – (*Theme TI) – **Valency/Voice** – Direction/Theme TA/TI – Possessed S (-*yi*)
[this paper, for Michif]

(16)   STEM – Possessed O (-*im*) – Direction/Theme – **Valency/Voice** – Possessed S (-*yi*)
[Bakker 2006, for Cree]

As it appears from (17) and (18), valency and voice derivative morphemes precede the transitive animate theme signs in Michif. In fact, the derivatives that output TA verbs (e.g. -*h* INCR/CAUS.TA, -*aw* TA, and -*amaw* APP.TA) consistently appear before the direction/TA theme signs:

(17)   *kii-**atoshkaa**-h̲-ee-w-ak*
PST-work.AI-CAUS.TA-DIR-IND.3-PL
'they made her work'

(18)   *ni-**peeht**-a̲w̲-aa-w*
1-hear.TI-TA-DIR-IND.3S
'I hear her'   [Mazzoli, elicitation]

---

5 If the obviative object marker -*im* is included in the template, voice and valency should precede it.

Also, derivatives that apply to TA bases attach to stems stripped of direction markers, as is the case for medio-passive -(i)kaashoo in (19) and Section 4.15 (cf. also II medio-passive -(i)kaatee in Section 4.16, middle-reflexive -oo in Section 4.14, and agentless passive -ikawi and -aa in Section 4.19):

(19) la   faam   awa   kaa-ohpikih-aa-t
      DEF.F.S   woman.F.AN   this.AN   CNJ-raise.TA-DIR-CNJ.3→4
      Cinderella   kii-**wiihkom**-ikaashoo-w
      Cinderella   PST-invite.TA-MED.AI-IND.3S
      'the woman who raised Cinderella had been invited to the feast'
      VAI < wiihkom-ee-w [vta] 'invite someone'

Table 2 lists twenty Michif derivatives (for fifteen attested derivative functions), and in Sections 4.1–4.20, I will discuss and exemplify their distribution. In Section 4.21, I single out their relative positions within slot 7 of the template in Table 1. In the examples, for each verb I will show the derivation process with respect to the features of animacy and transitivity of the original stem. The gloss of each simple stem (in bold) include the specifications of animacy and transitivity (either AI, AI+O, II, TI or TA), and the gloss of each derivative morpheme (underlined) include the derived features (either AI, II, TI or TA). Table 2 sums up all this information. The derivatives are subdivided in animacy-converter morphemes (-aw and -maka), morphemes that add to the valency of the original stem (-m, -h, -t, -amaw, -sht, -shtaw), those that reduce the valency of the original stem (-amaasho and -ikee), morphemes that alter verb voice (-itoo, -oo, -ishoo, -(i)kaashoo, -(i)ikaatee, -aakoshi, -aakwa, -ikawi, and -aa), and one valutative morpheme (-shkee).

Table 2: Derivatives in Michif.

Area	Section	Function	Form	Base input	Derivational output	Gloss
Animacy converters	4.1	animacy converter (O)	-aw	TI, AI+O	TA verbs	TA
	4.2	animacy converter (S)	-maka	AI	II	II
Valency (+)	4.3	comitative	-m	AI+O	TA	COM.TA
	4.4	transitivizer (valency increaser)	-h-(ee)	AI	TA	INCR.TA
	4.5	causative	-h	AI	TA	CAUS.TA

Area	Section	Function	Form	Base input	Derivational output	Gloss
	4.6	transitivizer	-t-(am)	AI	TI	TR-(THE.TI)
			-t-(ee)		TA	TR-(DIR/INV)
	4.7	applicative	(-am)-aw	TI, AI+O	TA	(THE.TI)-APP.TA
	4.8	benefactive	-sht	AI	TI	BEN.TI
	4.9	benefactive animate	-shtaw	AI	TA	BEN.TA
Valency(–)	4.10	actor focus	(-am)-aashoo	TI	AI	(THE.TI)-AC.FOC.AI
	4.11	non-specified goal	-ikee	TI, AI+O	AI	GEN.AI
Voice	4.12	reciprocal	-ito	TA	AI	REC.AI
	4.13	reflexive	-ishoo	TA	AI	RFLX.AI
	4.14	middle-reflexive	-oo	TA	AI	MID.RFLX.AI
	4.15	medio-passive AI	-ikaashoo	TA (also TI?)	AI	MED.AI
	4.16	medio-passive II	-ikaatee	TA, TI, AI+O	II	MED.II
	4.17	middle attributive predication AI	-aakoshi	TI	AI	PRED.II
	4.18	middle attributive predication II	-aakwa	TI	II	PRED.AI
	4.19	agent-less passive	-ikaawi (SAP)	TA	AI	PASS.AI
			-aa (3)		AI	PASS.AI
Valutative	4.20	accrescitive	-shkee	AI	AI	ACCR.AI

Animacy

4.1 -aw animacy converter

The derivative -aw applies to TI and AI+O and outputs TA verbs, as in (20)–(21). It also derives transitive animate stems from (syntactically transitive) AI+O stems, as in (22):

(20) li   praeñs   awa   kaahkwee-**mishk**-<u>aw</u>-aa-t
      DEF.M.S   prince.M.AN   that.AN   try-look.for.TI-TA-DIR-CNJ.3→4

  aniki kaa-kii-ohchi-nimi-h-aa-t
  those.AN CNJ-PST-from-dance.AI-INCR.TA-DIR-CNJ.3→4
  'the prince was trying to find the person that he had danced with'
  VTA < *mishk-am* [vti] 'to find s.t.'

(21) ni-**peeht**-<u>aw</u>-aa-w li bitor
  1-hear.TI-TA-DIR-IND.3>4 DEF.M.S bittern.M.AN
  ee-**kitoo**-t obor li laek
  CNJ-call.AI-3S on.edge DEF.M.S lake.M.INAN
  'I hear the bittern's call by the lake' [Laverdure and Allard 1983: 43]
  VTA < *peeht-am* [vti]

(22) sapraañ en faam **ay**-<u>aw</u>-a-t
  need INDEF.F.S woman.F.AN CNJ-have.AI-TA-CNJ.2S→3
  'you have to get married'
  VTA < *ayaa-w* [vai+o] 'to be, to have'

The animacy converter -*aw* is added to TI stems that lack the thematic sign -*am* (20)–(21) and to AI+O stems ending in abstract final -*aa*, but without the final (22).

4.2 -*maka* inanimate subject converter

The morpheme -*maka* applies to AI and outputs II verbs (Bloomfield 1946: 107). When applied to AI stems in -*ee/aa*, it attaches to the -*ee* variant (24)–(26).

(23) gii-naki-n-aan   dañ vil ee-**nipoo**-<u>maka</u>-hk
  1PST-stop.AI-IND.non3-PL.EXCL in city.F.INAN CNJ-die.AI-II-CNJ.OS
  'we stopped in a ghost town' [Laverdure and Allard 1983: 110]
  VII < *nipoo-w* [vai] 's/he dies'

(24) namo **pimohtee**-<u>maka</u>-n li fan
  NEG walk.AI-II-IND.OS DEF.M.S fan.M.INAN
  'the fan is inactive' [Laverdure and Allard 1983: 142]
  VII < *pimohtee-w* [vai] 's/he walks'

(25) **atoshkee**-<u>maka</u>-n
  work.AI-II-IND.OS
  'it works'   [Mazzoli, elicitation]
  VII < *atoshkee-w* [vai] 's/he works'

(26) li spacecraft **shipweehtee**-<u>maka</u>-n
  DEF.M.S spacecraft.M.INAN go.away.AI-II-IND.OS
  'the spacecraft started to go, it is going' [Mazzoli, elicitation]
  II < *shipweehtee-w* [vai] 's/he goes'

Valency

4.3 *-m* comitative

The derivative *-m* applies to AI and AI+O in *-ee/aa* and *-i* finals, outputs TA verbs with a comitative meaning (cf. Harrigan et al. 2017: 18 for Plains Cree). It is defined as a relational derivational affix in Cook and Muehlbauer (2010). When added to stems ending in *-ee/aa*, the comitative *-m* applies to the stem variant *-ee*, as in (27) and (29), just like the animacy converter *-maka* (Section 3.2). This behavior is in contrast to other markers, such as the valency increaser *-h* (28), (30) and Section 4.4, which applies to corresponding verbs that end in *-aa*:

(27) Harvey   **atoshkee**-m-ee-w   Elvis
     Harvey   work.AI-COM.TA-DIR-IND.3>4   Elvis
     'Harvey works with Elvis'   [Mazzoli, elicitation]
     VTA < *atoshkee-w* [vai] 's/he works'
     * *atoshkaa-m-ee-w*

(28) kii-**atoshkaa**-h-ee-w-ak
     PST-work.AI-CAUS.TA-DIR-IND.3>4-PL.SBJ
     'they made her work'   [Mazzoli, elicitation]
     VTA < *ni-atoshkaa-n* [vai] 'I work'
     * *atoshkee-h-ee-w*

This observation is confirmed in (29)–(30):

(29) **meetawee**-m-ikaashoo-w   la   kataeñ
     play.AI-COM.TA-MED.AI-IND.3S   DEF.F.S   doll.F.INAN
     'the doll is being played with'   [Mazzoli, elicitation]
     VTA < *meetawee-m-ee-w* [vta] 's/he plays with' < *meetawee-w* [vai] 's/he plays'

(30) **meetawaa**-h-ee-w
     play.AI-CAUS.TA-DIR-IND.3>4
     's/he makes someone work'   [Mazzoli, elicitation]
     VTA < *ni-meetawaa-n* [vai] 'I play'

Comitative *-m* also applies to AI stems ending in abstract AI final *-i*, like *kiyaashki-w* and *wiiki-w*:

(31) **wiiki**-m-ee-w
     dwell.AI-COM.TA-DIR-IND.3>4
     's/he marries someone' or 's/he lives with someone' [Mazzoli, elicitation]
     VTA < *wiiki-w* [vai] 's/he dwells'

4.4 -h general valency increaser/transitivizer

The general valency increaser applies to virtually any AI stems and outputs TA verbs (32)–(33):

(32) **paahpi-h-ee-w** li pchi baby
laugh.AI-INCR.TA-DIR-IND.3>4 DEF.M.S little.M baby.M.AN
'she laughs at the little baby' or 'she makes the little baby laugh' (causative cf. Section 4.5) [Mazzoli, elicitation]
VTA < *paahpi-w* [vai] 'he laughs'

(33) taanihki eekaa **(li-)ami-iwi-h-a-t**
why NEG (the-)friend-be.AI-INCR.TA-DIR-CNJ.2S→3S
'why won't you be friends with him?' [Bakker p.c.]
VTA < *li-ami-iwi-w* [vai] 'to be friend'

Differently than the causative (cf. [28] and [30] in Section 4.2.3), the general valency increaser -*h* applies to the -*aa* alternant of AI stems ending with -*ee/aa*, as in (34):

(34) safek Sandrieuz wiya maatoo-w, namo
so Sandrieuz 3EMP cry.AI-IND.3S NEG
shipweehtee-h-ikaashoo-w
leave.AI-INCR.TA-MED.AI-IND.3S
'so Cinderella, she was crying. They had not taken her along'
VAI < *shipweehtee-h-ee-w* [vta] 's/he leaves her' < *shipweehtee-w* [vai] 's/he leaves'

4.5 -h causative

The causative derivative -*h* applies to AI and outputs TA. I maintain that the -*h* valency increaser and -*h* causative are separate morphemes, since they appear to have a different distribution: while causative -*h* selects -*ee* variants of AI stems, the general increaser -*h* selects -*aa* variants of AI stems, as explained in Section 4.2.2. Some AI verb stems, for example ending in -*i*, when derived with TA -*h*, receive both readings (general valency increaser and causative) depending on context, as *paahpi-* ('to laugh') in (32) (cf. *paahpi-m-ee-w, *paahpi-t-ee-w). Some other verb stems like *atoshkee-* ('work.AI') and *pikshkwee-* ('speak.AI') take only a causative reading with derivative -*h* ([28], [35]), and then use different markers to increase valency with different semantics, cf. comitative -*m* for *atoshkee-* (27) and applicative/benefactive -*t* for *piikshkwaa-* (42).

(35) kii-**pikshkwaa**-*h*-*ee*-*w*-*ak*
 PST-speak.AI-CAUS-TA-DIR-IND.3-PL
 'they made her speak'
 VTA < *bikshkwaa-n* [vai] 'I speak'

As shown in (28) and (30) above, and (35) and (36) here, causative -*h* is added to the -*aa* alternant of the AI stems:

(36) mischet   kii-**nipaa**-*h*-*ee*-*w*-*ak*
 a.lot   PST-sleep.AI-CAUS.TA-DIR-IND.3→4-PL.SBJ
 lii   vash,   lii   kooshooñ...
 ART.PL   COW.F.AN   ART.PL   pig.M.AN
 'they slaughtered many cows, pigs...'
 VTA < *nipaa-w* [vai] 's/he sleeps'

(37) **nootin**-*ikee*-*h*-*ee*-*w*
 fight.TR-GEN.AI-CAUS.TA-DIR-IND.3>4
 's/he makes people quarrel'   [Mazzoli, elicitation]
 VTA < *nootin-ikee-w* [vai] 's/he fights' < *nootin-ee-w* [vta] 's/he fights him' / *nootin-am* [vti] 's/he fights something'

(38) **naton**-*ikee*-*h*-*ee*-*w*
 look.for.TR-GEN.AI-CAUS.TA-DIR-IND.3>4
 's/he makes people look for things'   [Mazzoli, elicitation]
 VTA < *naton-ikee-w* [vai] 's/he looks for things' < *naton-ee-w* [vta] 's/he looks for someone' / *naton-am* [vti] 's/he looks for something'

The functions of the causative and the valency increaser -*h* derivatives should not be confused with that of the final -*h* of TA and TI verbs (glossed as 'do by undetermined means', cf. Cook and Muehlbauer 2010; Wolfart 1973: 63), as used in (39):

(39) **kishiwaa**-*h*-*ee*-*w*
 angry-FIN.TR-DIR-IND.3>4
 's/he angers him/her, s/he makes someone mad'   [Mazzoli, elicitation]

Example (40) shows how the initial *kishiwaa*- ('related to anger') must be combined with another final (-*shi*, AI) to form a proper stem:

(40) **kishiwaa-shi**-*w*
 angry-FIN.AI-IND.3S
 's/he is angry'   [Mazzoli, elicitation]

4.6 -t(ee) or -t(am) transitivizer

The derivative -*t* applies to animate intransitive AI stems and transforms them into transitive stems, TA or TI. From the intransitive stem **kitoo**-*w* 's/he calls, makes a sound' (Laverdure and Allard 1983: 43), the suffix -*t* derives **kitoo**-*t*-*ee*-*w* 's/he talks to so, TA' (cf. 41) and **kitoo**-*t*-*am* 's/he talks to it, TI':

(41) asheeh-kiiwee-pahtaa-w aañ baa
 back-homewards-run.AI-IND.3S at down
 ee-doo-**kitoo**-*t*-aa-t ooñhiñ
 CNJ-go-call.AI-TR-DIR-CNJ.3>4 them.OBV
 'she ran back downstairs, to go and talk to them'
 VTA < **kitoo**-*w* [vai] 's/he calls'

If the AI stems end in the abstract final alternating in -*ee/aa*, -*t*- is added to the -*aa* alternant, as in (42):

(42) keekway anima **piikshkwaa**-*t*-am-eek?
 what that.INAN talk.AI-TI-THE.TI-CNJ.2PL
 'what [language] are the two of you speaking?' [Mazzoli, elicitation]
 VTI < *biikshkwaa-n* [vai] 'I speak'

4.7 -(am)-aw applicative

The derivative -*(am)-aw* applies to TI and VAI+O and outputs TA double object verbs.[6] Applicatives are valency operators that add a participant fulfilling a given semantic role in an event encoded by another verb. The role of the introduced participant can be a recipient ('to someone'), substitutive ('on behalf of someone'), or plain benefactive ('for someone') (Creissels 2010). The Michif suffix -*(am)-aw*, related to the valency converter -*aw* (Section 4.1), introduces a recipient or substitutive participant, at times in contrast to -*shtaw* (Section 4.9), which introduces a benefactive (cf. the minimal pair in [50]–[51]). The applicative -*aw* is added to transitive inanimate stems that end in the TI theme sign -*am*, forming double object verbs. The meaning of the derived verbs with -*(am)-aw* clearly reflects their morphological structure: the inanimate goal of the underly-

---

[6] Wolfart (1973: 74) notes that in Plains Cree, TI -*tot* and TA -*totaw* occur as applicatives with the -*ee* alternant of AI stems in -*ee/aa* (*kiiw-ee-w* AI 's/he goes home' > *kiiw-ee-totaw-ee-w* TA 's/he goes home to him'). These occurrences are not attested in Michif.

ing stem is still the primary object, and the animate goal of the derived stem is the secondary object.

(43) en   groo   taañd   darzhaañ
     INDEF.F.S   big.M   amount.of   money
     kii-**nakat**-<u>am-aw</u>-ee-w   sooñ   garsooñ
     PST-leave-THE.TI-APP.TA-DIR-IND.3>4   3POSS.M.S   son.M.AN
     'he left a great amount of money to his son'   [Laverdure and Allard 1983: 116]
     VTA < *nakat-am* [vti] 's/he leaves it'

(44) (ee)-kiimoochi-**wiiht**-<u>am-aw</u>-aa-t   anihi
     CNJ-secretely-tell.TI-THE.TI-APP.TA-DIR-CNJ.3>4   those.AN
     lii   fiiy
     ART.PL   girl.F.AN
     'as she was telling it secretly to those girls'
     VTA < *wiiht-am* [vti] 's/he tells it'

(45) **waapaht**-<u>am-aw</u>-ee-w
     look.it.TI-THE.TI-APP.TA-DIR-IND.3>4
     'he looks at something for or on him'   [Mazzoli, elicitation]
     VTA < *waapaht-am* [vti] 's/he looks at something'

Occasionally, the derived verb does not have a double object and keeps only the animate argument:

(46) **naat**-<u>am-aw</u>-ee-w
     get-THE.TI-APP.TA-DIR-IND.3>4
     's/he sticks up for someone, s/he sides with someone'   [Mazzoli, elicitation]
     VTA < *naat-am* [vti] 's/he gets something'[7]

I claim that the integral form of the derivative must include the TI theme sign because the suffix *-(am)-aw* applies also to non-TI stems, as in the two examples below. In fact, the double object verbs **asht**-<u>am-aw</u>-ee-w (47) and **atoshk**-<u>am-aw</u>-ee-w (48) are formed from the AI+O verbs *ashtaa-w* ('s/he puts it away') and *atoshkee-w* ('s/he works'). Unattested TI back formations **asht-am* and **atoshk-am* are created through the addition of a TI sign *-am* (slot 6), and the applicative feature is added through *-aw*:

(47) **asht**-<u>am-aw</u>-ee-w
     place-THE.TI-APP.TA-DIR-IND.3>4
     's/he puts it away for him/her'

---

7 Cf. *diloo chi-naat-ahk* 'that s/he gets the water' (Laverdure and Allard 1983: 69).

VTA < *ashtaa-w* [vai+o] 's/he places it right, puts it away'
asht-am [intended, vti] 's/he puts it away'

(48) **atoshk**-<u>am-aw</u>-*ee-w*
work-THE.TI-APP.TA-DIR-IND.3>4
's/he works on her/his behalf'
VTA < *atoshkee-w* [vai] 's/he works'
atoshk-am [intended, vti] 's/he works on it'

The -*(am)-aw* suffix applies to TI stems ending in the TI theme -*am*. It also originates back formations for VAI+O stems, by addition of the TI theme -*am*.

4.8 -*sht* (relative to an object)

The derivative suffix -*sht* applies to AI stems to derive TI verbs, for actions "relative to an object" (Bloomfield 1946: 117):

(49) li   tournoo   zel   roozh
     DEF.M.S   blackbird.M.AN   wing   red
     niikaanee-<u>sht</u>-*am*   li   praeñtaañ
     be.in.advance.AI-BEN.TI-THE.TI DEF.M.S spring.M.ANAN
     'the redwing blackbird is a harbinger of spring'
     VTI < *niikaanee-w* [vai] 's/he is advanced/ahead/first, s/he is the leader'
     [Laverdure and Allard 1983: 125]

4.9 -*shtaw* benefactive (relative to an animate entity)

The suffix -*shtaw* affixes to AI stems to derive TA verbs, when a new participant is included, having the role of the recipient or benefactive. The suffix is composed by -*sht* (Section 4.8) and -*aw* (Section 4.1):

(50) *kii-***atoshkee**-<u>shtaw</u>-*ee-w*
PST-work.AI-BEN.TA-DIR-IND.3>4
's/he works for or at him/her'   [Laverdure and Allard 1983: 339, 358]
VTA < *atoshkee-w* [vai] 's/he works'

The examples (50)–(51) show a minimal pair that highlights the differences between the applicative -*(am)-aw* and the benefactive -*shtaw*:

(51) *kii-***atoshk**-<u>am-aw</u>-*ee-w*
PST-work-THE.TI-DIR-IND.3>4
'she went in for her or him / she works on her behalf'   [Mazzoli, elicitation]

Both -*sht* and -*shtaw* apply to the -*ee* variant of AI stems alternating in -*aa/ee*.[8] Applicative -*(am)-aw* applies to the bare root.

4.10 (-am)-aashoo actor focus, 'for one's self'

The derivative suffix *(-am)-aashoo* applies to TI and outputs AI. It focuses the transitive action on the actor, so that the self becomes the goal. The suffix applies to TI stems that most of the times include the theme TI -*am*, as in (52)–(54):

(52) alantur di   vaeñt   aañ   naandaw
     around of   twenty year   something
     kii-**mishk**-*am-aashoo*-w-ak
     PST-find.TI-THE.TI-AC.FOC.AI-IND.3-PL
     'when they were around twenty, they found somebody for themselves'
     VAI < *mishk-am* [vti] 's/he looks for it'

(53) kii-**naat**-*am-aashoo*-w   aañ   kurazheu
     PST-get-THE.TI-AC.FOC.AI-IND.3S   in   courage
     'she gamely defended her rights'   [Laverdure and Allard 1983: 108]
     VAI < *naat-am* [vti] 's/he fetches it'

(54) si   booñ kaa-**kashkiht**-*am-aashoo*-hk   keekway
     it.is good REL-control.TI-THE.TI-AC.FOC.AI-CNJ.INDEF.AC   something
     'it's good to gain things for yourself'   [Laverdure and Allard 1983: 107]
     VAI < *kashkiht-am* [vti] 'able to do it' < *kashkihtaa-w* [vai+o] 'in control, able to do it'

It is unclear if the suffix's integral form is -*aashoo* or -*amaashoo* (with the preceeding TI theme, cf. the case of *(-am)-aw* in Section 4.7). There appears to be contradictory evidence on this respect. On the one hand, the simple suffix -*aashoo* is applied to the TI stem without the theme sign, in examples like *shiikahaaht-* in (55) and in a few other cases:

(55) ni-kii-**shiikahaaht**-*aashoo*-n   avik   diloo
     1-PST-spill.water.TI-AC.FOC.AI-IND.non3   with   water.INAN
     'I spilled water on myself'   [Rosen 2019]
     VAI < *shiikahaaht-am* [vti] 's/he splashes or pours water on it'

---

8 Wolfart (1973: 74) notes the same for Plains Cree, i.e. that both -*st* and -*staw* are added to the *ee*-alternants of AI stems. He also notes that Plains Cree stems ending in -*i* lengthen the vowel, as in *nahapi-w* AI 's/he sits down', which becomes TA *nahapii-staw-ee-w* 'he sits down by him', and TI *nahapii-st-am* 'he sits down by it'.

However, both (56) and (57) are cases of TI stem backformations (unattested *ohpikiht-am and *oshiht-am) created *ad hoc* to derive complex forms with -am-aashoo, parallel as to what is observed for -am-aw in Section 4.7:

(56) ga-**ohpikiht**-*am-aashoo*-n
 1FUT-raise.TI-THE.TI-AC.FOC.AI-IND.non3S
 'I will adopt her/him' (lit. I will grow it for myself)   [Mazzoli, elicitation]
 VAI < *ohpikihtaa-w* [vai+o] 's/he raises something'
 < **ohpikiht-am* [intended, vti] 's/he grows it', unattested

(57) mooñ   paeñ   d-**osh(ih)t**-*am-aashoo*–n
 1POSS.M.S bread.M.AN 1-make.AI-THE.TI-AC.FOC.AI-IND.non3S
 ma   galet   kahkiiyaaw
 1POSS.F.S bannock.F.AN everything
 'I make my own bread, my bannock, everything'
                              [Sammons 2018: 182, adapted]
 VAI < *oshihtaa-w* [vai+o] 's/he makes it, s/he prepares it, s/he builds it'
 < **oshiht-am* [intended, vti] 's/he makes it', unattested

This partially confirms the argument given in Section 4.7 for the applicative *(-am)-aw*, that a TI theme position should be assumed to occupy slot 6 (after the stem and before the derivative slot), as illustrated in Table 1.

4.11 *-ikee* general goal

The derivative *-ikee* applies to TI and AI stems and outputs AI verbs. It occurs mostly in transitive inanimate verbs (58)–(59) or in animate intransitive verbs (60) (cf. Wolfart 1973: 83 for Plains Cree). It transforms transitive actions on (inanimate) objects into intransitive events having a more general goal (cf. 'hit the door' vs. 'knock on the door', in [58]).[9]

(58) tudaeñku   kaa-**pakama**-*ikee*-t   awiyak
 suddenly   REL-hit.TI-GEN.AI-CNJ.3S   somebody
 dañ   leu   port
 in   3POSS.PL   door.F.INAN

---

[9] For Plains Cree, Wolfart (1973: 72) shows examples of *-ikee* used in the complex derivatives -*stamaakee* and -*amaakee*, which is also confirmed for Michif. Cf. **teepwee**-*shtamaa*-*kee*-w, 's/he acts as announcer (for people)' VAI < **teepwee**-*stama*-*ee*-w [vta] 's/he acts as announcer for her/him', lit. 's/he calls out to people on behalf of her/him'. Cf. also **wiiht**-*amaa*-*kee*-w 's/he makes predictions' VAI < **wiiht**-*amaw*-*ee*-w [vta] 's/he tells it for her/him' < **wiiht**-*am* [vti] 's/he tells about it'.

'suddenly somebody knocked on their door'
VAI < *pakamah-am* [vti] 's/he hit it' or *pakamahw-ee-w* [vta] 's/he hits him/her'

(59) ***ayamihc-ikee*-w**
      read.TI-GEN.AI-IND.3S
      's/he reads things'   [Mazzoli, elicitation]
      VAI < *ayamiht-aa-w* [vti] 's/he reads it'

(60) ***meetawaa-kee*-w**
      play.AI-GEN.AI-IND.3S
      's/he plays with things'
      VAI < *meetawee-w avik la kateñ* [vai+o] 's/he plays with the doll'

The *-ikee* derivative applies to TI stems without the TI theme *-am* (58) or *-aa* (59) and to the *-aa* version of the AI abstract final alternating in *-ee/aa* (60).

Voice

All derivatives in this section apply to transitive verbs to derive intransitive ones. Michelsen (1926: 370, cited in Wolfart 1973: 27) lists five voices for the Algonquian languages: active, middle, passive, reflexive, and reciprocal. Middle, reflexive, and reciprocal voices are expressed through derivational patterns (Section 4.12)–(4.18). The passive voice is realized by several strategies that include both inflectional morphemes (indicating direction in the TA conjugation) and derivational morphemes (cf. Section 4.19).

4.12 *-ito* reciprocal

The derivative *-ito* applies to TA stems and outputs AI verbs. It attaches to transitive animate verbs to form reciprocals. Since it has to attach to TA stems, it is sometimes preceded by the valency increaser *-h* (Sections 4.4 and 4.5) as in (61).

(61) *sapraañ   maaka   chi-**wiiki**-h-ito-yen*[10]
      need   however   CNJ-live.AI-INCR.TA-REC.AI-CNJ.2S
      'but then you will have to get married'

---

[10] It should be *-yeek* if it is plural. However, it seems common for reciprocals in Michif to conjugate in the singular (Bakker, p.c.).

VAI < *wiiki-*h*-ee-w* [vta] (unattested)[11], but cf. *wiiki-m-ee-w* [vta] 'marry him/her'

(62) *aeñ-kwashooñ-**mow**-ito-w-ak*
 INDEF.M.S-pig.M-eat.TA-REC.AI-IND.3-PL
 'they (animate) eat each other like a pig (greedily)'
 VAI < *mow-ee-w* [vta] 's/he eats him/her'

Among other examples, one finds **nipa**-*h*-*ito*-*wak* 'they kill each other' (< *nipa-h-ee-w* [vta] 'kill him/her), **kitima**-*h*-*ito*-*wak* 'they ruin each other' (< **kitim**-*h*-*ee-w* [vta] 'ruin him/her'), and **paahpi**-*h*-*ito*-*wak* 'they laugh at each other' (< **paahpi**-*h*-*ee-w* [vta] 'laugh at him/her').

4.13 *-ishoo* reflexive

The derivative *-ishoo* applies to TA stems, outputs AI verbs. It applies to transitive animate stems to transform them into reflexive animate intransitive verbs (cf. Wolfart 1973: 63, 73 for Plains Cree):

(63) **waapam**-*ishoo*-w   dañ   li   mirwa
 see.TA-REC.AI-IND.3S   in   DEF.M.S   mirror.M.INAN
 's/he sees her/himself in the mirror'
 VAI < *waapam-ee-w* [vta] 's/he sees her/him'

(64) *kii-**nipa**-h-ishoo-w*
 PST-sleep.AI-CAUS.TA-REC.AI-IND.3S
 's/he committed suicide', lit. 's/he caused him or herself to die'
 [Mazzoli, elicitation]
 VAI < *nipa-h-ee-w* [vta] 's/he kills her/him' < *nipaa-w* [vai] 's/he sleeps'

4.14 *-oo* middle reflexive

The morpheme *-oo* applies to TA stems and outputs AI verbs. It is used in both primary and secondary processes. In secondary derivation it functions as a middle-reflexive (Wolfart 1973: 65, 73 for Plains Cree). It is added to transitive animate stems without their TA themes to derive animate intransitive verbs.

---

11 This is probably a backformation.

(65) zha   parii   chi-**aachim**-<u>oo</u>-yaan
     I   ready   CNJ-tell.TA-MID.RFLX.AI-CNJ.1S
     mooñ   istwaer
     1POSS.M.S   story.M.INAN
     'I am ready to tell my story'
     VAI+O < *aachim-ee-w* [vta] 's/he tells of him'

(66) **atoshkee**-<u>m</u>-<u>oo</u>-w
     work.AI-COM.TA-MID.RFLX.AI-IND.3S
     's/he employs people'
     VAI < *atoshkee*-<u>m</u>-*ee-w* [vta] 's/he works with someone' < *atoshkee-w* [vai] 's/he works'

It is frequently found with stems ending in the complex intransitive animate final *-eyim-oo* 'think of her/himself' and *-payi-h-oo* ('move oneself', epenthetic *-h*).

4.15 -*(i)kaashoo* medio-passive

The morphemes *-(i)kaashoo*[12] and *-(i)kaatee* (Section 4.16) are described in the literature on Cree and Michif as middle-reflexive derivatives that apply to TA bases (Bloomfield 1946: 109; Cook and Muehlbauer 2010; Souter 2010). In Michif, *-(i)kaashoo* and *-(i)kaatee* are medio-passive derivatives that apply mainly to TA bases.

Medio-passive morphemes express a "middle" voice, that is, a voice that portrays events remaining in the dominion of the subject (Kemmer 1993). In middle voice, the syntactic subject cannot be categorized as either agent or patient but may have elements of both (e.g. in English, "my clothes soaked in detergent overnight"). The middle function can also indicate that the subject is interested in the action in terms of benefit (or emotionally), but the agent remains unspecified or is nonexistent. In many languages, the category shares some boundaries with the reflexive and the passive. In Michif, it often receives a passive reading.

---

12 The medio-passive *-(i)kaashoo* should be distinguished from the derivative *-(i)hkaashoo* 'pretending to be, make oneself, AI'. Therefore, one should distinguish between (a) **paahpi-<u>h</u>-<u>ikaashoo</u>**-w 's/he is laughed at' (context: the person did something funny and all the people now laugh at him or her), and (b) **paahpi**-<u>hkaashoo</u>-w 's/he pretends to laugh'. Also: (a) *Verna kii*-**nagamo**-<u>h</u>-<u>ikaashoo</u>-w 'Verna was sung to' (context: as in a serenade), and (b) *Verna* **nakamo**-<u>hkaashoo</u>-w 'Verna pretends to sing' (context: as in a playback).

The *-(i)kaashoo* morpheme applies to TA (and arguably also TI) and outputs AI middle verbs. As noted in the literature, it attaches to many TA bases, as in (67)–(71). Epenthetic *-i-* interrupts consonant clusters.

(67) ee-kii-**kitimah**-*ikaashoo*-t
CNJ-PST-abuse.TA-MED.AI-CNJ.3S
'she was abused'
VAI < *kitimah-ee-w* [vta] 's/he abuses him/her'

(68) **ich**-*ikaashoo*-w[13]
say.TA-MED.AI-IND.3S
'she was told'
VAI < *it-ee-w* [vta] 's/he says thus to him/her'

(69) Cinderella   eekwanima   **miiy**-*ikaashoo*-w[14]
Cinderella   that.INAN   give.TA-MED.AI-IND.3S
'Cinderella got it from them'
VAI < *miiy-ee-w* [vta] 's/he gives it to him/her'

(70) **nakamo**-*h*-*ikaashoo*-w[15]
sing.AI-TR-MED.AI-IND.3S
'she is sung to'   [Mazzoli, elicitation]
VAI < *nakamoo-h-ee-w [vta] < *nakamoo-w* [vai] 's/he sings'

(71) **kipah**-*ikaashoo*-w
close.TA-MED.AI-IND.3S
'she was locked up'   [Mazzoli, elicitation]
VAI < *kipah-ee-w* [vta] 's/he closes him/her'
kipah-am [vti] 'she closes/obstructs it'

However, *-(i)kaashoo* also appears after a TI stem in the lexicalized form *ishinikaashoo-* (72):

(72) Harvey   **ishin**-*ikaashoo*-w
Harvey   see.thus.TI-MED.AI-IND.3S
'he is called Harvey'   [Mazzoli, elicitation]
VAI < *ishin-am* [vti] 's/he sees something thus'

---

[13] Alveolar /t/ palatalizes as /c/ before high vowels in both Cree and Michif. The palatalization of /t/ to /c/ only applies before historical */i/ and not to */e/, which merged with /i/ in Cree.

[14] Double object verb *miiyeew* ('to give it to him/her') keeps its inanimate object (*eekwanima*) also in its medio-passive form.

[15] There appears to be variation, as in *nakamo-h-ikaashoo-w* and *nakamo-ikaashoo-w*. This does not entail any change in meaning. I interpret *-h* as a backformation of a VTA from which to regularly derive the medio-passive voice.

4.16 -(i)kaatee medio-passive

The medio-passive -(i)kaatee has similar features to -(i)kaashoo. It applies to TA, TI and AI+O stems but outputs II verbs. The bases to which -(i)kaatee attaches are TA (73) and TI with theme in -am (74) or AI+O stems with final -htaa (75)–(76). The suffix attaches to bare stems without direction markers for TA, without the theme signs -am for TI, and without the final portion -aa of AI+O stems.

(73) la   ash   **kitimah**-*ikaatee*-w
     DEF.F.S   axe.F.INAN   abuse.TA-MED.II-IND.O
     'the axe is misused'   [Mazzoli, elicitation]
     VII < *kitimah-ee-w* [vta] 's/he abuses him/her'

(74) la   rom   **taashkin**-*ikaatee*-w   aañ
     DEF.F.S   room.F.INAN   beat.TI-MED.II-IND.O   in
     deu   pchit   rom
     two   little.F   room.F.INAN
     'the room is divided into two small rooms' [Laverdure and Allard 1983: 77]
     VII < *taaskin-am* [vti] 's/he splits it'

(75) ee-**oshch**-*ikaatee*-k   anima   la   maeñzooñ[16]
     CNJ-build.AI+O-MED.II-CNJ.O   that.INAN   DEF.F.S   house.F.INAN
     VII < *oshiihtaa-w* [vai+o] 's/he makes it, s/he builds it'

(76) la   bol   **kiishihch**-*ikaatee*-w
     DEF.F.S   cup.F.INAN   complete.AI+O-MED.II-IND.OS
     avik   la   tool
     with   DEF.F.S   tool.F.INAN
     'the cup is made of metal'   [Rosen 2019]
     VII < *kiishihtaa-w* [vai+o] 's/he completes it'

4.17 -aakoshi middle attributive predication

The derivative -aakoshi applies to TI stems and outputs AI verbs. The pair of derivatives -aakoshi and -aakwa are described in the literature as medio-passive suffixes that attach to TI stems to create AI and II verbs, respectively (Wolfart 1973: 71; Cook and Muehlbauer 2010; Souter 2010). They are sometimes associated with the pair -(i)kaashoo and -(i)kaatee (Sections 4.15 and 4.16) and de-

---

[16] Also attested: *oshihch-ikaatee-w* (Fleury and Bakker 2004).

scribed as devices of the middle voice (medio-passive and middle-reflexive) having passive nuances (Bloomfield 1962: 299; Wolfart 1973: 71). Instead, I refer to -*aakoshi* and -*aakwa* as middle attributive predication derivatives, deriving stative attributive predicates from TI verbs, expressing middle voice. When applied to a base verb meaning 'X', their derivation results in predicative forms of the type 's/he or it is X-y'.

The -*aakoshi* derivative applies to TI stems and attaches to bare stems without the TI theme sign:

(77) *en*   *zheraef*   *noo*   **peeht**-*aakoshi*-*w*
      INDEF.F.S   giraff.F.AN   NEG   hear.TI-PRED.AI-IND.3S
      'a giraffe is soundless'   [Laverdure and Allard 1983: 307]
      VAI < *peeht-am* [vti] 's/he hears it'

(78) *li*   *Prizidaan*   *dela*   *Maenrik*
      DEF.M.S   president   of.the   America
      kishkeeyiht-*aakoshi*-*w*   *larzhaan*   *ee-manaachih-aa-t*
      know.TI-PRED.AI-IND.3S   money.AN   CNJ-save.TA-DIR-CNJ.3→4
      'the President of the United States is notable for saving money'
                                                   [Laverdure and Allard 1983: 194]
      VAI < *kishkeeyiht-am* [vti] 's/he knows it'

(79) *Cinderella*   *wiya*   **kitim**-*aakoshi*-*w*
      Cinderella   she   abuse.TR-PRED.AI-IND.3S
      'Cinderella, she was pitiful'
      VAI < *kitimah-am* [vti] 's/he abuses it' or *kitimah-ee-w* [vta] 's/he abuses him/her'

4.18 -*aakwa* middle attributive predication

The morpheme -*aakwa* applies to TI stems and outputs II verbs. It behaves like -*aakoshi*, but derives II stems from TI. It attaches to bare stems without their TI theme signs:

(80) ***kishkeeyiht***-*aakwa*-*n*   *taanshi*   *ee-kaahkwee-toot-aman*
      know.TI-PRED.II-IND.OS   how   CNJ-try-do.TI-CNJ.2S
      'it's obvious what you're trying to do'   [Rosen 2019]
      VII < *kishkeeyiht-am* [vti] 's/he knows it'

(81) ***kitim***-*aaka*-*n*   *ee-ishweepa-k*
      abuse.TR-PRED.II-IND.OS   CNJ-weather.BE.II-CNJ.OS

'it is pitiful the way the weather is' [Mazzoli, elicitation]
VII < *kitimah-am* [vti] 's/he abuses it' or *kitimah-ee-w* [vta] 's/he abuses him/her'

The two derivative affixes *-aakoshi* and *-aakwa* often combine to form verbs of sensory perception related to hearing and sight. In these forms, they combine with the stem-internal finals *-ht* (by.ear) and *-n* (by.sight) to form the complex finals *-naakoshi* AI, *-naakwan* II, *-htaakoshi* AI, and *-htaakwan* II. These four finals are quite common and must combine with initials to form well-formed stems.

4.19 *-ikawi* and *-aa* agent-less passive

The agent-less passives *-ikawi* and *-aa* apply to TA and output AI. Plains Cree and Michif have two passives. One is realized through the inverse forms of the TA conjugation, and in this way the agent is expressed or implicit (on the relation between voice and Algonquian direction for TA verbs, see Wolfart 1973: 24f.; Dahlstrom [1986] 2013: 68f.). The other is a passive form in which the agent/actor remains unspecified. The first strategy should be considered inflection. The second strategy, the agent-less passive, is derivational, and uses the suffix *-ikawi* for speech act participants and *-aa* for the third persons, as in (82) and (83):

(82) niishta   kaa-apishiishi-yaan   kii-**aachim**-oo-sta-ikawi-yaan
 I.too   REL-be.small.AI-CNJ.1S   PST-tell.TA-MID.RFLX.AI-BEN.TA-PASS.AI-CNJ.1S
 nohkom   ni-mushum-ipan   ee-kii-**aachim**-oo-ch-ik
 my.grandmother   my-grandpa-late   CNJ-PST-tell.TA-MID.RFLX.AI-CNJ.3-PL
 'I too, when I was small, was told stories by my late grandmother and grandfather when they were telling stories'
 VTA < *aachim-oo-staw-ee-w* [vta] 's/he narrates for her/him' < *aachim-o-w* [vai] 's/he narrates, tells stories' < *aachim-ee-w* [vta] 's/he narrates to her/him'

(83) la   Sandrieuz   kii-**it**-aa-w
 DEF.F.AN   Sandrieuz   PST-say.TA-PASS.AI-IND.3S
 'she was called Sandrieuz'
 VAI < *it-ee-w* [vta] 's/he says to her/him'

The agent-less passives *-ikawi* and *-aa* apply to TA stems that do not include the TA theme signs.

4.20 -shkee accrescitive

This valutative applies to AI stems and outputs AI verbs. Cook and Muehlbauer (2010) list *-iski* for Plains Cree as an habitual suffix that transforms AI into AI stems (e.g. *matoskiw* 's/he cries easily and often'; *kitohcikêskiw* 's/he plays often on a musical instrument'; *kihtimiskiw* 's/he is often lazy, s/he is lazy all the time'; *mitsoskiw* 's/he eats often'; *nikamoskiw* 's/he sings often'). In Michif, *-shkee* is used as a habitual/accrescitive derivational morpheme that transform AI stems into AI stems implying the action is performed 'too often' or 'too much':

(84) **minihkwee-shkee-w-ak**
drink.AI-ACCR.AI-IND.3-PL
'they drink too much' [Mazzoli 2019: 112]
VAI < *minihkwee-w* [vai] 's/he drinks'

(85) Mary kishiwaahtwaa-w akoos **nipaa-shkee-w**
Mary angry.AI-IND.3S because sleep.AI-ACCR.AI-IND.3S
'Mary is angry because she sleeps too much' [Mazzoli, elicitation]
VAI < *nipaa-w* [vai] 's/he sleeps'

4.21 Relative order of secondary derivatives in Michif

Based on the Michif occurrences listed in (20)–(85), the relative order of the Michif derivatives appears as in Table 3:

Table 3: Relative order of Michif derivatives within slot 7 of the template in Table 1.[17]

TA/MID.AI	GEN.AI	BEN.TA	APP.TA	REC.AI	CAUS.TA	RFLX.AI	AC.FOC.AI/PASS.AI/TR
-aw	-ikee	-st	-amaw	-ito	-h	-isho	-aashoo
-oo							-ikawi
							-t

In order to complete the table above, the following occurrences, among others, have been tested and confirmed for Michif:

---

[17] Note that the positions of the middle *-oo*, the actor focus *-aashoo*, the passive *-ikawi* and the transitivizer *-t* are provisional. The data just show that *-oo* precedes the benefactive *-st*, and that *-aashoo*, *-ikawi*, and *-t(ee)* follow the applicative, benefactive, and the general goal markers, respectively.

(86) **nootin**-*ikee*-*sht*-*am*-*aw*-ee-w
fight.TR-GEN.AI-BEN-THE.TI-APP.TA-DIR-IND.3→4
's/he fights (people) for him/her' [Mazzoli, elicitation]

(87) **wiiht**-*am*-*aa*-*to*-w-ak
tell.TI-THE.TI-TA-REC.AI-IND.3-PL
'they tell it to each other' [Wolfart 1973: 70; Mazzoli, elicitation]

However, the relative positions of the general goal -*ikee* and the applicative (-*am*)-*aw* appear inverted with respect to Table 3, in occurrences like (88):

(88) **osht**-*am*-*aw*-*kee*-hk
make.AI+O-THE.TI-APP.TA-GEN.AI-INDEF.AC
'accomodate, lit. makes for others in general'
[Laverdure and Allard 1983: 16]

5 Conclusions

In this paper, I have presented a verb template in 12 slots designed and tested specifically for Michif, which differs substantially from the templates previously presented for Michif and Plains Cree (Table 1). For instance, I do not include a slot for medials in the Michif stem. Also, I place the derivational slot 7 for voice and valency after the verb stem (slots 4–5), and the (first) position for the TI theme signs (slot 6), which is confirmed before the derivatives -*aw* and -*aashoo*. Finally, I place the theme signs of direction for TA verbs, and a second position for TI signs, in a separate slot (8) following the position for derivational morphemes like -*sht* and -*t*.

I make a case for splitting the class of the morphemes traditionally included in the category of finals in Michif into two different sets, based on their distributional and structural properties. The affixes which I refer to as finals are involved in primary derivation and define the bipartite verb stem for features of valency and animacy. The list of final morphemes for Michif is probably not too long and partially given in Section 3.4. Currently, there is no descriptive work that lists Michif (or Plains Cree) stem-internal final morphemes, although this important work may add significantly to typological research of word formation in polysynthetic languages. However, a typologically oriented descriptive enterprise of this kind may prove difficult for Michif, as well as for other Algonquian languages, given that the adequate synchronic morphemic treatment of most Algonquian finals is a matter of debate (Zúñiga 2016).

Secondary derivation is recognized as a distinct process with respect to primary derivation. It involves suffixes that attach to stems previously defined for features of transitivity and animacy, modifying those features in a predictable way. Secondary derivation conforms to processes of derivation described for many languages from diverse language families. The set of secondary derivatives in Michif includes 20 suffixes (Table 2) and includes morphemes that trigger animacy conversions, modulate voice, and affect verb valency, plus one valutative. In Table 3, I provide a provisional assessment of the derivatives' relative position within slot 7 of the template.

This work represents an advancement in the description of Michif verb morphology and how it compares to its Algonquian sources. It improves upon a traditional descriptive taxonomy that does not capture the structural properties of the morphemes involved in stem formation and further derivation. A purely templatic approach to Michif taxonomy runs the risk of generating linguistic descriptions that do not align with descriptions of similar phenomena in different languages. Instead, a more typologically-oriented perspective serves as a way to define descriptive categories for Michif (and other Algonquian languages) that capture the structural properties of the morphemes involved in verb formation, therefore allowing for crosslinguistic analyses. Undoubtedly, a similar shift in perspective will also help to provide descriptions that are more useful and accessible for language learners and community members interested in developing pedagogical resources.

Acknowledgments: This research was conducted with the support of the University of Bremen and the European Union FP7 COFUND under grant agreement n° 600411. I wish to thank Peter Bakker, Nicole Rosen, Dale McCreery, Dennis Davey, David "Doc" Brian, Lawrie Barkwell, and Heather Souter. The speakers who contributed their language knowledge for this paper are Verna DeMontigny, Harvey Pelletier (Brandon, Manitoba, Canada), and Ella McLeod (Turtle Mountain Reservation, USA).

Abbreviations

0	inanimate subject
12	first person plural inclusive (I and you)
2	second person
3	third person
4	third person obviative (fourth)

ACCR	accrescitive
AC.FOC	actor focus
AI	animate intransitive
AI+O	animate intransitive plus object
AN	animate
APP	applicative
ART	article
BE	'to be'
BEN	benefactive
CAUS	causative
CNJ	conjunct
COM	comitative
DEF	definite
DIR	direct (TA)
EPEN	epenthesis
EXCL	exclusive
F	feminine
FIN	final
FUT	future
GEN	general goal
II	inanimate intransitive
INAN	inanimate
INCL	inclusive
INCR	valency increaser
IND	independent
INDEF	indefinite
INDEF.AC	indefinite actor
INTR	intransitive
DIR	direct
M	masculine
MID.RFLX	middle-reflexive
MED	medio-passive
NEG	negative
OBJ	object
OBV	obviative
PASS	passive
POSS	possessive
PL	plural
PRED	predicative attributive
PST	past
REC	reciprocal
RED	reduplication
REL	relative
RFLX	reflexive
S	singular
SAP	speech act participants
SBJ	subject

SJ	subjunctive
TA	transitive animate
THE	theme sign for transitive verb stems
TI	transitive inanimate
TR	transitive
VOL	volitive

References

Armoskaite, Solveiga. 2010. On intrinsic transitivity in Blackfoot verb roots. *University of British Columbia Working Papers in Linguistics* 29. 60–69.

Bakker, Peter. 1997. *A language of our own: The genesis of Michif, the mixed Cree-French language of the Canadian Métis*. Oxford: Oxford University Press.

Bakker, Peter. 2004. The verb in Michif. In Lawrence Barkwell (ed.), *La lawng: Michif peekishkwewin. The heritage language of the Canadian Metis*. Vol 2: *Language theory*, 63–80. Winnipeg: Pemmican Publications/Manitoba Metis Federation Michif Language Program.

Bakker, Peter. 2006. Algonquian verb structure: Plains Cree. In Grazyna Rowicka & Eithne Carlin (eds.), *What's in a verb?*, 3–27. Utrecht: LOT.

Bakker, Peter. 2012. Ethnogenesis, language and identity. The genesis of Michif and other mixed languages. In Nicole St-Onge, Carolyn Podruchny, & Brenda Macdougall (eds.), *Contours of a people. Metis family, mobility, and history*, 169–193. Norman: University of Oklahoma Press.

Bakker, Peter. 2013. Michif. In Susanne M. Michaelis, Philippe Maurer, Martin Haspelmath & Magnus Huber (ed.), *The survey of pidgin and creole languages: Contact languages based on languages from Africa, Asia, Australia, and the Americas*, 3, 158–165. Oxford: Oxford University Press.

Bakker, Peter. 2017. Typology of mixed languages. In Alexandra Aikhenvald & R. M. W. Dixon (eds.), *The Cambridge handbook of linguistic typology*, 217–253. Cambridge: Cambridge University Press.

Bakker, Peter & Robert A. Papen. 1997. Michif: A mixed language based on Cree and French. In Sarah Thomason (ed.), *Contact languages: A wider perspective*, 295– 363. Amsterdam & Phiadelphia: John Benjamins.

Barkwell, Lawrence (ed.). 2004. *La lawng: Michif peekishkwewin. The heritage language of the Canadian Metis: Language theory*, vol. 1. Winnipeg: Manitoba Metis Federation/Michif Language Program.

Bloomfield, Leonard. 1946. Algonquian sketch. In Harry Hoijer et al. (eds.) *Linguistic structures of Native America*, 85–129. New York. The Viking Fund.

Bloomfield, Leonard. 1962. *The Menomini language*. New Haven: Yale University Press.

Brittain, Julie & Sara Acton. 2014. The lexicon-syntax interface: Root semantics as an indirect determinant of intransitive verb syntax in Cree. *International Journal of American Linguistics* 80. 475–506.

Comrie, Bernard. 2010. The role of verbal morphology in establishing genealogical relations among languages. In Lars Johanson & Martine Irma Robbeets (eds.), *Transeurasian verbal morphology in a comparative perspective: Genealogy, contact, chance*, 21–32. Wiesbaden: Harrassowitz.

Cook, Claire & Jeff Muehlbauer. 2010. A morpheme index of Plains Cree. Unpublished manuscript.

Creissels, Denis. 2010. Benefactive applicative periphrases: A typological approach. In Fernando Zúñiga & Seppo Kittilä (eds.), *Studies in ditransitive constructions*, 29–69. Amsterdam & Philadelphia: John Benjamins.

Dahlstrom, Amy. 2013. *Plains Cree morphosyntax*. London: Routledge. (originally, UC Berkeley PhD thesis 1986; also 1991 Garland Publishing).

Dryer, Matthew. 2007. Clause types. In Shopen, Timothy (ed.), *Language typology and syntactic description*, vol. I: *Clause structure*, 224–275. Cambridge: Cambridge University Press.

Edwards, Mary. 1954. *Cree, an intensive language course*. Meadow Lake, Saskatchewan: Northern Canada Evangelical Mission.

Fleury, Norman & Peter Bakker. 2004. *La pchit Sandrieuz an Michif*. Aarhus/Saskatoon/Winnipeg: private publication, CD. Also, Winnipeg: MMF Michif Languages Program 2007.

Frantz, Donald. 1991. *Blackfoot grammar*. Toronto: University of Toronto Press.

Frantz, Donald G. 2009. *Blackfoot grammar*, 2nd edn. Toronto: University of Toronto Press.

Genee, Inge. 2013. On the representation of roots, stems and finals in Blackfoot. In J. Lachlan Mackenzie & Hella Olbertz (eds.), *Casebook in functional discourse grammar*, 95–124. Amsterdam & Philadelphia: John Benjamins.

Gillon, Carrie & Nicole Rosen (with speaker Verna DeMontigny). 2018. *Nominal contact in Michif*. Oxford: Oxford University Press.

Goddard, Ives. 1990. Primary and secondary stem derivation in Algonquian. *International Journal of American Linguistics* 56. 449–483.

Golla, Victor. 2007. North America. In Christopher Moseley (ed.), *Encyclopedia of the world's endangered languages*, 1–96. New York: Routledge.

Harrigan, Atticus, Katherine Schmirler, Antti Arppe, Lene Antonsen, Trond Trosterud & Arok Wolvengrey. 2017. Learning from the computational modelling of Plains Cree verbs. *Morphology* 27(4). 565–598.

Junker, Marie-Odile. 2003. A Native American view of the "Mind" as seen in the lexicon of cognition in East Cree. *Cognitive Linguistics* 14(2/3). 167–194.

Kemmer, Suzanne. 1993. *The middle voice*. Amsterdam & Philadelphia: John Benjamins.

Laverdure, Patline & Ida Rose Allard. 1983. *The Michif dictionary*. John C. Crawford (ed.), Winnipeg: Pemmican Publications.

Macaulay, Monica & Joseph Salmons. 2017. Synchrony and diachrony in Menominee derivational morphology. *Morphology* 27(2). 179–215.

Mathieu, Eric. 2013. Denominal verbs in Ojibwe. *International Journal of American Linguistics* 79(1). 97–132.

Mattissen, Johanna. 2017. Sub-types of polysynthesis. In Nicholas Evans, Marianne Mithun & Michael Fortescue (eds.), *The Oxford handbook of polysynthesis*, 70–98. Oxford: Oxford University Press.

Mazzoli, Maria. 2019. Michif loss and resistance in four Metis communities (Kahkiyaaw mashchineenaan, "All of us are disappearing as in a plague"). *Zeitschrift für Kanada-Studien* 69. 96–117.

Mazzoli, Maria. 2020. Michif studies: Challenges and opportunities in collaborative language research. *Journal of Postcolonial Linguistics* 3. 43–63.

Mazzoli, Maria & Eeva Sippola (eds.). in press. *New perspectives on mixed languages: From core to fringe*. Berlin & Boston: De Gruyter Mouton.

Mazzoli, Maria, Peter Bakker & Verna DeMontigny. in press. Michif mixed verbs: Typologically unusual word-internal mixing. In Maria Mazzoli & Eeva Sippola (eds.). Berlin & Boston: De Gruyter Mouton.

Michelsen, Truman. 1926. The fundamental principles of Algonquian languages. *Journal of the Washington Academy of Sciences* 16. 369–371.

Muehlbauer, Jeff. 2008. *The representation of intentionality in Plains Cree*. Vancouver, B.C.: University of British Columbia Doctoral dissertation.

Pentland, David H. 1999. The morphology of the Algonquian independent order. In David H. Pentland (ed.), *Papers of the 30th Algonquian conference*, 222–266. Winnipeg: University of Manitoba.

Report of the Royal Commission on Aboriginal Peoples, Volume 1. 1996. Ottawa: Government of Canada.

Report of the Truth and Reconciliation Commission of Canada. 2015. Government of Canada.

Rhodes, Richard A. S. 1977. French Cree: A case of borrowing. In William Cowan (ed), *Actes du huitième congrès des algonquinistes*, 6–25. Ottawa: Carleton University.

Rhodes, Richard A. S. 1982. Algonquian trade language. In Cowan, William (ed.), *Papers of the thirteenth Algonquian conference*, 1–10. Ottawa: Carleton University.

Rhodes, Richard A. S. 2008. Ojibwe in the Cree of Métchif. In Karl S. Hele & Regna Darnell (eds.), *Papers of the 39th Algonquian conference*, 569–580. London: University of Western Ontario.

Rhodes, Richard A. S. 2016. On the semantics of abstract finals: 35 years later. In Monica Macaulay & Valentine J. Randolph (eds.), *Papers of the forty-fourth Algonquian conference*, 289–310. Albany, NY: SUNY Press.

Rosen, Nicole. 2007. *Domains in Michif phonology*. Toronto, ON: University of Toronto Doctoral dissertation.

Rosen, Nicole (ed.). 2019. *Michif Web dictionary*. https://dictionary.michif.atlas-ling.ca. (accessed 13/06/20)

Rosen, Nicole & Heather Souter. 2009. *Piikishkweetak añ Michif!*, 1st edn. Winnipeg, Manitoba: Louis Riel Institute.

Rosen, Nicole & Heather Souter. 2015. *Piikishkweetak aa'n Michif!*, 2nd edn. Winnipeg, Manitoba: Louis Riel Institute.

Russell, Kevin. 1999. The "word" in two polysynthetic languages. In T. Alan Hall & Ursula Kleinhenz (eds.), *Studies on the phonological words*, 203–221. Amsterdam & Philadelphia: John Benjamins.

Sammons, Olivia N. 2019. *Nominal classification in Michif*. Edmonton: University of Alberta Doctoral dissertation.

Slavin, Tanya. 2012a. *The syntax and semantics of stem composition in Oji-Cree*. Toronto: University of Toronto Doctoral dissertation.

Slavin, Tanya. 2012b. Phonological and syntactic evidence for stem structure in Oji-Cree. *International Journal of American Linguistics* 78(4). 497–532.

Souter, Heather. 2010. An index of verb finals in Michif. An inventory of abstract and complex verb finals using the Michif dictionary Turtle Mountain Chippewa Cree as corpus. University of Lethbridge. (Unpublished Term Project for Ling 5990: Michif Morphology.)

Spencer, Andrew. 2015. Derivation. In Peter O. Müller, Ingeborg Ohnheiser, Susan Olsen & Franz Rainer (eds.), *Word-formation. An international handbook of the languages of Europe*, vol. 1, 301–321. Berlin & Boston: De Gruyter Mouton.

Stewart, Jesse & Felicity Meakins. in press. Advances in mixed language phonology: An overview of three case studies. In Maria Mazzoli & Eeva Sippola (eds.). Berlin & Boston: De Gruyter Mouton.

Tollan, Rebecca & Will Oxford. 2018. Voice-less unergatives: Evidence from Algonquian. In Wm. G. Bennett, Lindsay Hracs & Dennis Ryan (eds.), *Storoshenko Proceedings of the 35th West Coast Conference on Formal Linguistics* (WCCFL 35), 399–408. Somerville, MA: Cascadilla.

Valentine, Randolph. 2001a. *Nishnaabemwin reference grammar*. Toronto: University of Toronto Press.

Valentine, Randolph. 2001b. Being and becoming in Ojibwe. *Anthropological Linguistics* 43. 431–470.

Wolfart, H. Christoph. 1973. Plains Cree: A grammatical study. In *Transactions of the American Philosophical Society, New Series* 63.5. Philadelphia: American Philosophical Society.

Wolfart, H. Christoph. 1996. Sketch of Cree, an Algonquian language. In Goddard, Ives (ed.), *Handbook of North American languages* 17, 390–439. Washington, DC: Smithsonian Institution.

Zúñiga, Fernando. 2016. Selected semitransitive constructions in Algonquian. *Lingua Posnaniensis* 58(2). 207–225.

Appendix

La pchit Sandrieuz aañ Michif is a Michif story first published by Norman Fleury and Peter Bakker in 2004. Currently, it is the only available source providing an audio recording, its transcription and the English translation for a Michif text. Here, I provide the linguistic analysis of the text of the story that served as a basis for my study of derivation in Michif as discussed in the main paper. In the following text, the first line is the original transcription (Fleury and Bakker 2004) and the second line is my transcription (and morpheme segmentation) following the spelling conventions proposed in Rosen and Souter (2009, 2015). The third line contains the glosses, and the fourth line is the original English translation. The list of abbreviations is provided at the end of the paper.

Excerpt 1

1 *Zha parii chi-achimoyaan mon istwaer*
   zha   parii   chi-aachimoo-yaan   moñ   istwaer
   1SBJ   ready   CNJ-tell.story.AI-CNJ.1S 1POSS.M.S   story.M.INAN
   'I am ready to tell my story

2 *pur awa la pchit fiy, la Sandrieuz*
   pur   awa   la   pchit   fiiy   la   Sandrieuz
   for   this.AN DEF.F.S   little.F girl.F.AN DEF.F.S   Sandrieuz
   about this little girl, Cinderella.

3 *kii-itaaw. Kii-ishinihkaashow.*
   kii-it-aa-w   kii-ishin-ikaashoo-w
   PST-say.TA-PASS.AI-IND.3S   PST-see.TI-MED.AI-IND.3S
   This was said about her. She was called like that.

4 *Eekiikitimaahikaashot, la pchitfiy awa,*
   ee-kii-kitimaah-ikaashoo-t   la   pchit   fiiy   awa
   CNJ-PST-abuse.TA-MED.AI-CNJ.3S   DEF.F.S   little.F girl.F.AN this.AN
   She was abused, the little girl,

5 *sitaet enn pchit orfalinn. O-paapaa-wa itekwenn*
   sitaet   en   pchit   orfalin   o-paapaa-wa   itekwenn
   she.was   INDEF.F.S   little.F   orphan.F.AN 3-father-POSS   apparently
   she was a little orphan. Her father apparently

6 *kii-wiikimeeyiw onhin la*
   kii-wiikim-ee-yi-w   ooñhiñ   la
   PST-marry.TA-DIR-POSS.SBJ-IND.3>4   that.AN.OBV   DEF.F.S
   had been married to this

7 *faam-a o-paapaa-wa sitet aen vaavv*
   faam-a   o-paapaa-wa   sitet   aeñ   vaav
   woman.F.AN-OBV   3-dad-POSS   was   INDEF.M.S   widow.M.AN
   woman. Her father was a widower.

8   *kii-wanih-ee-w sa faam.*
    kii-wanih-ee-w   sa   faam
    PST-loose.TA-DIR-IND.3>4   3POSS.F.S   woman.F.AN
    He had lost his wife.

9   *Site li mond rish nawachiko,*
    site   li   moond   rish   nawachiko
    it.was   DEF.M.S   people.M.AN   rich   reasonably
    They were reasonably rich people,

10 *kom tapishko daen pale kii-wiiki-wak:*
    kom   tapishko   dañ   palee   kii-wiiki-w-ak
    as   kind.of   in   palace.M.S   PST-live.AI-IND.3-PL
    they were living in a kind of castle:

11 *enn gran, gran maenzon aan rosh.*
    en   graañ   graañ   maeñzooñ   añ   rosh
    INDEF.F.S   big.M   big.M   house.F.INAN   in   stone
    a big, big stone house.

12 *Ee-oshch-ikaat-eek anima la maenzon,*
    ee-osh(ih)ch-ikaatee-k   anima   la   maeñzooñ
    CNJ-make.AI-MED.II-CNJ.OS   that.INAN   DEF.F.S   house.F.INAN
    This house had been built thus,

13 *ee-oshikaat-eek kayaash dan langleteer.*
    ee-osh-ikaatee-k   kayaash   dañ   langleteer
    CNJ-make. AI-MED.II-CNJ.OS   long.time   in   England
    it had been built thus a long time ago in England.

14 *Iyave yaenk la rosh kahkiyaw keekwee*
    iyave   yaeñk   la   rosh   kahkiyaaw   keekwee
    there.was   only   DEF.F.S   stone.F.AN   all   what
    It was only stones, all over the place.

15 *kaa-oshtaa-cik lii maenzon*
    kaa-osh(ih)taa-c-ik   lii   maeñzooñ
    CNJ-make.AI-CNJ.3-PL   ART.PL   house.F.INAN
    When they made houses,

16 *avec lii rosh kii-aapachihee-wak*
    avec   lii   rosh   kii-aapachihee-w-ak
    with   ART.PL   stone.F.AN   PST-be.used.AI-IND.3-PL
    they used rocks at that time

17 *kishpi ee-waashkahikee-cik.*
    kishpi   ee-waashkahikee-c-ik
    at.that.time   CNJ-make.houses.AI-CNJ.3-PL
    when they built houses.

18 *Safek awa lom, enn espes di rwe*
    safek   awa   lom   en   espes   di   rwe
    so   this.AN   man.M.AN   INDEF.F.S   kind   of   king.M.AN
    'So this man,'

19 *kaa-itaa-naan, site aen nom*
    kaa-it-aa-naan   site   aeñ   nom
    CNJ-say.TA-PASS.AI-IND.1PL.INCL it.was   INDEF.M.S   man.M.AN
    we call him a kind of a king, he was a

20 *baen site aen lord,*
    baeñ   site   aeñ   lord
    good   it.was   INDEF.M.S   lord.M.AN
    well-off man. He was a "lord",

21 *kaa-kii-itaa-cik kayaash li mond.*
    kaa-kii-it-aa-c-ik   kayaash   li   mooñd
    CNJ-PST-say.TA-PASS.AI-IND.3-PL long.time   DEF.M.S   people.AN
    'as the people would say long time ago.'

22 *Sa faam, sa pramyer faam*
    sa   faam   sa   pramyii   faam
    3POSS.F.S   woman.F.AN   3POSS.F.S   first   woman.F.AN
    His wife, his first wife

23 *kii-wanih-eew eekwa kiihtwam kii-wiiw-eew*
    kii-wanih-ee-w   eekwa   kiihtwam   kii-wiiwi-w
    PST-loose.TA-DIR-IND.3<4   and.now   again   PST-take.wife.AI-IND.3S
    he had lost her and now he had remarried.

24 *kii-wiikim-eew onhin la faam-a.*
    kii-wiikim-ee-w   ooñhiñ   la   faam-a
    PST-marry.TA-DIR-IND.3>4   this.OBV   DEF.F.S   woman.F.AN-OBV
    He had remarried this woman.

25 *Siten enn moves faam, enn moves faam,*
    site   en   moves   faam   en   moves   faam
    she.was   INDEF.F.S   bad.F   woman.F.AN   INDEF.F.S   bad.F   woman.F.AN
    She was a bad woman, a bad woman.

26 *kii-machi-manitowi-w ana la faam,*
    kii-machi-manito-wi-w   ana   la   faam
    PST-wicked-spirit-be.AI-IND.3S   that.AN   DEF.F.S   woman.F.AN
    She was a real devil, this woman. She was.

27 *pi ilave trwaa fiy ana*
    pii   ilave   trwaa   fiiy   ana
    and   there.were   three   daughter   that.AN
    And she had three daughters,

28 *kii-ayaw-eew la faam,*
    kii-ay-aw-ee-w   la   faam
    PST-have.AI-TA-DIR-IND.3>4   DEF.F.S   woman.F.AN
    she has this woman,

29 *pi lii pchit fiy, lii fiy anikik*
    pii   lii   pchit   fiiy   lii   fiiy   anikik
    and   ART.PL   little.F   daugther.F.AN   ART.PL   girl.F.AN   those.AN
    and these girls, these girls

30 *site lii fiy pa drol*
    site   lii   fiiy   pa   drol
    it.was   ART.PL   daughter.F.AN   NEG   funny
    were not nice.

31 *kii-machi-manitowi-wak wishtawaw.*
    kii-machi-manito-wi-w-ak   wishta-waw
    PST-wicked-spirit-be.AI-IND.3-PL   3EMP-PL
    They too were mean.

32 *Kii-kakwayikeeyimee-wak sakwa la pchit*
    kii-kakwaayik-eeyim-ee-w-ak   sakwa   la   pchit
    PST-great.hate-do.by.think.TA-DIR-IND.3>4-PL   and.so   DEF.F.S   little.F
    They really hated the little

33 *fiy awa, la Sandrieuz.*
    fiiy   awa   la   Sandrieuz.
    girl.F.AN   this.AN   DEF.F.S   Sandrieuz
    girl this Cinderella.

34 *kii-kwaayikeeyimee-wak la pchit*
    kii-kawaayik-eeyim-ee-w-ak   la   pchit
    PST-great.hate-do.by.think.TA-DIR-IND.AI.3>4-PL DEF.F.S   little.F
    They abused her

35 *fiy awa (ee)kii-kitamahee-wak sakwa*
    fiiy   awa   kii-kitamah-ee-w-ak   sakwa
    girl.F.AN   this.AN   PST-abuse.TA-DIR-IND.3>4   and.so
    this little girl. They treated her badly.

36 *eeka la Sandrieuz o-paapa-wa ekota*
    eeka   la   Sandrieuz   o-paapa-wa   ekota
    NEG   DEF.F.S   Sandrieuz   3-dad-POSS   there
    when Cinderella's father

37 *kaa-ayaa-yi-t. Kii-atoshkahee-wak*
    kaa-ayaa-yi-t   kii-atoshkaa-h-ee-w-ak
    CNJ-be.at.AI-POSS.SBJ-CNJ.3S   PST-work.AI-CAUS.TA-DIR-IND.3>4-PL
    was not there. They made her work

38. *parey kom aen nisklaav. Kii-kitimahee-wak.*
parey	kom	aeñ	nisklaav	kii-kitimah-ee-w-ak.
similarly	like	INDEF.M.S	slave.M.AN	PST-abuse.TA-DIR-IND.3>4-PL

    just like a slave. They abused her.

39. *Namoya lii bitaeñ eekwa kii-miyee-wak.*
namoya	lii	bitaeñ	eekwa	kii-miy-ee-w-ak
NEG	ART.PL	cloth.M.INAN	also	PST-give.TA-DIR-IND.3>4-PL

    And they did not give her any clothes.

40. *Lii bitaen kii-kishkam-wak*
lii	bitaeñ	kii-kishk-am-w-ak
ART.PL	cloth.M.INAN	PST-wear.TI-THE.TI-IND.3-PL

    They wore the clothes,

41. *li bel rob kahkiyaw keekwee*
lii	bel	rob	kahkiyaw	keekwee
ART.PL	nice.F	dress.F.INAN	all	that

    all the beautiful dresses.

42. *pi lii fiy anikik kii-tipeeyimee-wak*
pii	lii	fiiy	anikik	kii-tipeeyim-ee-w-ak
and	ART.PL	girl.F.AN	those.AN	PST-command.TA-IND.3>4-PL

    And those daughters were bossing around

43. *Cinderella la Sandrieuz-a*
Cinderella	la	Sandrieuz-a
Cinderella	DEF.F.S	Sandrieuz-OBV

    Cinderella.

44. *kii-mamishim-ee-wak maana*
kii-mamishim-ee-w-ak	maana
PST-RED-tell.on.TA-DIR-IND.3>4-PL.SBJ	usually

    They always used to tell on

45. *la Sandrieuz awa*
la	Sandrieuz	awa
DEF.F.S	Sandrieuz	this.AN

    Cinderella

46. *kii-kitimah-ikocik ashay.*
kii-kitimah-iko-c-ik	ashay
PAT-abuse.TA-INV-CNJ.4>3-PL.SBJ	already

    as if Cinderella abused them.

47. *Safek o-maamaa-yiwiwa-wa la faam ana,*
safek	o-maamaa-yi-wi-wa	la	faam	ana
therefore	3-mother-POSS.SBJ-be.AI-3S	DEF.F.S	woman.F.S	that.AN

    So this woman who was supposed to be her mother,

48 *kii-kichinoochihee-w ee-pakamahwaa-t.*
    kii-kichi-noochih-ee-w   ee-pakamahw-aa-t
    PST-big-treat.badly.TA-DIR-IND.3>4   CNJ-hit.TA-DIR-CNJ.3>4
    always treated her badly, hitting her.

49 *Kii-kitimahee-w anihi Sandrieuz-a*
    kii-kitimah-ee-w   anihi   Sandrieuz-a
    PST-abuse.TA-DIR-IND.3>4   this.OBV   Sandrieuz-OBV
    She abused this Cinderella.'

Excerpt 2

50 *kitahtawee piko taanshitikwe kaa-ishpayihk,*
    kitahtawee   piko   taanishi   eetikwe   kaa-ishpayi-k
    suddenly   but   how   NEG   CNJ-happen.INTR-CNJ.II.O
    'One day, however, I don't know how it happened,

51 *la Sandrieuz opaapaawa miina kiiwaniheew.*
    la   Sandrieuz   o-paapaa-wa   miina   kii-wanih-ee-w
    DEF.F.S   Sandrieuz   3-father.M.AN.POSS   also   PST-lose.TA-DIR-IND.3S
    Cinderella lost her father as well.

52 *Kiinipiw ana lom,*
    kii-nipi-w   ana   lom
    PST-die.AI-IND.3S   that.AN   man.M.AN
    He died,

53 *lom ana kiinipiw*
    lom   ana   kii-nipi-w
    man.M.AN   that.AN   PST-die.AI-IND.3S
    this man died.

54 *ekoshi, taandee chiwiikit?*
    ekoshi,   taandee   chi-wiiki-t
    so   where   CNJ-live.AI-3S
    Then, where was she to live?

55 *fule chi-wiicheeyaamaat onhin.*
    fule   chi-wiichee-am-aa-t   oonhin
    had.to   CNJ-live.with.TA-APP.TA-DIR-CNJ.3>4   these.AN.OBV
    She had to live with those people.

56 *la vyey ana,*
    la   vyey   ana
    DEF.F.S   old.woman.F.AN   that.AN
    The old lady,

57 *Cinderella site pa omaamaawa*
    Cinderella,   site   pa   o-maamaa-wa
    Cinderella   was   NEG   3-mother.F.AN-POSS
    she was not Cinderella's mother,

58 *me kii-ohpikihikohk, kaa-itwaanaan*
    me   kii-ohpikih-iko-hk   ki-itw-aan-aan
    but   PST-raise.TA-INV-INDEF.AC   2-say.AI-IND.2.INCL-PL
    but she was the one who had raised her, as we say,

59 *parey kom kaa-itwaayaahk*
    paree   kom   kaa-itw-aa-yaahk
    similarly as   CNJ-say-DIR-CNJ.TA.1PL>3S
    As it was told to us.

60 *Sa stepmother anihi kiiyaayi*
    Soñ   stepmother   anihi   kii-yaayi
    3POSS.M.S   stepmother.F.AN that.AN.OBV PST-?
    her stepmother she, ehm,

61 *kii-chiishiheew lom-a*
    kii-chiishih-ee-w   lom-a
    PST-fool.TA-DIR-IND.3>4   man.M.AN-OBV
    she had fooled the man

62 *avan chi-nipi-yit, itwew*
    avan   chi-nipi-yi-t,   itee-w
    before   CNJ-die.AI-OBV.S-CNJ.3S say.AI-IND.3S
    before he had died, it is said.

63 *"Ga-miyokanawaapamaaw*
    ni-a-miyo-kanawaapam-aa-w
    1-FUT-good-look.after.TA-DIR-IND.3>4
    "I will take good care of her

64 *ga-miyeukanaweeyimaaw ta fiy*
    ni-ka-miyo-kanaweeyim-aa-w   ta   fiiy
    1-FUT-good-take.care.TA-DIR-IND.SAP>3 2POSS.F.S daughter.F.AN
    I will keep your daughter well.

65 *kaya naandaw iteyihta*
    kaya   naandaw   iteeyiht-a
    NEG.IMP   anything   think.TI-IMP.2S
    Don't worry about that.

66 *ta fiy mitoni gakanaweeyimaaw*
    ta   fiiy   mitoni   ni-ka-kanaweeyim-aa-w
    2POSS.F.S daughter.F.AN really   1-FUT-take.care.TA-DIR-IND.SAP>3
    I will take care of your daughter very well.

67 *kamiyoayaaw avek niyanaan."*
    ka-miyo-ayaa-w   avek   niyaa-naan
    FUT-good-to.be.AI-IND.3S with   1-PL
    She will be well with us."

68 *"Gamiyokanawaapamaanaan."*
   ni-ka-miyo-kana-waapam-aa-n-aan
   1-FUT-good-after-look.TA-DIR-IND.SAP>3-PL
   "We will look after her very well."

69 *Maka kahkiyaashkit*
   Maaka   (kaa-)kah-kiyaashki-t
   but   (CNJ-)-RED-lie.AI-CNJ.3S
   But she was lying all the time

70 *kiichiishiheew anihi lom-a ekoshi*
   kii-chiishih-ee-w   anihi   lom   ekoshi
   PST-fool.TA-DIR-IND.3>4   that.AN.OBV   man.AN   at.that.time
   She deceived the man at that time.

71 *Ekoshi, kwayesh kii-ishi-miyonipiw lom ana*
   ekoshi   kwayesh   kii-ishi-miyo-nipi-w   lom   ana
   so   correct   PST-thus-good-die.AI-IND.3S   man.M.AN   that.AN
   Thus, precisely, the man died in peace,

72 *ekwa ekoshi kitahtawee piko*
   eekwa   ekoshi   kitahtawee   piko
   at.that.point   so   suddenly   but
   that is when, one day,

73 *mo wahyaaw ekota ohchi*
   mo   waahyaw   eekota   ohchi
   NEG   far   here   from
   not far from there,

74 *iyave aen rwe pi la renn*
   iyave   aeñ   rwe   pii   la   ren
   there.was   INDEF.M.S   king.M.AN   and   DEF.F.S   queen.F.AN
   there were a King and a Queen.

75 *pi aen garson kii-ayawaaweewak*
   pii   aeñ   garsoñ   kii-ayaw-ee-w-ak
   and   INDEF.M.S   boy.M.S   PST-have.TA-DIR-IND.3<4-PL
   And they had a boy,

76 *li praens awa.*
   li   praens   awa
   DEF.M.S   prince.M.AN   this.AN
   he was the prince.

77 *Ekoshpi li mond kii-wiikihitowak*
   ekoshpi   li   mooñd   kii-wiiki-ito-w-ak
   then   DEF.M.S   people.AN   PST-marry.TA-REC.AI-IND.3>4-PL
   At that time people married

78 *kankisonte zheunn naandaw*
    kankisooñte   zheunn   naandaw
    when.they.were   young   about
    when they were young,

79 *alantuur di vaen tan naandaw*
    alañtuur   di   vaeñ   tañ   naandaw
    around   of   twenty   year   about
    when they were around twenty.

80 *kii-mishkamaashowak*
    kii-mishk-am-aasho-w-ak
    PST-find.TI-THE.TI-AC.FOC.AI-IND.3-PL
    They found somebody for themselves

81 *pi ekiiwikitochik sheemaak*
    pii   ee-kii-wiki-ito-ch-ik   sheemaak
    and   CNJ-PST-marry.TA-REC.AI-CNJ.3-PL   now
    and got married right away.

82 *maaka ana li praens ilave*
    maaka   ana   li   praeñs   ilave
    but   that.AN   DEF.M.S   prince.M.AN   had
    But this Prince had...

83 *ilite pleu vyeu kisa awa*
    ilite   pleu   vyeu   kisa   ana
    he.was   more   old.M   then.that   this.AN
    he was already older than that,

84 *vaen deu, vaen trwaa zaan kii-ayaa-w*
    vaeñ   deu,   vaeñ   trwaa   zaañ   kii-ayaa-w
    twenty   two,   twenty   three   year   PST-have.AI-IND.3S
    he was 22, 23 years old.

85 *Pi li rwe eekwa la renn*
    pii   li   rwe   eekwa   la   ren
    and   DEF.M.S   king.M.AN   and   DEF.F.S   queen.F.AN
    And the King and the Queen

86 *iteewak*
    it-ee-w-ak
    say.TA-DIR-IND.3>4-PL.SBJ
    'they said to him'

87 *"sapran chiwiikihitoyenn*
    sapraañ   chi-wiikih-ito-yen
    it.is.necessary   CNJ-marry.TA-REC.AI-CNJ.2S
    "You have to get married.

88. *naandaw ishipayiyaani ti vayet*
 naandaw ishipayi-yaan-i ti vayet
 something.bad happen.II-CNJ.1S-COND you are.going.to.be
 If something will happen to me,

89. *ti vayet rwe pi tara pat faam*
 rwe pii tara pat faam
 king.M.AN and you.are.going.to.have NEG wife.F.AN
 You will be King and you have no wife.

90. *sapran enn faam chi-ayaawat*
 sapraañ en faam chi-aya-aw-a-t
 it.is.neccessary INDEF.F.S wife.F.AN CNJ-have.AI-TA-DIR-CNJ.3>4
 You have to have a wife.

91. *lii zaanfaan sapran kiishta chi-ayaawaachik*
 lii zaañfaañ sapraañ kiishta chi-aya-aw-a-chik
 ART.PL children.AN necessary you.too CNJ-have.AI-TA-DIR-2>3PL
 You too have to have children.

92. *namawiyek apre chi-otinahk opachip*
 (na)m(o)-awiyek apre chi-otin-ahk opachip
 NEG-somebody after CNJ-take.TI-CNJ.INDEF.AC ?
 There is nobody to take over,

93. *chi-kanaweehtahk oma not palae*
 chi-kanaweeyiht-ahk oma not palee
 CNJ-look.after.TI-CNJ.3S this.INAN 1POSS.PL palace.M.INAN
 To look after our palace

94. *pi tut notr terraen, noo sarvaan*
 pii tut not terraeñ noo sarvaañ
 and all 1POSS.PL property.M.INAN 1POSS.PL servant.M.AN
 and all our land, our servants,

95. *pi kahkiyaw noo solda.*
 pii kahkiyaw noo soldaa
 and all 1POSS.PL soldier.M.AN
 and all our soldiers:

96. *Sapran awiyek chikanaweyihtahk*
 sapraañ awiyek chi-kanaweeyiht-ahk
 it.is.necessary somebody look.after.TI-CNJ.3S
 we need somebody to take care of it.

97. *lii zanimo, lii zhvoo kishkohaanaanik*
 lii zanimoo lii zhvoo ki-shkoh-aa-naan-ik
 ART.PL animal.M.AN ART.PL horses.M.AN 2-?-DIR-IND.2>3PL
 We have a lot of cattle and horses.

98 *kitipeehteenaan anmas li terraen*
    ki-tipeeyiht-en-aan   aañmas   li   terraeñ
    2-own.TI-IND.non3-PL.INCL   a.lot.of   DEF.M.S   property.M.INAN
    We own a lot of land.

99 *kitipeehteenaan ota.*
    ki-tipeeyiht-en-aan   oota
    2-own.TI-IND.non3-PL.INCL   here
    We own it around here.

100 *Lii pesan okik eekwa atoshkeewak*
    lii   pesañ   ookik   eekwa   atoshkee-w-ak
    ART.PL   peasant.N.AN these.AN and   work.AI-IND.3-PL
    Those peasants are working.

101 *Sapra chitipeeyimaachik*
    sapraañ   chi-tipeeyim-a-ch-ik
    it.is.necessary   CNJ-rule.TA-DIR-CNJ.SAP>3-PL.OBJ
    You will have to own them.

102 *katipeeyihteen kahkiyaw oma.*
    ka-(ki-)tipeeyiht-en   kahkiyaw   oma
    FUT-(2-)rule.TI-IND.non3   all   this.INAN
    You will have to pay all of that.

103 *kiya kamiyitinaan*
    kiya   (ki-)ka-miy-iti-n-aan
    you.EMPH   (2-)FUT-give.TA-INV.1>2-IND.non3-PL.INCL
    We give it to you,

104 *sapra maaka chi-wiikihitoyen. Taapwee.*
    sapraañ   maaka   chi-wiikih-ito-yen   taapwee
    it.is.neccessary but   CNJ-marry.TA-REC.AI-CNJ.2S truly
    But then you will have to get married." It is true.

105 *Tudaenku li rwe itweew:*
    todaeñkuu   li   rwe   itwee-w
    suddenly   DEF.M.S   king.M.AN   say.AI-3S
    Suddenly the King said:

106 *"Kiishpin kiwiiweewin, sapran*
    kiishpin   ki-wii-wiw-in   sapraañ
    if   IND-INT-take.wife.AI-IND.2S necessary
    "If you want to take a wife, I will have

107 *enn mesazh kashipweetishahamaahk ota*
    en   mesazh   ka-shipwee-tishah-amaahk   oota
    INDEF.F.S   message.F.INAN CNJ-away-send.TI-CNJ.1PL.EXCL here
    a message to be sent away here

108 *kahkiyaw ookik lii fiy eekwanikik*
    kahkiyaw   ookik   lii   fiiy   eekwaanikik
    all   these.AN   ART.PL   daughter.F.AN   those.AN
    to all the girls.

109 *wiishtawaaw kaakahkihcheyahkichik*
    wiishta-waaw   kaa-kishchee(tee)ht-aa-ch-ik
    them.EMPH-PL   CNJ-respect.TA-PASS.AI-CNJ.3-PL
    Those who are esteemed highly,

110 *lii groo pale kaa-ayaachik wishtawaw.*
    lii   groo   palee   kaa-ayaa-ch-ik   wiishta-waw
    ART.PL   big.M   palace.M.INAN   CNJ-have.AI-CNJ.3PL   them.EMPH-PL
    those who have big palaces.

111 *Ekuta awiyak ka-kakweemishkaawaaw,*
    eekota   awiyak   (ki-)ka-kakwee-mishk-aw-aa-w
    then   somebody   (2-)FUT-try-find.TR-TA-DIR-IND.SAP>3
    There you will try to find someone,

112 *enn faam*
    en   faam
    INDEF.F.S   wife.F.AN
    a wife

113 *Pi kawiihkohkaanaan*
    pii   (ki-)ka-wiihkohk-aan-aan
    and   (2-)FUT-invite.people.to.feast.AI-IND.SAP-PL.INCL
    And we will invite people for a feast,

114 *kawiihkomaanaanik*
    (ki-)ka-wiihkom-aa-naan-ik
    (1&2-)FUT-invite.people.to.feast.TA-DIR-IND.SAP>3-PL.OBJ
    we will invite them

115 *chi-peeniimichik*
    chi-pee-niim-i-chik
    CNJ-come-dance.AI-CNJ.3-PL
    to come and dance.

116 *enn bal, enn gros bal*
    en   bal   en   gros   bal
    INDEF.F.S   ball.F.INAN   INDEF.F.S   big.F   ball.F.INAN
    A Ball, a Grand Ball

117 *ka-ushtaanaan*
    (ki-)ka-oshihtaa-n-aan
    (1&2-)FUT-prepare.AI+O-IND.SAP-PL
    we will organize,

118 *enn gros bal eekwanima*
en gros bal eekwa anima
INDEF.F.S big.F ball.F.INAN and that.INAN
this Grand Ball.

119 *site lii gros dans ekoshpi*
site lii gros dans ekoshpi
there.were ART.PL big.F dance.F.INAN at.the.time
They held big dances at that time.

120 *lii gros dans kii-ushihtaawak*
lii gros dans kii-oshiihtaa-w-ak
ART.PL large.F dance.F.INAN PST-prepare.AI+O-IND.3-PL
They organized big dances,

121 *enn gros gros silibraasyon*
en gros gros silibraasyoñ
INDEF.F.S big.F big.F celebration.F.INAN
A really big celebration.

122 *mihceet kiinipaheewak*
mishcheet kii-nipaa-h-ee-w-ak
many PST-kill.AI-CAUS.TA-DIR-IND.3>4-PL.SBJ
They slaughtered many

123 *lii vash, lii koshon, lii pul,*
lii vash lii kwashooñ lii pul
ART.PL cow.F.AN ART.PL pig.M.AN ART.PL chicken.M.AN
cows, pigs and chickens,

124 *kahkiyaaw chi-miichichik*
kahkiyaaw chi-miichi-ch-ik
all CNJ-eat.AI+O-CNJ.3-PL
all for them to eat.'

125 *la maanzhee aan mas*
la maañzhii aañ mas
DEF.F.S food.F.INAN in great.quantity
There was lots of food.

126 *mihcheet li moond safek taapwee*
mischeet li mooñd safek taapwee
many DEF.M.S people.M.AN so it.is.true
and many people, really.'

Excerpt 3

127 *iyonve pat telefoon ekoshpi*
iyooñve pat telefooñ ekoshpii
they.had NEG telephone.M.INAN at.the.time
'At that time they did not have telephones.

128. *pi iyonve pat lii let*
   pii iyooñve pat lii let
   and they.had NEG ART.PL letter.F.INAN
   And they did not have letters

129. *chishiipweechahahkik*
   chi-shipweeht-ah-ahk-ik
   CNJ-send.TI-?-CNJ.TI.3-PL
   to send things around.

130. *kiikwee ekoshpi li mond maana*
   keekwee ekoshpii li mooñd maana
   something at.the.time DEF.M.S people.M.AN usually
   At that time people

131. *kiipimbahteewak baendon*
   kii-pimbahtaa-w-ak obaeñdoñ
   PST-run.AI-IND.3-PL or
   would run around or

132. *aan zhwal eepaawihtamaawachik awiyak*
   aañ zhwal ee-paa-wiht-am-aw-aa-ch-ik awiyak
   in horse.M.AN CNJ-come-tell-THE.TI-TA-DIR-CNJ.3PL>4 someone
   or have someone on horseback to announce news

133. *chipaawiihkohkeechik. Taapwee*
   chi-paa-wiihkohkee-ch-ik taapwee
   CNJ-come-invite.people.to.feast.AI-CNJ.3-PL really
   to invite people to come. Really.

134. *la faam awa kaa-ohpikihaat Cinderella*
   la faam awa kaa-ohpikih-aa-t Cinderella
   DEF.F.S woman.F.AN this.AN CNJ-raise.TA-DIR-CNJ.3>4 Cinderella
   The woman who raised Cinderella

135. kii-wiihkomikaashow, *pii sii fiy*
   kii-wiihkom-ikaashoo-w pii sii fiiy
   PST-invite.TA-MED.AI-IND.3S and 3POSS.PL girl.F.AN
   was invited for the feast,

136. *pii sii fiy kii-wihtamaaweew maaka iteehtam*
   kii-wiht-am-aw-ee-w maaka iteeiht-am
   PST-say-THE.TI-TA-DIR-IND.3>4 but think.TI-THE.TI
   and she told her daughters about it. But she thought

137. *eeka Cinderella la Sandrieuz epeehtaakut*
   eeka Cinderella la Sandrieuz ee-peeht-aakwa-t
   NEG Cinderella DEF.F.S Sandrieuz CNJ-hear.TI-PRED.II-CNJ.3S
   little Cinderella should not hear it. (lit. that it is not heard by Cinderella).

138 *maka Sandrieuz kiipehtaweew*
    maaka   Sandrieuz   kii-peht-aw-ee-w
    but   Sandrieuz   PST-hear.TI-TA-DIR-IND.3>4
    But Cinderella heard her

139 *kiimonchiwihtamawaat*
    (ee-)kiimoochi-wiht-am-aw-aa-t
    (CNJ-)secretly-tell-THE.TI-TA-DIR-CNJ.3>4
    when she was telling it secretly

140 *anihi lii fiy*
    anihi   lii   fiiy
    those.AN.OBV   ART.PL   girl.F.AN
    to the girls.

141 *Pi sii fii kiimayatishiyiw*
    pii   sii   fiiy   kii-mayiaatishi-w
    and   3POSS.PL   girl.F.AN   PST-be.awful.AI-IND.3S
    And her girls were not pretty.

142 *si lii fiy led*
    si   lii   fiiy   led
    it.is   ART.PL   girl.F.AN   ugly
    They were ugly girls.

143 *iyonve li gran zaray, li gros babinn*
    iyonve   lii   graañ   zaray   lii   gros   babin
    they.had   ART.PL   big.M   ear.M.INAN   ART.PL   big.F   lip.F.INAN
    They had big ears, big lips.

144 *kiimayaatishiwak. Isonte lii fiy led*
    kii-mayiaatishi-w-ak   izooñte   lii   fiiy   led
    PST-be.ugly.AI-IND.3-PL   they.were   ART.PL   girl.F.AN   ugly
    They were not good looking. They were ugly girls.

145 *maka Cinderella, la Sandrieuz awa,*
    maaka   Cinderella   la   Sandrieuz   awa
    but   Cinderella   DEF.F.S   Cinderella   this.AN
    Cinderella, however,

146 *sitenn bel fiy enn bel fiy*
    site   en   bel   fiiy   en   bel   fiiy
    she.was   INDEF.F.S   pretty.F   girl.F.AN   INDEF.F.S   pretty.F   girl.F.AN
    she was pretty, a pretty girl.

147 *kiimiyonaakushiw.*
    kii-miyo-inaakoshi-w
    PST-good-look.AI-IND.3S
    She was good looking.

148 *Sitenn bel bel pchit fiy*
    sitet   en   bel   pchit   fiiy
    she.was   INDEF.F.S   pretty.F   little.F   girl.F.AN
    She was a very pretty little girl.

149 *taapwee la dans wii-itohtewak eekwa*
    taapwee   la   dañs   wii-itohtee-w-ak   eekwa
    really   DEF.F.S   dance.F.INAN   VOL-go.AI-IND.3-PL   now
    Really, now they would go to the dance.

150 *Sapran lii rob chi-oshihtaachik*
    sapraañ   lii   rob   chi-oshihtaa-ch-ik
    it.is.necessary   ART.PL   dress.F.INAN   CNJ-make.AI+O-IND.3-PL
    They had to make dresses.

151 *lii bel rob oonhin kii-oshihtaawak*
    lii   bel   rob   ooñhiñ   kii-oshihtaa-w-ak
    ART.PL   beautiful.F   dress.F.INAN   these.INAN   PST-make.AI-IND.3-PL
    They were making beautiful dresses

152 *chikishkahkik. Li rasaad, li paandaraj*
    chi-kishk-ahk-ik   lii   rasaad   lii   paandaray
    CNJ-wear.TI-CNJ.3-PL ART.PL   bead.F   ART.PL   earring F.INAN
    to wear. Beads, earrings

153 *kahkiyaw kiikwee kiikishkamwak*
    kahkiyaaw   keekwee   kii-kishk-am-w-ak
    all   something   PST-wear-THE-TI-IND.3-PL
    They were wearing all kinds of things.

154 *ekoshpi kahkiyaw kiikishkamwak*
    ekoshpi   kahkiyaaw   kii-kishk-am-w-ak
    at.the.time   all   PST-wear-THE-TI-IND.3-PL
    At that time they wore everything.

155 *lii gros reuban dan leu zhveu*
    lii   gros   reubaañ   dañ   lii   zhveu
    ART.PL   big.F   ribbon.F.AN   in   ART.PL   hair.INAN
    Big ribbons in their hair

156 *baen don kiikishkamwak kiikwee*
    obaeñdoñk   kii-kishk-am-w-ak   keekwee
    or   PAT-wear-THE-TI-IND.3-PL something
    or they wore things

157 *kom lii kuronn*
    kom   lii   karon
    like   ART.PL   crown.F.INAN
    like crowns

158 **ekushi aenkiishihuchik kayaash**
    ekoshi   ee-kii-ishiho-ch-ik   kayaash
    and.then   CNJ-PST-dress.AI-CNJ.3-PL   long.time.ago
    That is how they dressed a long time ago:

159 *lii bel gran rob*
    lii   bel   grañ   rob
    ART.PL   beautiful.F   long.M   dress.F.INAN
    beautiful long dresses,

160 *li gran rob baen kuloerii,*
    lii   grañ   rob   baeñ   kuleurii
    ART.PL   long.M   dress.F.INAN   well   colorful
    colorful dresses,

161 *lii bel rob*
    lii   bel   rob
    ART.PL   beautiful.F   dress.F.INAN
    pretty dresses.

162 *aan roon kiiushiteewan anihi lii rob*
    aañ   rooñ   kii-oshiht-ee-w-a   anihi   lii   rob
    in   round   PST-are.made-II-IND.3-PL   those.INAN   ART.PL   dress.INAN
    These dresses were made round.

163 *wiishta awa la faam,*
    wiishta   awa   la   faam
    she.too   this.AN   DEF.F.S   woman.F.AN
    The woman herself,

164 *wishta enn bel rob*
    wiishta   en   bel   rob
    she.too   INDEF.F.S   pretty.F   dress.F.INAN
    she too had a beautiful dress.

165 *kishkam. Sii fiy chiwiikimaayit*
    kishk-am   sii   fiiy   chi-wiikim-aa-yi-t
    wear-THE.TI   3POSS.PL   girl.F.AN   CNJ-to.marry.TA-DIR-OBV-CNJ.4>5
    As she was trying to marry her daughters off

166 *oonhin li praens-a*
    ooñhiñ   li   praens-a
    these.AN.OBV   DEF.M.S   prince.M.AN-OBV
    to this prince.

167 *kaakweewiikitaheew*
    kaakwee-wiikihtaa-h-ee-w
    try-get.married.AI-CAUS.TA-DIR-IND.3>4
    She would try to let him marry one of them,

168. *sii fiy kaakwee-meekit oonhin*
    sii   fiiy   kaakwee-meeki-t   ooñhiñ
    3POSS.PL   girl.F.AN   try-give.away.AI-CNJ.3S   these.AN.OBV
    as she would try and give her daughters as his wife.

169. *Cinderella wiya kitimaakoshiw.*
    Cinderella   wiya   kitimaa-koshi-w
    Cinderella   she.EMPH   abuse-PRED.AI-IND.3S
    Cinderella however was pitiful.

170. *namo kakii-ituhtew wiya.*
    moya   ka-kii-itohtee-w   wiiya.
    NEG   FUT-PST-go.AI-IND.3S   she.EMPH
    She was not be able to go.

171. *Namo wihkomikaashow.*
    moy(a)   wihkom-ikaashoo-w
    NEG   invite.TA-MED.AI-IND.3S
    She had not been invited.

172. *"mahpo" iteehtam la faam "namo kishkeehtam"*
    mahpo   iteeiht-am   la   faam   namo   kishkeeyiht-am
    ?   think.TI-THE.TI   DEF.F.S   woman.F.AN   NEG   know.TI-THE.TI
    "She wouldn't know," the woman thought. "She does not know about it",

173. *itwew taapwee teepwaateewak la Sandrieuz*
    itwee-w   taapwee   teepwaa-t-ee-w-ak   la   Sandrieuz
    say.AI-IND.3S   really   yell-TR-TA-IND.3>4-PL.SBJ   DEF.F.S   Sandrieuz
    she said. Really, they were yelling at Cinderella

174. *"not bitaen nata!"*
    not   bitaeñ   naat-a
    1POSS.PL   cloth.M.INAN   fetch.TI-IMP.2S
    '"Get our clothes!"'

175. *"shuushkohonn not rob!" Taapwee awa,*
    shooshkwah-en   not   rob   taapwee   awa
    iron-TI-IMP.2S   1POSS.PL   dress.F.INAN   really   this.AN
    '"Iron our dresses!" Really'

176. *Fule trwa lii fiy eekwa la faam*
    fule   trwaa   lii   fiiy   eekwa   la   faam
    necessary   three   ART.PL   girl.F.AN   and   DEF.F.S   woman.F.AN
    'The three girls and the woman,'

177. *omaamaawa fule chi-mitoni-chimiyohooyit*
    o-maamaa-wa   fulee   chi-mitoni   chi-miyo-ho-yi-t
    3-mother-POSS   it.was.needed   CNJ-true   CNJ-good-dress.AI-OBV-CNJ.3S
    'their mother, they had to be dressed very nicely.'

178 *chi-miyonaakushiyit so taapwee*
    chi-miyo-naakoshi-yi-t   so   taapwee
    CNJ-good-look.AI-OBV-CNJ.3S   so   really
    'So that they would look good really.'

179 *Me li boo zhvoo ayaaweew*
    mee   lii   boo   zhvoo   aya-aw-ee-w
    but   ART.PL   beautiful.M   horses.M.AN   have.AI-TA-DIR-IND.3S
    'But she had good horses,'

180 *awa la faam awa*
    awa   la   faam   awa
    this.AN   DEF.F.S   woman.F.AN   this.AN
    'this woman.'

181 *Li boo zhvoo kii-ayaaweew*
    lii   boo   zhvoo   kii-aya-aw-ee-w
    ART.PL   beautiful.M   horses.M.AN   PST-have.AI-TA-DIR-IND.3S
    'she had good horses'

182 *awa la faam rish*
    awa   la   faam   rish
    this.AN   DEF.F.S   woman.F.AN   rich
    'this rich woman.'

183 *Site lii zhvoo anihi Cinderella*
    site   lii   zhvoo   anihi   Sandrieuz
    it.was   ART.PL   horses.M.AN   those.AN.OBV   Sandrieuz
    These horses were Cinderella's

184 *opaapaawa sii zhvoo*
    o-paapaa-wa   sii   zhvoo
    3-father-POSS   3POSS.PL   horses.M.AN
    father's horses.

185 *kahkiyaaw sii vwacheur*
    kahkiyaaw   sii   vwacheur
    all   3POSS.PL   carriage.F.AN
    Also all the carriages.

186 *otaapaheew anihi*
    otaapah-ee-w   anihi
    ride.TA-DIR-IND.3>4   those.AN.OBV
    She was riding them,

187 *sii boo zhvoo.*
    sii   boo   zhvoo
    3POSS.PL   beautiful.M   horses.M.AN
    his good horses.

188 *Iyave aen servan.*
 iyave aeñ sarvaañ
 there.was INDEF.M.S servant.M.AN
 She had a servant.

189 *Iyave lii boo zhvoo.*
 iyave lii boo zhvoo
 there.was ART.PL beautiful.M horses.M.AN
 They had good horses.

190 *kii-shipweepayiwak la*
 kii-shipwee-payi-w-ak la
 PST-leave-move.AI-IND.3-PL DEF.F.S
 And they took off,

191 *asphinaen dan la bal oma*
 ashpi-n-aan dañ la baal oma
 go.away.AI-IND.3-PL to DEF.F.S ball.F.INAN this.INAN
 'Away to the ball.'

192 *ee-ituhteechik da li gran palae.*
 ee-itohtee-ch-ik dañ li graañ palee
 CNJ-go.AI-CNJ.3-PL to DEF.M.S big.M palace.M.INAN
 They went to the big palace.

193 *safek Sandrieuz wiya maatoow,*
 safek Sandrieuz wiya maatoo-w
 so Sandrieuz 3EMPH cry.AI-IND.3S
 So Cinderella, she was crying.

194 *namoya shipweehteehikaashow*
 namo shipweehtee-h-ikaashoo-w
 NEG leave.AI-INCR.TA-MED.AI-IND.3S
 They had not taken her along.

195 *maatoow kashkeeyihtam*
 maatoo-w kashkeeiht-am
 cry.AI-IND.3S be.sad.TI-THE.TI
 She was crying. She was sad about it.

196 *kashkeeyimeew omaamaawa, opaapaawa*
 kashkeeim-ee-w o-paapaa-wa
 miss.TA-DIR-IND.3S 3-father-POSS
 She missed her mother, her father.

197 *maachi-kishkishiw o-paapaa-wa.*
 maachi-kishkishi-w o-paapaa-wa
 begin-remember.AI-IND.3S 3-father-POSS
 She started to think about her father.

198 *"Baapaa kiinipiw"*
    b(p)aapaa   kii-nipoo-w
    father   PST-die.AI-IND.3S
    "My father is dead".

199 *"gitimaakishin, beyaakon"*
    ni-kitimaak-ishi-n   ni-peyaako-n
    1-miserable-AI-IND.non3S   1-be.alone.AI-IND.non3S
    "I am pitiful, I am alone!"

200 *"gitimaahikaawin."*
    kitimaah-ikaawi-n
    abuse.TA-PASS.AI-IND.1S
    "I am abused!"'

Excerpt 4

201 *Tudaenku la faam awa*
    tudaeñku   la   faam   awa
    suddenly   DEF.F.S   woman.F.AN   this.AN
    'Suddenly this woman

202 *lii mazhii gaa-ush(ih)tachik*
    lii   maazhii   kaa-osh(ih)taa-ch-ik
    ART.PL   magic   REL-make.AI+O-CNJ.3-PL
    who is able to perform magic appeared.

203 *kitahtawee kaawaapamaat oonhin la faam-a*
    kitahtawee   kaa-waapam-aa-t   ooñhiñ   la
    suddenly   REL-see.TA-DIR-CNJ.3S>4   this.OBV   DEF.F.S
    Suddenly she saw this woman.

204 *faam-a ekota niipawiw awa la faam*
    faam-a   ekota   niipawi-w   awa   la   faam
    woman.F.AN-OBV   there   stand.AI-IND.3S   this.AN   DEF.F.S   woman.F.AN
    There was this woman standing.

205 *iyave son bwaa anima*
    iyave   soñ   bwaa   anima
    there.was   3POSS.M.S   stik.M.INAN   that.INAN
    She had this stick of hers.

206 *aen pchi bwa aan noor kii-ayaaw*
    aeñ   pchi   bwaa   aañ   noor   kii-ayaa-w
    INDEF.M.S   little.M   stick.M.INAN   in   gold   PST-have.AI+O-IND.3S
    She had a little golden stick

207 *Ekwanahi enn faam aan mazhii*
    eekwa   en   faam   aañ   maazhii
    then   INDEF.F.S   woman.F.AN   in   magic
    She was a fairy

208 *sii mazhii ushihtaat awa la*
    sii   maazhii   oshihtaa-t   awa   la
    3POSS.PL   magic.INAN   make.AI+O-CNJ.3S   that.AN   DEF.F.S
    who performs magic.

209 *sit' enn bonn... enn bonn faam*
    sitet   en   bon   en   bon   faam
    it.was   INDEF.F.S   good   INDEF.F.S   good   woman.F.AN
    It was a good person, a good woman.

210 *Nawachiku la Sandrieuz sheek(ih)ikow*
    nawachiko   la   Sandrieuz   sheekih-iko-(t)
    to.some.extent   DEF.F.S   Sandrieuz   scare.TA-INV-CNJ.4>3
    To some extent Cinderella was scared by her.

211 *kushtam. Kikway uuma? Taanshi eekwa*
    kosht-am.   keekwee   oma   taanshi   eekwa
    to.be.afraid.TI-THE.TI   what   this.INAN   how   then
    She was afraid. "What is that? What is

212 *chi-ishipayiyaan? Taanshi eekwa chi-ishpayihk?*
    chi-ishipayi-yaan   taanshi   eekwa   chi-ishpayi-k
    CNJ-happen.AI-CNJ.1S   how   then   CNJ-happen.II-CNJ.0S
    going to happen to me now? What is going to happen?

213 *Ganipon ahpo eetikwee.*
    ni-ka-nipo-n   eetikwee
    1S-FUT-die.AI-IND.1S   apparently
    Maybe I am going to die.

214 *enn aanzh chi awa ee-peenaashit?"*
    en   aañzh   chiiñ   awa   ee-pee-naashi-t
    INDEF.F.S   angel.F.AN   Q   that.AN   CNJ-come-fetch.TA-CNJ.3>1
    Is she an angel who has come to get me?"

215 *Iteehtam eeniput. Maaka la*
    iteeiht-am-Ø   ee-nipo-t   maaka   la
    think.TI-THE.TI-IND.3S   CNJ-die.AI-CNJ.3S   but   DEF.F.S
    She thought she was going to die.

216 *faam awa itew: "Kaya sheekishi!*
    faam   awa   itee-w   kaaya   sheeki-sh-i
    woman.F.AN   that.AN   say.AI-IND.3S   IMP.NEG   fear-be.AI-IMP
    But this woman said: "Have no fear for me!

217 *Kaya kushta!" Aen-peewiichihitaan, itweew*
    kaaya   kosht-a   Ni-ka-pee-wiichih-it-aan   itwee-w
    IMP.NEG   afraid.TI-IMP   1-FUT-come-help.TA-DIR-CNJ.1>2   say.AI-3S
    Don't be afraid!" "I have come to help you," she said.

218 *La Sandrieuz wiya*
     la   Sandrieuz   wiiya
     DEF.F.S   Sandrieuz   her
     Cinderella,

219 *kihchiwiinaniyiw sa rob*
     kihchi-wiinan-iyi-w   sa   rob
     much-be.dirty.II-OBV.S-IND.O   3POSS.F.S   dress.F.INAN
     her dress was all dirty

220 *ayish ee-atushkee-t*
     ayish   ee-atoshkee-t
     because   CNJ-work.AI-CNJ.3S
     because she worked so hard.

221 *wiinaniyiw sa rob*
     wiinan-iyi-w   sa   rob
     be.dirty.II-OBV.S-IND.O   3POSS.F.S   dress.F.INAN
     Her clothes had become dirty.

222 *Tut dishirii, la rob anima*
     tut   dishirii   la   rob   anima
     all   apart   DEF.F.S   dress.F.INAN   that.INAN
     All torn apart, that's how her clothes were.

223 *lii vyeu suyii kiikishkam*
     lii   vyeu   suyii   kii-kishk-am
     ART.PL   old   shoe.INAN   PST.put.on.TI-THE.TI
     She was wearing old shoes.

224 *sii zhveu noochikowitew*
     sii   zhveu   noochiikoitew
     3POSS.PL   hair   everywhere.II-IND.O
     Her hair was all over the place.

225 *sii zhveu onhin ayishpayiniyiw*
     sii   zhveu   ooñhiñ   ash-payin-iyi-w
     3POSS.PL   hair   those.INAN   ?messed?-move.II-POSS.SBJ-IND.O
     Her hair was all messed up,

226 *ohpeeshtikwaneew ana la Sandrieuz*
     ohpw-ishtikwanee-w   ana   la   Sandrieuz
     up-head.AI-IND.3S   this.AN   DEF.F.S   Sandrieuz
     She has her head up in the air, Little Cinderella

227 *"Ah baen," itew,*
     ah   baeñ   itee-w
     INT   good   say.AI-IND.3S
     "Well", she said,

228 *"Kiishpin kinuuhtetuhtaan la daans -*
    kiishpin   ki-noohte-itohtaa-n   la   daañs
    if   2-wish-go.AI-IND.non3   DEF.F.S   dance.F.INAN
    ' "If you wish to go to the dance -'

229 *kimaaton eewiituhteeyin*
    ki-maato-n   ee-wii-itohtee-yen
    2-cry.AI-IND.non3   CNJ-INT-go.AI-CNJ.2S
    you are crying because you want to go to the

230 *la dans," itew, Ka-ituhtaan.*
    la   dans   itee-w   ka-itohtaa-n
    DEF.F.S   dance.F.INAN   say.AI-IND.3S   FUT-go.AI-IND.non3
    dance", she said, "then you will go.

231 *Kawiichiihitin." La Sandrieuz itweew:*
    ka-wiichih-iti-n   la   Sandrieuz   itwee-w
    FUT-help.TA-INV-IND.1>2   DEF.F.S   Sandrieuz   say.AI-IND.3
    I will help you." Cinderella said to her:

232 *"Maaka zha pat bitaen chi-ishinaakushiyaan", iteew*
    maaka   zha   pat   bitaeñ   chi-ish-inaakoshi-yaan   itee-w
    but   1S   NEG   cloth.M.INAN   CNJ-so-look.like.AI-CNJ.1S   say.AI-IND.3S
    "But I don't have clothes to make me look good," she said.

233 *"Zha pat zhvoo. Pa mwayaen nete kaa-ituhteeyaan",*
    zha   pat   zhvoo   pa   mwayaen   neete   kaa-itohtee-yaan
    1S   NEG   horses.AN   NEG   way   there   CNJ-go.AI-CNJ.1S
    "I have no horses. It is impossible for me to go there",

234 *itweew. "Awena kaa-itohtahit?*
    itwee-w   awena   kaa-itohtaa-h-it
    say.AI-IND.3S   who   CNJ-go.AI-CAUS.TA-CNJ.3>1
    she said. "who is going to take me there?"

235 *"Baen," itew: "Kamiyitin*
    baen   itee-w   ka-miyi-iti-n
    good   say.AI-IND.3S   FUT-give.TA-INV-IND.1>2
    "Well," she said to her: "I will give it to you.

236 *Kahkiyaw kaa-nihtaweehtaman*
    kahkiyaaw   kaa-nihtaw-eeyiht-aman   itwee-w
    everything   CNJ-able-do.by.thinking.TI-IND.2S   say.AI-IND.3S
    Everything that you need,

237 *kamiyitin," itwew.*
    ka-miy-iti-n   itwee-w
    FUT-give.TA-INV-IND.1>2   say.AI-IND.3S
    I will give you," she said.

238 *Enn shans taapweehtaweew*
 en shañs taapw-eeiht-aw-ee-w
 INDEF.F.S chance.F.INAN truth-do.by.thinking.TI-TA-DIR-IND.3>4
 A lucky thing that she believed her.

239 *Kiyaam taapweehtaweew*
 kiyaam taapw-eeiht-aw-ee-w
 so.it.be truth-do.by.thinking.TI-TA-TA.DIR-3>3'
 That is OK, she believed her.

240 *"gawiichihik", itwew*
 ni-ka-wiichih-ik itwee-w
 1-FUT-help.TA-IND.INV.3>1 say.AI-IND.3S
 "She will help me", she said

241 *"Kaskihtaa-chi gaawiichihik", itwew,*
 kaskaskihtaa-ch-ik ni-ka-wiichih-ik itwee-w,
 be.able.AI-CNJ.3-PL 1-FUT-help.TA-IND.INV.3>1 say.AI-IND.3S
 If she can, she will help me," she said.

242 *"Ana ga-taapweehtawaaw",*
 ana ni-ka-taapw-eeiht-aw-aa-w
 that.AN 1-FUT-truth-do.by.thinking.TI-TA-DIR-IND.1>3
 "I will believe her".

243 *iteehtam chi-ka-kiyaashkimikut*
 it-eeiht-am chi-ka-kiyaashkim-iko-t
 NULL-do.by.think.TI-THE.TI CNJ-FUT-lie.TA-INV-CNJ.4>3
 She thought she had been lying to her.

244 *taanshi ee-ohchi-payihk*
 taanishi chi-ishpayi-hk
 what CNJ-happen.II-CNJ.3S
 What is going to happen?

245 *taanishi chikakii-ushihaat awa lii zhvoo baendon*
 taanishi kaa-ishi-oshihaa-t awa lii zhvoo baendon
 what CNJ-so-make.AI+O-CNJ.3S this.AN ART.PL horse.AN or
 How could she make those horses,

246 *aen servan baendon enn kariol.*
 aeñ servaañ baeñdooñ en kariol
 INDEF.M.S servant.M.AN or DEF.F.S carriole.F.INAN
 or a servant or, or a carriole,

247 *baendon enn vwacheur? Taanishi*
 baeñdooñ en vwacheur taanishi
 or INDEF.F.S carriage.F.INAN how
 or a carriage? When can she make all that?"

248 *kaaishushihaat awa iteyihtam*
    kaa-ish-oshihaa-t awa it-eeiht-am
    CNJ-so-make.AI+O-CNJ.3S this.AN NULL-think.TI-THE.TI
    she thought.'

Excerpt 5

249 *Taapwee, avek soo bwaa anima, Tawayiwa!*
    taapwee avek soñ bwaa anima ataawaa-yi-wa
    in.truth with 3POSS.M.S stick.M.INAN that.INAN get.AI-OBV-IND.4S
    'Really, with her magic stick there it was!

250 *tahweew... eekoshi kaa-ishimiyohot*
    tahw-ee-w eekoshi kaa-ishi-miyoho-t
    point.to.TA-DIR-IND.3S>4 right.away CNJ-so-well.dressed-CNJ.3S
    She pointed at her. Right away she looked well!

251 *parey kom enn praenses ilave dii*
    paree kom en praeñses ilave dii
    similarly like INDEF.F.S princess.F.AN she.had INDEF.PL
    Just like a princess. She had

252 *bel rasaad pi dii pandaray pi enn*
    bel rasaad pii dii pandaray pii en
    beautiful.F beads.F and INDEF.PL earrings and INDEF.F.S
    beautiful beads and earrings and a

253 *bel kuronn kiiwaashishoow*
    bel kuron kishii-waashi-shoo-w
    beautiful.F crown.F.INAN intense-shine-AI.FIN-RFLX.AI-IND.3S
    beautiful crown. She was really glittering.

254 *la kuronn anima waashipayin*
    la kuronn anima waashi-payi-n
    DEF.F.S crown.F.INAN that.INAN light-move.INTR-IND.II.OS
    The crown was shining.

255 *lii boo suyii oohii*
    lii boo suyii ooñhiiñ
    ART.PL beautiful.M shoes.M.INAN these.INAN
    beautiful shoes

256 *kishkam. Aan vit mina*
    kishk-am-Ø aañ vit miina
    wear.TI-THE.TI-IND.3S in glass.F.INAN also
    she was wearing. Made of glass.

257 *lii boo suyii kishkam*
    lii boo suyii kishk-am-Ø
    ART.PL beautiful.M shoe.M.INAN wear.TI-THE.TI-IND.3S
    She was wearing beautiful shoes.

258 *iyave lii pchi pyii, awa la Sandrieuz*
iyave   lii   pchi   pyii   awa   la   Sandrieuz
there.was   ART.PL   small.M   feet.M.INAN   this.AN   DEF.F.S   Sandrieuz
She had small feet, Cinderella.

259 *Namo lii groo pyii kii-ayaaw*
namo   lii   groo   pyii
NEG   ART.PL   big.M   feet.M.INAN
She did not have big feet.

260 *lii pchi pyii kii-ayaaw ana.*
lii   pchi   pyii   kii-ayaa-w   ana
ART.PL   small.M   feet.M.INAN   PST-have.AI-IND.3S   that.AN
She had small feet.

261 *"Baen," itweew*
baeñ   itw-ee-w
well   say.AI-IND.3S
"Well," she said.

262 *"Kamiyitin miina enn vwacheur*
ka-miy-iti-n   miina   en   vwacheur
FUT-give.TA-INV.1>2   also   INDEF.F.S   car.F.INAN
"I will also give you a carriage,

263 *enn kariol eekwa kamiyitin*
en   kariol   eekwa   ka-miy-iti-n
INDEF.F.S   carriole.F.INAN   and   FUT-give.TA-INV-1>2
a carriole I will give you.

264 *iyave aen gros sitruj nda ashteew*
iyave   aeñ   gros   sitruj   anda   ashtee-w
there.was   INDEF.M.S   big.F   pumpkin.F.INAN   there   stand.II-IND.3S
There was a big pumpkin, it was right there

265 *enn pumpkin ekuta tawaham*
en   pumpkin   ekota   tawah-am-Ø
INDEF.F.S   pumpkin.F.INAN   there   point.TR-THE.TI-IND.3S
A pumpkin she pointed at

266 *eekwanima miina tawaham omishishi*
eekwanima   miina   tawah-am   omishish
that.INAN   also   point.TR-THE.TI   just.like.this
that as well. She pointed at it just like this

267 *kitahtawee aen bel vwacheur eekuta*
kiiitahtawee   aeñ   bel   vwacheur   eekota
suddenly.there.was   INDEF.M.S   beautiful.F   carriage.F.INAN   right.there
Suddenly there was a beautiful carriole.

268 *Aen kariol ita kaa-aashteek*
    aeñ   kariol   ita   kaa-aashtee-k
    INDEF.M.S   carriole.INAN   there   CNJ-stand.there.II-CNJ.3S
    A beautiful carriole was standing there.

269 *Baen, iyave pat zhvoo*
    baeñ   iyave   pat   zhvoo
    well   there.was   NEG   horses.AN
    Well, she did not have horses.

270 *Me iyave lii pchi frenn*
    me   iyave   dii   pchi   frend
    but   there.was   INDEF.PL   little.M   friend.M.AN
    But she had little friends.

271 *Awa la...la Sandrieuz iyave lii pchi zamii,*
    awa   la   Sandrieuz   iyave   lii   pchi   zamii
    this.AN   DEF.F.S   Sandrieuz   there.was   ART.PL   little.M   friend.M.AN
    Cinderella had small friends,

272 *lii pchi frenn.*
    lii   pchi   frenn
    ART.PL   little.M   friend.M.AN
    small buddies.

273 *Lii surii kii-ayaweew*
    lii   surii   kii-ayaaw-ee-w
    ART.PL   mice.M.AN   PST-have.TA-DIR-IND.3S>4
    She had mice.

274 *sis lii pchi surii kii-ayaweew.*
    sis   lii   pchi   surii   kii-ayaaw-ee-w
    six   ART.PL   little.M   mice.M.AN   PST-have.AI-IND.3S
    Six little mice, she had.

275 *"Ah baen," itweew*
    ah   baeñ   itwee-w
    ah   well   say.AI-IND.3S
    "Well," she (the fairy) said

276 *Akwanikik savayet tii zhvoo", itweew*
    akwanikik   savayet   tii   zhvoo   itwee-w
    those.AN   it.will.be   2POSS.PL   horses.AN   say.AI.IND.3S
    "Those ones will be your horses," she said

277 *Akwanikik savayet tii zhvoo.*
    akwanikik   savayet   tii   zhvoo
    those.AN   it.will.be   2POSS.PL   horses.AN
    "Those ones will be your horses

278 *Blaañ lii zhvoo ka-ayaawaawak, itweew,*
   blaañ   lii   zhvoo   ka-ayaaw-aa-w-ak   itwee-w
   white   ART.PL   horse.AN   FUT-have.TA-DIR-IND.SAP>3   say.AI-IND.3S
   White horses you will have", she said

279 *avek lii boo harnwe miina*
   avek   lii   boo   harnwe   miina
   with   ART.PL   beautiful.M   harness.M   as.well.as
   "with good harnesses as well as

280 *lii boo zartelaazh, itweew*
   lii   boo   zartelaazh   itwee-w
   ART.PL   beautiful.M   bridles.M.INAN   say.AI-IND.3S
   good bridles", she said.

281 *"Kamiyitin kahkiyaw miina", tahweew..*
   ka-miy-iti-n   kahkiyaaw   miina   tahw-ee-w
   FUT.give.TA-DIR-IND.1>2   all   as.well   point.TA-DIR.3>4
   "I will give you all that as well", and she pointed.

282 *Kitahtawee mænskuchipayiwak okik aan zhvoo*
   Kitahtawee   maenskuchi-payi-w-ak   ookik   aañ   zhvoo
   suddenly   change-move.INTR-IND.AI.3-PL   those.AN   in   horses.AN
   Suddenly they turned into horses

283 *lii boo zhvoo*
   lii   boo   zhvoo
   ART.PL   beautiful.M   horses.M.AN
   beautiful horses

284 *sis lii boo zhvoo otaapaheew*
   sis   lii   boo   zhvoo   otaapah-ee-w
   six   ART.PL   beautiful.M   horses.M.AN   drag.TA-DIR-IND.3>4
   six good horses They were hitched to

285 *uta dan la kariol, dan la vwacheur.*
   ota   dañ   la   kariol   dañ   la   vwacheur
   here   in   DEF.F.INAN   carriole.F.INAN in   DEF.F   car.F.INAN
   the carriage, the carriole.

286 *Taapwee awena chi-pamihaat eekwa*
   taapwee   awena   chi-pamihaa-t   eekwa
   really   who   CNJ-drive.AI-CNJ.3S   now
   Really, who was now going to drive

287 *ohi la kariol pi lii zhvoo?*
   oohiñ   la   kariol   pii   lii   zhvoo
   these.AN.OBV   DEF.F.S   carriole.F.INAN   and   ART.PL   horses.AN
   this carriage and the horses?

288 *Sapran awiyak chi-pamihaat.*
   sapraañ   awiyak   chi-pamihaa-t
   its.necessary   someone   CNJ-drive.AI-CNJ.3S
   She needed someone to drive.

289 *Iyave aen shyaen aen boo shyaen*
   iyave   aeñ   shyañ   aeñ   boo   shyañ
   there.was   INDEF.M.S   dog.M.AN   INDEF.M.S   good.M   dog.M.AN
   There was a dog, a good dog,

290 *kii-ayaweew aen vyeu shyaen*
   kii-ayaw-ee-w   aeñ   vyeu   shyañ
   PST-have.TA-DIR-IND.3>4   INDEF.M.S   old   dog.M.AN
   she had an old dog

291 *ana la Sandrieuz son shyaen*
   ana   la   Sandrieuz   soñ   shyañ
   that.AN   DEF.F.S   Sandrieuz.   3POSS.M.S   dog.M.AN
   it was Cinderella's dog.

292 *eekwa miina la faam twahikeew ite ekwani*
   eekwa   miina   la   faam   twah-ikee-w
   now   again   DEF.F.S   woman.AN.F   point.TR-GEN.AI-IND.3S
   Now again this woman pointed at things.

293 *site ekwani chi-paminaat*
   site   ekwani   chi-paminaa-t
   that.was   that   CNJ-drive.AI-CNJ.3S
   That was the one to drive

294 *lii zhvoo li draiv, ekwana lom*
   lii   zhvoo   li   draiv   ekwana   lom
   ART.PL   horses.AN   DEF.M.S   driver.INAN   this   man.AN
   the horses, the driver, this man

295 *ekwana servan kii-miyohoow*
   ekwana   servaañ   kii-miyoho-w
   this   servant.AN   PST-good.dress.AI-IND.3S
   this servant was well dressed

296 *miina lii boo bitaen kiikishkam*
   miina   lii   boo   bitañ   kii-kishk-am
   and.also   ART.PL   beautiful.M   clothes.M.INAN   PST.wear.TI-THE.TI
   He also had beautiful clothes

297 *aen boo shapoo ana li ga, hee*
   aeñ   boo   shapoo   ana   li   ga   hee
   INDEF.M.S   beautiful.M   hat.M.INAN   that.AN   DEF.M.S   guy.M.AN   INT
   A nice hat this guy had on.

298 *lii boo gaan kahkiyaw.*
    lii   boo   gaañ   kahkiyaaw
    ART.PL beautiful.M glove.M.INAN all
    He was wearing beautiful mittens and all.

299 *Ekuta pooshapiw dan li gran shiiz*
    ekota   poosh-api-w   dañ   li   graañ   shiiz
    there   get.aboard-sit-IND.3S in   DEF.M.S big.M   chair.M.INAN
    There he is sitting in the big seat

300 *aan laer nete "Haw," itweew*
    aañ   laer   neete   haw   itwee-w
    in   air   there   INT   say.AI-IND.3S
    up there. "Haw!", she said

301 *"Pooshi kishta," iteew "Pooshi*
    poosh-i   kiishta   it-ee-w   poosh-i
    get.aboard.AI-IMP you.too   say-DIR-IND-IND.3>4 get.aboard.AI-IMP
    "Embark, you too," she said to her. Get in here.

302 *nda. Ta tii zhvoo, ta too servan.*
    anda   ta   tii   zhvoo   ta   tii   servaañ
    there   you.have 2POSS.PL horses.AN you.have 2POSS.PL servant.AN
    "You have your horses, you have your servant

303 *Ta ta vwacheur," iteew*
    ta   ta   vwocheur   itee-w
    you.have 2POSS.F.S car.F.INAN say.AI-IND.3S
    You have your carriage," she said.

304 *"Ta pooshi eekwa, pooshapi," itweew*
    ta   poosh-i   eekwa   poosh-api   itw-ee-w
    you.have embark-IMP and.then get.aboard-sit-IMP say.TA-DIR-IND.3>4
    Get in now, sit down inside," she said.

305 *"Yaenk enn shooz kawiihtamaatin,"*
    yaeñk   en   shooz   ka-wiihtam-aa-ti-n
    only   INDEF.F.S thing.F.INAN FUT-tell.about.TI-TA-INV-IND.SAP>3
    "There is only one thing I have to tell you,"

306 *itweew*
    itw-ee-w
    say.TA-DIR-3>4
    she said.

307 *"Aashey sitaar oma la," itweew.*
    aashey   si   taar   oma   la   itw-ee-w
    already it.is   late   this.INAN ?   say.TA-DIR-IND.3>4
    "It is already late now," she said

308 *Kayaash kamaachipayik*
    kayaash   ka-maachi-payi-k
    long.ago   CNJ-start-move.INTR-CNJ.II.O
    A long time ago, it started

309 *anima li bal," iteew*
    anima   li   bal   itee-w
    that.INAN   DEF.M.S   ball.M.INAN   say.AI-IND.3S
    the Ball" she said to her

310 *"Niimiwak uma ashey," itweew.*
    niimi-w-ak   oma   ashey   itw-ee-w
    dance.AI-IND.3-PL   this.INAN   already   say.TA-DIR-IND.3>4
    "They are already dancing now," she said.

311 *"Maenwi kasheeweew ana la larloozh,"*
    maenwi   ka-sheewee-w   ana   la   larloozh
    midnight   FUT-ring.II-IND.O   that.AN   DEF.F.S   clock.F.INAN
    "At midnight that clock will ring",

312 *itweew,*
    itw-ee-w
    say.TA-DIR-IND.3>4
    she said.

313 *"duz fwe sapran kaasheeweet ana la lozh,"*
    duz   fwe   sapraañ   kaa-sheewee-t   ana   la   loozh
    twelve   times   it.takes   CNJ-ring.II-CNJ.3S   that.AN   DEF.F.S   clock.F.INAN
    "Twelve times it has to ring, this clock",

314 *itweew.*
    itw-ee-w
    say.TA-DIR-IND.3>4
    she said.

315 *"Sapran chi-peekiiweeyen*
    sapraañ   chi-pee-kiiwee-yen
    it.takes   CNJ-come-be.home.AI-CNJ.2S
    "Then you will have to come home.

316 *Sheemaak peekiiwee," iteew*
    sheemaak   pee-kiiwee   itee-w
    immediately   come-be.home.AI.IMP   say.AI-IND.3S
    Go home immediately," she said to her.

317 *maka noo wiiwiihtamaweew*
    maka   noo   wii-wiiht-amaw-ee-w
    but   NEG   VOL-tell.about.it-APP.TA-DIR-IND.3>4
    But she did not tell her

318 *taanishi chi-ishi-payihk kaya peekiiweechi.*
    taanishi   chi-ishpayi-hk   kaaya   pee-kiiwee-t-i
    in.what.way   CNJ-happen.II-CNJ.O   do.not   come-be.home.AI-CNJ.3S-SJ
    what would happen if she did not come home.'

Excerpt 6

319 *safek taapwee*
    safek   taapwee
    so   really
    'So really

320 *nda dan la dans, dan la bal nda*
    nda   dañ   la   dans   dañ   la   bal
    there   in   DEF.F.S   dance.F.INAN   in   DEF.F.S   ball.F.INAN
    there at the dance, at the ball,

321 *li praens awa kahkiyaw anihi*
    li   praens   awa   kahkiyaaw   anihi
    DEF.M.S   prince.M.AN   that.AN   all   those.OBV
    the prince was dancing with all of them,

322 *wichimushtaweew. Niimiw avek*
    wichi-moshtawee-w   niimi-w   avek
    together.with-dance.AI-IND.3S   dance.AI-IND.3S   with
    he dances with them. He dances with

323 *anihi lii fiy anihi.*
    anihi   lii   fiiy   anihi.
    those.AN.OBV   ART.PL   girl.F.AN   those.AN.OBV
    these girls.

324 *kaakweemishkawaat*
    (kaa-)kakwee-mishk-aw-aa-t
    (CNJ-)try-find.TI-TA-CNJ.3S
    He was going to try and find

325 *Enn faam chi-wiikimaat*
    en   faam   chi-wiikim-aa-t
    INDEF.F.S   woman.F.AN   CNJ-marry.TA-DIR-CNJ.3S
    a woman to marry with.

326 *me lii faam anihi*
    me   lii   faam   anihi
    but   ART.PL   woman.F.AN   those.AN.OBV
    But these women,

327 *lii fiy anihi kaa-mayaatishichik*
    lii   fiiy   anihi   kaa-mayaatishi-ch-ik
    ART.PL   girl.F.AN   those.AN.OBV   CNJ-be.ugly.AI-CNJ.3-PL
    these girls were all looking bad.

328 *lii fiy led aniki ekuta ayaawaawak*
    lii   fiiy   led   anikik   ekota   ayaa-w-ak
    ART.PL   girl.F   ugly   those.AN   there   be.there.AI-IND.3-PL
    Those ugly girls were there.

329 *shemaak wii kaakweemushtaweewak chikakweeniimit*
    shemaak   wii-kakwee-moshtaw-ee-w-ak   chi-kakwee-niimi-t
    right.away   VOL-try-dance-AI-IND.3-PL   CNJ-try-dance.AI-CNJ.3S
    Immediately they were trying to dance

330 *avek ana li praens tutdaenku*
    avek   ana   li   praens   tudaenku
    with   that.AN   DEF.M.S   prince.M.AN   suddenly
    She tried to dance with the prince. Suddenly,

331 *meekwach li praens awa aen-niimit*
    meekwach   li   praens   awa   ee-niimi-t
    while   DEF.M.S   prince.M.AN   this.AN   one-dance.AI-CNJ.3S
    while the Prince was dancing,

332 *keekway peehtam*
    keekway   peeht-am
    what   hear-THE-TI
    he heard something

333 *teepweew ana li gaa dan la port*
    teepwee-w   ana   li gaa   dan   la   port
    call.AI-IND.3S   that.INDEF.M.S   man.M.AN   in   DEF.F.S   door.F.INAN
    The man at the door was calling.

334 *iyave lii zom eekwa*
    iyave   lii   zom   eekwa
    there.were   ART.PL   man.M.AN   also
    There were men

335 *kanaweehtahkik la port*
    kanaw-ee(yi)ht-ahk-ik   la   port
    look.after-do.by.mind.TI-CNJ.3-PL   DEF.F.S   door.F.INAN
    who guarded the door

336 *nda niipawiwak oki lii solda*
    nda   niipawi-w-ak   ookik   lii   solda
    there   stand.AI-IND.3-PL   these.AN   ART.PL   soldier.M
    They were standing there, these soldiers

337 *Iteew li rwe, iteew*
    it-ee-w   li   rwe   it-ee-w
    say.TA-DIR-IND.3S>4   DEF.M.S   king.M.AN   say.TA-DIR-IND.3S>4
    The King, he said to him.

338 "*Peeyak miina ota takopayiw enn fiy*"
    peeyak   miina   oota   tako-payi-w   en   fiiy
    one.more   also   here   arrive-move.AI-IND.3S   INDEF.F.S   girl.F.AN
    "One more girl has arrived here",

339 *itweew, "aen-pee-niimit," itweew.*
    itw-ee-w   aen-pee-niimi-t   itwee-w
    say.AI-THE.AI-IND.3S CNJ-come-dance.AI-CNJ.3S   say.AI-IND.3S
    he said, "who comes for the dance," he said.

340 *Waapameew awa ee-teepweeyit*
    waapam-ee-w   awa   ee-teepwee-yi-t
    see.TA-DIR-IND.3S>4   this.AN   CNJ-call.AI-OBV-CNJ.3S
    He saw the one who had been calling.

341 *peehtaaweew li praens aapaanaapiw*
    peeht-aw-ee-w   li   praens   aapam-api-w
    hear.TI-TA-DIR-IND.3>4 DEF.M.S   prince.M.AN   see.TA-sit.AI-IND.3S
    The Prince heard him. He was observing her.

342 *waapameew. Boy, katawaashishishiw awa*
    waapam-ee-w   boy   katawaashishi-w   awa
    see.TA-DIR-IND.3>4   boy   was.beautiful.AI-IND.3S   this.AN
    He saw her. Boy, she was good-looking.

343 *enn bel fiy, iyave lii boo*
    en   bel   fiiy   iyave   lii   boo
    INDEF.F.S   beautiful.F   girl.F.AN   she.had   ART.PL   beautiful.M
    A pretty girl, she had beautiful

344 *bitaen kiishkam aen-miyohoot*
    bitañ   kiishk-am   ee-miyohoo-t
    clothes.M.INAN   wear.TI-THE.TI-IND.3S   CNJ-dress.well.AI-CNJ.3S
    clothes, she was wearing them, looking well-dressed.

345 *Lii rasaad kahkiyaw sa kuronn ayaaw,*
    lii   rasaad   kahkiyaw   sa   kuronnayaa-w
    ART.PL   bead.F   all   3POSS.F.S   crown.F have.AI+O-IND.3S
    All beads, she had her crown,

346 *sheemaak akaawaateew akaawaateew*
    sheemaak   akaawaa-t-ee-w   akaawaat-ee-w
    right.away   wish.AI-TR-DIR-IND.3>4   wish.AI-TR-DIR-IND.3>4
    right away he desired her. He desired her.

347 *kawaapishin nda, kaawaapamaat*
    aka(a)w-aapishi-n   nda   kaa-waapam-aa-t
    wish-be.by.sight.AI-IND.3S there   CNJ-see.TA-DIR-CNJ.3S
    He liked the way she looked right there, when he saw

348 *awa la bel fiy anihi*
    awa   la   bel   fiiy   anihi
    this.AN   DEF.F.S   beautiful.F   girl.F.AN   that.AN.OBV
    this beautiful girl.'

Excerpt 7

349 *Sheemaak anihi la faam pooni-niimiw*
    sheemaak   anihi   la   faam   pooni-niimi-w
    now   that.AN.OBV DEF.F.S   woman.F.AN quit-dance.AI-IND.3S
    'Right away he quit dancing with the woman

350 *Dan li boor ashiweepineew*
    dañ   li   bor   shiweepin-ee-w
    in   DEF.M.S   side.M.INAN   throw.TA-DIR-IND.3>4
    He threw her aside,

351 *oonhin kaaniimiyit avek*
    oonhiñ   kaa-niim-iyi-t   avek
    these.AN.OBV   CNJ-dance.TA-OBV.S-CNJ-3>4 with
    the one he was dancing with,

352 *Ana la fiy ana*
    ana   la   fiiy   ana
    that.AN   DEF.F.S   girl.F.AN   that.AN
    That girl

353 *La fiy ana kaamayaatishit ana.*
    la   fiiy   ana   kaa-mayaatishi-t   ana
    DEF.F.S   girl.F.AN   that.AN   CNJ-ugly.be.AI-3S.F.S   that.AN
    That girl was ugly.

354 *Naateew anihi la fiy*
    naat-ee-w   anihi   la   fiiy
    go.get-TA-IND.3>4   that.AN.OBV DEF.F.S   girl.F.AN
    He went for the other girl

355 *Sheemaak kaawaapashin*
    sheemaak   kaawaapishin-Ø
    immediately   CNJ-attracted.by.sight.AI-IND.3S
    immediately he found something beautiful in her.

356 *Ila tombe aan namur*
    ila   tombe   aañ   namur
    he.has   fallen   in   love.F.INAN
    He had fallen in love.

357 *shakiheew onhi sheemak niimiwak*
    shakih-ee-w   oonhiñ   sheemak   niimi-w-ak
    love.TA-DIR-IND.3>4   that.AN.OBV   right.away   dance.AI-IND.3-PL
    He was in love with that one, right away, they were dancing

358 *Tweehoniimiwak wiikaakweekitoteew*
     tweehoo-niimi-w-ak   wii-kakwee-kitoo-t-ee-w
     bird(landing)-dance.AI-IND-3S.PL   VOL-try-talk.AI-TR-DIR-3>4
     They were dancing like birds. He wanted to try and talk to her.

359 *maaka namo sheemaak kitoteew chi-kaakweechimaat*
     maaka   namo   sheemak   kitoo-t-ee-w   chi-kaakwee-chim-aa-t
     but   NEG   right.away   talk.AI-TR-DIR-3>4   CNJ-ask.TA-DIR-CNJ.3>4
     But he does not speak right away to ask her

360 *"Taanishi ishinihkaashoyen? Taande ohchichiyen?"*
     taanishi   ishin-ikaashoo-yen   taande   ohchii-yen
     what   call.TR-MED.AI-CNJ.2S   where   be.from.AI-CNJ.2S.S
     What is your name? Where do you come from?

361 *Namoya kakweechimeew*
     namoya   kakwee-chim-ee-w
     NEG   try-ask.TA-DIR-IND.3>4
     He does not ask her

362 *taapwee chiihkeehtamwak chiihki-niimiwak*
     taapwee   chiihk-ee(yi)ht-am-w-ak   chiihki-niimi-w-ak
     really   enjoy-do.by.think.TI-THE.TI-IND.3-PL   enjoy-dance.AI-IND.3-PL
     really, they were happy, they were dancing happily

363 *Miyeuhtamwak.*
     miyeuht-am-w-ak
     like.TI-THE.TI-IND.3-PL
     they liked it

364 *Chiihkeehtamwak la meuzeuk*
     chiihk-ee(yi)ht-am-w-ak   la   meuzik
     enjoy-do.by.think-TH.TI-IND.3-PL   DEF.F.S   music.F.INAN
     they enjoyed the music

365 *miyeuhtamwak ana kaa-nakishkaatochik*
     miyeuht-am-w-ak   ana   kaa-nakishk-aa-to-ch-ik
     like.TI-THE.TI-IND.3-PL   that.AN   CNJ-meet-TA-REC-CNJ.3-PL
     they were happy to meet each other

366 *wiishta Cinderella la Sandrieuz anihimiyaapishin,*
     wiishta   Cinderella   la   Sandrieuz   anihi   miy-aapishin-Ø
     her.too   Cinderella   DEF.F.S   Sandrieuz   that.AN.OBV   like.by.sight.AI-IND.3S
     Cinderella too she liked the way he looked

367 *shakiheew ohi la praens-a wishta*
     shakih-ee-w   oohiñ   li   praens-a   wishta
     love.TA-DIR-IN3>4   that.AN.OBV   DEF.F.M   prince.M.AN-OBV   him.too
     she loved the prince too

368 *nama naandaw maaka wii-itweew*
    ma   naanda-w   maaka   wii-itwee-w
    NEG   happen.II-IND.OS   but   VOL-say.AI-IND.3S
    but she was not going to say that

369 *tutdaenku la klosh ana,*
    tudaeñku   la   klosh   ana
    suddenly   DEF.F.S   bell.F.AN   that.AN
    suddently that clock,

370 *larlozh ana kaashiweet*
    larlozj   ana   kaa-sheewee-t
    clock.F.AN that.AN   CNJ-ring.AI-CNJ.3S
    that clock was ringing

371 *si kom en gros klosh anima ee-shiweet*
    si   kom   en   gros   klosh   anima   ee(ñ)-sheewee-t
    it.is   as   INDEF.F.S   big.F   bell.F.AN   that.INAN   CNJ-ring.AI-CNJ.3S
    it was, like, a big bell that sounded

372 *ana la relozh: klong, klong! Tudaenku wah*
    ana   la   rlozh   klong   klong   tudaeñku   wah
    that.AN   DEF.F.S   clock.F.AN   klong   klong   suddenly   wah
    The clock did: klong, klong! Suddenly: wah

373 *Sapran chi-kiiweeyaamooyaan chi-kiiweeyaan*
    sapraañ   chi-kiiwee-yaamoo-yaan   chi-kiiwee-yaan
    necessary   CNJ-home-flee.AI-CNJ.1S   CNJ-go.home.AI-CNJ.1S
    I have to run home to go home

374 *Gii-ishi-wihtamaak*
    ni-kii-ishi-wiihtam-aa-ik
    1-PST-so-tell.TI-TA-IND.INV.3S>1
    that was told to me

375 *ana la bon faam ana itwew*
    ana   la   bon   faam   ana   itw-ee-w
    that.AN   DEF.F.S   good.F   woman.F.AN   that.AN   say.TA-DIR-IND.3>4
    by the fairy, she had said that to her

376 *taapwee, tapashiiw*
    taapwee   tapashii-w
    really   flee.AI-IND.3S
    really, she fled

377 *Wayawiiyaamow nda dan la palae ohchi*
    wayawii-yaamoo-w   anda   dañ   la   palee   ohchi
    go.out-flee.AI-IND.3S   there   in   DEF.F.S   palace.F.INAN   from
    she ran out of the palace

378 *li praens awa teepweew, teepwaatikow*
    li   praens   awa   teepwee-w   teepwaa-t-ikoo
    DEF.M.S   prince.M.AN   this.AN   yell.AI-IND.3S   yell.AI-TR-IND.INV.4>3
    the prince was shouting, calling to her

379 *"Pee-asheekiiwee! Pee-asheekiiwee", iteew*
    pee-ashee-kiiwee   pee-ashee-kiiwee   itee-w
    come-back-return.AI   come-back-return.AI   say.AI-IND.3S
    come back here! come back here!, he said

380 *"Kaashichipiteek!" iteew sii solda.*
    kaashchi-pit-ihk   it-ee-w   sii   soldaa
    grab.pull.TR-IMP.2PL>3S say.TA-DIR-IND.3S>4   3POSS.PL   soldier.M.AN
    Grab her!", he said to his soldiers

381 *pamwayaen.*
    pamwayaen.
    no.way
    it is impossible

382 *Eekwa piistikwashkwahteew dan so kariol nda*
    eekwa   piihti-kwashkwahti-w   dañ   soñ   kariol   anda
    then   enter-jump.AI-IND.3S   into   3POSS.M.S   carriage.F.AN there
    She jumped into her carriage there

383 *li draiver awa, li servan*
    li   draiver   awa   li   servaañ
    DEF.M.S   driver.M.AN   this.AN   DEF.M.S   servant.M.AN
    the driver, the servant

384 *pashiteehweew lii zhvoo*
    pashiteehw-ee-w   lii   zhvoo
    whip.TA-DIR-IND.3S>4   ART.PL   horses.AN
    He whipped the horses

385 *pashiteehweew kut fwet tapashiiwak*
    pashiteehw-ee-w   kud   fwet   tapashii-w-ak
    hit.TA-DIR-IND.3S   shot.of   whip.INAN   flee.AI-IND.3S-PL
    He hit them with the whip, they fled

386 *shuuhkeeyaamowak sako shuuhkeepayiwak*
    shoohki-yaamo-w-ak   sako   shoohki-payi-w-ak
    strong-flee.AI-IND.3S-PL   really   strong-move.AI-IND.3S-PL
    they ran fast, really they moved quickly

387 *avan chitakoshihk wiikiwahk*
    avañ   chi-takoshi-hk   wiiki-w-ak
    before   CNJ-arrive.AI-CNJ.3   be.home.AI-IND.INDEF.AC
    before they arrived at the house

388 kahkiyaw ana mishchikopayiw ana miina
    kaahkiyaw   ana   meeshkochi-payi-w   ana   miina
    all   that.AN   change-move.AI-IND.3S   that.AN   again
    all of her had turned back to normal again

389 la sitruy ekuta kaapahkishihk
    la   sitruy   ekota   kaa-pahkishi-hk
    DEF.F.S   pumpkin.F.AN   there   CNJ-fall.AI-CNJ.3S
    The pumpkin fell there

390 lii surii ekuta kaapahkishikihkik
    lii   surii   ekota   kaa-pahkishi-hk-ik
    ART.PL   mice.AN   there   CNJ-fall.AI-CNJ.3-PL
    The mice fell there.

391 lom awa, kaakiilomiwit
    lom   awa   kaa-kii-lom-iwi-t
    man.AN   this.AN   CNJ-PST-man.AN-become.AI-CNJ.3S
    The man, who had turned into a man

392 li shyaen wishta kiihtwam
    li   shyaeñ   wiishta   kiihtwam
    DEF.M.S   dog.M.AN   him.too   again
    he was a dog again.

393 mishchikopayiw aan shyaen.
    meeshkochi-payi-w   aeñ   shyeñ
    change-move.AI-IND.3S   INDEF.M.S   dog.M.AN
    The dog too had turned into a dog.

394 Aah, la poovr Cinderella.
    ah   la   poovr   Cinderella
    INT   DEF.F.S   poor   Cinderella
    Oh, poor Cinderella.'

Excerpt 8

395 ekwanima piko kaa-kanaweehihtahk site
    ekwanima   piko   kaa-kanaweeiht-ahk   site
    and.that   only   CNJ-look.after.TI-CNJ.3S   it.was
    'The only thing that she had kept was

396 soo suyii, aan vit.
    soñ   suyii   aañ   vit
    3POSS.M.S   shoe.M   of   glass.F
    her shoe, made of glass.

397 Maaka henn kiiwanihtaaw
    maaka   hen   kii-wanihtaa-w
    but   one   PST-lose.AI(t)-IND.3S
    She had lost one

398 *kaa-tapashiit kiiwanihtaw*
kaa-tapashii-t   kii-wanihtaa-w
CNJ-flee.AI-CNJ.3S   PST-lose.AI(t)-IND.3S
She had lost one when she was hurrying away. She had lost it

399 *dret da la palae nda dan lii zeskalyii*
dret	dañ	la	palee	anda	dañ	lii	zeskalyii
right	in	DEF.F.S	palace.F.INAN	there	on	ART.PL	stairs

right in the palace on the stairs.

400 *ekuta kii-wanihtaaw*
ekota   kii-wanihtaa-w
so.there   PST-lose.AI(t)-IND.3S
It was there she had lost it.

401 *muushahkinam ekwanima li præns*
mooshahkin-am   ekwanima   li   praens
pick.up.TI-IND.3S   right.that.INAN   DEF.M.S   prince.M.AN
He picked it up, the Prince.

402 *eekwanima kii-waapahtam li suyii eetikwee*
eekwanima	kii-waapaht-am	li	suyii	eetikwe
right.that.INAN	PST-see.TI-IND.3S	DEF.M.S	shoe.M.INAN	apparently

He apparently saw the shoe.

403 *"A baen la, taanishi kaa-tootamaahk?"*
ah   baeñ   la   taanishi   kaa-toot-am-aahk
INT   well   there   what   CNJ-do.TI-THE.TI-CNJ.1PL
"Well, now, what do we do?"

404 *Itweew awa li praens.*
itwee-w   awa   li   praeñs
say.AI-IND.3S   this.AN   DEF.M.S   prince.M.AN
Said the Prince.

405 *"hen aen suyii dayaan, maaka"*
hen   aeñ   suyii   d-ayaa-n   maaka
one   INDEF.M.S   shoe   1-have.AI(t)-IND.non3   but
"I have one shoe, however."

406 *opaapa-wa itweew*
o-paapa-wa   itw-ee-w
3-father-POSS   say.TA-DIR-IND.3>4
He said to his father,

407 *li rwe: "Aa, mahpo gikisheewimaw*
li   rwe   Aa   mahpo   gii-kisheeyim-aa-w
DEF.M.S   king   INT   even   1PST-know.TA-DIR-IND.SAP>3
the King: "I don't even know her.

408 *namoya giikakweechimaaw son non,*
    namo   gii-kakwee-chim-aa-w   soñ   noñ
    NEG   1PST-manage-ask.TA-DIR-IND.SAP>3   3POSS.M.S   name.M.AN
    I did not ask her name,

409 *taandee ee-wiikit, taanishi ee-ishinihkaashut*
    taandee   ee-wiiki-t   taanishi   ee-ishin-ikaashoo-t
    where   CNJ-live.AI-CNJ.3S   how   CNJ-see.TI-MED.AI-CNJ.3S
    where she lives, how she is called."

410 *Nakataweehtamwak eekwa. Kiyaam....*
    naakataweeiht-am-w-ak   eekwa   kiyaam
    ponder.TI-THE.TI-IND.3-PL   now   let.it.be
    They were trying to figure it out. What can you do?

411 *"Omishi ka-tahkamikishonaan", iteew,*
    oma   ishi-ka-tahkamikishi-naan   itee-w,
    this.INAN   thus-FUT-behave.AI-IND.1PL.INCL   say.AI-IND.3S
    "This is what we will do," he said to him.

412 *"li suyii uma kaa-kanaweehtaman*
    li   suyii   oma   kaa-kanaweeiht-aman
    DEF.M.S   shoe.M.INAN   this.INAN   CNJ-look.after.TI-CNJ.2S
    "This shoe that you kept,

413 *kapapaawiicheewaawak*
    (ki-)ka-papaa-wiicheew-aa-w-ak
    (2-)FUT-wandering.around-go.with.TA-DIR-IND.2>3-PL
    You will go around with

414 *ookik tii servan*
    ookik   tii   servaañ
    these.AN   2POSS.PL   servant.AN
    your servants.

415 *dan lii palae oonhin papaakiyokaan,*
    dañ   lii   palee   oonhiñ   (ki-)ka-papaa-kiyokaa-n
    in   ART.PL   palace.F.INAN   these.INAN   (2-)FUT-around-visit.AI-IND.non3
    Visit the people in the palaces,"

416 *itweew*
    itw-ee-w
    say.TA-DIR-IND.3>4
    he said.

417 *"Kapapaadawahchikaan, itew kaakishkeehtaman*
    (ki-)ka-paa-ndawahchikaa-n   itee-w   kaa-kishkeeiht-aman
    (ki-)FUT-around-scout.AI-IND.non3   say.AI-IND.3S   CNJ-know.TI-CNJ.2S
    "You will scout around. So that you will know it.

418 *mishkawachi ana la fiy chiteepishaahk*
mishk-aw-a-ch-i ana la fiiy chi-teepishk-ahk
find.TI-TA-DIR-CNJ.2>3-SJ that.AN DEF.F.S girl.F.AN CNJ-fit.TI-CNJ.3S
If you find the girl whom fits

419 *uma li suyii ka-wiikimaaw",*
oma li suyii ka-wiikim-aa-w
this.INAN DEF.M.S shoe.M.INAN FUT-marry.TA-DIR-IND.3>4
this shoe. You will marry her",

420 *itweew,*
itw-ee-w
say.TA-DIR-IND.3>4
he said,

421 *"Savayet ana la fiy".*
savayet ana la fiiy
will.be that.AN DEF.F.S girl.F.AN
"That will be the girl."

422 *Safek taapwee kiiweew awa la faam*
safek taapwee kiiwee-w awa la faam
so really go.home.AI-IND.3S this.AN DEF.F.S woman.F.AN
So really the woman had gone home,

423 *La mazhisyenn ana la vyey,*
la mazhisyenn ana la vyey
DEF.F.S witch.F.AN that.AN DEF.F.S old.F.AN
The old lady was a witch,

424 *la faam ana,*
la faam ana
DEF.F.S woman.F.AN that.AN
this woman.

425 *kaa-machimanitu-iwit avek sii fiy,*
kaa-machi-manito-iwi-t avek sii fiiy
CNJ-evil-spirit-be.AI-CNJ.3S with 3POSS.PL daughter.F.AN
that devilish woman with her daughters,

426 *kiiweew avek sii trwa fiy.*
kiiwee-w avek sii trwa fiiy
go.home.AI-IND.3S with 3POSS.PL three daughter.F.AN
She had gone home with her three daughters.

427 *Ekota ee-takushihkik*
ekota ee-takoshi-hk-ik
there CNJ-arrive.AI-CNJ.3-PL
When they had arrived there,

428 *namoya kii-kishkeehtamwak*
   namoya   kii-kishkeeiht-am-w-ak
   NEG   PST-know.TI-THE.TI-IND.3-PL
   they did not know

429 *eekwa taanshi kaa-kii-tahkamihkak*
   eekwa   taanshi   kaa-kii-tahkami-hk
   and   what   CNJ-PST-behave.AI-CNJ.INDEF.AC
   what had happened to her

430 *eewako la dans,*
   awa   la   dans
   this.AN   DEF.F.S   dance.F.AN,
   at the dance.

431 *la bal eekii-itohteet,*
   la   bal   ee-kii-itohtee-t
   DEF.F.S   ball.F.AN   CNJ-PST-go.AI-CNJ.3S
   That she had been to the ball,

432 *namoya kiishkeehtamwak Cinderella wiya*
   namoya   kiishkeeiht-am-w-ak   Cinderella   wiiya
   NEG   know.TI-THE.TI-IND.3-PL   Cinderella   her.EMPH
   they did not know. Cinderella, however

433 *la Sandrieuz maatoow,*
   la   Sandrieuz   maatoo-w
   DEF.F.S   Sandrieuz   cry.AI-IND.3S
   Cinderella was crying,

434 *nawachiko sheekishiiw*
   nawachiko   sheekishi-w
   partly   be.scared.AI-IND.3S
   she was a little scared.

435 *kiikway kiishpin kishkeehtahkik?*
   keekway   kiishpin   kishkeeiht-ahk-ik
   what   if   know.TI-CNJ.3-PL
   "What if they know?",

436 *itweew kakishkeehtamwak*
   itw-ee-w   ka-kishkeeiht-am-w-ak
   say.TA-DIR-IND.3>4   FUT-know.TI-THE.TI-IND.3-PL
   She said. "They will know it."

437 *gamooshtinikwak ahpotikwee gamooshtinikwak,*
   ga-mooshtin-ik-ok   ahpotikwee   ga-mooshtin-ik-ok
   1FUT-catch.TA-IND.3>SAP-PL   maybe   1FUT-catch.TA-IND.3>1-PL
   "They may even catch me, maybe. They may even catch me",

438 *itweew*
   itw-ee-w
   say.TA-DIR-IND.3>4
   she thought.

439 *sapran kaya naandaw chii-itweeyaan itweew*
   sapraañ   kaaya   naandaw   chi-itwee-yaan   itwee-w
   it.is.necessary   NEG   anything   CNJ-say.AI-CNJ.1S   say.AI-IND.3S
   "I am not going to be able to say anything", she said

440 *ngakaataan ooma li suyii.*
   ni-ka-kaataa-n   oma   li   suyii
   1FUT-hide.AI(t)-IND.non3   this.INAN   DEF.M.S   shoe.M.S
   "I will hide the shoe."

441 *Taapwee kii-kaataaw.*
   taapwee   kii-kaataa-w
   really   PST-hide.AI(t)-IND.3S
   So she hid the shoe.'

Excerpt 9

442 *ah tutdaenku kaapakahamikeet awiyek*
   ah   tudaeñku   kaa-pakah-am-ikee-t   awiyek
   oh   suddenly   CNJ.hit.TI-THE.TI-GEN.AI-CNJ.3S someone
   'Oh suddenly somebody knocked

443 *dan leu port nda*
   dañ   leu   port   anda
   on   3PL.POSS.PL   door.F.INAN   there
   on their door

444 *pi kii-kiishkeehtamwak lii nuvel*
   pii   kii-kiishkeeiht-am-w-ak   lii   nuvel
   and   PST-know.TI-THE.TI-IND.3-PL   ART.PL   news.INAN
   And right there they heard the news.

445 *ashay kii-peehtamwak*
   ashay   kii-peeht-am-w-ak
   already   PST-hear.TI-THE.TI-IND.3-PL
   They had already heard about it,

446 *ee-aachimochik nda dan li vilazh*
   ee-aachimoo-ch-ik   anda   dañ   li   vilaazh
   CNJ-tell.AI-CNJ.3-PL   there   in   DEF.M.S   village.M.INAN
   because people spoke about it in the village.

447 *La faam awa kiipeehtam*
   la   faam   awa   kii-peeht-am-Ø
   DEF.F.S   woman.F.AN   this.AN   PST-hear.TI-THE.TI-IND.3S
   The woman had heard it.

448 *maaka wiitahkamikiishichik*
    maaka   wii-tahkamikiishi-ch-ik
    but   VOL-be.up.to.something.AI-CNJ.3-PL
    But they were going to retrieve the shoe.

449 *li praens awa kaakweemishkawaat*
    li   praeñs   awa   kaakwee-mishk-aw-aa-t
    DEF.M.S   prince.M.AN   this.AN   try-find.TI-TA-DIR-CNJ.3S
    The prince was trying to find

450 *aniki kaakiiohchinimihaat*
    anihi   kaa-kii-ohchi-nimi-h-aa-t
    that.AN.OBV   CNJ-PST-with-dance.AI-TA-DIR-CNJ.3>4
    the person that he had danced with.

451 *aen-kii-ohchimushtawaat ooñhiñ.*
    aeñ   kii-ohchi-moshta-w-aa-t   ooñhiñ
    INDEF.M.S   PST-with-dance.TA-DIR-IND.3>4   this.AN.OBV
    The one he had danced with.

452 *Tudaenku la vyey ana itwew:*
    tudaeñku   la   vyey   ana   itwee-w
    suddenly   DEF.F.S   old.one.F.AN   that.AN   say.AI-IND.3S
    Suddenly the woman said:

453 *"hee, takoshiniwak!*
    hee   takoshini-w-ak
    INT   arrive.AI-IND.3-PL
    "Hey, they are coming!"

454 *Takopayiwak ookik!*
    tako-payi-w-ak   ookik
    arrive-move.AI-IND.3-PL   these.AN
    "They arrive!"

455 *Ngakataaw la Sandrieuz!*
    ni-ka-kaat-aa-w   la   Sandrieuz
    1-FUT-hide.TR-DIR-IND.SAP>3   DEF.F.S   Sandrieuz
    I will hide Cinderella.

456 *Gakataw!", itweew*
    ga-kaat-aa-w   itwee-w
    FUT-hide.TR-DIR-SAP>3   say.AI-IND.3S
    Put her away!" she said.

457 *Gapishcheeminaaw dan la shamb aan laer,*
    ni-ka-(paash)chi-weepin-aa-w   dañ   la   shañb   aañ   leer
    1-FUT-over-throw.TR-DIR-IND.SAP>3   in   DEF.F.S   room   in   air
    "I will throw her in the attic,"

458 *itweew.*
    itwee-w
    say.AI-IND.3S
    she said.

459 *Kii-paapishkaham la port.*
    (kii-)kipaapishkah-am-Ø   la   port.
    (PST-)lock.TI-THE.TI-IND.3S   DEF.F.S   door.F.INAN
    She locked the door.

460 *Kiidoo-ashtaaw.*
    kii-doo-ashtaa-w
    PST-go-place.AI(t)-IND.3S
    She went and placed it there.

461 *iyave enn tab nda*
    iyave   en   taab   anda
    there.was   DEF.F.S   table.F.INAN   there
    There was a table there.

462 *uta ashtaw anima la klii*
    oota   ashtaa-w   anima   la   klii
    there   put.there-AI(t)-IND.3S   that.INAN   DEF.F.S   key.F.INAN
    And that is where she put the key

463 *asheehkiiweepahtaw aañ baa*
    ashee-kiiwee-pahtaa-w   aañ   baa
    backwards-home-run.AI-IND.3S   in   low
    She ran back downstairs,

464 *aen-doo-kitotaat onhin: "haw*
    eeñ-doo-kito-t-aa-t   ooñhiñ   haw
    CNJ-go-talk.AI-TR-DIR-CNJ.3>4   these.AN.OBV   hi
    to go and talk to them. "Hi!

465 *"Parey-ishok!", iteew sii fiy*
    pree-isho-k   itw-ee-w   sii   fiiy
    ready-be.AI-IMP.2PL   say.TA-DIR-IND.3>4   3POSS.PL   daughter.F.AN
    Get yourselves ready", she said to her daughters

466 *"parey kayaanawaaw", itweew*
    pree   ki-ayaa-n-awaaw   itweew
    ready   2-be.AI-IND.non3-PL   say.TA-DIR-IND.3>4
    "You prepare yourselves", she said

467 *"sapran parii kaa-ayaayeek," itweew*
    sapraañ   parii   kaa-ayaa-yeek   itweew
    necessary   ready   CNJ-be.AI-CNJ.2PL   say.TA-DIR-IND.3>4
    "You have to be ready," she said.

468 *"Kakweekishkamok anima li suyii*
    kaakwee-kishk-am-ok   anima   li   suyii
    try-fit.TI-THE.TI-IMP.2S   that.INAN   DEF.M.S   shoe.M.INAN
    "Try to fit the shoe.

469 *kiishpin kaawiikimaawaaw ana li praens,*
    kiishpin   ki-wiikim-aawaaw   ana   li   praeñs
    if   2-marry.TA-IND.2PL>3   that.AN   DEF.M.S   prince.M.AN
    If the prince will marry one of us,

470 *onvayet baen, on va yet rish,"*
    on   vayet   baeñ   on   vayet   rish
    1PL   will.be   well   1PL   will.be   rich
    we will be well, we will be rich,"

471 *iteew kiimiyeuhtamwak*
    itweew   kii-miyeuht-am-w-ak
    say.TA-DIR-IND.3>4   PST-like.TI.THE.TI-IND.3-PL
    she said to them. They liked

472 *ee-liirishiwichik ookik*
    ee-li-rish-iwi-ch-ik   ookik
    CNJ-DEF.M.S-rich-be.AI-CNJ.3-PL   these.AN
    to be rich, these people

473 *safek taapwee tahkunamwak*
    safek   taapwee   tahkon-am-w-ak
    so   truly   hold.TI-THE.TI-IND.3-PL
    So truly they held

474 *anima li suyii daen tetdariyee.*
    anima   li   suyii   dañ   tetdariyee
    that.INAN   DEF.M.S   shoe.M.INAN   in   pillow
    that shoe on a pillow.

475 *daen kusaen kii-ayaawak.*
    dañ   aeñ   kusaeñ   kii-ayaa-w-ak.
    on   INDEF.M.S   cushion.M.INAN   PST.have.AI(t)-IND.3-PL
    On a cushion they had it.

476 *ekuta kii-ashtaaw anima li suyii.*
    ekota   kii-ashtaa-w   anima   li   suyii
    right.there   PST-place.AI(t)-IND.3   that.INAN   DEF.M.S   shoe.M.INAN
    That's where they had that shoe.

477 *Li praens ayaaw eekwa.*
    li   praeñs   ayaa-w   eekwa
    DEF.M.S   prince.M.AN   be.there.AI-IND.3S   also
    The prince was there as well.

478 *Taapwee kaakweekishkam ookik.*
   taapwee   kaakwee-kishkam-Ø   ookik
   indeed   try-fit.TI-THE.TI-IND.S3 these.AN
   Indeed they tried to fit it.

479 *Lii gran pyii lon kii-ayaawak*
   lii   graañ   pyii   looñ   kii-ayaa-w-ak
   ART.PL   big.M   foot.M.INAN long   PST-have.AI-IND.3-PL
   They had big, long feet,

480 *anikik lii fiy*
   anikik   lii   fiiy
   those.AN   ART.PL   girl.F.AN
   those girls.

481 *Lii groo pyi graa henn ana,*
   lii   groo   pyii   graañ   hen   ana
   ART.PL   big.M   foot.M.INAN fat.M   one   that.AN
   One of them had big fat feet,

482 *lii pyii maeg henn oot.*
   lii   pyii   maeg   henn   oot
   ART.PL   foot   skinny   one   other
   fat feet,

483 *pi ana aen gro pyii*
   pii   ana   aeñ   groo   pyii
   then   that.AN   INDEF.M.S   big.M   foot.M.INAN
   The one with big feet,

484 *kishkam mooo*
   kishkam-Ø   moo
   wear.TI-THE.TI-IND.3S   NEG
   she tried it. Ay!

485 *pii kaakweekishkam "no, namo kashkihtaan*
   pii   kaakwee-kishk-am-Ø   no   namo   (ki-)kashkihtaa-n
   then   try-fit.TI-THE.TI-IND.3S   no   NEG   (2-)able.AI-IND.NON3.S
   Then she tried and fit it. "No, you are not able

486 *chi-kishkaman anima", ichikaashow.*
   chi-kishk-am-an   anima   ich-ikaashoo-w
   CNJ-fit.TI-THE.TI-CNJ.2S   that.INAN   say.AI-MED.AI-IND.3S
   to fit that one," she was told.

487 *"wii, gateepishkeen," iteew.*
   wii   ni-ka-teepishk-een   itee-w
   yes   1-FUT-fit.TI-IND.non3S   say.AI-IND.3S
   "Yes, it fits my feet," she said to them.

488 *Li suyi tudaenku*
　　li　　　　　suyii　　　　　　tudaeñku
　　DEF.M.S　　shoe.M.INAN　　suddenly
　　Suddenly the shoe

489 *kashkweepayihk oote li suyii.*
　　kwaashkwee-payi-hk　　oota　　li　　　　　suyii
　　jump-move.AI-CNJ.OS　　here　　DEF.M.S　　shoe.M.INAN
　　flew off right there.

490 *Ayish namo kwayesk kiishkam, heen*
　　ayish　　　namo　kwayesh　kiishk-am-Ø　　　　　　heeñ
　　because　　NEG　　correct　　fit.TI-THE.TI-IND.3S　　INT
　　Because she did not fit it.

491 *keekach patinamwak.*
　　keekaach　　patin-am-w-ak
　　almost　　　drop.TR-THE.TI-IND.3-PL
　　They almost dropped it.

492 *Safet yaenk aan vit anima li suyii*
　　safet　　　yeñk　　aañ　vit　　　　　　anima　　　li　　　　　suyii
　　it.was　　only　　in　　glass.F.INAN　that.INAN　DEF.M.S　　shoe.M.INAN
　　It was made of only glass, this shoe.

493 *kaakiipiikohtin.*
　　kaa-kii-piikohti-n
　　CNJ-PST-break.while.falling.II-IND.OS
　　It could have fallen into pieces.

494 *Kashchipitam anima li suyii.*
　　kahchipit-am-Ø　　　　　　anima　　　li　　　　　suyii
　　grab.TI-THE.TI-IND.3S　　that.INAN　DEF.M.S　　shoe.M.INAN
　　He grabbed the shoe.

495 *"Okee," iteew.*
　　okay　　itw-ee-w
　　okay　　say.TA-DIR-IND.3>4
　　"Okay," he said to her,

496 *Namo kashkihtaan.*
　　mo　　　(ki-)kashkihtaa-n　　　　　　　　anima
　　NEG　　(2-)be.able.AI-IND.non3　　that.INAN
　　"You cannot wear it."

497 *"Kiya eekwa",*
　　kiiya　　eekwa
　　you　　　now
　　"It's your turn",

498 *itew loot ana la fiy.*
    itw-ee-w   loot   ana   la   fiiy
    say.TA-DIR-IND.3>4   other   that.AN DEF.F.S girl.F.AN
    he said to the other girl.

499 *Kahkiyaaw anihi lii trwa fiy*
    kahkiyaaw   anihi   lii   trwa   fiiy
    all   those.AN.OBV   ART.PL   three   girl.F.AN
    All of these three girls

500 *namo kiiteepishkamwak.*
    mo   kii-teepishk-am-w-ak
    NEG   PST-fit-THE.TI-IND.3-PL
    they did not fit it.'

Excerpt 10

501 *La Sandrieuz wiya kaakweekiichiiw neetee ohchi.*
    la   Sanderieuz   wiya   kakwee-kichii-w   neetee   ohchi
    DEF.F.S   Sandrieuz   she.EMPH   try-escape.AI-IND.3S   over.there from
    'Cinderella, she tried to escape from there.

502 *Kipahikaashow. Lii surii anikik*
    kipah-ikaashoo-w   lii   surii   anikik
    lock.TI-MED.AI-IND.3S   ART.PL   mice.M.AN   those.AN
    She was locked up. The mice

503 *pii li shyaen kaakweewiichihikow.*
    pii   li   shyaeñ   kakwee-wiichih-iko-w
    and   DEF.M.S   dog.M.AN   try-help.TA-DIR-IND.4>3
    and the dog tried to help her.

504 *Pi i yave aen groo sha nwaer nda.*
    pii   iyave   aeñ   groo   shaa   nwaer   anda
    and   there.was   INDEF.M.S   big.M   cat.M.AN   black   there
    And there was a big black cat there.

505 *La faam ana soo sha,*
    la   faam   ana   soñ   shaa
    DEF.F.S   woman.F.AN   that.AN   3POSS.M.S   cat.M.AN
    It was the woman's cat,

506 *aen vrae moo– machimanituwit*
    aeñ   vrae   moo/   machi-manito-wi-t
    INDEF.M.S   right   ?   bad.spirit.AI-be.AI-CNJ.3S
    a real da.... devil was

507 *ana li sha,*
    ana   li   shaa
    that.AN   DEF.M.S   cat.M.AN
    this cat,

508 *parey kom la faam ana.*
    parey   kom   la   faam   ana
    same   like   DEF.F.S   woman.F.AN   that.AN
    he was just like the woman.

509 *Kaakweenipaaheew anihi lii surii, haeñ*
    kaakwee-nipah-ee-w   anihi   lii   surii   haeñ
    try-kill.TA-DIR-IND.3>4   those.AN.OBV   ART.PL   mice.M.AN   INT
    He tried to kill these mice,

510 *lii surii anihi kaakweenipaaheew.*
    lii   surii   anihi   kaakwee-nipa-h-ee-w
    ART.PL   mice.M.AN   those.AN.OBV   try-kill.TA-DIR.IND.3>4
    he wanted to kill them.

511 *Li shyaen awa, aen vyeu shyaen aata,*
    li   shyaeñ   awa   aeñ   vyeu   shyaeñ   aata
    DEF.M.S   dog.M.AN   this.AN   INDEF.F.S   old   dog.M.AN   although
    The dog, even though he was an old one,

512 *nashahawateew anihi li sha-wa.*
    na(wa)shwaa-t-ee-w   anihi   li   shaa-wa
    chase.AI-TR-DIR-IND.3>4   that.AN.OBV   DEF.M.S   cat.M.AN-OBV
    he ran after this cat.

513 *Li sha ana kiipahkishin*
    li   shaa   ana   kii-pahkishi-n
    DEF.M.S   cat.M.AN   that.AN   PST-fell.down.AI-IND.3S
    The cat fell down

514 *aan laer nda ohchi.*
    aañ   laer   anda   ohchi.
    in   air   there   from
    from up in the air.

515 *kii-nipaahishin ana ahpo eetikwee,*
    kii-nipaa-ishi-n   ana   ahpo   etikwee
    PST-sleep.AI-AI-IND.3S   this.AN   maybe   I.guess
    Maybe he fell dead, I don't know,

516 *ubaendoon kiiwiishakishin naandaw li sha*
    obaeñdooñ   kii-wiishakishi-n   naandaw   ana   li   shaa
    or   PST-hurt.bad.AI-IND.3S   something   that.AN   DEF.M.S   cat.M.AN
    or else the cat was badly hurt.

517 *"Aahkameeyimok", iteew.*
    ahkameeyim-ok   it-ee-w
    keep.on.work.TA-IMP.2PL   say-TA-IND.3>4
    "Go on", she said.

518 *"Aahkameeyimok", iteew lii surii oonhin.*
    ahkameeyimo-k   itee-w   lii   surii   ooñhiñ
    keep.on.AI-IMP.2PL   say-TA-IND.3>4   ART.PL   mice   these.AN.OBV
    "Keep on," she said to the mice.

519 *"Kaakweemishkamok anima la klii",*
    kakwee-mishkam-ok   anima   la   klii
    try-find.TI-IMP.2PL   that.INAN   DEF.F.S   key.F.INAN
    "Try to find the key!"

520 *iteew.*
    it-ee-w
    say.TA-DIR-IND.3>4
    she said to them.

521 *Taapwee, andisur la port sheekoyaamoowak*
    taapwee   andisur   la   port   sheekoyaamoo-w-ak
    really   underneath   DEF.F.S   door.F.INAN   ???.AI-IND.3-PL
    Really, they run underneath the door,

522 *aniki li surii,*
    aniki   lii   surii
    those.AN   ART.PL   mice.M.AN
    these mice,

523 *kwashkohtiwak dan la tab*
    kwaashkwati-w-ak   dañ   la   tab
    jump.AI-IND.3-PL   on   DEF.F.S   table.F.INAN
    they jumped on the table.

524 *nda mishkamwak.*
    anda   mishk-am-w-ak
    there   find.TI-THE.TI-IND.3S-PL-AI
    There they found it.

525 *Sapran chi-kaakwee-otapeechik.*
    sapraañ   chi-kaakwee-otaapee-ch-ik.
    necessary   CNJ-try-drag.AI(t)-CNJ.3-PL
    They had to try and drag it.

526 *Kishikwan anima la klii.*
    kishikwa-n   anima   la   klii
    be.heavy.II-IND.OS   this.INAN   DEF.F.S   key.F.INAN
    It was heavy, this key.

527 *Enn gros klii.*
    en   gros   klii
    INDEF.F.S   big.F   key.F.INAN
    It was a big key.

528 *Kishikwan, wiichihiitowak eekwa.*
    kishikwa-n   wiichih-ito-w-ak   eekwa
    be.heavy.II-IND.OS   help.TA-REC.AI-IND.3-PL   then
    As it was heavy, they helped each other.

529 *Cinderella eekwanima miiyikashow.*
    Cinderella   eekwanima   miiy-ikaashoo-w.
    Cinderella   that.INAN   give.TA-MED.AI-IND.3S
    Cinderella got it from them.

530 *Paashtenam la port.*
    paashteen-am-Ø   la   port
    open.TI-THE.TI-IND.3S   DEF.F.S   door.F.INAN
    She opened the door.

531 *Meeshchi wii-shipweehteechik*
    Mishchit   wii-shipweehtee-ch-ik
    just.about   VOL-leave.AI-CNJ.3-PL
    They were just about to go out,

532 *ookik li praens pi sii servan,*
    ookik   li   praens   pii   sii   servaañ
    these.AN   DEF.M.S   prince.M.AN   and   3POSS.PL servant.M.AN
    the prince and his servants,

533 *otee waapamiku*
    otee   (ee-)waapam-iko-w
    over.there   (CNJ)-see.TA-INV-CNJ.4>3
    when they realized she was there.

534 *la faam ana teepweew:*
    la   faam   ana   teepwee-w
    DEF.F.S   woman.F.AN that.AN   shout.AI-IND.3S
    The woman shouted:

535 *"aenh, sipa! Moo. no peeyak aen ...*
    aeñ   sipa   moo   no   peeyak   aeñ
    INT   I.don't.know   NEG   NEG   one   INDEF.M.S
    "Yes, I don't know, no, she is no...

536 *La fiy ana,*
    la   fiiy   ana
    DEF.F.S   girl.F.AN   that.AN
    That girl,

537 *site yaenk aen servant ana. Kiyaam.*
    site   yaeñk   aeñ   servaañ   ana   kiiyaam
    she.is   only   INDEF.M.S servant.M.AN that.AN think.nothing.of.it
    she is just a servant. It doesn't matter.

538 *Kaya nipaachiihkaw awa la fiy", iteew.*
    kaaya   napaachiihkaw   ana   la   fiiy   it-ee-w
    do.not   molest.TA   this.AN DEF.F.S girl.F.AN say.TA-DIR-IND.3>4
    Don't bother that girl," she said to them.

539 *"No, noo," iteew li praens.*
    no   noo   it-ee-w   li   praens
    NEG   NEG   say.TA-DIR-IND.3>4   DEF.M.S   prince.M.AN
    "No, no," the Prince said to her.

540 *Tut lii fiy nyweehtam chi-kaakweekishkahkik*
    tot   lii   fiiy   nd-weeiht-aen   chi-kaakwee-kishk-ahk-ik
    all   ART.PL   girl.F.AN   1-want.TI-IND.non3   CNJ-try-fit.TI-CNJ.3-PL
    All the girls have to try

541 *anima li suyi", iteew.*
    anima   li   suyii   it-ee-w
    that.INAN DEF.M.S   shoe.M.INAN   say.TA-DIR.IND.3>4
    the shoe," he said to her.

542 *Taapwee, teepwaateew.*
    taapwee   teepwaa-t-ee-w
    really   shout.AI-TR-DIR-IND.3>4
    Really, he called her.

543 *Lii fiy ookik kishiwasiwak.*
    lii   fiiy   ookik   kishiwaashi-w-ak
    ART.PL   girl.F.AN these.AN   angry.AI-IND.3-PL
    They daughters were angry.

544 *weepineewak.... Cinderella la Sandrieuz.*
    weepin-ee-w-ak   Cinderella   la   Sandrieuz
    pushed.TA-DIR-IND.3>4-PL.SBJ Cinderella   DEF.F.S   Sandrieuz
    They pushed Cinderella.

545 *Aahkweepiniwak.*
    (k)weepin-ee-w-ak
    pushed.TA-DIR-IND.3>4-PL.SBJ
    They pushed her.

546 *Kiyaam.*
    kiiyaam
    never.mind
    Never mind.

547 *Kishkam anima*
    kishk-am-Ø   anima
    put.on.TI-THE.TI-IND.3S   that.INAN
    She put it on,

548 *teepishkam li suyi.*
    teepishk-am-Ø   li   suyii
    fit.TI-THE.TI-IND.3S   DEF.M.S   shoe.M.INAN
    and the shoe fitted her.'

Excerpt 11

549 *Eekoshi la Sandrieuz tutdaenku sitaen enn praenses.*
    eekoshi   la   Sandrieuz   todaeñku   sitaen   en   praeñses
    thus   DEF.F.S   Sandrieuz   suddenly   she.was   INDEF.F.S   princess.F.AN
    'Thus Cinderella suddenly became a Princess.'

550 *Kiiwiikimeew ana li praens.*
    kii-wiikim-ee-w   ana   li   praeñs
    PST-marry.TA-DIR-IND.3>4   that.AN   DEF.M.S   prince.M.AN
    She married the Prince.

551 *Kiipeepichiweew dans li palae.*
    kii-piihtikweepichi-w   dañ   li   palee
    PST-move.AI-IND.3S   in   DEF.M.S   palace.M.INAN
    She moved into the palace.

552 *kii-shipweehtaheew sii suurii,*
    kii-shipweehta-h-ee-w   sii   surii
    PST-leave.AI-CAUS.TA-DIR-IND.3>4   3POSS.PL   mice.M.AN
    She took her mice

553 *pi so shyaen,*
    pii   soñ   shyaeñ
    and   3POSS.M.S   dog.M.AN
    and her dog along,

554 *ite laa, ite baen pur tut bon,*
    ite   laa   ite   baeñ   pur   tot   boñ
    they.were   there   there.were   good   for   all   good
    then they were well forever,

555 *eekoshi kii-kishinipiw.*
    eekoshi   kii-ishi-nipo-w
    until   PST-thus-die.AI-IND.3S
    until she died of old age.

556 *Sitenn renn apre.*
    Site   en   renn   apre
    s/he.was   INDEF.F.S   queen.F.AN   after
    She became a Queen after.

557 *Pii moohkaach kiihtwaam kiiwaapameew*
    pii   moo-hkaach   kiihtwam   kii-waapam-ee-w
    and   NEG-ever   again   PST-see.TA-DIR-IND.3>4
    And never again she saw

558 *anihi la moves faam*
    anihi   la   moves   faam
    that.AN.OBV   DEF.F.S   bad   woman.F.AN
    the evil woman

559 *pi sii fiy.*
    pii   sii   fiiy
    and   3POSS.PL   daughter.F.AN
    and her daughters.

560 *zhame kiihtwam kii-waapameew.*
    zhamee   kiihtwam   kii-waapam-ee-w
    never   again   PST-see.TA-DIR-IND.3>4
    Never again she saw them.

561 *Eekoshi kiimiyeuyihtam.*
    eekoshi   kii-miyeuiht-am-Ø
    finally   PST-like.TI-THE.TI-IND.3S
    Finally she was happy.

562 *ekwanima listweer kaakii-aachimoyaan*
    ekwanima   listweer   kaa-kii-aachimoo-yaan
    that.INAN   story.F.INAN   CNJ-PST-tell.AI-CNJ.1S
    This story that I told you

563 *kayaash niishta kaa-apishiishiyaan*
    kayaash   niishta   kaa-apishiishi-yaan
    long.ago   me.too   CNJ-be.small.AI-CNJ.1S
    when I too, long ago, was small,

564 *kii-achimostaakowiyaan*
    kii-achim-oo-staa-ikawi-yaan
    PST-tell.TA-MID.RFLX.AI-BEN.TA-PASS.AI-CNJ.1S
    was told by

565 *nuhkum pii ni-mushum-ipan*
    nohkom   pii   ni-moshom-ipan
    my.gradmother.F.AN and   my-grandpa-late
    my late grandmother and grandfather

566 *ekii-aachimochik. Eekoshi.*
    ee-kii-aachim-oo-ch-ik   eekoshi.
    CNJ-PST-tell.TA-MID.RFLX.AI-CNJ.3-PL   that.is.it
    when they were telling stories. That's it.'

Danae Maria Perez
Social conditioning for the transmission of adstrate features in contact varieties of Spanish in the Central Andes

Abstract: This chapter introduces new data on an underdocumented contact language in the Bolivian Andes: Afro-Yungueño Spanish. This highly endangered variety of Spanish is spoken by a small African-descendant community and surrounded by Aymara and Andean Spanish. In this region, certain areal features are prominent in both Andean Spanish as well as in the local indigenous languages, and the chapter analyzes to what degree Afro-Yungueño Spanish displays them as well. The analysis is based on lexical and grammatical features and shows that even though Afro-Yungueño Spanish is geographically Andean, its typological setup displays relatively few areal structures, as only the lexicon shows a substantial Andean component. The chapter closes in arguing that social isolation has prevented areal features from becoming part of Afro-Yungueño Spanish.

Keywords: areal features, Andes, social isolation, endangerment, Afro-Yungueño Spanish

1 Introduction

This chapter focuses on the region around the Bolivian high plateau *Altiplano* and Lake Titicaca, also known as the Central Andes. The indigenous languages spoken in this area share a number of areal features that are likely to have spread from one language to the other due to their millennia-long contact (Adelaar 2012: 586). For nearly 500 years, also Spanish has been in contact with these languages, and two new varieties of Spanish have emerged here: Bolivian Highland Spanish (henceforth BHS) and Afro-Yungueño Spanish (henceforth AYS). BHS is spoken in the metropolitan area of La Paz, where approximately 3 million people are living in 2020 (Instituto Nacional de Estadística). AYS, by contrast, is a highly endangered isolated enclave variety. It is spoken by a small African-descendant com-

---

Danae Maria Perez, Zurich University of Applied Sciences, Department of Applied Linguistics, Theaterstr. 15c, P.O Box, 8401 Winterthur, Switzerland. E-mail: peze@zhaw.ch

https://doi.org/10.1515/9783110723977-006

munity at approximately 120kms from La Paz and counted no more than 200 individuals in 2010 and was close to extinction in 2020. This community differs from other Andean communities because of its unusual social history and its origins in coca plantation slavery (Perez 2015: 313).

Both BHS and AYS are Andean varieties of Spanish that have been claimed to diverge from patrimonial Spanish in many ways. Yet, while BHS is known to display features that mostly stem from local indigenous languages (cf. Escobar 2011; Clements 2021), AYS diverges from any other variety of Spanish to a much greater extent (e.g. Lipski 2008: 63). The linguistic input and contact history of BHS and AYS are as follows: the adstrate languages of BHS are Bolivian Aymara and Southern Quechua, the former being the more dominant one, and AYS has Bolivian Aymara as the relevant adstrate language, while the assumed defunct substrates were Kikongo and (Afro-)Portuguese (Perez 2015: 318; for the taxonomy, cf. Yakpo 2017). AYS can thus be expected to be linguistically rather unrelated to other Andean languages, including BHS. In addition, cultural and attitudinal factors, such as geographical and social isolation, are said to determine language change in isolated varieties as much as contact and demographics do (Jourdan 2008; Schreier 2009), and a lack of bilingualism and interaction may have caused AYS to remain distinct despite its geographical proximity to Aymara in the heart of the Central Andes. The exploration of the Andean character of these two varieties is therefore expected to help determine whether social factors, such as isolation, condition the transmission of areal patterns not only from one indigenous language to another but also to new contact varieties.

In this chapter, I will therefore look at these two neighboring Central Andean varieties, i.e. BHS and AYS, with a particular focus on features typically found in varieties of Aymara and Quechua, to see to what extent they are present in these two varieties today. This will allow us to better understand what the social conditioning for their transmission may be. I will start in Section 2 by outlining some typological features of Aymara and Quechua which are said to be areal features, i.e. features that languages in geographical proximity have in common due to prolonged contact. I do this in order to explain the structures that may be at the root of certain features found in BHS or AYS on the basis of the assumption that the Aymara adstrate does have an influence on both of them as a result of intense language contact. Section 3 and 4, respectively, will look at how these structures are reflected in BHS and AYS. Section 5 will discuss what social conditions may influence the evolution of these varieties and how they adopted these areal features.

AYS data are difficult to collect because most AYS-speakers also speak BHS and avoid AYS in the presence of outsiders. The present study is based on data that were collected in the field adhering to the most unintrusive anthropological field methods and in close collaboration with community members, who assisted in the collection and analysis of the data. The data presented here stem from prolonged fieldwork of several months in the Yungas region as well as La Paz between 2009 and 2016, which yielded approximately eight hours of recordings of naturally occurring conversations plus a considerable amount of fieldnotes. All the data were collected in naturally occurring conversations in order to stimulate the use of AYS features, and monolingual BHS-speakers were frequently present in the conversations. The recordings thus contain data of both varieties as well as switches between the two. The data presented here are consistent with the literature (e.g. Mendoza 1991; Angola 2008; Lipski 2008; Perez 2015; Quartararo 2017).

2 Areal features in the Central Andes

The Andes cover vast territories and diverse climatic zones, and they were settled by diverse communities in several waves and over several millennia. This historical development is assumed to explain the high linguistic diversity found in this region. There is, however, one language family that is most prominent in the Andes: the Quechuan language family. During the era of the *Tawantinsuyo*, the four-fold Inca Empire with Cusco at its center, the Cusco variety of Quechua became dominant (Itier 2011). In the region around the Central Andes, which was part of the *Collavina*, or *Chinchaisuyo*, area, Aymara is the most dominant indigenous language (Cerrón-Palomino 2008: 26). Map 1 shows the principal areas of Quechua in the North and Southeast and Aymara at the center of the Central Andes.

The two languages are structurally very similar and share the same cultural space. This structural similarity is likely to be the outcome of the linguistic and cultural contact between the speech communities over an extended period of time (cf. Cerrón-Palomino 2008: 26; Adelaar 2012: 575). The synchronic morphological and semantic parallelisms between these two languages are outstanding to the point of allowing a morpheme-by-morpheme translation between the two languages in most cases, and their lexical material overlaps to a considerable degree (Adelaar and Muysken 2004: 267; Cerrón-Palomino 2008; Adelaar 1986, 2012: 594).

From a typological perspective, varieties of Quechua and Aymara are very similar. They are both agglutinative (or concatenating) languages in which suffixes are added to a stem, often producing sentences consisting of one single

Map 1: The distribution of indigenous languages and AYS in the Central Andes during the 20th century (cf. Adelaar and Muysken 2004: 168).

and at times highly complex word (Hardman 2001: 100). They both follow an (S)OV syntactic structure with nominative-accusative alignment. Neither Aymara nor Quechua have grammatical gender, and they mark plural with a (not obligatory) suffix, i.e. *-naka* in Aymara and *-kuna* in Quechua. The pronominal system is fourfold as it is based on the inclusion or non-inclusion of the speaker and addressee, i.e. 1) + speaker − addressee, 2) − speaker + addressee, 3) − speaker − addressee, 4) + speaker + addressee, the latter representing what is generally known as an inclusive first-person plural when pluralized with the suffix *-naka* (Adelaar and Muysken 2004: 269).

(1) singular   plural
     naya 'I'   *nanaka* 'us without you'
     juma 'you'   *jumanaka* 'you (all)'
     jupa 's/he, they'   *jupanaka* 'they'
     jiwasa 'me or us, and you'   *jiwasanaka* 'us and you (all)'
                                                    [Cerrón-Palomino 2008: 118]

Aymara and Quechua both mark possessives twice, as the modifier receives the genitive case marker and the head noun the grammatical person of the possessor, as in (3), an example from Aymara (cf. Adelaar and Muysken 2004: 278; Adelaar 2012: 595):

(2) *naya-n(a)*   *uta-ja*
     1SG.NOM-GEN   house.1SG-POSS   [Hardman 2001: 155]

On the phonological level, both show similarities in that they have a three-vowel system based on /i/–/u/–/a/; Aymara, however, shows up to 22 allophonic variants of these vowels. Aymara and Southern Quechua (probably as a result of its close contact with Aymara), distinguishes between plain, aspirated, and glottalized consonants, as in *tanta* 'meeting', *tʰanta* 'cloth', and *t'anta* 'bread'. This distinction is said to be a feature that is particular to the Central Andes (Adelaar 2012: 606). Furthermore, complex morpho-phonological rules in Aymara often lead to the suppression of certain vowels in preceding morphemes, which produces highly complex consonant clusters (cf. Hardman 2001: 20–21; Adelaar and Muysken 2004: 195, 264–271; Cerrón-Palomino 2008: 43). Adelaar and Muysken (2004: 278) provide an example of the rich directional and spatial inflection in Aymara with the verb stem *ira-* 'to carry small objects', which illustrates the complex nature of vowel omission conditioned by the following suffix: *-nta-* and *-qa-* do not suppress the preceding vowel, whereas *-su-* and *-ta-* do:

(3) *ira-nta-*   'to introduce small objects'
     ir(a)-su-   'to take out small objects'

ir(a)-ta-	'to lift up small objects'
ira-qa-	'to put down small objects'

There are also semantic and cultural aspects that are particular to this region. One Aymara feature that sets it apart is the perception of time and its reflection in the grammar. Time in Aymara is conceived of as linear, and the principal distinction is made between the future and the non-future; while the non-future, i.e. the past and the present, is in front of one's eyes and thus *visible* to the speaker and their interlocutor, the future is behind the speaker's back and hence unknown (Apaza Apaza 2008: 130). Also, time is seen as fluid, and "the future is said to flow over one's shoulder and become manifest before one's eyes" (Hardman 2001: 112). Accordingly, in Aymara, *nayra* means at once 'eye, sight' as well as 'before', and an expression as *nayra mara* 'last year, front year' is understood as the past year that lies in front of us. This perception is also translated into gestures, as Aymara-speakers point towards their back when talking about future events, while pointing towards the space in front of them when talking about the past (Evans 2010: 169–170). This distinction between future and non-future is fundamentally different from Spanish, which, along with many Indo-European languages, sees the future as lying ahead of the speaker, and in which morphological future forms have only relatively recently been grammaticalized (cf. the evolution of the synthetic future tense from medieval Latin to Spanish, Penny 2004: 236–238), while the past is behind and has been grammaticalized with different degrees of temporal depth and aspectual distinctions for over two millennia.

This perception of time and the importance of the visibility and thus evidence of what is said and known are reflected in the Aymara grammar and its system of evidentiality. Evidentiality encompasses many different expressive means of making reference to the reliability or truthfulness of the source of a piece of information on which a statement is based (Aikhenvald 2004). In other words, evidentials are grammatical resources – typically free or bound morphemes – which allow the speaker to indicate where their knowledge on what they are saying comes from and with what certainty they are upholding their point. This is grammaticalized in the morphology of Aymara by means of verbal suffixes and discourse markers in different categories, which include a) statements made with certainty and based on personal knowledge or b) statements based on indirect evidentiality that is either inferred or conjectural and for which the speaker does not want to be held accountable (Hardman 2001: 105; Adelaar and Muysken 2004: 286; Adelaar 2012: 599; Quartararo 2017: 87; cf. for Quechua Adelaar and Muysken 2004: 210). This grammaticalized marking of evidentiality, i.e. the importance of whether one has personally witnessed an event or is retelling a story they have heard of or assume, is salient in discourse practices, such as politeness strategies and the expression of deference and respect, and thus deeply entrenched in Andean culture. Hardman (1988: 167, my translation) explains that speakers of Aymara are often mistaken as being distrustful and that

> ...they are quick to accuse others of lying ... yet this is simply an issue of being correct regarding the source of their information. In fact, the reputation of a person within the community may depend heavily on not committing mistakes concerning their source of information, on not saying that they have personal knowledge when they don't have, and vice versa.

These discourse practices of trustworthiness and reliability are likely to be stressed in inter-community communication, especially in the context of trade relations and negotiations. It is therefore similarly likely that the prolonged linguistic and cultural contact has led to linguistic convergence that perpetuated evidentiality as an areal feature of the languages in the Central Andes (cf. Adelaar 2012: 612).

3 Adstrate features in Bolivian Highland Spanish

The Spaniard Francisco Pizarro invaded the region of *Alto Perú* 'Upper Peru' in 1532. Though the Hispanization of the population in this area was rather slow, the socio-political and cultural changes introduced by the Spaniards have undoubtedly triggered intense processes of language change. Not only did they establish Spanish as the language of colonial administration, but they also needed supraregional *lingua francas* to communicate with, and to Christianize the population of more peripheral regions. They therefore declared the Cusco variety of Quechua and Aymara each a regional *lengua general* (Cerrón-Palomino 2003: 85; Andrien 2011: 115–116). Most of the indigenous population remained Aymara- or Quechua dominant until well into the 20th century (Clements 2021). By today, however, Spanish has become dominant, while many local languages, such as Atacameño, have become extinct. Yet these languages have left, and continue to leave, many traces in Andean varieties of Spanish.

Andean Spanishes are today among the most fascinating varieties of Spanish that diverge considerably from Standard Spanish and are intensely intertwined with their cultural context. Given their historical importance, Quechua and Aymara are the most important adstrate languages that have had, and continue to have, influence on BHS. While Andean Spanish in other parts of the Andes has received considerable attention, this region is still underresearched.

The situation is, however, similar to locations where Spanish is in contact with Quechua only. The literature on La Paz Spanish is still scarce, Laprade (1981), Mendoza (1991), and Quartararo (2017) being the only noticeable exceptions. Given that Quechua and Aymara are structurally very similar to the extent of having been labelled as one, i.e. as "Quechumara" by Cerrón-Palomino (2003), I therefore also consider the literature on Quechuan-influenced Spanish for the present chapter. While most of the features discussed here may be more prominent among bilingual speakers of a lower degree of education (cf. Quartararo 2017), it is important to notice that the features discussed here are part of the speech of monolingual L1 speakers of Spanish.[1]

When compared to the typological features mentioned in Section 2, Spanish shares the syntactic nominative-accusative alignment with Aymara and Quechua, yet SVO is the most common, i.e. unmarked, word order (Olarrea 2012: 603). Spanish is an inflectional or fusional language, which means that it makes use of pre- and suffixes that mark more than one grammatical category at once, as in the verbal first-person singular indicative suffix *-o* in *bebo* (from Spanish *beber*) 'I drink'. Spanish has three grammatical persons and two genders (yet three in the pronominal system), and unlike Aymara and Quechua, it has no double possessives and marks possession by means of either the preposed possessive pronouns *mi, tu, su, nuestro/a, vuestro/a* as in *mi casa* 'mi casa', or else the preposition *de* 'of' as in *la casa **de** Pedro* 'Peter's house' (Penny 2004: 169).

There are of course many Aymaran and Quechuan lexical items that were introduced into the local Spanish lexicon. They often refer to concepts unknown to the Spanish-speaking world outside this context, such as *chuño* 'dried potato' (from Aymara *ch'uñu*) or *yapa* 'supplement given by the salesperson as a gift' (from Aymara *yapa*). There are however also loanwords that replace existent Spanish terms, such as *chaqui* 'hangover' (from Aymara *ch'akhi*), which is more common than Spanish *resaca*, or *achuntar* 'to hit' from Aymara *chonta*, the name of a tree from which arrows and tools are made, instead of Spanish *atinar*. Most of these words are phonologically Hispanicized, which means that the

---

[1] For instance, irregularities in gender and number agreement, which have stabilized to a certain degree and are also used by first-language speakers of Spanish with a rather low level of formal education, are frequent in rural varieties where relatively unmonitored L2 acquisition is likely to be the origin of these features (Klee 1996; Cerrón-Palomino 2003: 40–42; Clements 2009: 177–178; Perez 2014). Speakers who display these features in their speech commonly suffer from social stigmatization. The problematic view behind this social stigmatization is that these features are often said to stem from the rural people's "bruteness", i.e. a low degree of formal education and lesser familiarity with European culture, rather than being an adstrate feature (cf. Cerrón-Palomino 2003: 40–42).

glottalized and aspirated as well as post-velar consonants become plain velar ones, and high vowels are often lowered to mid-vowels. *Kuka* 'coca' thus became *coca* and *ch'arkhi* 'dried meat' became *charque* in BHS (borrowed to English as *jerky*).

Apart from loanwords, the phonological particularities of the varieties spoken in the Andes are one of the key features to differentiate them from other postcolonial dialects of Spanish. Spanish dialectology mostly deals with variation in the realization of consonants, since its five-vowel system is relatively stable across varieties (cf. e.g. Lipski 2007). When looking at the consonantal systems of Andean varieties of Spanish, the retention of *lleísmo*, i.e. the phonological distinction between the palatal lateral /λ/ and the palatal glide /j/ as in *pollo* 'chicken' versus *poyo* 'stone bench', which have merged to /j/ (called *yeísmo*) in most dialects of Spanish, is particularly characteristic. This feature is said to be due to colonization patterns with influence from the heart of the Iberian Peninsula, rather than from the coastal South and Andalusia (e.g. Catalán 1989; Pöll 2021); in the case of BHS, however, the retention of this sound is certainly reinforced by the presence of this phoneme in the adstrate languages (Mendoza 1991: 67).

Similarly noticeable is the maintenance of syllable- and word-final consonants, above all implosive *-s* (Lipski 2007: 211). This feature is relevant as it stands out among other American varieties of Spanish for two reasons. On the one hand, most dialects of Spanish from Southern Spain and the Americas have a rather weak realization of syllable-final *-s*; some of them, such as Caribbean Spanish, even experienced their complete loss (Lorenzino et al. 1998). This phonological process has strong repercussions for the morphosyntax of these varieties, since the realization of Standard Spanish number agreement is altered if the plural *-s* is not phonetically realized. The fact that many American varieties of Spanish have lost syllable-final *-s* is generally ascribed to this feature's dialectal origin in the Southern part of the Iberian Peninsula, i.e. also this feature is said to have been brought to the New World by a large proportion of colonizers originally stemming from Southern Spain and the Canary Islands, or because people from other parts of Spain would spend time in the South waiting to board a ship to America. Scholars maintain that the Southern varieties had a more limited impact on Andean varieties of Spanish due to the colonizers' origin in other parts of Spain rather than the South (Lapesa 1980: 372; Alvar 2000; Pöll 2021).

There is, however, an additional reason to the maintenance of syllable-final and word-final *-s* in Highland Bolivia: Aymara. As explained in Section 2, Aymara often removes vowels producing consonant clusters to the point of displaying long chains of consonants. Spanish, by contrast, has a general CV(C) syllable pattern, where the formation of consonant clusters is usually restricted to syllable breaks (Hualde 2012). In BHS, unstressed vowels, particularly those in word-final syllables, are often removed, thus producing consonant clusters that are highly unusual for Spanish. *Vamos* 'we go, let's go' is often reduced to *vams*, producing the *-ms-* sequence that is inexistent in the phonotactics of patrimonial Spanish. The morpho-phonological process of vowel deletion, rather than consonant weakening, in Aymara is likely to be at the root of the omission of unstressed vowels and the retention of *lleísmo* and implosive *-s* in BHS. BHS is thus a highly distinct variety that differs considerably from most other varieties of Spanish on the phonological level.[2]

On the level of morphosyntax, BHS is similarly different from Patrimonial Spanish. BHS has re-ordered, for instance, the order of elements on the sentence level according to the Quechua and Aymara (S)OV system, as in (4). The origin of this structure is likely to be the direct transfer from Aymara, which generally places verbs and also the declarative sentence suffix *-wa* at the end of the sentence. In example (5a), which is an analysis of the sentence 'your house is very big' in Aymara and how this would be expressed in BHS and patrimonial Spanish in (5b–c), respectively (cf. also Cerrón-Palomino 2003: 188), illustrates the re-ordering in BHS:

(4) mal   puesta   la   mesa   **estaba**
     wrong   placed   DET   table   **COP**
     'The table was in the wrong position'   [Mendoza 1991: 125]

(5) a.   Aymara
         uta.ma.xa   sinti   jach'a.**wa**
         house.2SG-POSS.TOP   very   big.**DECL**
    b.   BHS
         Tu   casa   muy   grande   es.
         2SG-POSS   house   very   big   COP
    c.   Spanish
         Tu   casa   es   muy   grande.
         2SG-POSS   house   COP   very   big
         'Your house is very big.'   [Cerrón-Palomino 2008: 120]

---

2 Phonological processes that affect the stable five-vowel system of Spanish, i.e. the frequent confusion of the mid vowels with high vowels, are not discussed here as they are not commonly found among L1 speakers of Spanish. For example, rural speakers with lesser exposure to Spanish often realize /i/ as a variant closer to [e] and /u/ similar to [o], producing forms like *cora* instead of *cura* 'priest' and *mesa* instead of *misa* 'mass'. This feature is the result of influence from the Aymaran and Quechuan vocalic systems having no more than three phonemic vowels /i/–/a/–/u/ with a wide range of allophonic variants.

Example (5b) would be *tu casa es muy grande* in patrimonial Spanish as in (5c). *Tu casa muy grande es* is not possible in standard-nearer varieties of Spanish, not even as a topicalized sentence (cf. Olarrea 2012). In BHS, this sentence is unmarked, and it is likely to be the result of the (S)OV word order in Aymara (Cerrón-Palomino 2003: 191–197; Clements 2009: 174). The same presence of sentence-final verbs is also attested in La Paz Spanish with its strong Aymara adstrate (Mendoza 1991: 196–197). This makes clear that there are profound typological differences between BHS and standard-nearer varieties.

Possessives are another intriguing area where processes of contact-induced change can be observed. Unlike in patrimonial Spanish, the double marking of possession, which is present in both adstrates, is also evident in BHS. The pattern is based on the combination of *de* 'of' together with a redundant possessive pronoun, which corresponds to the double marking in the adstrate languages. Accordingly, in Aymara-influenced La Paz Spanish, double possessives are the common form, as in **su** hijito **de** la María 'Maria's son' instead of patrimonial Spanish **el** hijito **de** María (Mendoza 1991: 105). Clements (2009: 176–177), with reference to this identical pattern in Quechua-influenced Spanish, explains that this is the result of the adstrate languages marking possession twice, as in examples (6a–b), which represent Peruvian Andean Spanish and Quechua, respectively. Examples (7a–b) reproduce the same double possessive structure in Aymara and Aymara-influenced Spanish. Patrimonial Spanish, in contrast, would only mark possession once as in (6c) and (7c):

(6) a. *De* **mi** *mamá* *en* **su** *casa* *estoy* *yendo.*
   of my   mom   in   her   house I-am   going
 b. *Mamaa.pa*   *wasi.n.tam*   *liyaa*
   mom.of   house.3SG-POSS.LOC   go
 c. *Estoy yendo a la casa de mi mamá.*
   'I am going to my mom's house.'   [Clements 2009: 176–177]

(7) a. **su**   *perro*   **de**   *mi*   *padre*
   3SG-POSS   dog   of   1SG-POSS   father
 b. *tata.ja.**na***   *anu.**pa***
   father.1SG-POSS.GEN   dog.**3SG-POSS**
 c. *el perro **de** mi padre*
   'My father's dog'   [Cerrón-Palomino 2008: 121]

This feature could be the result of the adstrate languages' grammaticalized information on who precisely the possessive is referring to. Given that *su* is ambiguous in Spanish as it refers to several different persons (3SG, 2PL, 3PL, plus 2SG and 2PL in the deferential form), speakers of Quechuan and Aymara, which make this distinction in their L1, may feel a need to specify and thus add the information of who they are referring to at the end of the sentence.

In fact, there are reasons to assume that for this cultural reasons, possessives in general pose a challenge to speakers of Spanish in a Quechuan- and Aymara-speaking area. Also Dankel and Gutiérrez Maté (2020) propose that the complex pronominal system of Quechua with four grammatical persons has a repercussion on the use of *vuestro/a* in Cusco Spanish. *Vuestro/a*, as its corresponding second-person plural subject pronoun *vosotros*, is usually not found in American varieties of Spanish, where *su* (along with *ustedes*) is the common form. The authors assume that its use in Cusco Spanish is tied to a more deferential expression of respect. In the light of the specification of the person in BHS and also Andean Spanish, it is also possible that this structure is a strategy to compensate for a lack of specification in Spanish that has now been grammaticalized in the varieties spoken in the Andes.

A less apparent yet perhaps even more remarkable feature of Andean Spanish is its grammaticalized system of evidentiality. As outlined in Section 2, the obligatory marking of evidentiality is an areal feature found in both adstrate languages, and its repercussion in Spanish is undeniable. BHS marks reportative, non-testimonial information on the verb. Thus, when the speaker talks about information they did not have before and only heard from secondary sources, they will indicate this. The grammatical resource employed for this in BHS is the remote past, or pluperfect past (Mendoza 1991: 155–156). In other words, the use of the remote past in BHS does not only, or not at all, express that the proposition happened in the remote past, but that the content of the proposition is new, or recently inferred, information for the speaker. As shown in examples (8)–(9), the pluperfect form has thus in addition to its temporal reference to the remote past also the function of an indirect evidential:

(8) *Había   llegado   a   la   hora   convenida.*
    had   arrived   on   the hour   agreed
    '[I didn't know and just learned that] he arrived on time.'
    [Mendoza 1991: 156, my translation]

(9) *Le   había   hecho   comer   trigo.*
    ACC   had   made   eat   corn
    '[I didn't know and just learned that] she made him eat wheat.'
    [Sánchez 2004: 158, my extended translation]

In addition to this altered use of the remote past, Babel (2009) reports that the variety of Spanish spoken in the surroundings of Cochabamba, where Quechua is the strongest adstrate, has grammaticalized the use of different forms of *dice(n)* 's/he/they say' and *dizque* 'so-called, said' to indicate inferential and conjectural evidentiality. In statements like *no hace su tarea dice* 'she does not do her homework, it is said (s/he says)' (Babel 2009, my translation), in which *dice* is phonotactically integrated into the sentence and not a tag, *dice* is added to indicate that the speaker does not have full knowledge of an event, i.e. that the speaker has not witnessed it personally. Similar language-internal reportative elements were present in medieval Spanish, above all the form *dizque*, and their use in South America has been attested in colonial documents as early as the 17th century (Gutiérrez Maté 2016: 211). This grammaticalized use of *dice* is also common in Aymara-influenced BHS today, including the La Paz variety (Mendoza 1991: 156; Quartararo 2017: 185), and the importance of marking the origin of one's knowledge is likely to be a pattern that is part of this region's cultural ecology. Evidentiality marking can thus be taken as an indigenous feature that has been adopted into BHS.

To sum up, the widespread bilingualism and massive shift from Quechua and Aymara to Spanish during the 20th century increased the influence of these languages on Spanish over the past few decades (cf. Clements 2021). Apart from its lexical particularities, the most striking features of BHS are its grammaticalized expression of evidentiality, the use of double possessives, and the unusual presence of (S)OV sentence structure that have resulted from this particular linguistic and cultural context.

4 Adstrate features in Afro-Yungueño Spanish

AY is a contact variety of Spanish with a very unusual social history. Enslaved Africans slaves first arrived in the steep and lush Yungas valleys on the Eastern slopes of the Andes from the Portuguese slave trade in the course of the 18th century. They arrived over the River Plate route from Angola and Brazil, which entailed that AYS was influenced by African substrate languages (probably Kikongo and perhaps other Bantu languages) as well as some Portuguese. At the hacienda in the Yungas valleys, the slaves were in contact with their Spanish-speaking slave holders and the Aymara-speaking indigenous population of the region (Perez 2015: 324). The first group of slaves consisted of approximately twenty individuals and grew to over 100 until 1805. They worked on the coca plantations of a number of scattered haciendas and remained in social and geographical seclusion until the Agrarian Reform in 1953. Afterwards, the AY speech community opened up and came into close contact with other, standard-nearer varieties of Spanish, above all BHS, and accordingly, AYS experienced rapid changes and an approximation towards BHS during the second half of the 20th century (Perez 2014, 2015).

4.1 Aymara influences in the AYS phonology and lexicon

Phonetically, AYS is highly distinct from any Andean variety of Spanish, including BHS. First and foremost, while BHS shows a tendency to omit unstressed vowels, AYS has a strong preference for CV syllable structures. This includes the introduction of glides between two syllabic vowels, as in *hwidéyu* (from Spanish *fideo* [fi'ðeo] > [hwi'deju]), or the loss of word-final consonants. The only word-final consonant in AYS apart from those present in place names and ideophones is *-l*, as in *cocal* 'coca plantation'.[3] Furthermore, a highly pronounced form of *yeísmo* (the neutralization of <y> /j/ and <ll> /ʎ/ to /j/) produces forms that also merge the /lj/ cluster when the preceding vowel is high, as in *hwamía* 'family' (from Spanish *familia* [fa'milja] > [hwa'mia]). Other features of AYS are the raising of unstressed final mid-vowels /e/ to [i] and /o/ to [u], as in *mastuku* 'corpulent' (probably from Sp. *masto* 'male animal'). The most striking feature may be the use of multiple high intonational peaks and lengthened vowels (Lipski 2008: 74–80), as well as falsetto for the expression of contextual meaning and breathy voice for grammatical information, such as intensification (Perez and Zipp 2019). The combination of these features clearly distinguish AYS from BHS and, in fact, also from most other varieties of Spanish.

The main bulk of the AYS lexicon is clearly Spanish, and the Portuguese and African input is small: the former provided a number of lexical and grammatical items, such as *rir* (<Port. *rir*) 'to laugh', *kwasi* (<Port. *quase*) 'almost', and *ki laya* (<Port. *que laia*) 'how', whereas the latter only seems to have left traces of grammatical morphemes, such as the Kikongo pluralizer *ané* in *otene* 'you-PL', which is also found in Papiamentu (Perez 2015: 321). Most of the Aymara items are either verbs or nouns which refer to the immediate context of coca cultivation and life in the Yungas region. While also BHS uses many Aymara items, the proportion of them in AYS is particularly high, and the list presented in Table 1 only includes Aymaran and Quechuan lexemes that are exclusive to AYS and not shared with BHS. With the exception of <ch> representing the affricate [tʃ] and <y> representing [j], the transcribed items do not adhere to the Spanish orthography but to the more simplified IPA forms, and unless otherwise indicated, the stress is on the penultimate syllable.

---

3 Lipski (2008: 73) claims that also paragogic vowels are used to achieve CV structure. He gives two examples: *ele* 's/he' (instead of Spanish *él*) and *ayere* 'yesterday' (instead of Spanish *ayer*). I believe that these examples do not support a general pattern of paragogic vowels in AYS: while *ele* could be originally Portuguese words like *ayere*, appear in rural BHS rather than AYS and are thus not to be included into the phonology of AY. *Ayere* may, in fact, have been introduced into AYS by L2 speakers of Aymara (see below).

Table 1: Items of Aymara or Quechua origin in AYS.

AY word	Meaning	Aymara (or Quechua) etymon	Derivates and comments
akuyi	'act of chewing coca leaves'	akhulli 'break during work shift on coca plantation'	akuyiká 'to chew coca during a work break'
ampe	'please'	ampi (courtesy particle to ask for something)	
awaykiá	'abuse of someone among many'	awqaña 'to fight between (ethnic) groups'	
awicho	'grandmother'	awicha	(originally mamarande, mama 'mother' + Sp. grande 'big')
ayni	'reciprocal work exchange'	ayni 'reciprocity, mutual corresponence'	
kachi	'space covered with shale to dry the coca'	kachi	
chahmiá	'to collect the last leaves/fruit'	chaxmaña 'to harvest the leftovers of a field'	
chiriri	'a curly (black) person'	chhiri-iri 'curly-AGENTIVE'	The agentive suffix -iri is not productive in AYS.
chirmí	'to look from the corner of one's eyes'	(Quechua) ch'irmiy 'to close one's eyes'	
cho	interjection to call attention	chhuy	
chohtata	'black [sunburnt] coca'	origin unknown	
chúa	'tasteless, watery'	(Quechua) chuma	
chumi	'bush'	ch'umi	inchumá 'get covered by bush'
churko	'wavy, curly hair'	chhurkhu 'opaque'	
chuya	'one part of a couple'	ch'ulla 'uneven, unequal'	
kochaya	'eye booger, sleep'	q'uchalla (ADJ) 'full of eye booger' (q'ucha 'eye booger')	
koriá	'clean with a hoe'	origin unknown	perhaps from Sp. corear 'to do something in a group'
hantako	'cloth to sit on'	hant'aku	
haukaña	'stick to play the drum'	hauq'aña 'to whip'	
hay	emphatic marker, exclamation in response to a call	hay (particle used to respond to a call)	Shift of function from response to emphasis
huntucha	'heated food'	hunt'uchaña 'to heat up'	huntuchá 'to eat leftovers'

AY word	Meaning	Aymara (or Quechua) etymon	Derivates and comments
mamita	'indigenous woman'	mama 'madam' + Spanish female diminutive suffix -ita (this suffix is also present in Aymara as a Spanish loan)	Refers to indigenous women (with a negative connotation) only with the diminutive suffix; mama 'mother' is likely to be of Kikongo origin.
masi	'weeding'	masiña	masí 'to weed the coca field'
mato	'recently harvested coca leaves'	matu	
matwasi	'room to store the coca leaves'	matu + (Quechua) wari 'house'?	
minga	'wage worker on a coca field'	mink'a	
miyuchiá	'to bewitch'	milluchaña	
muchi	'rotten with worms'	muchi 'worm eggs'	
payá	'to harvest, collect'	pallaña 'to collect one by one'	
pihcho	'ball of coca leaves in mouth'	(Quechua) pihchu	
pusaña	'tube to blow the fire'	phusaña 'to blow, tube to blow the fire'	
puti	'plantain'	phuti	
kere	'fireplace'	qhiri	
kepe	'cloth to carry things on back'	q'ipi	
keyi	'angry at someone'	origin unknown	asé keyi 'to be angry'
kichí	'to collect coca leaves'	probably from qichiña 'to carry water'	
sarta	'act of proposing to a woman'	sart'aña 'to visit, to ask for a girl's hand'	
sayaña	'parcel of land'	sayaña	
seke	'row, pit'	siq'i 'with lines'	Also used for 'corn rows (hairstyle)'
tamata	'fermented urine'	t'amata	
tatito	'indigenous man'	tata 'sir' + Sp. masculin diminutive suffix -ito (this suffix is also present in Aymara as a Spanish loan)	This refers to indigenous men (with a negative connotation) only with the diminutive suffix.

AY word	Meaning	Aymara (or Quechua) etymon	Derivates and comments
tuna	'demolished'	t'una	
wacho	'a row of coca plants'	wachu 'plow, furrow'	
waracha	'bed'	waracha	
waska	'whipping'	(Quechua) waskha 'rope, chain'	waskiá 'to whip'
yapa	'small rodent [hunted for food]'	yapa 'supplement of food offered by a salesperson'	yapa in BHS has its original, not the AYS, meaning (the animal's name is sari in BHS)
yuyu	'green, not ripe'	perhaps yuyu 'type of plant found in swamps'	A different origin of this item is possible.

Most examples from this list, such as *akuyiká* 'to chew coca leaves', make clear that all lexical items are phonologically altered according to the AYS phonological repertoire: the aspirated and glottalized plosives are always plain, the postvelar consonants are velar, and the palatal lateral /λ/ is adapted according to the untypically strong *yeísmo* (merger of the lateral and the glide) characteristic of AYS. The high vowels /i/ and /u/ are usually adapted as /e/ and /o/ as in *kere* 'fireplace' like in BHS, and only occasionally get a raised realization in unstressed syllables. This lack of systematic vowel raising is rather surprising given the fact that AYS does occasionally raise unstressed mid-vowels to /i/ and /u/, respectively, which would make an integration of the original vowel more likely (cf. also Lipski 2008: 74, who observes that AYS vowel raising is different from the more regular pattern in Aymara-influenced L2 Spanish). Similarly, *mato* 'recently harvested coca leaves', for instance, is *matu* in Aymara, yet its AYS form is *mato* according to the Spanish pronunciation even though this word is likely to have been present in its original form in the context of the coca plantation. This suggests that these lexical items were not directly taken from L1 speakers of Aymara, but rather from a previously Hispanicized source, such as second-language speakers of Aymara who were present on the haciendas during the time when AYS emerged.

The semantics of this list corroborate this observation. Many of the Aymara items in AYS have a somewhat altered, though related, meaning when compared to the meaning of the Aymara etymon. *Kochaya* 'eye booger', for instance, is an adjective in Aymara meaning 'full of eye booger', yet AYS has adopted the adjective instead of the noun *q'ucha*. Also *yapa* 'small rodent' (instead of *sari*, which is the local name of this animal) as well as *yuyu* 'green, not ripe' (which refers to a plant, rather than a degree of ripeness), have undergone semantic shift. This suggests that they were not introduced by competent Aymara speakers, perhaps bilinguals, but rather by second-language speakers of Aymara.

In addition, a closer examination of the grammatical items in this list points in a similar direction. It reveals that no bound morphemes from Aymara's rich morphology were integrated into AYS, neither in their original form, nor in a calqued translation. This is in line with the general patterns of AYS, which show a tendency towards the use of independent morphemes rather than bound ones (cf. Perez and Zipp 2019). Accordingly, the derivational agentive suffix *-iri* 'person of', for example, is not productive in AYS and only exists in Aymara words that were adopted as a chunk (according to rules of matter borrowing, according to Matras and Sakel 2007), such as *chiriri* 'curly (i.e. black) person'. The only grammatical morphemes included into the AYS system are free grammatical morphemes, such as *ampe*, which is a deferential marker of respect or courtesy, and the interjections *cho* 'hey, oh!' and *hay* 'hey, what?' This inclusion of only independent Aymara items into AYS, added to the phonologically adapted forms and the semantic change, suggests that these elements themselves stem from an already Hispanicized variety of Aymara, probably the L2 Aymara spoken by the majordomos on the hacienda, who addressed the Aymara-speaking wage laborers in Aymara, or a variety of Spanish that made use of many Aymara items (Perez 2015: 315).

4.2 Aymara influence on AYS morphosyntax

When the two morphological systems are compared, AYS seems 'simpler' than BHS (or 'reduced', cf. Bakker 2008: 138; McWhorter 2011; Perez and Zipp 2019). There is no grammatical gender, meaning that apart from certain lexified formulaic forms, such as *santa virgen*, there is only one grammatical gender for nouns and pronouns, and adjectives usually only take the masculine form. Similarly, plurality on nouns is only marked by means of the free pre-nominal marker *lu*,[4] which can be combined with a possessive, as in *su lu wawa* 'her children'. The verb is marked for time usually by means of an invariant suffix without person agreement, while person is indicated with an overt subject pronoun, as in *yo tosta* 'I roast' instead of patrimonial Spanish *(yo) tuesto*.[5] Example (10) provides

---

[4] While *lu* has so far been assumed to stem from Spanish *los*, it may in fact rather be the Kikongo nominal classifier *lu* (Perez and Wall 2017).
[5] The lack of diphthongs in verbs is another feature of AYS that is likely to stem from a Portuguese substrate (Perez 2015: 330).

another example of how person gets marked by means of an overt subject pronoun rather than with a verbal ending as in Spanish, and example (11) further shows that an overt subject (i.e. *awasero* 'rain') may even be added in constructions that lack a subject in patrimonial Spanish. It also shows that regularized forms replaced the Standard Spanish irregular past tense forms (*ponyó* instead of *puso*). The added translations for BHS show that AYS codes less grammatical information morphologically than the lexifier.

(10) Nohotro yegó la pwente.
we arrive.PAST LOC bridge
Llegamos al puente. (BHS)
'We arrived at the bridge.'

(11) Awasero ponyó yobé.
rain(n) start.PAST rain(v)
Se puso a llover. (BHS)
'It started to rain.'

These patterns show that the AYS morphology generally prefers isolating structures, which is in sharp contrast with both BHS and Aymara. Example (10) further illustrates that only few prepositions exist in AYS, i.e. *kun* 'with' and *y* 'of', i.e. the Spanish possession-marking preposition *de* 'of'. The latter was phonologically reduced to a suffix-like -*i*, as in *kasay Juan* 'John's house', and it is attached to the possessum as in Spanish, which is different from the double possessives common in BHS. Thus, AYS shares basic structures of its lexifier language that are distinct from BHS. Furthermore, AYS has a clear preference for SVO word order that is common in Atlantic contact languages (Winford 2008: 21), and its pronominal system has forms that are not found in BHS, such as *oté* (<Sp. *usted*) 'you' (*bo* <Port. *você* or <Sp. *vos* may also appear; Perez 2015: 321):

(12) a. yo 'I' nohotro 'we'
oté 'you' otene 'you-PL'
ele 's/he', eyu 'they'
b. yo 'I' nosotros 'we'
tú/vos 'you' ustedes 'you-PL'
él/ella 's/he', elos/ellas 'they'

These features are thus different from both BHS and Aymara. The most striking difference, however, is its isolating morphology, which suggests a possible creole or creoloid status of AYS (Lipski 2008: 196; Perez 2015; Perez and Zipp 2019; for more details on the typological features setting AYS apart from other post-colonial dialects of Spanish, cf. Perez et al. 2017).

As seen in Section 3, one of the most characteristic areal features of the languages of the Central Andes is the marking of evidentiality, a discourse-related feature that has become part of the cultural space and was hence also grammaticalized in BHS. Unlike BHS, however, the reduced inflectional morphology of AYS does not use the remote past to mark non-testimonial, reportative evidentiality. In fact, there are generally no patrimonial Spanish analytic past tense verb forms combined with a conjugated auxiliary verb, and past tense is marked on the basis of a synthetic form unmarked for person.

In line with the use of independent morphemes in AYS, there is, however, an independent marker that represents the non-testimonial origin of a piece of information: *disi* 's/he says', and particularly the phonetically altered form *dihi*. Examples (13)–(15) are taken from two different speakers of AYS, and most of their use of *dici/dihi* indicates non-involvement or hearsay-knowledge:

(13) Nway   komo   dentrá dihi.
     there-is-not how   go-in   EVID
     'There doesn't seem to be a way to get in.'

(14) Nohotro yegó   abaho San Joaquín andi   ehe
     we   arrive.PAST down   San Joaquín where DET
     lu   tiyito   disi.
     PL   uncle.DIM   EVID
     'We arrived in San Joaquín where apparently the elderly black men live.'

(15) Lu   moso   nomá disi ke tyene ke bibí **dihi** Mururata.
     PL   black-people only QUOT   have-to   live EVID   Mururata
     'They say that allegedly only black people should live in Mururata.'

These examples show that *dici/dihi* is a marker of distance or non-involvement similar to what is found in BHS (Quartararo 2017; cf. Babel 2009 for Quechua-influenced Spanish). It is used to indicate that the speakers do not know from personal experience what they are talking about. It is important to note that phrase-final *dihi* is phonotactically integrated into the utterance and often also appears in post-verbal position where *disi* as a sentence-final discourse marker would not appear. This suggests that it is grammaticalized beyond being an independent discourse marker. Phrase-initial and rather standard-like *disi ke* in (15), by contrast, can be understood as introducing indirect speech, rather than a non-testimonial reportative. This evidential use of post-verbal, often phrase-final, *disi* as an indicator of the source of information shows that the marking of evidentiality has also been integrated into AYS, and it is likely to stem from Aymara, or L2 Aymara. Its morphosyntactic properties as an independent post-verbal or sentence-final marker may have made *disi/dihi* easier to integrate into AYS than the morphologically less isolating constructions of the remote past.

In a nutshell, Aymara seems to have had little grammatical impact on AYS, as only certain free grammatical morphemes, such as the marker of respect and courtesy *ampe* and the calqued, i.e. translated, marker of non-testimonial evidentiality *dici* were integrated into the rather isolating morphology of AYS. The most substantial Aymara contribution to AYS is thus found on the lexical level, where, in addition to lexemes referring to the immediate context, also discourse-related and cultural elements were integrated. In other words, AYS did adopt cultural elements that belong to the Central Andean space while its isolating morphology differentiates AYS substantially from its linguistic surroundings from a typological perspective. The same applies to AYS phonology, whose preference for open syllables and reduced number of consonants differ from BHS and Aymara (Perez and Zipp 2019). A classification of AYS as an Andean variety is therefore only to a limited extent applicable: geographically yes, areally no.

5 Discussion

The foregoing discussion has shown that BHS is a postcolonial variety of Spanish that is deeply entrenched with its sociocultural and linguistic context. The considerable influence of Aymara and Quechua on BHS are likely to be the result of the prolonged bilingualism in the region during more than four centuries, as the main proportion of the population was dominant in an indigenous language until the 20th century (Clements 2021). The influence of these languages on Spanish was substantial in that it altered certain syntactic structures, such as the highly unusual SOV sentence structure, the appearance of double possessives, or the grammaticalized marking of evidentiality. Furthermore, a distinction seems to be possible between features that have stabilized in BHS as an L1 and varieties that are L2 varieties having emerged in contexts of limited access to formal education. For example, while the former maintain distinctions and agreement patterns typical of patrimonial Spanish, such as the five-vowel system or number and gender agreement, the latter display a higher degree of variation in the areas of phonology and grammar. Overall, it has become clear that the sustained and intense contact with Aymara has had a strong effect on the grammar of BHS.

AYS, by contrast, is typologically rather foreign to this linguistic area. It has preserved a distinct phonological system, its syntactic SVO structure, as well as an isolating morphology, which stands in stark contrast with the indigenous adstrates and even the superstrate. The only aspects taken from the indigenous languages are lexical items as well as free grammatical morphemes, which seem indispensible when speakers seek to survive in a particular social context. In this case, the need of expressing respect, politeness, and truthfulness that is particular to this specific cultural context was instrumental. Thus, while cultural aspects have certainly been adopted, most grammatical ones have not. Even evidentiality, a strong areal feature that has been integrated into the morphosyntax of BHS, is only expressed by means of a free morpheme instead of verbal inflection.

The relevance of social factors in the evolution of contact languages should never be underestimated, as they may determine the use or avoidance of certain features (cf. Jourdan 2008). The reasons for this limited integration of adstrate features in AYS can be manifold. In the first place, the limited impact of Aymara corroborates the social and geographic isolation in which the AYS speech community existed for over two centuries. Aymara lexical items seem to have been Hispanicized phonologically before they were integrated into the AYS lexicon, which is likely to have happened via the speech of the slave overseers and hacienda owners, who were said to have spoken Aymara, or an L2 variety thereof (Perez 2015: 315). This piece of information may thus allow us insights into language practices on the coca-producing haciendas during the 18th century.

Also, and in sharp contrast to the substantial impact of Aymara on BHS, the lack of Aymara influence on the grammar of AYS is conspicuous. Given that Afro-Bolivians formed a small community that was surrounded by a majority of Aymara speakers, demographic dominance does not seem to correlate with linguistic impact. Rather, the lack of adstrate features in AYS suggests that there was a social distance between speakers of different ethnic groups, which caused AYS speakers to resist linguistic dominance or influence. This in turn corroborates that the two groups were, in fact, not only ethnically but also socially separate during colonial times and until the opening of the community in the 1950s. This hypothesis is reinforced by the fact that the African slaves and the indigenous wage laborers were kept in separate quarters on the haciendas, i.e. they lived in different villages and did not have their work breaks at the same time in the plantation, in order to avoid conspiracies or riots on the hacienda (Crespo 1995 [1977]: 125). In fact, there were nearly no Aymara-AYS bilinguals, and a certain animosity between the indigenous and the African-descendant populations persists until today (Perez 2015: 315). Depreciative designations in AYS, such as *indio* and *tatito* 'indigenous man', and *india* and *mamita* 'indigenous woman' attest to these rather negative attitudes. A similarly conspicuous absence of indigenous structures was observed by Kouwenberg (2013), who found that Berbice Dutch, a Dutch-based creole spoken in Dutch Guiana, experienced limited impact from Arawak. She concludes that "neither the presence in substantial numbers of particular groups of speakers nor their sustained contact with superstrate speakers necessarily determine their roles in linguistic creolization" (Kouwenberg 2013: 14). This suggests that creolization is a rather unpredictable process that is determined by often unexpected extra-linguistic factors, as high speaker numbers of the adstrate language, for instance, as well as intense physical and linguistic contact may not be enough to ensure the adoption of adstrate features in a contact variety. The limited impact of first-language Aymara on AYS undermines such a hypothesis, and suggests that attitudinal factors and issues of ethnic and linguistic identity play an important role as well (cf. Schreier 2009). In other words, motivation and language ideologies may trump demographic factors in the emergence of new languages (cf. Parkvall 2000: 195), and the importance of contextual factors should not be underestimated (Jourdan 2008).

From an areal and typological perspective, the AYS data presented here provide further evidence to see evidentiality as an important areal feature (cf. Babel 2009: 496; Adelaar 2012: 612) of the region. Significantly, it is the only feature that has also been adopted by this small enclave community. This is likely to be the result of cultural practices that are important beyond ethnic boundaries, which corroborates the strong impact cultural practices, can have on grammatical systems. Other features, such as double possessives were not adopted by this enclave variety. Despite its low number of speakers, the unique social history of AYS thus allows us to shed new light on the sociolinguistic history and the relevance of ecological factors in the transmission of features in the Central Andes.

Abbreviations

ACC	accusative
COP	copula
DECL	declarative
DET	determiner
EVID	evidentiality
GEN	genitive
LOC	locative
NOM	nominative
PAST	past tense
POSS	possessive
PL	plural
QUOT	quotative
SG	singular
TOP	topic

References

Adelaar, Willem F. H. 1986. La relación quechua-aru: Perspectivas para la separación del léxico. *Revista Andina* 4(2). 379–426.

Adelaar, Willem F. H. 2012. Languages of the Middle Andes in areal-typological perspective: Emphasis on Quechuan and Aymaran. In Lyle Campbell & Verónica Grondona (eds.), *The indigenous languages of South America. A comprehensive guide*, 575–624. Berlin & Boston: De Gruyter Mouton.

Adelaar, Willem F. H. & Pieter Muysken. 2004. *The languages of the Andes*. Cambridge: Cambridge University Press.

Aikhenvald, Alexandra Y. 2004. *Evidentiality*. Oxford: Oxford University Press.

Alvar, Manuel. 2000. *Manual de dialectología hispánica. El español de América*. Barcelona: Ariel.

Andrien, Kenneth. 2011. The Bourbon reforms. In Paul Heggarty & Adrian J. Pearce (eds.), *History and language in the Andes*, 113–133. New York: Palgrave Macmillan.

Angola, Juan. 2008. *Comunidad Dorado Chico. Nuestra Historia*. La Paz: Comunidad Dorado Chico, Traditions pour Demain.

Apaza Apaza, Ignacio. 2008. *Estructura metafórica del tiempo en el idioma aymara*. La Paz: Instituto de Estudios Bolivianos.

Babel, Anna M. 2009. Dizque, evidentiality, and stance in Valley Spanish. *Language in Society* 38. 487–511.

Bakker, Peter. 2008. Pidgins versus creoles versus Pidgincreoles. In Silvia Kouwenberg & John Victor Singler (eds.), *The handbook of Pidgin and Creole studies*, 130–157. Oxford: Blackwell.

Catalán, Diego. 1989. *El español. Orígenes de su diversidad*. Madrid: Paraninfo.

Cerrón-Palomino, Rodolfo. 2003. *El castellano andino: aspectos sociolingüísticos, pedagógicos y gramaticales*. Lima: Fondo Editorial.

Cerrón-Palomino, Rodolfo. 2008. *Quechumara. Estructuras paralelas del quechua y del aimara*. La Paz: Plural Editores.

Clements, J. Clancy 2009. *The linguistic legacy of Spanish and Portuguese: Colonial expansion and language change*. Cambridge: Cambridge University Press.

Clements, J. Clancy. 2021. Some (unintended) consequences of Colonization: The rise of Spanish as a global language. In Danae Perez, Daniel Schreier, Marianne Hundt & Johannes Kabatek (eds.), *English and Spanish: World languages in interaction*. Cambridge: Cambridge University Press.

Crespo, Alberto. 1995 [1977]. *Esclavos negros en Bolivia*, 2nd ed. La Paz: Editorial Juventud.

Dankel, Philipp & Miguel Gutiérrez Maté. 2020. Vuestra atención, por favor ('your attention please'). Some remarks on the usage and history of plural vuestro/a in Cusco Spanish. In Martin Hummel & Célia dos Santos Lopes (eds.), *Address in Portuguese and Spanish. Studies in diachrony and diachronic reconstruction*, 317–359. Berlin & Boston: De Gruyter Mouton.

Escobar, Anna María. 2011. Spanish in contact with Quechua. In Manuel Díaz-Campos (ed.), *The handbook of Hispanic sociolinguistics*, 323–352. London: Blackwell.

Evans, Nicholas. 2010. *Dying words. Endangered languages and what they have to tell us*. Oxford: Wiley Blackwell.

Gutiérrez Maté, Miguel. 2016. Reconstructing the linguistic history of palenques. On the nature and relevance of colonial documents. In Armin Schwegler, John McWhorter, & Liane Ströbel (eds.), *The Iberian challenge. Creole languages beyond the plantation setting*, 205–229. Frankfurt & Madrid: Vervuert & Iberoamericana.

Hardman, Martha J. 1988. Jaqi Aru: La lengua humana. In Xavier Albó (ed.), *Raíces de América. El mundo aymara*, 155–216. Madrid: Alianza América & UNESCO.

Hardman, Martha J. 2001. *Aymara*. München: Lincom.

Hualde, José Ignacio. 2012. Stress and rhythm. In José Ignacio Hualde, Antxon Olarrea & Erin O'Rourke (eds.), *The handbook of Hispanic linguistics*, 153–171. Malden & Oxford: Blackwell.

Instituto Nacional de Estadística de Bolivia. http://wd.ine.gob.bo/. (checked 04/19/2020)

Itier, César. 2011. What was the lengua general of colonial Peru? In Paul Heggarty & Adrian J. Pearce (eds.), *History and language in the Andes*, 63–85. New York: Palgrave Macmillan.

Jourdan, Christine. 2008. The cultural in Pidgin genesis. In Silvia Kouwenberg & John V. Singler (eds.), *The handbook of Pidgin and Creole studies*, 359–381. London: Wiley Blackwell.

Klee, Carol A. 1996. The Spanish of the Peruvian Andes. The influence of Quechua on Spanish language structure. In Ana Roca & John B. Jensen (eds.), *Spanish in contact. Issues in bilingualism*, 73–92. Somerville: Cascadilla.

Kouwenberg, Silvia. 2013. The historical context of creole language emergence in Dutch Guiana. *Revue Belge de Philologie et d'Histoire* 91(3). 695–711.

Lapesa, Rafael. 1980. *Historia de la lengua española*, 9th edn. Madrid: Gredos.

Laprade, Richard. 1981. Some cases of Aimara influence on La Paz Spanish. In Martha James Hardman (ed.), *Aymara language in its social and cultural context*, 207–227. Gainesville: University Presses of Florida.

Lipski, John. 2007. *El español de América*, 5th edn. Madrid: Cátedra.

Lipski, John. 2008. *Afro-Bolivian Spanish*. Frankfurt & Madrid: Vervuert & Iberoamericana.

Lorenzino, Gerardo, Alexandra Alvarez, Enrique Obediente & Germán de Granda. 1998. El español caribeño: antecedentes sociohistóricos y lingüísticos. In Matthias Perl & Armin Schwegler (eds.), *América negra: panorámica actual de los estudios lingüísticos sobre variedades hispanas, portuguesas y criollas*, 25–69. Frankfurt: Vervuert.

Matras, Yaron & Jeanette Sakel. 2007. *Grammatical borrowing in cross-linguistic perspective*. Berlin & New York: De Gruyter.

McWhorter, John. 2011. *Linguistic simplicity and complexity. Why do languages undress?* Berlin & Boston: De Gruyter Mouton.

Mendoza, José G. 1991. *El castellano hablado en La Paz. Sintaxis divergente*. La Paz: Talleres Gráficos de la Facultad de Humanidades y Ciencias de la Educación.

Olarrea, Antxon. 2012. Word order and information structure. In José Ignacio Hualde, Antxon Olarrea & Erin O'Rourke (eds.), *The handbook of Hispanic linguistics*, 603–628. London: Blackwell.

Parkvall, Mikael. 2000. Reassessing the role of demographics in language restructuring. In Ingrid Neumann-Holzschuh & Edgar W. Schneider (eds.), *Degrees of restructuring in creole languages*, 185–213. Amsterdam & Philadelphia: John Benjamins.

Penny, Ralph. 2004. *Gramática histórica del español*. Barcelona: Ariel.

Perez, Danae. 2014. Contact languages in contact. On the challenges of documenting Afro-Yungueño Spanish. *Workshop on Afro-Latin Varieties*, University of Aarhus, December 4–6.

Perez, Danae. 2015. Traces of Portuguese in Afro-Yungueño Spanish? *Journal of Pidgin and Creole Languages* 30(2). 307–343.

Perez, Danae & Albert Wall. 2017. Bareness and nominal semantics in Afro-Yungueño Spanish. Annual meeting of the *Societas Linguistica Europaea*, University of Zurich, September 10–13.

Perez, Danae & Lena Zipp. 2019. On the relevance of voice quality in contact varieties. Non-modal phonation type in Afro-Yungueño Spanish. *Language Ecology* 3(1). 3–27.

Perez, Danae, Sandro Sessarego & Eeva Sippola. 2017. Afro-Hispanic varieties compared. New light from phylogeny. In Peter Bakker, Fynn Borchsenius, Carsten Levisen & Eeva Sippola (eds.), *Creole languages – Phylogenetic approaches*, 269–291. Amsterdam & Philadelphia: John Benjamins.

Pöll, Bernhard. 2021. Spanish today. Pluricentricity and codification. In Danae Perez, Daniel Schreier, Marianne Hundt & Johannes Kabatek (eds.), *English and Spanish: World languages in interaction*. Cambridge: Cambridge University Press.

Quartararo, Geraldine. 2017. *Evidencialidad indirecta en aimara y en el español de La Paz. Un estudio semántico-pragmático de textos orales*. Stockholm: University of Stockholm unpublished doctoral dissertation.

Sánchez, Liliana. 2004. Functional convergence in the tense, evidentiality, and aspectual systems of Quechua Spanish bilinguals. *Language and Cognition* 7. 147–162.

Schreier, Daniel. 2009. Language in isolation, and its implications for variation and change. *Blackwell Language and Linguistics Compass* 3. 682–699.

Winford, Donald. 2008. Atlantic creole Syntax. In Silvia Kouwenberg & John Victor Singler (eds.), *The handbook of Pidgin and Creole studies*, 19–47. Malden and Oxford: Blackwell.

Yakpo, Kofi. 2017. Towards a model of contact and change in the English-lexifier Creoles of Africa and the Caribbean. *English World-Wide* 38. 50–76.

Ana Paulla Braga Mattos
The Afro-Brazilian community Kalunga: Linguistic and sociohistorical perspectives

Abstract: This study analyzes the variety of Portuguese spoken in Kalunga, an Afro-Brazilian community located in the state of Goiás, Brazil. It investigates the sociohistorical background of this community and the linguistic situation that we encounter in Kalunga today. Based on a corpus of recordings of spoken language, it describes features of the vernacular of the Kalunga community and provides an account of the sociolinguistic and sociohistorical situation of the Kalunga communities. The data show that Kalunga Portuguese shares many linguistic and sociohistorical features with other Afro-Brazilian varieties. These are marginalized varieties socially and linguistically far removed from the so-called Standard Brazilian Portuguese varieties. This study thus contributes to the linguistic and cultural documentation of the Kalunga community of Goiás in particular, and to the studies on Brazilian Portuguese varieties and language contact in general.

Keywords: Kalunga, Afro-Brazilian Portuguese, Afro-Brazilian community, grammar, sociolinguistics, fieldwork

1 Introduction

This chapter focuses on the variety of Portuguese spoken in Kalunga, an Afro-Brazilian community located in the state of Goiás, Brazil. Kalunga is one out of a total of 2,958 recognized *quilombola* communities in Brazil, and it is recognized by the Brazilian government as the biggest Brazilian *remanescente quilombola* 'remnant maroon community'. It consists of approximately 4,200 people (Almeida 2015: 50), who live in villages spread over an area of 2,632 km^2, and some of these villages are culturally and geographically isolated. As many other Afro-descendants in rural communities, the majority of the elderly people in Kalunga are illiterate and the young inhabitants have, usually, a low level of formal education. In the rich diversity of linguistic and cultural groups in Brazil, the Kalunga rural community is a prototypical example of a *remanescente quilombola*, and it represents a postcolonial legacy from colonial structures in Brazil.

Ana Paulla Braga Mattos, Aarhus University, Jens Chr. Skous Vej 7, bygning 1467 – 323, 8000 Aarhus C, Denmark, E-Mail: mattos@cas.au.dk

Research on the Kalunga's sociohistorical configuration is highly relevant for both social and linguistic studies. From a social perspective, linguistic and sociohistorical investigations help communities like Kalunga to be recognized as minority groups, and this recognition gives the communities access to governmental support, as established by Brazilian laws (Brazilian Federal Constitution 1988: art. 68; Brazilian Presidential Decree 7.387 2010).[1] In addition, it may increase public awareness about the multilingual contexts in Brazil. From a linguistic perspective, it is important to consider that the level of isolation in which Kalunga people have lived has led to the preservation and independent evolution of cultural and linguistic features that are not present in other (rural) communities.

In the last few decades, the varieties spoken by Afro-descendants in Brazil have been documented and analyzed (see, e.g. Lucchesi et al. 2009; Petter and Oliveira 2011; Byrd 2012; Vogt and Fry 2013 [1996]). However, although Kalunga land tenure, land rights, identity, health and fauna and flora have been studied[2], the language spoken by the community had not until recently been brought to the attention of linguists (see Mattos 2019 for a study on Kalunga Portuguese language, Mattos 2020 for a study on negation in Kalunga Portuguese and Mattos and Oliveira 2020 for a comparative study between Kalunga Portuguese and other Portuguese varieties). This paper examines both linguistic and sociohistorical aspects of the variety of Portuguese spoken by the Kalunga community. The main goals are to show linguistic features found in Kalunga Portuguese and to place it on a dialectal continuum of postcolonial Brazilian Portuguese varieties.

This paper is organized as follows: Section 2 gives an overview of the Brazilian varieties of Portuguese. The materials and methods are presented in Section 3. Section 4 discusses the sociohistorical background of the community. Section 5 presents the current sociolinguistic situation of Kalunga and perceptions and attitudes towards the varieties. The analysis of grammatical features follows in Section 6, covering observations about the phonological processes, restructur-

---

1 In the Brazilian Constitution, Article 68 (*Art. 68 Ato das disposições constitucionais transitórias*) ensures Afro-descendants the land titles of *quilombola* community areas. In 2010, the Brazilian government published Decree 7.387 (Brazilian Presidential Decree 7387 2010), which established the National Inventory of Linguistic Diversity, which explicitly includes the speech varieties of *quilombo* communities. Another policy adopted by the Brazilian government towards Afro-descendants and their legacy is the approval of the Brazilian Federal Law 10.639 of January 9th, 2003 (Brazilian Federal Law 10.639/03 2003). This law states that all schools must teach Afro-Brazilian culture and history.
2 For published and unpublished academic works on Kalunga community, please access https://odonto.ufg.br/n/45140-trabalhos-academicos-sobre-a-comunidade-kalunga (checked 16/06/20).

ing of the verb phrase, negation, possessive constructions, peculiarities of the noun phrase, and prepositions. Sections 7 and 8 cover the discussion and the conclusions.

2 Brazilian Portuguese varieties

Scholars agree on the existence of a number of dialectal varieties in the Portuguese spoken in Brazil. Bortoni-Ricardo (1985), Mello (1996) and Petter (2008) suggest that Brazilian Portuguese (BP) should be referred to with the concept of a continuum of dialects, based on studies on different varieties of Portuguese spoken in the country. These show the results of different levels of restructuring. According to Mello (1996: 18), Brazilian Vernacular Portuguese (BVP) "refers in reality to a continuum of dialects", in which there are varieties that diverge from Standard Brazilian Portuguese (SBP) to a greater or lesser extent. She claims that the varieties spoken in some Afro-Brazilian communities, which are also included in the BVP spectrum, are the dialects that diverge most from SBP.

Figure 1 shows an adapted version of a dialectal continuum of Brazilian Portuguese varieties proposed by Campos (2014: 58). It includes Afro-Indigenous Brazilian Portuguese (Oliveira et al. 2015) together with Afro-Brazilian Portuguese (henceforth ABP, Lucchesi et al. 2009) and Indigenous Portuguese (Maher 1998), all on the left side of the continuum, being the varieties farthest removed from SBP to the right. In-between these extremes, we also find rural varieties of Portuguese and non-standard urban and regional forms of speech.

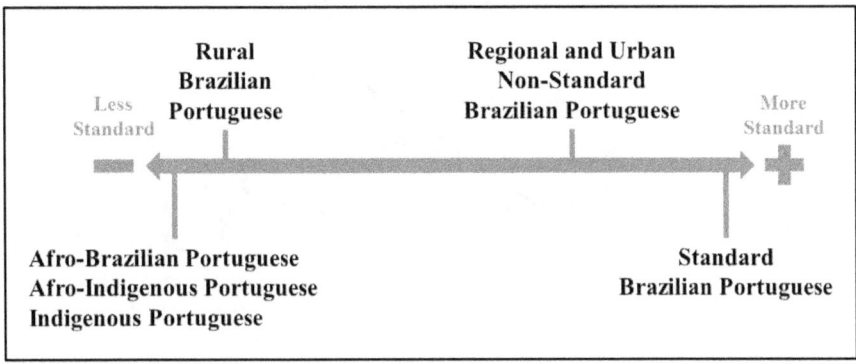

Figure 1: Dialectal continuum of BP varieties (based on Campos 2014: 182).

In this paper, I use the term BVP to refer to the varieties found in rural areas whose speakers are usually illiterate or near-illiterate, as well as varieties of urban areas whose speakers have a low level of formal education. SBP refers to the varieties spoken in urban areas by educated speakers in formal contexts, while ABP refers to forms of speech of four African-descendant communities in Bahia (Lucchesi et al. 2009: 30–33). BP is used to refer to all the varieties spoken in Brazil (for a discussion of the terms, see, e.g., Mello 1996: 18).

3 Sociohistorical context

The following maps show the geographical position of Kalunga in relation to the state of Goiás and Brazil (Map 1), and the Kalunga community (Map 2). It is important to point out that the Kalunga area is very large and that it consists of many villages. The Kalunga site is part of three municipalities: Cavalcante, Monte Alegre, and Teresina de Goiás. The two villages I visited, Vão de Almas and Vão do Moleque, are shown in Map 2.

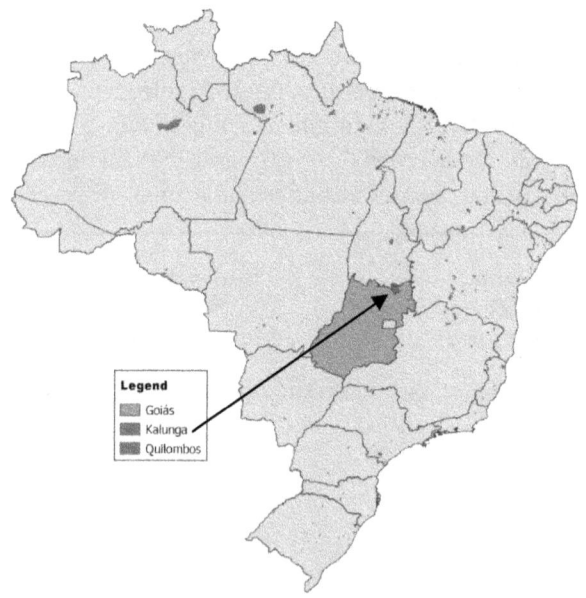

Map 1: Location of the Kalunga historical site in Goiás, Brazil.

Map 2: Kalunga (Vão de Almas and Vão do Moleque villages) and Paranã River.

The African diaspora in Brazil goes back to 1538 (Mattoso 2003). The state of Goiás, however, became home to a number of African-descendants in the early 18th century, when slaves were sent to work in the gold mines during the gold rush. During the first half of the 18th century, more than half of the population of Goiás was enslaved, and a large number of *quilombos* 'maroon slave communities' were established in Goiás (Palacin 1994; Silva 2001). Palacin (1994: 79) in fact claims that in the 18th century "there was not a village in Goiás without the shadow of a *quilombo*".

After 1770, due to the socioeconomic conditions of the region, the number of slaves sent to Goiás decreased, and in 1808, African slaves no longer constituted the majority of the population. The Goiás population became mostly mixed – i.e., the children of a black parent (usually the mother) and a white parent (usually the father) –, as well as free and freed blacks. It is also important to point out that many different indigenous groups lived in Goiás, especially speakers of *Jê* languages (Bertran 2011). They had established contacts with the *Bandeirantes* in the 17th and 18th centuries (Araújo 2014), i.e., Europeans or descendants of Europeans who went to the innermost areas of the country to enslave indigenous peoples and to search for precious metals and stones.

There is no consensus among researchers about the formation process of the Kalunga community. Some scholars believe that the community originates from runaway slaves, while others argue against this hypothesis. Baiocchi (1999) argues that there were settlements established in Cavalcante and Monte Alegre from 1740 to 1769 to explore the possibilities of gold mining. Slaves escaped from these mines and formed *quilombos* in the surrounding valleys and hills, and according to this author, Kalunga communities would originate from these *quilombos*. Brito Neto (2002), by contrast, argues that there is no historical register of a large *quilombo* in the northeast of Goiás, i.e., in the Kalunga territory. There is only one mention of a *quilombo* in a much smaller area near the Paranã River in the 18th century. According to Brito Neto (2002), the Kalunga community was probably formed by groups of black families that had obtained their freedom and who continued to live close to the mines. Araújo (2014: 14–15), finally, argues that Kalunga is a community that started with runaway slaves or freed-workers that looked for a refuge. He bases this argument on the fact that there were gold mines in Cavalcante and Monte Alegre (see Map 2). Therefore a large number of enslaved people were brought to Goiás, and afterwards many of them ended up in the rural areas close to the mines. He claims that Kalunga's ancestors spread over the Paranã valley and lived in small groups. The bases of their lives were subsistence culture and preservation of particular cultural characteristics. Velloso (2007) proposes a third hypothesis which combines aspects of both theories presented above. He claims that only a few areas of Kalunga were *quilombos* at some point, as for instance the area of Vão de Almas, whereas other territorial areas were actually formed by a number of farms. After the gold rush in Goiás towards the end of the 18th century, it was very common that the poor, mostly black people would start agricultural activities and form *quilombos* or collective farms.

Due to this uncertainty, some scholars question whether the term *remanescente quilombola* 'quilombo remnant' is adequate and whether it can be applied to characterize all the Kalunga villages spread over an area of ca. 253 thousand hectares. Marinho (2008), in her work on Kalunga identity and territory, claims that the use of the name *Kalunga* as a group that shares an identity and its recognition as a *quilombo* community may be motivated by the need to solve land right problems and not so much by the need to affirm themselves as a historical and cultural group. In fact, the anthropologist Mari de Nasaré Baiocchi was the one to name all the villages jointly *Kalunga* (Baiocchi 2001: 71–75). Based on a study of the surnames of the dwellers, interviews, and historical documents, Baiocchi (1991) concludes that the families in the farms spread over the Kalunga area today were part of the same family groups in the beginning, i.e., they were relatives. Only in 1991 did the government of Goiás recognize the area as a Cultural Heritage asset and give the Kalunga the right of the territories. The Kalunga community was recognized by *Fundação Cultural Palmares*[3] as a *quilombo* community on April 19th, 2005.

4 Materials and methods

My analysis is based on a corpus of spoken data collected among the eldest speakers in two villages in the Kalunga community. I conducted ethnographic fieldwork and sociolinguistic interviews in the two most isolated villages – identified according to studies based on historical documents and interviews (Marinho 2008: 74) and local information – in the community: Vão de Almas and Vão do Moleque. The corpus consists of 28 hours of speech and ethnographic data. I use as main guidelines for grammatical description Basic Linguistic Theory (Dixon 2009a, b), while the comparative analysis takes into account previous studies on Afro-Brazilian communities and other Brazilian Portuguese varieties (e.g., Mello 1996; Lucchesi et al. 2009; Petter and Oliveira 2011; Byrd 2012).

I interviewed 21 speakers (12 men and 9 women) ranging in age from 51 to 98 years. Each interview lasted between 30 minutes and one hour, and all interviews were recorded. The interviewees were encouraged to talk as much as they wanted and about topics of their choice, stimulated by questions from the interviewer. The topics were about their life experiences like marriage(s), health problems, danger of death, stories involving poisonous animals, religious parties, just to mention a few. The topic list was inspired by *Projeto Vertentes* (Lucchesi et al. 2009: 160–161), and the sociolinguistic questionnaire was inspired by the project on the ethnolinguistic survey on the Afro-Brazilian communities in Pará and Minas Gerais (Petter and Oliveira 2011). Both the topic list and the questionnaire were very suitable and applicable to the Kalunga's social, economic, and environmental reality.

---

[3] *Fundação Cultural Palmares* 'Palmares Cultural Foundation' is a governmental organization connected to the Ministry of Culture in Brazil.

Spending time in this community and getting into closer contact with the villagers by means of interviews, a semi-structured questionnaire, and observations was a good way to achieve the goals of collecting cultural and linguistic data and extracting the vernacular (Labov 1972; Meyerhoff et al. 2012). I attempted at interviewing elderly people from the most remote villages who have rarely left the community, in order to get data from speakers who are most likely to preserve the traces of language contact that may be present in Kalunga.

To guarantee the consultants' anonymity, while making sure that the reader is aware of the relevant sociolinguistic background information about the interviewees, I use the following codes to identify the village, the gender, and the age of the consultants.
– **Village:** Vão de Almas (A) or Vão do Moleque (M);
– **Gender:** Female (F) or Male (M);
– **Age:** two digits corresponding to the participant's age.

For example, the code AF74 corresponds to a 74-year-old (74) female (F) consultant from *Vão de Almas* (A). The names used in the examples and in interview extracts are fictitious.

5 Sociolinguistic situation

5.1 Kalunga today

As mentioned previously, Kalunga is a large rural community formed by many villages, and it is legally recognized as a *quilombo* remnant community. Within the large Kalunga area, there are clear differences in lifestyle, house construction, and infrastructure between the villages. Vão de Almas and Vão do Moleque are geographically and socially more isolated than the others because of the lack of electricity[4] and the fact that their location is more difficult to access. Therefore they preserve a more traditional way of life when compared to the surrounding region. The adobe houses with straw roofs, subsistence farming, and certain aspects of everyday life reflect a way of life that is rather uncommon nowadays, even when compared to the rural areas around the community. This includes preparing meals using custom-made clay ovens, washing clothes and doing the dishes in the river, bathing in the river before the night-

---

[4] In December 2017, some houses had recently been connected to the electrical grid. Some other houses were on the way to be connected.

fall, and staying around an oil or kerosene lamp to tell stories instead of watching television. Furthermore, there is no formal health care infrastructure in the Kalunga villages, and despite some basic governmental support, such as health agents, the people have to travel to the nearby cities to be treated, and the community members therefore mostly use home remedies. In fact, folk medicine and the use of plants in rituals to cure diseases are typical of Afro-Brazilian and other minority communities in Brazil (e.g., Camargo 1998; Medeiros Costa Neto 2000; Coelho-Ferreira 2009; Santos Sales et al. 2009).

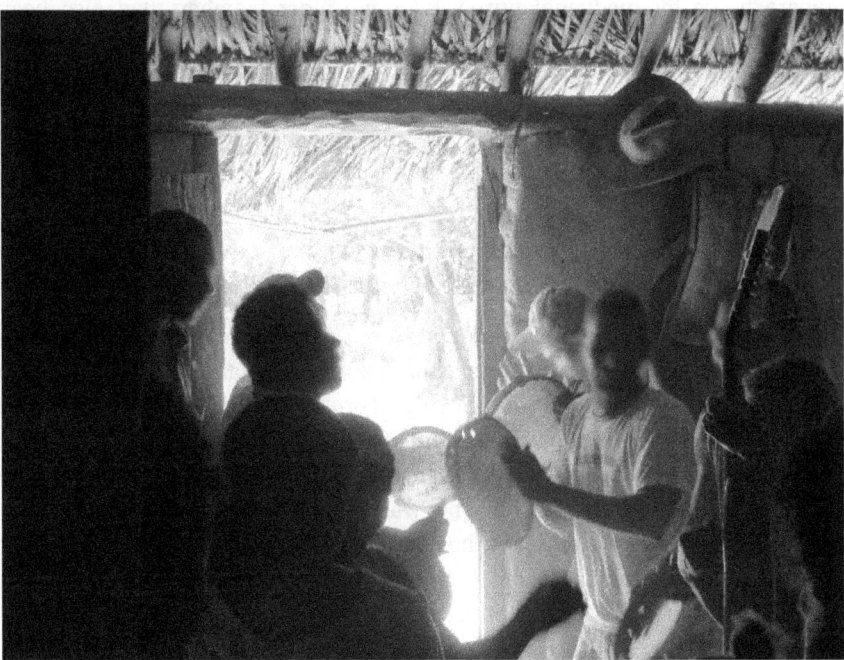

Figure 2: Folia dos Reis celebration in Vão de Almas (Field Picture 2014).

Traditions associated with their past are very vivid in cultural practices in Kalunga. In Vão de Almas community, for instance, members take very seriously the celebration of *Folia dos Reis*, which is a worship celebration for *Santo Reis* (based on the Three Wise Men according to the Catholic religion). The dances like *sussa* and *curralera*[5], the songs, the ornamentation, and the rituals are high-

---

5 For more on the cultural manifestations *sussa* and *curralera* and their relation to African traditions, see for instance, Siqueira (2006), Silva Junior (2008), or Rodrigues (2011).

ly important to the Kalunga. However, although many traditional activities are still practiced in the community, most speakers claimed that they have lost many festivities and prayers over the years, because the new generations do not want to continue the traditions.

The villagers in Vão de Almas and Vão do Moleque are small farmers and mostly produce crops for their own basic needs, but many of the people (i.e., men over 60 years of age and women over 55 years) are retired.[6] Other common occupations are midwifery and *raizeira or raizeiro*, i.e., people who know how to prepare herbs for medicinal purposes. Some older members had also been salespersons and traders, and they used to travel for days on foot or by horse to sell their produce, such as manioc flour, rice, and beans, in nearby villages outside the community.

The majority of elder people in the villages are illiterate. The interviewees are between 51 and 98 years of age, and 16 out of 21 of them are illiterate, while two of the five literate interviewees have only basic literacy skills, such as writing their names. In previous years, teachers were sent to the community, but the villagers did not have a formal teaching process, as AF66 explains in ex. (1):

(1) *Eu estudei, mas num aprendi porque o estudo naquele tempo o estudinho vinha um fulano diz qu'é professor, nós foi, mas antes de interar um ano ele, antes de interar um ano ele foi embora, nós ficou com livrinho, eu a vez de sair eu mesmo perguntando, ah, num liguei não.*
'I studied, but I didn't learn because, at that time, someone used to come [to the village] and say that [he] was a teacher, we went [to the school], but before one year, before he completed one year, he left, we were left with a little book. Instead of asking around myself [to learn by myself from others], ah, I didn't care.' [AF66]

It was very common that families did not allow their children to have formal education because they needed their work contribution in the fields and at home. In addition, families believed that studying was not as important as working in the fields. The speakers mentioned that they wished they had studied, as in ex. (2).

(2) *Pois é minha dona eu sinto muito num saber a leitura (...) meu pai era um homem que trabaiador demais, minha dona, ele ele pensava que jogava só nós no serviço assim né pensava que era mais vantagem.*

---

[6] According to the current Brazilian legislation, minority groups such as *quilombola* people and indigenous people have the right to receive pension support from the government when men and women complete 60 and 55 years of age respectively.

'So it is, m'am, I feel so sorry that I can't read (...). My dad was a man who worked very hard [a hard-work kind of man], m'am, he only thought of putting us to work, you know, he thought there were more gains'. [AF59]

Today, there are primary schools in the two villages, yet they still face organizational problems; e.g., there are not enough teachers, the quality of didactic material is low, and many students do not complete the primary level. The students also travel long distances to school on foot and sometimes even cross big rivers, which is a challenge during the frequent floodings. If the children manage to finish the elementary level and want to continue their studies and attend high school, they move to urban centers. Therefore, many young people leave the community to continue their studies or to find jobs and other opportunities after they finish primary school. The lack of infrastructure in the form of schools, jobs, and health care seems to be the main reason for the emigration from the countryside to the city.

Most of the challenges faced by the community have to do with the lack of infrastructure (e.g., running water, electricity, bridges, health care system, and educational system) and natural disasters, such as floods and droughts, as well as issues regarding land rights and the construction of a river dam. Corruption and embezzlement are also common. Violence against young women is also a problem in Kalunga. Nevertheless, there seems to be a positive view on their community in general among those who remain. Many community members said that "I was born and raised here, I want to stay here until I die" (MF98) and "I'll only leave this place in a coffin" (AM73).

5.2 Language perception and attitudes

Both Kalunga members and people outside the community claim that Kalunga speech is different from other varieties of Portuguese in Brazil. Inhabitants of the cities in Goiás, like São João D'Aliança, Cavalcante, and Alto Paraíso, share the opinion that the people in Kalunga have a "special speech", "a different way of speaking", and that sometimes they use some "strange words" which make it difficult to understand Kalunga speakers, especially when talking to the elderly. Even in the rural areas around the aforementioned cities, the dwellers say that the people from Kalunga speak "strangely", and that "it is not the same Portuguese" they speak.

In line with outsiders' perceptions, Kalunga people consider the way they speak different from other people's ways of speaking. They also say that there is variation between the villages in Kalunga. Some speakers referred to their variety as *o português errado* 'the wrong Portuguese'. When describing their way of speaking in comparison to radio speech or the people in Cavalcante, both representing BVP, they say:

(3) *É porque tem diferença... ela não eu num sei muito negócio só sei que tem, já mudou um pouco. (...) eu num sei dizer explicar pro'cê não.*
'There is a difference... I don't know a lot [much thing], I just know that there is a difference. And it has changed a bit (...) I don't know, [I can't] explain it to you.' [AF75]

(4) *A gente vê falar dona mas a gente, aqui nós é só a fala é essa mesma. Tratar senhora senhora ninguém trata de você né, trata só trata senhora é só a senhora, senhoro senhoro (...) É aí vê que tem mas na memória a gente nu nu num tá lembrando né?*
'We heard it, m'am, but for us it is just the speech, it is like this. We say *senhora* 'lady' no one says *you* [using *você*], right, only say *senhora* 'lady' to *senhora* 'lady', *senhoro* 'sir' to *senhoro* 'sir'. Yeah, maybe there are [different words], but in our memory we don't remember, right?' [AM65]

The speakers usually recognize that there are differences between the varieties, but they find it difficult to specify, as in ex. (3). In (4), the speaker makes a metalinguistic commentary when he mentions the use of the address form *senhora* 'lady' instead of the pronoun *você* 'you'. It is a feature that this Kalunga speaker recognizes as different from other forms of speech.

(5) *A diferença que tem é porque aqui depois que a gente entende um pouco e a gente conhece bem que essas região de Cavalcante tem muito lugar que tem muitas pessoa que conversa errado, mas é o Português que a pessoa entende né é que tem umas pessoa que a vez conversa errado acha algum de fora acha que tá errado né mas a gente da região sabe que num é errado que é o português que conhece é esse né tem muitos animal que a pessoa conhece por exemplo sucuri muito aqui num sabe falar sucuri é sucluiu, porco é poico.*
'The difference is that here, after we understand a bit, we know well that in this region of Cavalcante there are many places where many people speak wrongly, but that's the Portuguese they know, right, it is like there are people who sometimes speak wrongly. Some outsiders think it is wrong, right, but we from this region know that it is not wrong. The Portuguese that is known is like that, right, there are many animals that people know for example *sucuri* [anaconda] they say *sucluiu, porco* [pig] is *poico*.' [AM67]

In ex. (5), the speaker discusses the existence of different varieties in the region of Cavalcante, and he mentions some phonological processes, such as, alternation /r/>/i/, which will be addressed in the next section. The statement shows that the speakers perceive distinct features of Kalunga Portuguese.

However, both outsiders and insiders see the speech of Kalunga as a stigmatized variety of Brazilian Portuguese: they consider Kalunga Portuguese to include words that are not said "correctly", and it is referred to as a "strange language" and "the wrong Portuguese". It is considered to be different from other varieties known in the surrounding areas. Yet because of seasonal migration (i.e., study, work, tourism, radio, formal education), Kalunga Portuguese is experiencing more external influences from other varieties today similar to other Afro-descendant communities in Brazil, where access to new media played a significant role in the shift to BVP (Lucchesi et al. 2009). The lack of electricity and the absence of television and internet access in Vão de Almas and Vão do Moleque has been a factor that slowed down the process of implementation of a more urban-like variety in this community.

6 Selected linguistic features of Kalunga Portuguese

I here focus on selected phonological and morphosyntactic features that are particular to the Kalunga speech variety when compared to SBP. I compare my data to other varieties of BVP and ABP whenever this is relevant and information is available. All the examples include a SBP version after glossing. The aim of this description is to show linguistic features found in Kalunga Portuguese and help place Kalunga Portuguese in a dialectal continuum of Brazilian Portuguese varieties.

6.1 Phonological characteristics

When compared to other varieties of BVP, there are a number of peculiar features present in Kalunga. For example, the palatalization of /t/ and /d/ may occur after the high vowel [i], as /aproveita/ > [pɾu'veɪtʃa] 'enjoy', /oito/ > ['oɪtʃu] 'eight' and /leitura/ > [leɪ'tʃuɾa] 'reading' and in the context of a complex onset, as in /trabalha/ > [tʃa'baɾe] 'work' and in /atras/ > [a'tʃas] 'behind'. Palatalization is a common phenomenon in BVP varieties and it usually occurs before /i/, e.g., [ˈdʒiɐ] 'day' and [ˈtʃiɐ] 'aunt', as in the varieties of the Goiás region. In Kalunga, however, palatalization before /i/ is not a categorical feature.

There is no occurrence of the palatal /ʎ/ in my data. In the context in which the phoneme /ʎ/ is used in other varieties of BVP, it may be that in Kalunga, it either merged with /i/, as in /meʎorar/ > [mioˈɾa] 'to improve' and /famiʎa/ > [faˈmiɐ] 'family', or it was replaced with /i/, as in /muʎer/ > [muiˈɛ] 'woman' and /oʎa/ > [ˈɔia] 'look'.

Final vowels are generally added to consonant-final words to avoid closed syllables and in accordance to the general consonant-vowel (CV) tendency. Normally, the high vowels [ʊ] and [ɪ] appear in both tonic and atonic final syllables. The phenomenon occurs in the context of final /r/, /l/, /s/, /z/, as /profesor/ > [pɾofeˈsoɾʊ] 'teacher', /sol/ > [ˈsolʊ] 'sun', /igual/ > [iˈgʊalʊ] 'same', /deus/ > [ˈdeʊsʊ] 'God', /qual/ > [ˈqʊalɪ] 'which', /vez/ > [ˈvezɪ] 'turn', /fez/ > [ˈfezɪ] 'did/made' /diz/ > [ˈdizɪ] 'says'.

In addition, we find consonant and vowel alternations or consonant-consonant alternations in different pairs, as the following examples show:

- In word-internal coda, /r/>[ɪ], as in curso > [ˈkuɪsʊ] 'course', amargando > [maɪˈgãnʊ] 'embittering'.
- In coda position, /s/>[h], as in umas > [ˈũmɐh] 'some.F', festa > [ˈfɛhtɐ] 'party', mesmo > [ˈmehmʊ].
- In word-internal coda, / l/>[ɪ], as in Cavalcante > [kaˈvaɪkãtɪ] 'Cavalcante', almocim > [ˈaɪmusĩ] 'lunch'.
- In some words, /v/>[b], as in varrendo > [baˈxẽdʊ] 'sweeping', brava > [ˈbɾabɐ] 'mad'.
- /v/>/h/, as in vantagem > [hãˈtaʒɪ] 'advantage', tava > [ˈtahɐ] 'was'.

Also, there is vowel quality change in /i/>/e/ and /a/>/e/, which could be an assimilation phenomenon in the context of high and mid vowels, as in primeiro > [pɾeˈmeɾʊ] 'first', artesanato > [tezeˈnatʃʊ] 'craftwork', ribeirão > [xebeˈɾãʊ] 'stream'.

Another trait is the tendency to simplify complex onsets, such as /kl/ and /tr/. Examples in Kalunga are [xeˈkama] 'complain' (/xeclama/ in SBP), [ˈotʊ] 'other' (/outro/ in SBP), [aleˈgeɪ] 'rejoiced' (/alegrei/ in SBP). This feature is common in other varieties of BVP, as the Caipira dialect[7] (Amaral 1976: 48) and other Afro-Brazilian varieties (Byrd 2012: 168).

---

[7] The broadest definition of the term refers to the vernacular Portuguese spoken in the countryside area of Minas Gerais, São Paulo and Goiás. The term caipira might carry a pejorative meaning in the Brazilian context.

6.2 Morphosyntatic features

The morphological and syntactic features presented here are meant to show the differences and similarities between Kalunga and other varieties of BVP, especially ABP varieties, in order to help place Kalunga in the Brazilian linguistic scenario.

6.2.1 Person and number marking on the verb

Verbal agreement paradigms in BVP are well studied, especially by sociolinguists, and the BVP varieties show mainly differences in the suffixes marking person on the verb (as examples, see Monguilhott and Coelho 2002; Souza 2005; Lucchesi et al. 2009: ch. 14; Monte 2012; Rúbio 2012). The more frequent the person suffix is marked on the verb, the more standard-like the variety is considered by BP speakers. Verbal paradigms in Kalunga follow the general aspects of BVP in that person agreement is altered, i.e. the same suffix/form is used for several persons, whereas in SBP, there is a different verbal form/suffix for each of the six subject forms. This phenomenon is also connected to the subject pronouns that show variation in BVP. The varieties differ in the frequency in which agreement is marked on the verb with a verbal suffix. In my sample, first person plural and third person plural are almost never marked with a verbal suffix, while first person singular is usually marked with a verbal suffix.

In first person singular, BVP verbs generally have a first person suffix marking. In my sample, there are some exceptions to this tendency. Examples of this exception are shown in (6) to (8):

(6) Eu   num   **tem**   fio.
    I   NEG   **have**[8]   son
    'I don't have a son.'
    (SBP: *Eu não tenho filho*)   [AF66]

(7) Eu   já   **fez**   o   café,   eu   lavo.
    I   already   **make.PST**   the.M   coffee   I   wash
    'I made the coffee, I wash [the dishes].'
    (SBP: *Eu já fiz o café, eu lavo*)   [AF59]

---

8 As verbs are not conjugated, I gloss them as main verbs without any number and person mark on the verb.

(8) – O senhor **faz** a farinha?
    the.M sir **make** the.F flour
   'Do you make manioc flour?'
   (SBP: *O senhor faz a farinha?*)
   – **Faz.**
     Make
   'I do.' [AM65]
   (SBP: *Faço*)

The first person singular is usually not marked on the verb in present and past tense, as shown in (6) and (7). As (8) shows, answering a polar question can be a trigger for the absence of first person singular marking on the verb. In my sample, the constituent order – the subject (immediately) before or after the verb – and the presence or the absence of an overt subject do not seem to affect the use or not of verbal marking in the first person singular.

Although there are only a few occurrences of first person singular without a suffix on the verb, it is still an interesting phenomenon. This feature is also found in the ABP variety of Helvécia (Lucchesi et al. 2009), but not in the other varieties of BVP, not even in the non-standard rural varieties (Lipski 2007: 37). In Helvécia, this phenomenon was presented as one of the strongest arguments in favor of a previous creolization stage in the community (Lucchesi et al. 2009).

The occurrences of plural marking on the first person in the Kalunga data are very low. The overt subject seems to play a role in this case, as (9) and (10) show.

(9) Só **peguemo** a estrada desse
    just get.PST.1PL the road this
   'we just got this road' [MF98]
   (SBP: *Nós só pegamos essa estrada*)

(10) Nós saiu foi pra fora **viemo** embora
     we exit.PST go to outside come.PST.1PL away
    'We got out [of the river] we came back [home]' [MF94]
    (SBP: *Nós saímos e viemos embora*)

In (9), the subject (first person plural) is only marked by the suffix *-emo* in the verb *pegu-emo* '[we] got'. In (10), there are two verbs referring to the first person plural subject. The first one, which has a pre-verbal subject, does not have first person plural marking, while the second verb, which does not have a pre-verbal overt subject, has the first person plural morpheme *-mo*. In these examples, when there is no overt pronoun, the first person plural is marked on the verb with a verbal suffix.

In all the occurrences of the morphologically marked first person plural, the morphemes used by the speakers are forms other than the standard *-mos*. The allomorphs used are either *-mo*, like in *vamo* '[we] go', *somo* '[we] are', which is also used in other varieties like urban varieties, or *-emo*, which is common in rural communities (Lucchesi et al. 2009: 364), and is considered stigmatized and pejoratively typical of rural varieties, like in *fiquemo* '[we] stayed', *peguemo* '[we] took'.

Third person plural marking is almost absent in Kalunga. Examples (11) and (12) are sentences without the SBP third person plural suffix *-m* in the third person plural.

(11) *Os   menino   **vai**   e   **liga***
     the.PL.M   boy   **go**   and   **turn.on**
     'The boys go (to the river) and turn on (the water pump)'   [AF66]
     (SBP: *Os meninos vão e ligam*)

(12) ***Eles**   conta   um   caso   aí,   **eles**   num   entende*
     they   tell   a   story there,   **they**   no   understand
     'They tell a story, they don't understand'   [AM73]
     (SBP: *Eles contam um caso aí, eles não entendem*)

In (11), the third person singular verbs *vai* 'go' and *liga* 'turn on' refer to the plural subject *os menino* 'the.PL.M boy'. Thus, unlike SBP where plural is expressed multiple times, the only plural suffix in the sentence is present on the definite article *os* 'the.M.PL'. In (12), the two pronouns *eles* '3PL' are the only signs of overt plural marking in the sentence.

6.2.2 Negation

In the Kalunga data, as in other BVP varieties, there are three forms of expressing a negative verbal phrase: (i) NEG+VP; (ii) NEG+VP+NEG; (iii) VP+NEG (Sousa 2015; Schwenter 2005). What follows are examples of negative constructions in Kalunga that are not common in other BVP varieties. The examples show sentences with negative words/expression of negation, such as the adverbs *nunca* 'never', *nem* 'not even', and the indefinite pronouns *ninguém* 'nobody' and *nada* 'nothing'. The form *num* is used as a negative marker as well.

(13) *Nesse   lugar   aqui   **ninguém**   **num**   tem   futuro   **não***
     in this   place   here   **nobody**   **NEG**   have   future   **NEG**
     'In this place nobody has a future'   [AF59]
     (SBP: *Nesse lugar aqui ninguém tem futuro*)

In (13), there are three elements that indicate negation, the subject *ninguém* 'nobody', and the two negation particles *num* 'not' and *não* 'not'. The use of the negative indefinite pronoun with another negator occurs also in other varieties of BVP, although it is not a very common phenomenon (Nascimento 2014: 88). However, in other BVP varieties, except in Helvécia, I did not find evidence of the negative indefinite pronoun as *ninguém* 'nobody' in the subject position followed either by the negator *não* 'not' (or its variants), as in (13), or by a double negation, as in (14).

(14) **Ninguém num** ranjava dado
       nobody NEG get.PST given
       'Nobody used to get [baby stuff] given away' [AF59]
       (SBP: *Ninguém conseguia nada doado*)

Occasionally, the negator *não* 'no' co-occurs in the corpus with the word *nem* 'not even', as in (15) and (16). Usually *nem* 'not even' is used to emphasize a negative sentence.

(15) Tinha ano que ele **nem num** vinha
       have.PST year that he NEG NEG come.PST
       'There were years that he did not even come' [AM65]
       (SBP: *Havia ano que ele nem vinha*)

(16) **Nem** peixe eu **num** como
       NEG fish I NEG eat
       'I don't even eat fish' [MM94]
       (SBP: *Nem peixe eu como*)

The use of *num* 'no' before the verbs *vinha* 'he came' and *como* 'I eat', respectively in (15) and (16), is an addition of a negator in a negative sentence. It does not seem to convey a new meaning or emphasis to the sentence. Sentences like (16) occur usually with the topicalization of a complementizer or an adverb in the corpus.

Other particular negative constructions present in the sample are sentences with the adverb *nunca* 'never'. *Nunca* usually means 'something never done before', as exemplified in the following sentence:

(17) Rede eu **nunca** fiz **não**
       hammock I NEG do.PST NEG
       'I have never made a hammock' [MF94]
       (SBP: *Eu nunca fiz rede*)

In (18) and (19), *nunca* is used with somewhat different meanings when compared to (17).

(18) *Num   destruiu   porque   roça   nós   **nunca**   tinha*
     NEG   destroy.PST because   harvest   we   NEG   have.PST
     plantado   né?
     planted   PART
     'It [the rain] didn't destroy because we hadn't planted the crops, right?'
     (SBP: *Não destruiu porque nós não tínhamos plantado a roça*)   [AF59]

(19) ***Nem*   água   **nunca**   bebeu   quanto   mais   pra   comer*
     NEG   water   NEG   drink.PST   even   more   PREP   to eat
     'Water she never drank, not even ate (anything)'   [MF98]
     (SBP: *Nem água bebeu quanto mais comeu algo*)

In both (18) and (19) *nunca* seems to be used simply as clausal negator, and it does not have the meaning of 'something never done before', as in (17), nor an emphatic meaning. In (19), *nem* 'not even' and *quanto* 'even' are emphasizers. For more on negation patterns in Kalunga, see Mattos (2020).

6.2.3 Possession

In the Kalunga sample, the analytic form *de* 'of' + pronoun is a way of expressing possession, as (20) shows:

(20) *A   valência   **de**   **nós**   aqui   é   aquele   Jonas*
     the.F   salvation   of   we   here   is   that   Jonas
     'The salvation of us here is that Jonas'   [AM65]
     (SBP: *A nossa ajuda aqui é aquele Jonas*)

This analytic form to indicate possession is not common in BVP varieties for the first person. In an urban spoken corpus analyzed by Neves (2000), the author did not find any occurrence of this form referring to first persons. In SBP, the analytic form of the possessive is used for third person singular *dele*[9] 'his' and *dela* 'her' and third person plural *deles* 'their.M' and *delas* 'their.F', and with the second person forms *de você* 'of you.SG' and *de vocês* 'of you.PL' (cf. Neves 2000: 471–489).

---

9 *Dele, deles* and *dela, delas* are, originally, periphrastic forms *de ele(s)* and *de ela(s)*. Nowadays, these forms are considered possessive pronouns (Neves 2000), so that they will be glossed, respectively, as 'his, her, their.M, their.F'.

Although the analytic form is found in Kalunga to indicate possession in first person singular, the possessive pronoun is much more common. In first person plural, however, there are no occurrences of possessive pronouns to indicate possession in my corpus, only the analytic form. In (21) and (22), the analytic form indicates possession in first person singular and plural, respectively.

(21) Naquele   tempo   **de** eu   qualé   escola que   tinha
     PREP.DEM   time   **of** I   which.is school that have.PST
     'In my old days, which school was there?'   [AF66]
     (SBP: *No meu tempo, qual escola que havia?*)

(22) Carregou   uma   vaca   **de** nós   bem   ali   embaixo
     carry.PST one.F   cow   **of** we   well   there   below
     'It [the flood] carried one of our cows just down there'   [AM73]
     (SBP: *Carregou uma vaca nossa bem ali embaixo*)

One relevant aspect concerning the use of possessive pronouns is that, in SBP, the possessive pronoun usually precedes the noun. However, in my sample, it is common to have the first person possessive pronoun after the noun, as in (23). A similar phenomenon was reported by Mello (1996: 38) as a shared feature of Lanc Patuá – a French-based creole language spoken in the state of Amapá, Brazil – and in the Caipira dialect.

(23) Salário   **minha**   é   pouco
     salary   **my.F**   is   little
     'My salary is low'   [AF75]
     (SBP: *Meu salário é pouco*)

Besides the position of the pronoun in (23), the non-gender agreement between the possessive pronoun *minha* 'my.F' and the noun *salário* 'salary.M' is another feature that distinguishes this variety from other BVP varieties and SBP.

6.2.4 The indefinite pronoun system

In Kalunga, the use of *tudo* 'all' is preferred over the pronouns *todo* 'all.M.SG' and *toda* 'all.F.SG', i.e., gender and number are usually not marked in the quantifier. Plural forms *todos* 'all.M.PL' and *todas* 'all.F.PL' do not occur in the sample. There are occurrences of *toda* 'all.F.SG' in the sample and it usually occurs with a subset of feminine nouns, as in *toda vida* 'all life' and *toda coisa* 'everything'. *Todo* 'all.M.SG' occurs usually together with masculine words like *dia* 'day' and *mundo* 'world', as in *todo dia* 'everyday' and *todo mundo* 'everybody'. Some of the occurrences of *todo* 'all.M.SG' and *toda* 'all.F.SG' are answers from questions that are constructed with these pronouns. There is one occurrence of *tuda* 'tudo.F', as in *tuda coisa* 'everything'. Examples (24) and (25) illustrate occurrences of the pronoun *tudo*:

(24) Ah   ano   passado mesmo nós perdeu   a   roça   **tudo**
     INTJ   year   last   even   we   lose.PST **the.F** **small.farm.F** **all**
     'Last year we lost the whole harvest'   [AM65]
     (SBP: *Ah! Ano passado mesmo nós perdemos a roça toda*)

(25) *É*   **deles**   **tudo**   aí
     is   **their.M**   **everything**   there
     'All of them there'   [AF75]
     (SBP: *É deles todos aí*)

In (24), *tudo* refers to *roça* 'small farm' and means 'totality, a whole'. In (25), the speaker answers the question 'which festivity do you like the most?', the pronoun *tudo* refers to the object pronoun *deles* 'their.M' and means 'all types of festivities'. In the sample, the pronoun *tudo* 'all/everything' may be used to express the totality of something, the totality in numbers or the idea of inclusion, unlike the way it occurs in SBP.

6.2.5 Double object constructions

Double object constructions are not very common in my data, but they do occur a few times and are a relevant phenomenon to be discussed. According to Lucchesi et al. (2009: 427), the phenomenon is strongly indicative of a more heavily restructured process of contact in ABP varieties, since it does occur in many creole languages and is not shared among Romance languages. Examples (26) to (28) illustrate the phenomenon in Kalunga:

(26) Ele   mostrou   **nós**   o   lugar
     he   show.PST   **we**   the.M   place
     'He showed us the place'   [AF59]
     (SBP: *Ele nos mostrou o lugar*)

(27) Se   desse   nós   **uma**   **pessoa**   pra   carregar
     if   give.SUBJ   we   a.F   person   to   to carry
     'If [she] gave us **someone** to carry [us]'   [MF98]
     (SBP: *Se nos dessem a uma pessoa para carregar*)

(28) Num   dava   prejuízo   **ninguém**
     NEG   give.PST   loss   **nobody**
     'It [the flood] didn't cause a loss to anyone'   [AM73]
     (SBP: *Não dava prejuízo a ninguém*)

In (26), the dative complement *nós* 'we' occurs without a preposition and precedes the accusative complement *lugar* 'place'. In standard-nearer BP, the dative complement could be constructed both by the pronoun *nos* 'us' or by adding the preposition *a* 'to' before *nós* 'we'. In Kalunga, as in other BVP varieties, the preposition *pra* is the most common preposition form used before the pronouns. In (27), the dative complement *uma pessoa* 'a person' also occurs without a preposition, but it follows the accusative complement *nós* 'we'. In the data, all double object constructions have a pronoun as an object. In the last ex. (28), the dative complement *ninguém* 'nobody' follows the accusative complement *prejuízo* 'loss' without preposition.

The double object construction is not common in other BVP varieties, even in rural varieties, and many scholars study the possible influence of African substrate languages in this phenomenon (see, for instance, Baxter et al. 2014). For a creole perspective, see Michaelis et al. (2013: ch. 60).

6.2.6 Gender agreement within a NP

Grammatical gender is irregularly marked in Kalunga, as in (23), where *salário* 'salary' is a masculine noun, and *minha* 'my.F' a feminine possessive pronoun. Examples (29) to (32) illustrate other occurrences within the NP.

(29) Tive   lá   **n-um**   reunião
     have.PST   there   PREP-ART.IND.M   meeting.F
     'I was there in a meeting'   [AF59]
     (SBP: *Eu estive lá em uma reunião*)

(30) Eles   foi   esconder   **d-o**   revolta
     they   be.PST   to hide   PREP-ART.DEF.M   rebellion.F
     'They were trying to hide from the rebellion'   [MM94]
     (SBP: *Eles foram se esconder da revolta*)

(31) Tinha   **muit-o**   enchente
     have.PST   **many-M**   flood.F
     'There were many floods'   [AM73]
     (SBP: *Havia muita enchente*)

(32) Tem   **um-a**   **monte**   de   menino
      have   **a-F**   **bunch.M** of   boy
      'There is a bunch of boys'   [AF75]
      (SBP: *Há um monte de menino*)

In BVP, gender agreement is common. Its lack has only been reported for a few varieties: very isolated rural communities, such as ABP (Lucchesi et al. 2009: 305), and the variety of Portuguese spoken in Cuiabá, in the state of Mato Grosso (Dettoni 2005). This phenomenon was also reported earlier for Kalunga by Baiocchi, as cited in Lucchesi et al. (2009: 305).

6.2.7 Prepositions

In Kalunga, adverbial constructions and possessive constructions in the analytic form do not always use the SBP prepositions, although analytic forms with prepositions are the most common ones. Examples (33) to (35) indicate, respectively, time, purpose and possession, and they occur without a preposition.

(33) Nós   também   levantava   **madrugada**
      we   too   wake-up.PST   dawn
      'We also used to wake up early in the morning'   [MM94]
      (SBP: *Nós também nos levantávamos de madrugada*)

(34) Ele   morreu   **coração**
      he   die.PST   heart
      'He died of a heart attack'   [MM94]
      (SBP: *Ele morreu de coração*)

(35) E   a   **luz**   **nós**   aqui   é   a   lamparina
      and   the   light   we   here   is   the   lamp
      'And the light [of] us here is oil lamp'   [AM65]
      (SBP: *E a nossa luz aqui é a lamparina*)

Another interesting aspect is the extensive use of some prepositions like *ni* 'in' and *mais* 'with'. According to Gonçalves and Pires (2015: 5), *ni* is a nonstandard stigmatized form of the preposition *em* 'in' and may indicate, for instance, direction and location (for more studies on this preposition, see, e.g., Lucchesi et al. 2009; Souza 2015).

In Kalunga, there are instances of the preposition *ni* indicating location, direction, and time. In (36) and (37), the prepositions indicate location of a body part and time/situation, respectively. Ex. (38) seems to be a generalized locative construction.

(36) Colocou   o   soro   **ni**   minha   veia
     put.PST   the   serum   PREP   my   vein
     'They injected a serum in my vein'   [AF75]
     (SBP: *Colocaram o soro na minha veia*)

(37) É   negócio   de   gente   tá   dormindo   e   sair
     is   thing   of   people   is   sleeping   and leave
     ni   chuva
     PREP   rain
     'It is because we are sleeping and leave [the house] in the rain' [AF75]
     (SBP: *É porque a gente está dormindo e sai na chuva*)

(38) Fizeram   empréstimo   **ni**   meu   salário
     Make.PST   loan   PREP   my.M   salary
     'Someone made a loan on my salary'   [AF75]
     (SBP: *Fizeram empréstimo no meu salário*)

In addition, *mais* is used in the Kalunga data in comitative phrases, as in (39). This is common, for instance, in rural varieties in the regions of Goiás and Minas Gerais. In (40) and (41), this usage seems to be extended to other meanings.

(39) Aí   veio   pra   cá   juntou   **mais**   o   pai   dela
     then   come.PST   PREP   here   gathered   PREP   the   father her
     'So [she] came here and got together with her father'   [MF98]
     (SBP: *Aí veio para cá e juntou-se com o pai dela*)

(40) Ele   dividiu   **mais**   mãe   e   tomou   eu
     he   divide.PST   PREP   mom   and   take.PST   I
     'He separated from mom and took me [from her]'   [AF75]
     (SBP: *Ele se separou da minha mãe e me tomou*)

(41) Minha   mãe   largou   **mais**   meu   pai
     my   mom   leave.PST   PREP   my   father
     'My mom left my father'   [AM73]
     (SBP: Minha mãe largou do meu pai

In both (40) and (41), the meaning of the sentences is that the couples separated. *Mais* 'from', in (40) and (41), does not give the sense of togetherness and accompaniment, especially because of the meaning of the verbs *dividir* 'to divide' and *largar* 'to leave', which indicate the opposite of being together. In both sentences, *mais* connects two participants in the same event. It seems that there is an expansion of the meaning of the preposition. It is thus not only used with the typical comitative functions, as in (39).

7 Concluding remarks: Kalunga Portuguese, a colonial heritage language

My analysis suggests that Kalunga shares sociohistorical and linguistic data with other ABP varieties and differences from other BVP varieties. Many of the features that Kalunga shares with other ABP varieties have been defined by other scholars as resulting from a strong influence of African languages, especially when they are also found in different restructured languages, such as creole languages. Some instances of these shared features are (i) altered or irregular gender agreement, (ii) altered or irregular nominal agreement, (iii) altered or irregular verbal agreement, and (iv) analytic forms of possessive relationships with first person pronouns. In comparison with the speech of Helvécia (another more heavily restructured variety), Kalunga further shares the following features: (i) double object constructions, (ii) omission of prepositions in NP, (iii) lack of gender agreement in the NP, and (iv) verbal negation with subject negatively marked.

There are features in Kalunga that appear in other BVP varieties as well, but the less standard occurrences are more noticeable in Kalunga and ABP than in other varieties. For instance, reduction of pronoun systems, non-agreement markers, non-morphological plural markers on the verbs, and the phonological processes described in Section 6.1.

The discussion about sociohistorical and linguistic features of Kalunga presented here sheds light on the classification of this variety with regard to other BVP varieties and contact varieties in general. The isolated way of life in the heritage community, with physical and cultural distance from the mainstream society, is manifested in the language spoken in Kalunga. Both analyses of the structural features as well as insiders' and outsiders' attitudes toward the language variety spoken in Kalunga point to this language as being a distinct variety in comparison to other varieties of BVP. Archaisms and innovations present in Kalunga are socially marked features, and they are not present in the varieties closer to SBP. The study gives, therefore, evidence of a high level of marginalization of the variety spoken in Kalunga, similar to other black communities in Brazil.

Regarding the status of Kalunga, I suggest to place Kalunga on the left end of the dialect continuum of BP varieties (Campos 2014: 58), and farthest from SBP, as Figure 3 shows.

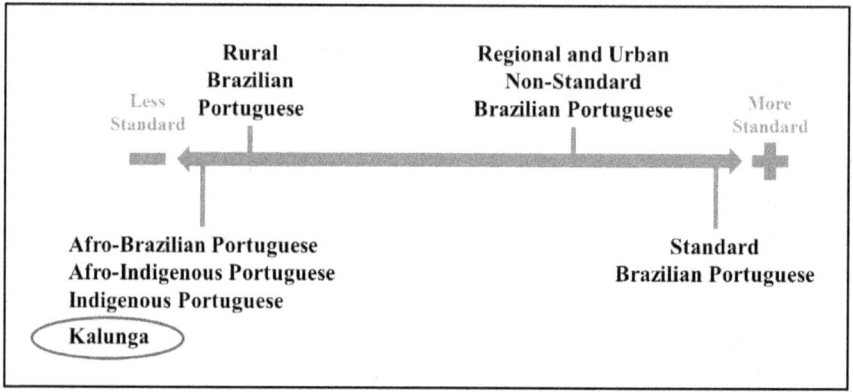

Figure 3: Dialectal continuum based on Campos (2014: 182) including Kalunga speech.

Abbreviations

ABP	Afro-Brazilian Portuguese
ART	article
BP	Brazilian Portuguese
BVP	Brazilian Vernacular Portuguese
DEF	definite
DEM	demonstrative
F	feminine
IND	indefinite
M	masculine
NEG	negation
PART	particle
PL	plural
PREP	preposition
PST	past
SBP	Standard Brazilian Portuguese
SUBJ	subjunctive

References

Almeida, Maria Geralda de 2015. *O território e a comunidade Kalunga: quilombolas em diversos olhares*. Goiânia: Gráfica UFG.
Amaral, Amadeu. 1976. *O dialeto caipira*, 3rd edn. São Paulo: HUCITEC.
Araújo, Gilberto Paulino de. 2014. *O conhecimento etnobotânico dos Kalunga: uma relação entre língua e meio ambiente*. Brasília: Universidade de Brasília PhD thesis.
Baiocchi, Mari de Nasaré. 1991. *Kalunga: estórias e textos*. Goiânia: Secretaria de Estado da Educação de Goiás.
Baiocchi, Mari de Nasaré. 1999. *Kalunga: povo da terra*. Brasília: Ministério da Justiça.
Baiocchi, Mari de Nasaré. 2001. *Uma história do povo Kalunga*. Brasília: Ministério da Educação.
Baxter, Alan, Camila Ferreira de Mello & Natali Gomes de Almeida Santana. 2014. A construção de objeto duplo e as influências do substrato no português afrobrasileiro (e africano). *PAPIA* 24(2). 283–306.
Bertran, Paolo. 2011. *História da terra e do homem no Planalto Central: eco-história do Distrito Federal*. Brasília: Universidade de Brasília.
Bortoni-Ricardo, Stella Maris. 1985. *The urbanization of rural dialect speakers: A sociolinguistic study in Brazil*. Cambridge: Cambridge University Press.
Brazilian Federal Constitution, Art. 68 *Ato das disposições constitucionais transitórias*. 1988. http://www.planalto.gov.br/ccivil_03/constituicao/constituicao.htm. (checked 16/06/20)
Brazilian Federal Law 10.639/03. 2003. http://www.planalto.gov.br/ccivil_ 03/leis/2003/L10.639.htm. (checked 16/06/20)
Brazilian Presidential Decree 7.387. 2010. http://www.planalto.gov.br/ccivil_03/_Ato2007-2010/2010/Decreto/D7387.htm. (checked 16/06/20).
Brito Neto, Joãmar Carvalho de. 2002. A informação na construção da cidadania entre os calungas. Presented at XXV Congresso da INTERCOM (Comunicação e Cidadania), Salvador-BA, 2002.
Byrd, Steven. 2012. *Calunga and the legacy of an African language in Brazil*. Albuquerque: University of New Mexico Press.
Camargo, Maria Thereza L. de Arruda 1998. *Plantas medicinais e de rituais afro-brasileiros*. São Paulo: Icone.
Campos, Ednalvo Apostolo. 2014. *A sintaxe pronominal na variedade afro-indígena de Jurussaca: uma contribuição para o quadro da pronominalização do português falado no Brasil*. São Paulo: University of São Paulo PhD dissertation.
Coelho-Ferreira, Márlia. 2009. Medicinal knowledge and plant utilization in an Amazonian coastal community of Marudá, Pará State (Brazil). *Journal of ethnopharmacology* 126(1). 159–175.
Dettoni, Rachel do Valle. 2005. A concordância de gênero no falar cuiabano: a trajetória de uma mudança linguística em curso. In Manuel M. Santiago Almeida & Maria Inês P. Cox (eds.), *Vozes cuiabanas: estudos linguísticos em Mato Grosso*, 51–68. Cuiabá: Cathedral Publicações.
Dixon, R. M. W. 2009a. *Basic linguistic theory: Methodology*. Oxford: Oxford University Press.
Dixon, R. M. W. 2009b. *Basic linguistic theory: Grammatical topics*. Oxford: Oxford University Press.
Gonçalves, Clézio Roberto & Luís Ricardo Rodriges Pires. 2015. A variação no uso da preposição "em" no município de Ouro Preto (MG). *Revista Philologus* 63(21). 33–41.

Labov, William. 1972. *Sociolinguistic patterns*, vol. 4. Philadelphia: University of Pennsylvania Press.

Lipski, John M. 2007. Afro-Yungueño speech: The long-lost "Black Spanish". *Language in Context* 4(1). 1–43.

Lucchesi, Dante, Alan Baxter & Ilza Ribeiro. 2009. *O português afro-brasileiro*. Bahia: Universidade Federal da Bahia (EDUFBA).

Maher, Terezinha de Jesus Machado. 1998. Sendo índio em português.... In Inês Signorini (ed.), *Língua(gem) e identidade. Elementos para uma discussão no campo aplicado*, 115–138. Campinas: Mercado de Letras/Fapesp.

Marinho, Thais Alves. 2008. *Identidade e Territorialidade entre os Kalunga do Vão do Moleque*. Goiás: Universidade Federal do Goiás MA thesis.

Mattos, Ana Paulla Braga. 2019. *Kalunga: An Afro-Brazilian Portuguese variety*. PhD Thesis Aarhus: Aarhus University.

Mattos, Ana Paulla Braga. 2020. Nunca and other negative aspects in Kalunga Portuguese. *Journal of Ibero-Romance Creoles (JIRC)* 10. 1–30.

Mattos, Ana Paulla Braga & Márcia Santos Duarte Oliveira. 2020. Kalunga in the lusophone context: A phylogenetic study. *Journal of Portuguese Linguistics* 19(2). 1–24.

Mattoso, Kátia 2003. *Ser escravo no Brasil*. São Paulo: Brasiliense.

Medeiros Costa Neto, Eraldo. 2000. Conhecimento e usos tradicionais de recursos faunísticos por uma comunidade afro-brasileira. Resultados preliminares. *Interciencia* 25(9). 423–431.

Mello, Heliana Ribeiro de. 1996. *The genesis and the development of the Vernacular Brazilian Portuguese*. City University of New York: University of New York PhD dissertation.

Meyerhoff, Miriam, Chie Adachi, Golnaz Nanbakhsh & Anna Strycharz. 2012. Sociolinguistic fieldwork. In Nick Thieberger (ed.), *The Oxford handbook of linguistic fieldwork*, 121–146. Oxford: Oxford University Press.

Michaelis, Susanne M., Philippe Maurer, Martin Haspelmath & Magnus Huber (eds.). 2013. *Atlas of Pidgin and Creole language structures online*. Leipzig: Max Planck Institute for Evolutionary Anthropology.

Monguilhott, Isabel & Izete L. Coelho. 2002. Um estudo da concordância verbal de terceira pessoa em Florianópolis. In Paulino Vandresen (ed.), *Variação e mudança no português falado na Região Sul*, 189–216. Pelotas: EDUCAT.

Monte, Alexandre. 2012. *Concordância verbal e variação: um estudo descritivo-comparativo do português brasileiro e do português europeu*. São Paulo: Universidade Estadual Paulista PhD thesis.

Nascimento, Cristiana Aparecida Reimann do Nascimento. 2014. *A negação no português falado em Vitória/ES*. Vitória, ES: Universidade Federal do Espírito Santo MA thesis.

Neves, Maria Helena de Moura. 2000. *Gramática de usos do português*. São Paulo: Editora UNESP.

Oliveira, Márcia Santos Duarte, E. A. Campos, J. F. Cecim, F. J. Lopes & R. A. Silva. 2015. O conceito de português afro-indígena e a comunidade de Jurussaca. In Juanito Ornelas de Avelar & Laura Álvarez-López (eds.), *Dinâmicas afro-latinas: línguas e histórias*, 149–178. Stockholm: Stockholm University Press.

Palacin, Luis. 1994. *O século do ouro em Goiás, 1722–1822: estrutura e conjuntura numa capitania de Minas*. Goiânia: UCG Editora.

Petter, Margarida Maria Taddoni. 2008. *Variedades lingüísticas em contato: português angolano, português brasileiro, português moçambicano*. São Paulo: São Paulo University (USP) Associate Professorship thesis.

Petter, Margarida Maria Taddoni & Márcia Santos Duarte Oliveira. 2011. *Relatório final do projeto piloto: levantamento etnolinguístico de comunidades afro-brasileiras de Minas Gerais e Pará*. São Paulo: University of São Paulo.

Rodrigues, Clênio G. 2011. *Sussas e Curraleiras Kalunga: na Folia do Divino Pai Eterno da cidade de Cavalcante-GO e na Festa de Santo Antônio da comunidade do Engenho II*. Goiás: Universidade Federal de Goiás MA thesis.

Rúbio, Cássio Florêncio. 2012. *Padrões de concordância e de alternância pronominal no português brasileiro e europeu: estudo sociolinguístico comparativo*. São Paulo: Universidade Estadual Paulista "Júlio de Mesquita Filho" PhD thesis.

Santos Sales, Giovana Patricia dos, Helder Neves de Albuquerque & Mário Luiz Farias Cavalcanti. 2009. Estudo do uso de plantas medicinais pela comunidade quilombola Senhor do Bonfim-Areia-PB. *Revista de Biologia e Ciências da Terra* 1. 31–36.

Schwenter, Scott A. 2005. The pragmatics of negation in Brazilian Portuguese. *Lingua* 115 (10). 1427–1456.

Silva, Martiniano José da 2001. *Quilombos do Brasil central: violência e resistência escrava, 1719–1888*. Goiânia: Kelps.

Silva Junior, Augusto Rodrigues da. 2008. Dança Kalunga: a Suça, o Batuque, o Redemunho. *Anais Abrace* 9(1).

Siqueira, Thaís Teixeira. 2006. *Do tempo da sussa ao tempo do forró, música, festa e memória entre os Kalungas de Teresina de Goiás*. Brasília: Universidade de Brasília MA thesis.

Sousa, Lilian Teixeira de. 2015. Three types of negation in Brazilian Portuguese. *Lingua* 159. 27–46.

Souza, Pedro Daniel dos Santos. 2005. *A variação na concordância verbal na primeira fase do período arcaico da língua portuguesa: séculos XIII – XIV*. Bahia: Universidade Federal da Bahia MA thesis.

Souza, Emerson Santos. 2015. *A preposição 'ni' no continuum rural-urbano de comunidades baianas*. Feira de Santana: Universidade Estadual de Feira de Santana MA dissertation.

Velloso, Alessandra D'Aqui. 2007. *Mapeando narrativas: uma análise do processo histórico espacial da comunidade do Engenho II – Kalunga*. Brasília: Universidade de Brasília MA thesis.

Vogt, Carlos & Peter Fry. 2013 [1996]. *Cafundó: A África no Brasil*, 2nd edn. Campinas: Editora da Unicamp.

Iwan Wyn Rees
Hispanicization in the Welsh settlement of Chubut Province, Argentina

Some current linguistic developments

Abstract: Patagonian Welsh, which has been in contact with Spanish to various degrees for over 150 years in Chubut Province, Argentina, provides a fascinating case study for examining different outcomes of language contact. However, very few previous studies have attempted to provide a systematic analysis of the linguistic characteristics of Patagonian Welsh, and the linguistic repercussions of the revival of Welsh in Chubut since the 1990s have never been investigated before. This study therefore constitutes the first attempt to analyze several linguistic features of the variety of Welsh currently spoken in Chubut, mainly from a contact perspective. The results establish a number of differences (as well as similarities) between various speaker types, namely heritage speakers, heritage learners and L2 learners. Consequently, the implications of the data for pedagogical practices in Chubut and for heritage languages generally will be explored.

Keywords: language contact, phonetic and phonological convergence, loanwords, heritage speakers, second-language acquisition, standardization, Hispanicization, Patagonian Welsh

1 Introduction

Despite substantial emigration from Wales in the mid-nineteenth century, especially to North America (Jones and Jones 2001), Welsh is not commonly regarded as a colonizer language in the Americas today. Nevertheless, this Celtic language which is spoken by around 19 % (562,000) of the population of Wales according to the 2011 Census (Office for National Statistics 2012) has existed ceaselessly in Chubut Province (Patagonia) in Argentina since the establishment of a Welsh settlement there over 150 years ago in 1865. The exact number

---

Iwan Wyn Rees, Ysgol y Gymraeg/School of Welsh, Cardiff University, John Percival Building, Cardiff. CF10 3EU, Wales, E-Mail: ReesIW2@cardiff.ac.uk

of Welsh speakers in Chubut is in fact not known, but some recent sources suggest that as many as 5,000 still speak Welsh in the province today (James 2014; Eberhard et al. 2019). Even so, the case of Patagonian Welsh is particularly interesting since it has witnessed considerable (and some unexpected) changes in terms of its status, domains of use and the nature of its contact with Spanish.

Although some recent sociolinguistic studies have been inspired by the revitalization of Welsh in Chubut since the 1990s, for instance in the fields of ethnolinguistic vitality (Johnson 2009, 2010), linguistic landscaping (Coupland and Garrett 2010) and code-switching (Carter et al. 2011), it is surprising that no detailed analyses of the Welsh spoken in this region today have hitherto been available. The aim of this study therefore is to address this gap by analyzing a number of linguistic features of Patagonian Welsh predominantly from a language contact perspective. Since the dominant contact language in question is Spanish, as opposed to the situation of Welsh in Wales whereby levels of contact with English vary geographically (Morris 2017), this unique case allows us to identify several structural differences between varieties of Welsh in Wales and Patagonian Welsh that arise from contact with Spanish.

As documented by Thomason (2001: 8–13), examples of contact-induced changes from around the world are not by any means confined to lexical items, and according to Matras (2009: 222), one of the most common results of long-term contact is phonetic transfer. This study will thus focus on the effects of language contact on the use of several phonetic and/or phonological features, in addition to some loanwords, among speakers of various types, e.g. heritage speakers[1] and second-language speakers (henceforth, L2 speakers). Since this study will be the first to consider the linguistic repercussions of the revival of Welsh in this region and thereby draw comparisons between L2 speakers of Patagonian Welsh and different kinds of native speakers, the relevance of concepts relating to the field of second-language acquisition (SLA) will also be probed. Indeed, some of the results obtained suggest that different linguistic processes – some of which relate to language contact and others more associated with L2 acquisition – can lead to (partly) the same outcome in some instances, but to a different outcome in other cases. Consequently, the implications of the data presented in this chapter, especially for current pedagogical practices in Chubut, will be explored.

The remainder of this section will be divided into two subsections: the first will introduce key theoretical concepts that are relevant to this study and the

---

[1] The concept of "heritage speakers" is defined and discussed in more detail in Section 3 below.

second subsection will present details on previous work conducted on Patagonian Welsh. Section 2 will then provide a historical background of the Welsh settlement in Chubut and will be followed by the methodological details of this study in Section 3. Section 4 will then outline the variables analyzed, which will lead into the empirical results of Section 5. These data will be followed by a discussion of this study's findings in Section 6 and a summary of its conclusions in Section 7.

1.1 Key concepts

Thomason (2001: 1) notes that **language contact** is characterized by "the use of more than one language in the same place at the same time" and, unsurprisingly, studies of contact situations around the globe usually focus on communities where at least some speakers use more than one language. As mentioned above, the effects of language contact are wide-ranging (Thomason 2001: 8–13), and phonetic transfer from one language to another is one of the most common results of long-term contact (Matras 2009: 222). A highly relevant process associated with language contact is **structural convergence** defined by Thomason (2001: 262) as "a process through which two or more languages in contact become more similar to each other [...]". **Contact-induced change** is therefore the outcome of convergence and, according to Matras (2009: 222), "[...] contact-induced change in phonology is the result of speakers' inability or reluctance to maintain complete and consistent separation among the phonological systems of two languages". In a detailed analysis of processes that can lead to contact-induced phonological change, Matras (2009: 223–226) specifies that two systems may converge "in a situation of established and prolonged bilingualism" whereby "speakers of one language, often a minority language, may adjust the inventory of sounds and the rules that govern their distribution to match those of another, often a dominant contact language [...]". Since Welsh has been in contact with Spanish to various degrees for over 150 years in Chubut Province, it is plausible to argue that this kind of process arising from a long-term, intensive bilingual situation can account for the linguistic changes which have occurred (and which may well be ongoing) among native speakers of Patagonian Welsh.

Other concepts from the field of SLA seem to be more pertinent when accounting for some of the phonological features that arise among Chubut's learners of Welsh. First, **interlanguage** refers to a learner's communicative system which is expected to change over time as the L2 speaker gradually acquires a full knowledge of the target language (Selinker 1972). Thus, short-term errors that tend to become less frequent as the learner progresses are integral elements of a learner's interlanguage and may be regarded as examples of "interference" as defined below by Grosjean. **Fossilization** is another related phenomenon described as a "permanent lack of mastery of a target language (TL) despite continuous exposure to the TL input, adequate motivation to improve, and sufficient opportunity for practice" (Han 2004: 4). It appears therefore that both "interlanguage" and "fossilization" may be relevant concepts for the analysis of the results that follows, especially when differences arise between individual L2 speakers that vary in terms of their learning experiences.

The terms **interference** and **transfer** have been used interchangeably in several previous studies, but more recently, specialists in the field of SLA have favored the latter form since "['interference'] impl[ies] that knowledge in the first language hinders L2 development" (Ortega 2013: 31). However, in this chapter, I will follow Grosjean (2011: 14–5) who suggests that we use the term "transfer" for static phenomena "which reflect permanent traces of one language (La) on the other (Lb)" (with a "foreign" accent being "probably the clearest manifestation of a permanent trace of the other language"), and the term "interference" for dynamic phenomena "which are elements of the other language which slip into the output of the language being spoken (or written) and hence interfere with it". As will be seen, this distinction between "transfer" and "interference" as defined here will be helpful when accounting for some differences between the patterns of heritage speakers (i.e. those who have acquired Welsh at home) and those of L2 speakers (i.e. those who have learnt Welsh as adults).

1.2 Previous work on Patagonian Welsh

Although very few previous studies have provided a systematic analysis of the linguistic characteristics of Patagonian Welsh, R. O. Jones's (1976, 1984, 1988) accounts of phonological developments in the town of Gaiman, Chubut in the early 1970s are particularly relevant to my own study: some of the variables investigated here were initially identified by R. O. Jones,[2] and this allows for useful comparisons to be drawn between the situation of almost 50 years ago and the current one.

Since R. O. Jones's study attempted to examine the relationship between linguistic variation and the social stratification of Welsh in this community, a random sampling technique was applied, based mainly on speakers' gender

---

[2] All the phonological variables examined in this study are outlined in detail in Section 4 below.

and age, but their cultural orientation was also considered. The latter social dimension took into account their religious and educational background, as well as their cultural affiliation.

In Table 1 below, the Welsh-speaking sample obtained is divided into four main age-groups as follows: I = Elderly (60+); II = Middle-aged (45–60); III = Young Middle-aged (30–45); IV = Young (under 30). It is also shown that age-group II has been further divided into two sub-groups according to their cultural orientation: category A speakers are more likely to be prominent members of a Welsh chapel for instance whilst category B informants tend to be more involved with Spanish-medium religious establishments. R. O. Jones (1984: 245) also states that "[...] social network patterns coincide with these social strata divisions in that informants A tended to socialize far more with other Group A speakers but not to the exclusion of rapport with Group B speakers or with non-Welsh speaking members of the community".

The data presented in Table 1 show how the phonetic realizations of four specific variables vary between the various groups of speakers due to the influence of Spanish.

Table 1: The phonetic realizations of 4 variables (adapted from Jones 1976: 60).

	I	II A	II B	III	IV
chi 'you'	[χiː]	[χiː]	[xiː]	[xiː]	[xiː]
chwaer 'sister'	[χwaːir]	[χwaːir]	[xwaːir]	[xwaːir]	[xwaːir]
te 'tea'	[tʰeː]	[tʰeː]	[teː]	[teː]	[teː]
tân 'fire'	[tʰaːn]	[tʰaːn]	[taːn]	[taːn]	[taːn]
pont 'bridge'	[pʰontʰ]	[pʰontʰ]	[pont]	[pont]	[pont]
siŵr 'sure'	[ʃuːr]	[ʃuːr]	[siuːr]	[siuːr]	[siuːr]
siwgr 'sugar'	[ʃugur]	[ʃugur]	[siugur]	[siugur]	[siugur]
Spanish	[spaniʃ]	[spaniʃ]	[spanis]	[spanis]	[spanis]
machine	[maʃiːn]	[maʃiːn]	[masiːn]	[masiːn]	[masiːn]
mynydd 'mountain'	[mənɨð]	[mənɨð]		[mənɨð]	[minið]
yn y tŷ 'in the house'	[ən ə tiː]	[ən ə tiː]		[ən ə tiː]	[in i tiː]
fy afal i 'my apple'	[ən aval i]	[ən aval i]		[ən aval i]	[in aval i]

It is clear from the results that age played a crucial role with younger speakers appearing to be much more likely to incorporate Hispanicized variants in their Welsh than the older generation who seem to be identical to Welsh speakers in Wales. However, the differences between sub-groups IIA and IIB confirm that age was not the only relevant social factor in the early 1970s, and that speakers' cultural orientation, and thus their social networks, were also important elements that conditioned the extent of Spanish influence. Although the data in Table 1 are useful for us today, it should be stressed that it is largely a generalization of the main tendencies of the different groups rather than a detailed quantitative analysis; variation within the language of groups and individual speakers must surely have existed, but the amount of such variation in these variables were not probed. However, it is important to add that a quantitative analysis of "h-dropping" was carried out by R. O. Jones (1984: 250–258), and although age was again found to play an important role in the case of this variable too, even more significant differences were shown to be attributable to speakers' cultural orientation within age-groups I, II and III.

2 Historical background of the Welsh settlement in Chubut in Patagonia

The Welsh settlement in Patagonia, or *Y Wladfa (Gymreig)* (literally 'The [Welsh] Colony') as it is commonly called in Welsh, is located in Chubut Province, southern Argentina (see the lower right-hand corner map of Figure 1). The settlement does not consist of the entire province however, and today it is generally considered that *Y Wladfa* is confined to two distinctive parts of Chubut, namely the Lower Chubut Valley (*Dyffryn Camwy* in Welsh), which extends from Rawson to Dolavon in the east of the region, and the Cordillera de los Andes region (*Godre'r Andes* in Welsh), which borders with Chile and comprises Esquel and Trevelin (as shown in Figure 1). Although separated by over 550km, numerous family connections and Welsh cultural links remain between these two major districts.

On the 28th of July 1865, 153 Welsh emigrants, most of whom were from the coalfields of south-east Wales and English urban centers, arrived in Patagonia aboard the Mimosa, a converted tea-clipper. The establishment of a Welsh colony in this remote region of South America was not only in response to the increasing dominance of the English language and the Anglican Church in Wales (Williams 1991: 23; Jones 2009), but also resulted from concerns that considerable emigration from Wales in the mid-nineteenth century, mainly to North America, ultimately led to the loss of Welsh speakers' language, culture and religion (Johnson 2009: 141). Indeed, Michael D. Jones, the Welsh Congregationalist minister and principal of a theological college who was key to the idea and implementation of the Welsh settlement, had previously spent some years in the United States where he observed that Welsh immigrants tended to assimilate very quickly compared with people of other nationalities (R. O. Jones 1998: 291–292; Williams 1991: 22–26). Consequently, he believed that it was necessary to establish a Welsh settlement in a more isolated location away from the influence of the British Empire where Welsh immigrants could preserve their language, culture and religion. Eventually, the Argentine government's offer of Lower Chubut Valley was accepted in exchange for the Welsh settlers' occupation of the land which would secure Argentine sovereignty over the region (Coupland and Garrett 2010: 8).

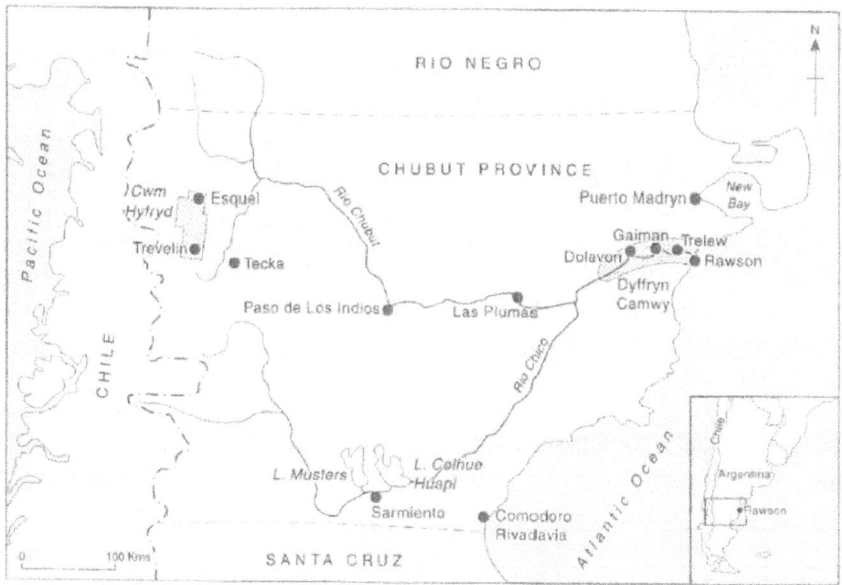

Figure 1: Chubut Province's main locations, including places in the Welsh settlement, and its location in Argentina (from R. O. Jones 1998: 296).

Around 3,000 Welsh emigrants travelled to Patagonia between 1865 and 1911, when immigration from Wales ceased (Johnson 2009: 142). Initially, the Welsh settlement was largely self-sustaining and independent and managed its own education system, its own local political and legal institutions, its religious buildings, as well as its own economic co-operative company and irrigation society (R. O. Jones 1998: 297–307). Unsurprisingly, Welsh was established as the exclusive language of all these establishments, and it cannot be overemphasized how revolutionary this sudden and substantial expansion in the language's domains of use was bearing in mind that Welsh was largely confined to the home and the chapel in Wales until the second half of the twentieth century. Moreover, several Welsh-language newspapers were published regularly soon after the establishment of *Y Wladfa* (Williams 1962: 123–126, 169, 198; Brooks 2012), and the early Welsh settlers even had their own constitution written in Welsh (R. O. Jones 1998: 298).

The domination of Welsh in all domains of public and personal life was not to continue however, and by the end of the nineteenth century, the Argentine state increased its pressures on the Welsh community to integrate into the wider community, and education through the medium of Spanish became a legal requirement for all public schools. Gaiman was the only area which came into direct confrontation with the Argentine government over the education issue, but even here, the government finally took over the school in 1899. Another consequence of this resistance by the Welsh community was that Welsh-speaking teachers were relocated away from Lower Chubut Valley to other regions in Argentina (Coupland and Garrett 2010: 9).

Nevertheless, instruction through the medium of Welsh did not cease to exist completely in the twentieth century since a campaign got under way for an independent secondary school which was eventually opened in Gaiman in 1907 and remained operative until 1947. As R. O. Jones (1984: 239) points out, this school, *Ysgol Ganolraddol y Gaiman*, was pioneering in that "[...] its syllabus was patterned on that of the British grammar school system but the education was trilingual – Welsh, Spanish and English in contrast to the English monoglot education current at the same period in Wales". It could therefore be interpreted that a reluctant acceptance of Spanish coincided with a degree of Anglicization, at least in the case of this school in Gaiman.

On the whole then, it appears that the Argentine education system was successful in its attempt to Hispanicize the children of the Welsh settlers. Interestingly, during his visit to Chubut in 1971/2, Davies (1976: 77) observed that levels of bilingualism varied among female speakers, specifying that several women over the age of 70 years old hardly had any knowledge of Spanish, whilst generally those under the age of 70 were able to communicate fluently through the medium of Argentina's national language. He also claims that the same levels of differences were not observed by male speakers due to the influence of Argentina's compulsory *servicio militar* (from 1901 onwards). It follows that members of the Welsh community in Chubut were not necessarily Hispanicized after the turn of the twentieth century; indeed, this initial chapter of the settlement has even been described as "the period of independence for the Welsh language" (Davies 1976: 69; my translation). However, Davies concludes that an influx of immigrant groups other than the Welsh during the first decades of the twentieth century was ultimately the most effective medium to Hispanicize the Welsh settlement in Chubut Valley, remarking that "the older generation can still remember the time when almost all of the natives were Welsh, referring to the odd Italian shopkeeper in Gaiman, or even in Trelew, who would also learn a bit of Welsh for commercial purposes" (Davies 1976: 77; my translation).

A substantial increase in the non-Welsh population was not the only factor that contributed to the decline of the Welsh language in Chubut, however. Because of economic developments in Argentina between the 1920s and 1930s, the Welsh settlers also witnessed a decline in their political influence. G. Williams (1991: 156) for instance states that the Welsh settlers "[...] lost their institutional power base through the collapse of the Co-operative Society, the nationalization of the Irrigation Society, the Railway Company, and the flour mills and their loss of control of the local municipalities". Furthermore, intermarriage became increasingly common too, leading to a reduction in the intergenerational transmission of the language. After the Second World War, as the Argentine government promoted monolingualism in the country, Welsh became increasingly restricted to Welsh speaking families and some religious meetings.

Even attendance at Welsh-speaking chapels decreased since their function as local welfare agencies became less necessary due to the Argentine government's introduction of medical insurance for the self-employed from the 1940s onwards (Williams 1991: 126–127, 257). Ultimately, a conflict concerning the involvement of missionaries from the Methodist Episcopal Church from the United States who encouraged the use of Spanish as the medium of communication served to practically separate the remaining members of the Welsh chapels into two factions in the early 1960s (Williams 1991: 131–132). As G. Williams highlights, "[c]ertainly the conflict served to speed up the process of cultural assimilation by further reducing the Welsh-language domains and also by weakening the internal cohesion of the ethnic group in formal institutional terms".

However, it is claimed that the 1965 centenary of the establishment of the Welsh settlement led to an improvement in attitude towards the Welsh ethnic group, as well as a renewed interest in the Welsh language and culture (Brooks and Lublin 2007; Johnson 2009: 142; Coupland and Garrett 2010: 9). The Eisteddfod, a competition-based Welsh cultural festival dedicated to literature, music and dance, was revived during the celebrations of the 1965 centenary for instance. However, it was not until the early 1990s that the Welsh language seemed to be on the increase (Jones 1996), largely due to the support of voluntary Welsh-speaking teachers from Wales. This revived enthusiasm for Welsh ultimately led to the initiation of a formal project to promote the language in

Chubut in 1997 funded by the Welsh Office (now the Welsh Government), the British Council and the Wales-Argentina Society. Over 20 years later, the Welsh Language Project in Chubut is reported as being an astounding success with the highest ever number of learners being noted in its 2016 annual report (Arwel 2016). The most recent milestone in the project's development has been the establishment of *Ysgol y Cwm* in 2016, Chubut's third Welsh-Spanish primary bilingual school. Since the inception of this project in 1997, three teachers from Wales have been assigned to different regions of Chubut each year to teach Welsh to adults and school pupils at various levels, as well as to co-ordinate cultural activities through the medium of Welsh.

However, despite the growth of Welsh language classes in the province, Welsh speakers still constitute a very small minority of the 500,000+ inhabitants of Chubut today (as noted above, the exact number of Welsh speakers in Chubut is not known). The long-term future of Welsh as a heritage language is far from clear, and interestingly, Birt (2005: 148) viewed that "[l]earning Welsh in Patagonia is not an attempt at reversing language shift but rather, [a means of] enabling participation in Welsh-language cultural events [...]". Nonetheless, several children today have claimed in interviews with me to have acquired Welsh (partly) at home, and it remains to be seen whether the transmission of the language will be common among future generations.

3 Data collection and analysis

The results presented in this chapter are based on fieldwork conducted in Chubut Province, Argentina in 2016 for a pilot study upon which a larger project on language contact and dialect contact phenomena may be based.[3] The simple aim of this field trip was to record a range of Welsh speakers from a variety of linguistic backgrounds to establish the amount and nature of language variation present, not only as between different speaker types, but also within the language of individual speakers.

Informants were selected in different areas of Chubut using the "friend of a friend" technique that enabled me to draw on people's pre-existing social rela-

---

[3] This fieldwork was made possible by a small grant from the *Coleg Cymraeg Cenedlaethol* (the Welsh-language National College) and it subsequently led to the development of an educational online resource that aims to introduce the traditional dialect forms of Patagonian Welsh to teachers working in the province (see Rees 2017 for further details).

tionships (Milroy 1987: 66).⁴ Contact was thus made with prominent local community members who agreed to function as "brokers" in the area and helped me to persuade suitable speakers to participate in interviews with me. The brokers explained to the participants that I was a native speaker of Welsh from Wales seeking for conversations with Welsh speakers in Chubut. In this way I was able to access local social networks, and to be recognized first and foremost, not as a researcher, but as an acquaintance of the "brokers" from Wales. It must be acknowledged however that this technique was not completely successful in persuading every person contacted to take part in my research: claims of inability to speak "proper Welsh" or even to remember the language were the most common reasons for such refusals. Future work on the sociolinguistics of Welsh in Chubut should bear this challenge in mind, especially when the objective is to obtain representative samples of the Welsh-speaking population in these communities. Random sampling was not used in this study: as noted above, Welsh speakers constitute a very small minority of the population of each community in the Welsh settlement, and sociolinguists working on varieties of Welsh in Wales have found this technique to be impractical in the context of a minority language (e.g. M. C. Jones 1998: 49; Thomas 1998: 92).

For the purpose of this pilot study, and due to time limitations, an accurate representative sample of the whole Welsh-speaking population in Chubut was not considered to be practical nor necessary; rather, the aim was to record a cross-section of speaker types. As for the classification of speakers, I decided to distinguish between "heritage speakers" (including "heritage learners"), defined by Polinsky and Kagan (2007: 368) as "people raised in a home where one language is spoken who subsequently switch to another dominant language", and L2 learners of Welsh who have been raised through the medium of Spanish only. The advantage of engaging with the concept of heritage speakers (rather than employing the more superficial term "L1 speakers") is that it acknowledges the considerable inter-individual differences that exist among this group of speakers. Indeed, Polinsky and Kagan (2007: 370–372) have proposed a continuum of speaking abilities among heritage speakers that ranges from "acrolectal" (high-proficiency near-native) speakers to "basilectal" (lowest-proficiency) speakers. Although placing various heritage speakers on the continuum goes beyond the scope of this pilot study, it should be borne in mind that the heritage speakers of Patagonian Welsh are not uniform in terms of their speaking competencies and that a mixture

---

4 This technique has previously been used in several sociolinguistic studies around the world, e.g. in Wales (Jones 1982; M. C. Jones 1998), England (Britain 1997), New Zealand (Holmes et al. 1991), Austria (Lippi-Green 1989), Australia (Horvath 1985) and Brazil (Bortoni-Ricardo 1985).

of "heritage speakers" (who have never formally been educated in Welsh) and "heritage learners" can be found today in Chubut.

Ultimately, a total number of 35 speakers were interviewed, and were divided into four specific speaker types according to the way in which they had acquired Welsh (see Table 2 below). For this specific study however, only six of these speakers form the basis of my analysis; three from group A (heritage speakers), one from group B (a type a heritage learner who had the opportunity to study Welsh in Wales in the 1990s),[5] and two from group C (L2 adult learners). Members of group D, namely L2 pupils currently learning Welsh (mainly) at bilingual schools, are not included in this study; these speakers were recorded conversing with their peers and Welsh teacher at Colegio Camwy in Gaiman, but further individual interviews would be required for the data of this group to be comparable with the results obtained for the other speaker types.

Table 2: The number of speakers interviewed in each group

Speaker types	No.
A – Heritage speakers; raised through the medium of Welsh; received no formal Welsh education	12
B – Heritage learners; (some) Welsh during upbringing; followed Welsh courses in Chubut and/or Wales	10
C – L2 adult learners; followed Welsh courses in Chubut and/or Wales	9
D – L2 pupils currently learning Welsh in Chubut	4

Further details of each individual speaker analyzed for this study are found in Table 3 below where it is shown that male and female informants are included within groups A and C. Despite gender and age differences within the sample, speakers' mode of acquisition was considered the most pertinent factor in this investigation of linguistic variability. As for the single individual in group B, it was originally intended to include her in group A; however, it became apparent that this speaker, who claimed to have always spoken Welsh to her grandmother (but mostly Spanish to her parents), had spent two years studying in Wales. Interestingly, she was able to distinguish between some words that she used with her grandmother during her childhood and other forms that she believed

---

[5] It is worth highlighting that heritage learners who have studied Welsh (mainly) in Chubut are not included in this pilot study, but would be useful in future work in assessing the extent to which the Welsh Language Project in Chubut is influencing heritage speakers' use of Welsh.

herself to have acquired whilst studying in Wales. It was thus decided that this speaker would be very appropriate as a representative of an intermediary group, i.e. a type of "heritage learner" between the two main groups. As for the other two groups, it should be emphasized that differences relating to the use or experience of Welsh exist within the same category of speakers.[6] For instance, the two female speakers of group A (A1 and A3) were noted to be more involved in local Welsh language activities than male speaker A2. In the same way, among the L2 learners of group C, speaker C1 is an experienced tutor and one of Chubut's early learners who started learning Welsh in the early 1990s, whilst speaker C2 had been studying Welsh for less than five years at the time of the interview.

Table 3: Informants' details.[7]

Group	Speaker	Male/female	Living in/Brought up in	Date of birth
A	A1	F	Esquel/Trevelin	10/03/1928
	A2	M	Esquel/Bryn Gwyn (near Gaiman)	12/01/1943
	A3	F	Gaiman/Bryn Gwyn	21/06/1927
B	B1	F	Gaiman/Treorci (near Gaiman)	23/02/1965
C	C1	M	Gaiman	25/04/1971
	C2	F	Gaiman/Buenos Aires and Gaiman	17/11/1967

The decision to focus on a relatively small sample of speakers reflects the fact that a holistic approach to language variation was adopted in this study; rather than concentrating on a limited number of linguistic features in a quantitative manner, the aim was to identify as many relevant phonological and lexical variables as possible. Accordingly, the phonological variables were auditorily analyzed using a broad phonetic transcription and transcribed in a series of audit trails; in a similar way, the variants obtained for the lexical variables were noted (in phonetic transcription initially) for each speaker in the same order (to facilitate comparisons). Consequently, the interviews were not transcribed in their entirety; since each audit trail focused on a certain number of linguistic varia-

---

[6] The implications of these individual differences will be explored further in Section 6 below.
[7] The order in which the speakers appear in this table is similar to that of Tables 4 and 5 in Section 5.

bles, the probability of including every single relevant token in the transcriptions was maximized. Since the identification of new variables (especially among the L2 learners) required me to cross-check with all the other recordings, it was necessary to confine the analysis to a limited number of speakers. However, a broad investigation of this kind will certainly provide a foundation upon which larger datasets can be used to conduct more specific (or narrower) examinations of certain linguistic features.

The "friend of a friend" method proved to be an effective way of obtaining hours of natural and mostly unprompted speech. Each individual interview was recorded in WAV format using a Zoom H2N Handy Recorder and generally lasted for at least 60 minutes. The informants of this study were interviewed individually at their homes, and the interviews consisted mainly of informal conversations on topics which were of interest to the speakers. At the end of each interview, informants were asked to describe what they saw in a series of pictures and translate some basic Spanish sentences into Welsh (my elementary knowledge of Spanish was not shown until this point); the aim of these exercises was to obtain comparable data relating to several lexical and syntactical variables. The formality of the speakers' speech during these exercises was not found to be significantly different from that of the informal conversations.

4 The variables

In the case of each phonological variable summarized below, comparisons will be drawn between Welsh and Spanish phonological systems. Such detailed comparisons between these two languages have not previously been documented and are in fact necessary for us to prove that language contact (rather than any internal linguistic factor) is the source of variation in the case of each feature (see for example Thomason 2001: 93–94; Bybee 2015: 249–250). Note that the phonological variables below are numbered in the same way as they appear in the results in Table 4 below.

4.1 Fronting of uvular /χ/

In varieties of Welsh, the uvular fricative [χ] (represented orthographically as <ch>) is common throughout Wales, and appears in initial, medial and final positions, e.g. [χiː] *chi* 'you', [kɔχi] *cochi* 'to blush' and [saːχ] *sach* 'sack' (G. E. Jones 1984: 47). In Spanish on the other hand, whilst the phoneme /x/ is usually articulated as a uvular fricative or trill [χ], for instance in [χorχe] *Jorge*, it is reported that the primary allophone of /x/ remains [x] in Argentina, as well as in some other Latin American countries (Tuten et al. 2016: 389). It is therefore plausible to argue that a change from a uvular fricative [χ] to a fronted velar [x] in Welsh is due to contact with varieties of Argentinean Spanish.

4.2 Unaspirated variants of unvoiced plosives /p, t, k/

Phonological accounts of Welsh normally distinguish between a set of three unvoiced plosives, i.e. /p, t, k/, and a corresponding set of voiced plosives, i.e. /b, d, g/. However, G. E. Jones (1984: 41) emphasizes that voicing is not a consistent feature in the articulation of the so-called "voiced" plosives, and that it is rather the "[...] aspiration/non-aspiration [that] is the constant feature distinguishing the two series of stops". This contrast between aspirated [pʰ, tʰ, kʰ] and unaspirated [b, d, g] is common in Welsh dialects throughout Wales. Conversely, although Spanish varieties also distinguish between the phonemes /p, t, k/ and /b, d, g/, the voiceless plosives are typically unaspirated (Tuten et al. 2016: 387). Consequently, a change from the aspirated variants [pʰ, tʰ, kʰ] to the unaspirated variants [p, t, k] in varieties of Welsh is most likely to originate from contact with Spanish.

4.3 Substitution of the palato-alveolar fricative /ʃ/ by /s/

All of Wales's dialects of Welsh today have the palato-alveolar fricative /ʃ/ as well as the alveolar fricative /s/ as elements of their inventory sets (G. E. Jones 1984: 46–7). In Spanish on the other hand, the palato-alveolar /ʃ/ is absent in most modern varieties of the language; however, the phoneme /j/ is reported as being articulated as [ʃ] or [ʒ] in Buenos Aires, with younger speakers preferring [ʃ] (Chang 2008; Tuten et al. 2016: 387), e.g. [poʃo] ~ [poʒo] for /pojo/ *pollo* 'chicken'. A change from /ʃ/ to /s(j)/ in Welsh, e.g. /ʃuːr/ > /sjuːr/ *siŵr* 'sure', /paʃo/ > /pasjo/ *pasio* 'to pass' and /sbaniʃ/ > /sbanis/ 'Spanish', may therefore be assumed to derive from Spanish.

4.4 Absence of the schwa vowel /ə/

Welsh has the short schwa vowel /ə/ in several contexts, for example in monosyllabic grammatical items and in stressed penultimates, e.g. /ən/ *yn* 'in' and

/kəvan/ *cyfan* 'entire' (Awbery 1984: 76–78). On the contrary, the five-phoneme vowel system of Spanish does not include the schwa vowel /ə/. The replacement of /ə/ by a fronter vowel, e.g. /e/ or /i/, in Patagonian Welsh is most certainly due to contact with Spanish.

4.5 H-dropping

The glottal fricative /h/ is common in most dialects of Welsh and in the standard language, and it appears in initial and medial positions, e.g. /hi:/ *hi* 'she/her' and /gwahanɔl/ *gwahanol* 'different'. However, /h/ is usually absent from the inventory set of traditional dialects in south-east Wales (G. E. Jones 1984: 47). In Spanish on the other hand, /h/ is absent from the consonantal systems of most varieties, including prestige varieties despite retention of <h> in the orthography, e.g. /aɾina/ *harina* 'flour' (Tuten et al. 2016: 389). Certainly, contact with Spanish is the most plausible reason for extensive "h-dropping" in Patagonian varieties of Welsh; however, it must be acknowledged that some non-/h/ Welsh dialects would have formed part of the original dialect mixture. Unfortunately, it is impossible to determine whether the influence of "h-dropping" in Spanish on Patagonian dialects of Welsh was reinforced in any way by the consequences of dialect contact (see Trudgill 2006: 5 for further details of problems when disentangling the influences of language contact and those of dialect contact). Nevertheless, since R. O. Jones's (1984) study of this feature (based on his fieldwork in 1973/4) concluded that "[a]s one progresses from the older generation to the younger generation the incidence of (h) decreases", there can be no doubt that the extent of contact with Spanish is the most (if not the only) relevant factor in the use of /h/ in Chubut's contemporary varieties of Welsh.

4.6 Substitution of the approximant [ɹ] by the tap [r] in /tr/

Although the Welsh /r/ is commonly reported as being a voiced alveolar trill [r], the post-alveolar approximant variant [ɹ] is commonly articulated in the consonant clusters /tr/ and /dr/ in Welsh dialects throughout Wales (G. E. Jones 1984: 44, 49). In Spanish on the other hand, the tap /ɾ/ and trill /r/ are separate phonemes in intervocalic positions (cf. /peɾo/ *pero* 'but' as opposed to /pero/ *perro* 'dog'), and it is the tap which is usual in consonant clusters, for instance in [tɾen] *tren* 'train' (Tuten et al. 2016: 390–391). We may therefore assume that a change in Patagonian varieties of Welsh from an approximant to a tap in /tr/, i.e. [tɹ] > [tr], is again due to contact with Spanish.

4.7 Frication of voiced plosive /d/

In Welsh, the unaspirated phonemes /b, d, g/ are always pronounced as plosives in citation / radical forms,[8] i.e. as [b, d, g], but as mentioned above, voicing is not a consistent feature in their articulation (G. E. Jones 1984: 41). Fricatives such as /v, ð, χ/ are therefore separate phonemes in Welsh, as exemplified by minimal pairs such as [boːd] *bod* 'to be' / [boːð] *bodd* 'satisfaction', [ban] *ban* 'peak' / [van] *fan* 'van' and [koːg] *cog* 'cuckoo' / [koːχ] *coch* 'red'. In contrast, the Spanish phonemes /b, d, g/ have plosive and fricative allophones in complementary distribution (Tuten et al. 2016: 388): /b/ (orthographic <b> or <v>) is realized as either [b] (after pauses and nasals only) or [β] (in all other contexts), e.g. [enbiar] *enviar* 'to send' vs. [leβe] *leve* 'light'; /d/ is articulated as either [d] (after pauses, nasals and laterals only) or [ð] (in all other contexts), e.g. [kaldo] *caldo* 'broth' vs. [kaða] in *cada* 'each'; and /g/ is either [g] (after pauses and nasals only) or [ɣ] (in all other contexts), e.g. [maŋga] *manga* 'sleeve' vs. [maɣo] *mago* 'wizard'. Clearly then, the traditional phonological system of Welsh is considerably different from that of Spanish in terms of their articulations of /b, d, g/, and the frication of these voiced plosives (at least in Welsh forms which are not subjected to word-initial consonant mutations) can undoubtedly be attributed to the influence of Spanish.

4.8 Devoicing of voiced plosives to [k, p, t]

In Welsh, although the phonemes /b, d, g/ are not always (fully) voiced, they are never realized as unvoiced [p, t, k] in initial or final positions in any of Wales's varieties of Welsh. As for medial positions however, the devoicing of /b, d, g/ is only possible in some traditional dialects in south-east Wales following a stressed vowel (Hannahs 2013: 15), e.g. *cadw* 'to keep' may be pronounced as [katu]. In Spanish on the other hand, devoicing of voiced plosives is reported as being common, with syllable-final positions favoring the greatest variation. In the case of syllable-final /b/ for instance, Tuten et al. (2016: 388) note that "in *obtener* 'to obtain' [...] [it] may be articulated as any of a range of variants between prototypical [β] and emphatic [p]". It appears therefore that the devoicing

---

[8] It is important to note however that Welsh has a complex system of consonant mutations whereby the initial consonants of secondary forms can change in some morphological and syntactical environments (see Ball and Müller 1992). Examples of soft mutations include [p] > [b], [d] > [ð] and [b] > [v] for instance. Since mutations relate to speakers' acquisition of grammatical rules, their use in Chubut will not be investigated in this study.

of voiced plosives in Spanish relates to a continuum of variants ranging from voiced fricatives to unvoiced /p, t, k/ with voiced /b, d, g/ appearing between the two extremes. Such a continuum can certainly account for the devoicing of voiced plosives in new varieties of Patagonian Welsh.

4.9 Labialization/plosification of fricative /v/ to [β]/[b]

As noted above, the fricatives /v, ð, χ/ are separate phonemes in Welsh, and never interchangeable with the voiced plosives /b, d, g/ in unmutated forms. Spanish on the other hand does not have labiodental /v/ as part of its inventory; nevertheless, bilabial [β] turns up as an allophone of /b/. Without any doubt, [β] or [b] can be considered as approximations of Welsh /v/ deriving from Spanish.

4.10 Insertion of /e/ before the alveolar sibilant /s/ + plosive

Consonant clusters comprising of the alveolar sibilant /s/ + plosive (+ liquid) sequences, e.g. /sb, sg, sd/, appear regularly in initial positions in all varieties of Welsh (as well as in other positions), e.g. /sbaːin/ *Sbaen* 'Spain', /sgiːɔ/ *sgïo* 'to ski' and /sdriːd/ *stryd* 'street'. Conversely, varieties of Spanish rule out tautosyllabic /s/ + plosive (+ liquid) in onsets and require resyllabification and prosthetic /e/ (Tuten et al. 2016: 391). Clearly then, insertion of /e/ word-initially before the clusters /sb, sg, sd/ in Welsh words would originate from contact with Spanish.

4.11 Lexical variables

Lastly, it should be mentioned that the lexical variables targeted through a series of pictures were intended mainly to investigate the phenomenon of dialect contact; in this study however, the analysis of lexical features in Table 5 below will be limited to the use of loanwords in Patagonian Welsh and their relationship with the phonological data of the various groups of speakers will be probed. Since instances of English loanwords occur (as well as Spanish ones), it is important to emphasize that these are also common in Wales (especially among older generations): it may therefore be assumed that loanwords from English formed part of the initial mixture of dialect forms. Interestingly, several heritage speakers informed me that they were unaware of the English origins of some loanwords until the arrival of teachers from Wales.

5 Results

We will now turn to the results of this study, looking first at the phonological variables outlined above, and then at the use of some loanwords in Patagonian Welsh. Note that the implications of these results are not discussed here but are left to the next section.

For ease of comparisons, three distinct symbols are used in Table 4 and are complemented by three different background colors which aim to highlight differences and similarities between the groups and individual speakers: the tick ✓ (on light grey background) in the first instance indicates that the feature in question originating from Spanish is used constantly by a speaker; ~ (on dark grey background) then reflects that variation within the language of an individual exists in the case of the feature under consideration, for example the interchange in [sbanis] ~ [sbaniʃ] 'Spanish' was noted for speakers A1 and A3; lastly, the cross ✗ (on white background) denotes that a variant deriving from Spanish is not present in the language of a speaker.

Looking first at the variables which were also examined by R. O. Jones (1976, 1984, see Section 1.2 above), i.e. features I to V in Table 4 below, it is clear from the results of the first two variables, i.e. the fronting of uvular [χ] to [x] and the non-aspiration in the unvoiced plosives [p, t, k], that the Hispanicized variants occur normally (if not consistently) by heritage speakers and learners alike. Variation between fronted [x] and uvular [χ] was identified in the speech of speaker A3 though, e.g. [xiː] ~ [χiː] *chi* 'you'. In the same way, some instances of aspirated [tʰ] in word-initial position were noted by speakers A3 (e.g. [tʰeː] *te* 'tea') and B1 (e.g. [tʰaːt] *tad* 'father'), although unaspirated [t] was far more common by these two informants too. In the case of speaker A3, it could be proposed that the emergence of [χ] and [tʰ] in some of her forms may relate to the fact that her father was born and raised in Wales; similarly, the use of [tʰ] by speaker B1 in a minority of her forms might have been influenced by her two years of residency in Wales.

However, a very unexpected result is shown for the third variable in Table 4, namely the substitution of the palato-alveolar fricative /ʃ/ by /s/, whereby the gradual decline of /ʃ/ seems to have been reversed. Indeed, informant B1 and the two L2 speakers in group C seem to use the palato-alveolar fricative /ʃ/ consistently, as opposed to the variation seen in the language of informants A1 and A3 (e.g. [sbanis] ~ [sbaniʃ] 'Spanish'), or the consistent use of /s/ by speaker A2.

Conversely, with regard to the fourth feature, an opposite trend is seen in Table 4: the schwa vowel /ə/ is always articulated by the heritage speakers of groups A and B, but is frequently absent in the language of the two L2 speakers (although not in all of their forms), for instance in [en] *yn* 'in', [eved] *yfed* 'to drink' and [desgi] *dysgu* 'to learn'. (Note that /ə/ was found to be supplanted by [e] rather than the [i] noted above in Section 1.2).

As for the fifth feature, i.e. "h-dropping", Table 4 indicates that this phenomenon was found to be widespread by speakers of each group, but variation between [h] and [Ø] was the norm rather than consistent "h-dropping". Several examples of interchange within the word for individual speakers were therefore noted, e.g. [eðju] ~ [heðju] *heddiw* 'today' by A1, [heːn] ~ [eːn] *hen* 'old' by A2 and [ogan] ~ [hogan] *hogan* 'girl' by C1. As noted also by R. O. Jones (1984: 251), occurrence of [h] may be associated with emphatic stress, but that was not always found to be case. Moreover, hypercorrections were identified in the language of each speaker (except for speaker C2), i.e. the insertion of /h/ word-initially in forms that would normally have vowels at their onsets, e.g. [hanoð] for *anodd* 'difficult' by A1 and [hemlað] for *ymladd* 'to fight' by C1. Clearly then, the similarities seen here between the three group's use of /h/ (and hypercorrections) are attributable to the phonological system of Spanish.

We turn next to the five phonological variables which have not previously been identified. First, the sixth variable in Table 4, namely the substitution of the approximant [ɹ] by the tap [ɾ] in the cluster /tr/, shows a very uniform picture whereby all the speakers use the alveolar tap [ɾ] consistently in this context. Since Welsh varieties in Wales also have the tap [ɾ] and the trill [r] in other contexts, it is unlikely that language tutors from Wales would "correct" speakers' articulation of [tr] to [tɹ].[9]

The remaining four variables of Table 4 are important in that they show a significant amount of variation as between the various groups of speakers. As for the seventh variable, only speakers in group C were found to fricate the voiced plosive [d] (but not in every relevant form), and examples of this phenomenon were obtained for initial, medial and final positions, e.g. [ən ðaŋos] *yn dangos* 'showing', [raðjo] *radio* 'radio' and [boːð] *bod* 'to be'. Although the first example could be interpreted as a hyper-mutation in Welsh (see footnote 8 above), the frication seen word-medially/-finally here increases the likelihood that the use of [ð] for /d/ is a phonological phenomenon rather than a grammatical error.

---

9 Interestingly, I am informed by a colleague from Patagonia that [ɹ] (with the approximant variant) used to appear in the Spanish varieties of some older rural Welsh speakers about 20 years ago. It remains to be discovered however whether this articulation is still heard in any varieties of Welsh or Spanish in Chubut today.

Table 4: The use of 10 phonological/phonetic variables related to contact with Spanish by three speaker types, namely "heritage speakers" (Group A), "heritage learner" (Group B) and "L2 adult learners" (Group C).

	Group	A			B	C	
	Speaker	A1	A2	A3	B1	C1	C2
I	Fronting of uvular [χ] "ch"	✓	✓	~	✓	✓	✓
II	Unaspirated variants of unvoiced plosives	✓	✓	~	~	✓	✓
III	Substitution of the palato-alveolar fricative /ʃ/ by /s/	~	✓	~	✗	✗	✗
IV	Absence of the schwa vowel /ə/	✗	✗	✗	✗	~	~
V	H-dropping	~	~	~	~	~	~
VI	Substitution of the approximant [ɹ] by the tap [r] in /tr/	✓	✓	✓	✓	✓	✓
VII	Frication of voiced plosive [d]	✗	✗	✗	✗	~	~
VIII	Devoicing of voiced plosives to [k, p, t]	✗	✗	✗	~	~	~
IX	Labialization/plosification of fricative /v/ to [β]/[b]	✗	✗	✗	✗	~	~
X	Insertion of /e/ before clusters comprising of fricative + plosive sequences	✗	✗	✗	✗	✗	✓

Similarly, the results of the eighth variable in Table 4 show that the devoicing of voiced plosives is common (although not completely consistent) among group C speakers. This phenomenon was noted to occur word-initially, -medially and -finally, e.g. [tim] for *dim* 'nothing', [kaɬi] for *gallu* 'to be able', [kanolpuintjo] for *canolbwyntio* 'to concentrate', [ki:k] for *cig* 'meat' and [gwait] for *gwaed* 'blood'. Interestingly, some occasional examples of this feature were also identified in the language of speaker B1, e.g. [tʰa:t] for *tad* 'father'. Since instances of the frication of [d] have just been established, one possible interpretation of the devoicing of [d] is that [t] represents a type of hypercorrection, i.e. a conscious effort to resist the frication of voiced plosives may well result in devoicing them altogether. Nonetheless, it should also be borne in mind that unvoiced plosives, voiced plosives and fricatives are very much on a continuum in phonological systems of Spanish (see Section 4 above for further details), so we may conclude that the devoicing observed here may well originate from a combination of Spanish-based phenomena.

As for the ninth feature, Table 4 shows again that it is only in the varieties of group C informants that we find that the fricative /v/ is regularly (but not entirely consistently) labialized or even plosified. Examples such as [βɛl] for *fel* 'like', [gaβr] *gafr* 'goat' and [riu baːθ] *rhyw fath* 'some kind' were noted for instance.

The last phonological variable shown in Table 4 involves the insertion of /e/ before clusters comprising of the alveolar sibilant /s/ + plosive sequence in word-initial position, and the results show that this feature only turned up in the Welsh of one of the learners recorded (speaker C2), e.g. in the forms [esbaineg] *Sbaeneg* 'Spanish' and [esgiːo] *sgïo* 'to ski'.

Turning lastly to the loanwords investigated, Table 5 shows the responses obtained for eight separate pictures. Again, to facilitate comparisons, different font types are applied: loanwords from Spanish are italicized and emboldened; loanwords from English are italicized only, and Standard Welsh forms (or at least common dialect forms) appear in a roman conventional font. Note also that distinct background colors are used: light grey signifies loanwords and white indicates that Standard Welsh words are used; in a few instances, a dark grey background is applied to show variation between a loanword and a Standard Welsh term.

A glance at Table 5 then reveals that Spanish and English loanwords appear constantly on the left-hand side but are absent on the right-hand side. In other words, the L2 speakers of group C who have learnt Welsh as adults are much more likely to use Standard Welsh words than the heritage speakers of group A who have acquired Welsh during their upbringing. However, the data obtained from informant B1 (i.e. the heritage learner) is valuable in that she was able to distinguish between the words that she would use when conversing with her grandmother during her childhood on the one hand, and the forms that she claims to have used regularly following her time studying in Wales. What is striking about the results of speaker B1 is that most of her "childhood forms" (on the left-hand side) mirror those obtained from group A speakers; conversely, her self-reported current usage of Standard Welsh words seems to connect her with the adult learners of group C. Consequently, the similarities seen between B1's "new forms" and the Standard Welsh words used by group C speakers appear to confirm that Welsh language instruction is a significant factor insofar as lexical variation and change in Chubut's contemporary varieties of Welsh is concerned.

Table 5: The use of loanwords for eight variables by three speaker types.

Speaker	Group A			Group B		Group C	
	A1	A2	A3	B1		C1	C2
				With grand-mother	Today		
I	*galpón*	*galpón*	*galpón*	*galpón*	beudy	sgubor/ beudy	sgubor/ beudy
II	strawberries	strawberries/*frutilla*	*frutilla*	strawberries	mefus	mefus	mefus
III	stairs	*escalera*	stairs	?	grisiau	grisiau	grisiau
IV	sweets	sweets	sweets/ *caramelos*	sweets	loshin/ da-das	loshin	loshin
V	carrots [karɔts]	carrots	carrots [karɛts]	carrots [karɛts]	moron	moron	moron
VI	plums	plums	*siniguelas* /plums	plums	eirin/ plums	eirin	eirin
VII	*carbón*	*carbón*/glo	*carbón*	?	glo	glo	glo
VIII	cabbage [kabɛts]	cabbage [kabɛts]	cabbage [kabɛts]	cabbage [kabɛts]		bresych	bresych

6 Discussion

The implications of the various trends emerging from the results above remain to be discussed and are divided into three subsections. 6.1 focuses on the similarities that all speaker types share, 6.2 then highlights the differences between the groups, and 6.3 explores other phenomena associated with the patterns of variability yielded (e.g. the effects of social networks and standardization).

6.1 Similarities

Several similarities exist as between the various groups of speakers (as well as differences). With regard to the phonological variables summarized above in Table 4, the results obtained for variables I, II, V and VI show that the three groups of informants share a significant amount of common features. Since variables I, II, and VI relate to phonetic modifications arising from contact with Spanish, and that the first two features were previously reported to be widespread in the early 1970s by some groups of speakers (Jones 1976, 1984), it is perhaps not surprising to discover a general increase in the influence of phonetic characteristics originating from Spanish. In this respect, it is worth emphasizing that none of the speakers analyzed shows a consistent use of the original Welsh variants for phonetic variables I, II and VI, as opposed to the reported situation of the 1970s (cf. Section 1.2 above).

It appears therefore that "transfer" (as defined by Grosjean 2011), which relates to "permanent traces" of one language on another, is a very useful concept in this instance, at least as far as the heritage speakers of groups A and B are concerned. Similarly, there is no doubt that phonological structural convergence (Matras 2009: 221–226) is a process that can account for the considerable overlap that exists between the phonological systems of the speakers' two languages, and that the most plausible mechanism by which this process has occurred (especially among the heritage speakers) is the prolonged and intensive bilingual situation that Matras refers to. However, it must be acknowledged that it is difficult to ascertain the extent to which these phenomena, i.e. "transfer" and "convergence", are relevant to L2 speakers of Welsh in Chubut; further quantitative and acoustic methods would be required to disentangle the effects of long-term convergence and individual bilingualism among Chubut's learners of Welsh (see Mayr et al. 2017 for instance).

6.2 Differences

Despite the parallels that we have thus far established as between the different groups of speakers, some considerable phonological and/or phonetic differences exist between them too. Generally, these differences are attributable to a greater degree of Hispanicization by the L2 speakers of group C than which is seen by the heritage speakers of groups A and B (except for variable IV, which will be discussed in detail below). Indeed, in the case of no less than five of the ten phonological features analyzed, i.e. variables IV, VII, VIII, IX and X, speakers in group C are clearly incorporating elements originating from Spanish into their Welsh which do not appear to be common among heritage speakers of Welsh. However, the processes involved in these changes are not similar in the case of each feature: variable IV (i.e. the absence of /ə/) could be described as a phonemic change since it concerns a loss of contrast between /ə/ and /e/; variables VII, VIII and IX are more related to phonetic modifications that resemble allophonic distributions in Spanish; finally, variable X has more to do with the influence of phonotactic constraints in Spanish whereby prosthetic vowels are essential before clusters comprising alveolar sibilant /s/ + plosive sequences in word-initial position. On the whole then, it is plain to see that the Welsh of group C is converging with the Spanish phonological system to a far greater extent than which is seen among the heritage speakers of groups A and B.

Certainly, the substantial differences that exist between the various groups (most of which involve newly identified variables, i.e. variables VII, VIII, IX and X) provide a basis for future studies on the acquisition of Welsh as an L2 in Chubut. Indeed, quantitative approaches may be adopted to trace the ongoing variation and change patterns of new speakers of Welsh in the province. In this way, further analyses of this kind will be able to examine the development of learners' "interlanguage" (Selinker 1972) and thereby establish the way in which the use of various phonological features is varying and changing at different stages of the learning process of L2 speakers.

It would seem from the variation patterns of the two group C speakers in Table 4 above that variables VII, VIII and IX represent instances of "interference" (as defined by Grosjean 2011), i.e. the slippages that are characteristic of most L2 varieties. However, since the new Hispanicized variants of these variables turn up regularly in the language of speaker C1, an experienced tutor who was among the first adult learners in Chubut to study Welsh from the early 1990s, it appears that variables VII, VIII and IX (all of which relate to phonetic modifications as noted already) may well be subjected to "fossilization" (Han 2004: 4). On the other hand, the difference seen between speakers C1 and C2 in the case of variable X may well point to the fact that speaker C2 is at a much earlier stage in the language learning process than her C1 counterpart. Thus, it could be argued that the difference between the two group C speakers in the instance of variable X (which involves phonotactic constraints in Spanish rather than any fine phonetic qualities in the L1) most probably indicates that the new variants, e.g. /esb/ rather than /sb/, are in fact short-term "errors" that form part of some learners' interlanguage. It would then follow that the absence of such "errors" in the speech of speaker C1 suggests that this new phenomenon is less likely to be fossilized than the phonetic modifications of variables VII, VIII and IX. It should be emphasized though that further fieldwork with a greater sample of L2 speakers would be necessary to confirm these initial hypotheses more accurately.

So far, all the differences noted as between the various groups of speakers have been related to an increase in the use of Hispanicized variants in L2 varieties of Welsh. However, it must be emphasized that variable III in Table 4 above is a striking exception of this general tendency whereby the gradual loss of /ʃ/ to /s/ seems to have been reversed. One possibility for the re-emergence of /ʃ/ is that L2 and heritage learners following Welsh courses have been "corrected" in class (either by teachers from Wales or even by tutors from Chubut who have studied in Wales). Furthermore, several younger and older speakers have informed me of their awareness of [ʃ] in Buenos Aires Spanish for orthographic <ll> and <y>, e.g. in [poʃo] for *pollo* 'chicken' (Chang 2008; Tuten et al. 2016: 387; see full details in Section 4 above), and that this pronunciation is also common in Chubut due to immigration from Argentina's capital. It is thus plausible to argue that [ʃ] is less "foreign" today among Chubut's monolingual Spanish speakers than it was when informants in group A were being brought up through the medium of Welsh. Consequently, if the use of [s] for /ʃ/ is found to appear among early beginners of Welsh in Chubut today, this may well have more to do with grapheme–phoneme correspondences in Spanish (whereby orthographic <si> or <is> are always pronounced as [si] or [is], e.g. in [siglo] *siglo* 'century') than any supposed inability to articulate [ʃ] due to Spanish interference. Clearly, further fieldwork with early learners and class observations are required to analyze in more detail how the re-emergence of /ʃ/ may be related to pedagogical practices in Chubut.

Since at least one phonemic change, i.e. /ʃ/ > /s/, seems to be witnessing a reversal, it is noteworthy that R. O. Jones (1984: 249), based on four linguistic changes that he observed in the 1970s (see Table 1 above), concluded that "[i]n terms of "apparent time" it would seem that phonetic or allophonic modification occurred prior to phonemic change". The reversal of the phonemic merger that I have just discussed certainly reinforces this interpretation and it also suggests that phonemic changes are less stable than changes in fine phonetic qualities. Furthermore, since I have also observed some attempts by teachers (originally from Wales) to increase pupils' awareness of the contrast between /ə/ and /e/, it seems that phonemic changes are more salient. In other words, the loss of phonemes appears to be more prone to catch the attention of language instructors and inspire them to develop "correction" strategies, which enhances the revitalization of traditional forms.

6.3 Other phenomena

Since some individual differences have already been established within group C, it is also important to note that linguistic uniformity was not found to be the norm among the heritage speakers either. For example, in the case of variable III in Table 4 above, intraindividual variation between [ʃ] and [s] was common by female speakers A1 and A3, whilst [s] was used consistently by male speaker A2. This difference may well be related to the speakers' social networks and general usage of Welsh: the two female speakers (A1 and A3) for instance participated regularly in Welsh-speaking and chapel events and often encountered visitors from Wales; the male speaker on the other hand was very much on the fringe of Welsh-speaking networks and associated the language mostly with the past and his late mother who had refused to speak Spanish to him during his childhood.

As Milroy and Milroy (1978: 23) have argued, "[...] the degree to which individuals approximate to a vernacular speech norm seems to correlate to the extent to which they participate in close-knit networks. It should not be surprising that a close-knit group tends to be linguistically homogeneous [...]". Whilst older speakers of Patagonian Welsh in the early 1970s exhibited a substantial degree of linguistic uniformity, i.e. a consistent use of features associated with the homeland (see Section 1.2 above), it follows that an absence of such homogeneity among Chubut's present-day heritage speakers of Welsh strongly suggests that the close-knit Welsh social networks that existed a generation or so ago have ceased to be due to intense Hispanicization. In other words, the increased amount of variability seen among speakers of groups A and B certainly points to the fact that Chubut's heritage speakers of Welsh engage mostly (if not exclusively) in Spanish-speaking communities of practice. This finding therefore concurs with Milroy and Milroy's hypothesis, but contrasts with Nagy's (2017: 101) investigation of heritage languages in Toronto in which no correlations were found between speakers' "strength of ties to the outgroup and [contact-influenced] linguistic patterns in the heritage language".

Finally, turning to the results of the lexical variables of Table 5 above, the clear pattern of decline that was seen in the use of Spanish and English loanwords is undoubtedly an indication of the standardization that is taking place amid L2 and heritage learners of Welsh as a result of Welsh language instruction (in both Chubut and Wales). In this respect, it is worth highlighting that a shift towards lexical standardization appears to coincide with an increased level of phonological Hispanicization among new speakers of Patagonian Welsh.

7 Conclusions

This pilot study constitutes the first attempt to analyze the development of several phonological and lexical features of the variety of Welsh currently spoken in Chubut, mainly from a language contact perspective. This study is also the first to explore the linguistic repercussions of the revitalization of Welsh in Chubut Province, and the new empirical results presented above have thus established a number of differences (as well as similarities) between various speaker types, namely heritage speakers, heritage learners and L2 learners. Consequently, this study has important implications for pedagogical practices and curricula in Chubut (and the Welsh Language Project in particular), for instance in distinguishing common L2 pronunciation "errors" from heritage speakers' more stable use of Hispanicized features arising from long-term contact. In the same way, and in view of the significant differences that have been shown to exist between L2 and heritage learners (who are often taught together), future training programs and course materials should facilitate instructors in accommodating the needs of learners from all language backgrounds, ensuring that the use of non-standard features by heritage speakers in Chubut is not undermined. Certainly, these considerations raise important questions about the way in which heritage languages generally can be promoted in post-colonial contexts. Finally, since the current situation of Patagonian Welsh has provided an excellent case study for examining different outcomes of contact, it is hoped that this study will open the field for further research on the ongoing linguistic developments in this understudied variety of Welsh, including quantitative and acoustic analyses of some of the newly identified phonological variables investigated here.

Acknowledgements: I am indebted to a number of people for help in preparing this study: to Dr Jonathan Morris, Prof. Diarmait Mac Giolla Chríost, Dr Gwenllian Awbery and two anonymous reviewers for their useful comments on previous versions; for the University of Wales Press for their permission to reproduce the map in Figure 1; to the *Coleg Cymraeg Cenedlaethol* (the Welsh-language National College) for their grant that made my visit to Argentina possible, and of course, to all members of the Welsh-speaking community in Chubut who gave of their time to help me with this project.

References

Awbery, Gwenllian M. 1984. Phonotactic constraints in Welsh. In Martin J. Ball & Glyn E. Jones (eds.), *Welsh phonology: Selected readings*, 65–104. Cardiff: University of Wales Press.
Ball, Martin J. & Nicole Müller. 1992. *Mutation in Welsh*. London: Routledge.
Birt, Paul. 2005. The Welsh language in Chubut Province, Argentina. In Diarmuid Ó Néill (ed.), *Rebuilding the Celtic languages: Reversing language shift in the Celtic countries*, 115–151. Talybont: Y Lolfa.
Bortoni-Ricardo, Stella Maris. 1985. *The urbanization of rural dialect speakers: A sociolinguistic study of Brazil*. Cambridge & New York: Cambridge University Press.

Britain, David. 1997. Dialect contact and phonological reallocation: "Canadian Raising" in the English Fens. *Language in Society* 26. 15–46.

Brooks, Walter Ariel. 2012. *Welsh print culture in y Wladfa: The role of ethnic newspapers in Welsh Patagonia, 1868–1933*. Cardiff: Cardiff University unpublished PhD thesis.

Brooks, Walter Ariel & Geraldine Lublin. 2007. The Eisteddfod of Chubut, or how the reinvention of a tradition has contributed to the preservation of a language and culture. *Beyond Philology* 4. 245–59.

Bybee, Joan. 2015. *Language change*. Cambridge: Cambridge University Press.

Carter, Diana, Margaret Deuchar, Peredur Davies & María del Carmen Parafita Couto. 2011. A systematic comparison of factors affecting the choice of matrix language in three bilingual communities. *Journal of Language Contact* 4. 153–183.

Chang, Charles B. 2008. Variation in palatal production in Buenos Aires Spanish. In Maurice Westmoreland & Juan Antonio Thomas (eds.), *Selected Proceedings of the 4th Workshop on Spanish Sociolinguistics*, 54–63. Somerville, MA: Cascadilla Proceedings Project.

Coupland, Nikolas & Peter Garrett. 2010. Linguistic landscapes, discursive frames and metacultural performance: The case of Welsh Patagonia. *International Journal of the Sociology of Language* 205. 7–36.

Davies, Gareth Alban. 1976. *Tan tro nesaf: Darlun o Wladfa Gymreig Patagonia*. Llandysul: Gomer.

Grosjean, François. 2011. An attempt to isolate, and then differentiate, transfer and interference. *International Journal of Bilingualism* 16(1). 11–21.

Han, ZhaoHong. 2004. *Fossilization in adult second language acquisition*. Clevedon: Multilingual Matters.

Hannahs, Stephen J. 2013. *The phonology of Welsh*. Oxford: Oxford University Press.

Holmes, Janet, Alan Bell & Mary Boyce. 1991. *Variation and change in New Zealand English: A social dialect investigation*. Wellington: Victoria University.

Horvath, Barbara M. 1985. *Variation in Australian English*. Cambridge & New York: Cambridge University Press.

Johnson, Ian. 2009. How green is their valley? Subjective vitality of Welsh language and culture in the Chubut Province, Argentina. *International Journal of the Sociology of Language* 195. 141–171.

Johnson, Ian. 2010. Tourism, transnationality and ethnolinguistic vitality: The Welsh in the Chubut Province, Argentina. *Journal of Multilingual and Multicultural Development* 36(6). 553–68.

Jones, Aled & Bill Jones. 2001. *Welsh reflections: Y Drych and America 1851–2001*. Llandysul: Gomer.

Jones, Ann E. 1982. Erydiad Geirfaol: Astudiaeth Ragarweiniol. *Cardiff Working Papers in Welsh Linguistics* 2. 25–42.

Jones, Glyn E. 1984. The distinctive vowels and consonants of Welsh. In Martin J. Ball & Glyn E. Jones (eds.), *Welsh phonology: Selected readings*, 40–64. Cardiff: University of Wales Press.

Jones, Mari C. 1998. Language obsolescence and revitalization: *Linguistic change in two sociolinguistically contrasting Welsh communities*. Oxford: Clarendon Press.

Jones, Robert Owen. 1976. Cydberthynas Amrywiadau Iaith a Nodweddion Cymdeithasol yn y Gaiman Chubut – Sylwadau Rhagarweiniol. *Bwletin y Bwrdd Gwybodau Celtaidd* XXVII. 51–64.

Jones, Robert Owen. 1984. Change and variation in the Welsh of Gaiman, Chubut. In Martin J. Ball & Glyn E. Jones (eds.), *Welsh phonology: Selected readings*, 237–261. Cardiff: University of Wales Press.

Jones, Robert Owen. 1988. Language variation and social stratification: Linguistic change in progress. In Martin J. Ball (ed.), *The use of Welsh: A contribution to sociolinguistics*, 289–306. Clevedon & Philadelphia: Multilingual Matters Ltd.

Jones, Robert Owen. 1996. *A report on the Welsh language in Argentina's Chubut Province 1996 / Adroddiad ar yr iaith Gymraeg yn nhalaith Chubut, yr Ariannin 1996*. Cardiff: British Council.

Jones, Robert Owen. 1998. The Welsh language in Patagonia. In Geraint H. Jenkins (ed.), *Language and community in the nineteenth century*, 287–316. Cardiff: University of Wales Press.

Jones, R. Tudur. 2009. Michael D. Jones a Thynged y Genedl. In E. Wyn James & Bill Jones (eds.), *Michael D. Jones a'i Wladfa Gymreig*, 60–84. Llanrwst: Gwasg Carreg Gwalch.

Lippi-Green, Rosina L. 1989. Social network integration and language change in progress in a rural alpine village. *Language in Society* 18. 213–234.

Matras, Yaron. 2009. *Language contact*. Cambridge: Cambridge University Press.

Mayr, Robert, Jonathan Morris, Ineke Mennen & Daniel Williams. 2017. Disentangling the effects of long-term language contact and individual bilingualism: The case of monophthongs in Welsh and English. *International Journal of Bilingualism* 21(3). 245–267.

Milroy, James & Lesley Milroy. 1978. Change and variation in an urban vernacular. In Peter Trudgill (ed.), *Sociolinguistic patterns in British English*, 19–36. London: Edward Arnold.

Milroy, Lesley. 1987. *Observing and analysing natural language*. Oxford: Basil Blackwell.

Morris, Jonathan. 2017. Sociophonetic variation in a long-term language contact situation: /l/-darkening in Welsh-English bilingual speech. *Journal of Sociolinguistics* 21(2). 183–207.

Nagy, Naomi. 2017. Cross-cultural approaches: Comparing heritage languages in Toronto. *University of Pennsylvania Working Papers in Linguistics* 23(2). 95–103.

Ortega, Lourdes. 2013. *Understanding second language acquisition*. Oxon & New York: Routledge.

Polinsky, Maria & Olga Kagan. 2007. Heritage languages: In the 'Wild' and in the classroom. *Language and Linguistics Compass* 1(5). 368–395.

Selinker, Larry. 1972. Interlanguage. *International Review of Applied Linguistics in Language Teaching* 10(3). 209–232.

Thomas, Ann Elizabeth. 1998. *Ynys Fach o Gymreictod: Astudiaeth Sosioieithyddol o'r Gymraeg ym Mhont-rhyd-y-fen*. Cardiff: The University of Wales unpublished PhD thesis.

Thomason, Sarah Gray. 2001. *Language contact: An introduction*. Edinburgh: Edinburgh University Press.

Trudgill, Peter. 2006. *New-dialect formation: The inevitability of Colonial Englishes*. Edinburgh: Edinburgh University Press.

Tuten, Donald N., Enrique Pato & Ora R. Schwarzwald. 2016. Spanish, Astur-Leonese, Navarro-Aragonese, Judaeo-Spanish. In Adam Ledgeway & Martin Maiden (eds), *The Oxford guide to the Romance languages*, 382–410. Oxford: Oxford University Press.

Williams, Glyn. 1991. *The Welsh in Patagonia: The state and ethnic community*. Cardiff: University of Wales Press.

Williams, R. Bryn. 1962. *Y Wladfa*. Caerdydd: Gwasg Prifysgol Cymru.

Websites/Online resources

Arwel, Rhisiart. 2016. Welsh language project in Chubut: 2016 Annual Report (British Council Wales). https://wales.britishcouncil.org/sites/default/files/welsh_language_report_english.pdf. (checked 20/03/2019)
Eberhard, David M., Gary F. Simons & Charles D. Fennig (eds.). 2019. *Ethnologue: Languages of the world*. Twenty-second edn. Dallas, Texas: SIL International.
https://www.ethnologue.com/country/AR/languages. (checked 20/03/2019)
James, E. Wyn. 2014. Viewpoint: The Argentines who speak Welsh. *BBC News Magazine*.
https://www.bbc.co.uk/news/magazine-29611380. (checked 20/03/2019)
Office for National Statistics. 2012. 2011 Census: Key Statistics for Wales, March 2011.
https://www.ons.gov.uk/peoplepopulationandcommunity/populationandmigration/populationestimates/bulletins/2011censuskeystatisticsforwales/2012-12-11. (checked 20/03/2019)
Rees, Iwan Wyn. 2017. Cyflwyno Tafodieithoedd Cymraeg y Wladfa. *Llyfrgell Adnoddau'r Coleg Cymraeg Cenedlaethol*. https://llyfrgell.porth.ac.uk/Default.aspx?catid=528. (checked 20/03/2019)

Danae Maria Perez and Mirjam Schmalz
Complex patterns of variety perception in the Eastern Caribbean

New insights from St. Kitts

Abstract: This chapter presents the sociolinguistic situation in St. Kitts, an island in the Lesser Antilles of the Eastern Caribbean. St. Kitts is officially English-speaking, yet most of the population speaks a creole variety thereof in their everyday conversation. In this chapter, we first outline the history of the island and the current situation of language use in St. Kitts, as well as the typological differences between St. Kitts English and St. Kitts Creole. We then present a study of language attitudes among Kittitians toward their own as well as other Caribbean varieties and also the more metropolitan varieties of English, above all British and American English. The results show that even though Kittitians do appreciate their own variety of English, the metropolitan ones still carry the highest prestige.

Keywords: St. Kitts and Nevis, Lesser Antilles, Caribbean English, language attitudes, English-based creoles

1 Introduction

This chapter tackles the sociolinguistic situation in the island state of St. Kitts and Nevis located in the Lesser Antilles of the Eastern Caribbean. Since 1782, St. Kitts and Nevis has been officially English-speaking; its sociolinguistic situation, however, is rather complex. A local standard variety of English is used alongside an English-lexifier creole, and the creole is the preferred code in informal everyday conversation while Standard English is used in formal contexts. This situation is the result of its population having been highly mobile since colonial times. Historically, settlers and enslaved people moved frequent-

---

Danae Maria Perez, Zurich University of Applied Sciences, Department of Applied Linguistics, Theaterstr. 15c, P.O Box, 8401 Winterthur, Switzerland. E-mail: peze@zhaw.ch
Mirjam Schmalz, University of Zurich, English Department, Plattenstr. 47, 8032 Zurich, Switzerland, E-mail: mirjam.schmalz@es.uzh.ch

ly between St. Kitts and other locations in the region. Today, it is the search for tertiary education and job opportunities that motivates Kittitians to leave, while business people from other Caribbean societies and overseas arrive and invest in the local tourist industry. These continuous migrational patterns lead to intense dialect and language contact, which shapes the local varieties of English and the perceptions thereof. St. Kitts and Nevis is thus an interesting postcolonial setting with very particular linguistic and sociolinguistic dynamics.

This situation is interesting not only for English dialectology and typology, but also for perceptual research in postcolonial contexts. Research on attitudes, which can be defined as "any affective, cognitive or behavioral index of evaluative reactions towards different varieties and their speakers" (Ryan et al. 1982: 7), has been gaining ground over the past few decades across the Caribbean. Since Winford's (1976) study on perceptions of teachers in Trinidad and Rickford's (1985) study on the perception of English and Creole in Guyana, the field has branched out to deepen the attitudinal knowledge of those two locations, as well as to cover the perceptual landscape of other territories within the region. Those studies have shown that communities in Trinidad and Tobago (cf. Deuber 2009; Deuber and Leung 2013), Jamaica (Westphal 2017) or the Bahamas (Hackert 2016) are slowly moving away from the complete orientation towards exonormative standards, i.e. U.S.-English or British English, towards a stronger endonormative orientation and more positive evaluation of the respective local Caribbean variety. This supports the view that, as Deuber and Leung state, "standard English is becoming not only a more pluricentric, but also a more complex phenomenon in today's world" (Deubert and Leung 2013: 311).

Within this complex situation of Standard English(es), it is of great importance to look at different language domains and the perceptions attached to them individually. In line with this, Deuber and Leung (2013) showed in their study on the perception of news broadcasters' speech in Trinidad that the locally influenced standard variety was favored over the U.S.-influenced variety and the local creole. This shows that even though the local creole variety was still disfavored in the context of news broadcasting, so was the exonormatively influenced variety. Thus, even though the local creole is still restricted in its usage to certain socially defined language domains, the locally influenced variety of English has recently been gaining strength and is more widely accepted than, or even favored over, exonormative standards in certain language domains. At the same time, as Hackert states, creoles are still often regarded "as 'bad' or 'broken' English and oppose[d] to 'proper' English" (Hackert 2016: 93). They are often associated with "backwardness and a lack of education", as well as "obstacles of modernization", which hinder their speakers of the "participation in the global economy" (Hackert 2016: 93). This connection of English and the possibility for social, educational, and economic advancement in life is pronounced up to the present day and also influences the attitudes held towards the locally spoken creoles. However, it must be noted that these findings and developments represent the situation in the more populous areas in the Caribbean. Neither an in-depth typological analysis nor an attitudinal study has so far been carried out in St. Kitts and Nevis.

The present chapter therefore sets out to add fresh data to both, the description of the sociolinguistic situation in St. Kitts today as well as the perceptual landscape on the island in the context of the speakers' mobility. After delineating a number of typological features of Kittitian English and Kittitian Creole, we will explore language attitudes in St. Kitts in order to gain a better understanding of how different regional and also overseas varieties are perceived there today. Our aim is to see to what extent St. Kitts is similar to other societies in the Caribbean where a creole and a standard-nearer variety coexist in a diglossic situation and what the roles of the two varieties are (cf. Devonish 2003). In the part of the chapter focusing on attitudes, we will investigate how different exonormative and endonormative varieties are perceived by Kittitians based on a verbal guise test. Furthermore, we will analyze sociolinguistic interviews in order to look for attitudinal patterns connected to the language varieties spoken in St. Kitts.

This chapter is based on first-hand data collected during two field trips to St. Kitts and Nevis in 2018 and 2019, during which we collected two types of data: recordings of elicited speech for the description of the linguistic varieties present in St. Kitts, and interviews and experiments for the linguistic perceptions and attitudes of the speakers. We will begin by sketching the particular linguistic ecology in St. Kitts in Section 2, in order to better understand the Kittitian perspective on the varieties under scrutiny. Section 3 outlines a number of key typological features of the Kittitian varieties to illustrate their relatedness with other regional varieties and their typological distance from Standard English. Section 4 then looks at language perceptions and attitudes. In this section, special attention is paid to Kittitian English, Jamaican English, as well as the more traditionally researched varieties from the UK and the US. Based on these findings, we propose that the perception of certain varieties that were traditionally seen as being of a rather low status, especially other Caribbean vernaculars (Hackert 2016), is being re-negotiated. The conclusion will bring these findings into the context of current knowledge and research on the region.

2 Location and the population's history

St. Kitts and Nevis belong to the smaller and less populated islands of the Eastern Caribbean and the Lesser Antilles. St. Kitts is more densely populated than Nevis with little over 40,000 inhabitants and a size of approximately 168 km². St. Kitts was officially settled by the English in 1623 and shortly after by the French in 1625. The two powers subsequently split the island into "four cultivable areas of equal size [...] leaving the dry south eastern extremity containing the salt pond as common property" (Baker 1999: 338). The local population present prior to the Europeans' arrival was almost entirely extinguished in a joint attack in the second half of the 1620s that was only survived by those who fled to neighboring islands (Parkvall 1999: 63). St. Kitts was the first West Indian island colony of England, and other islands, such as Nevis, Barbados, Anguilla, and Montserrat were colonized from there (Cooper 1999: 382; Smith 1999: 148). The island thereafter served as a point of dispersal of African laborers to other English territories in the area and "[d]ata compiled from Deerr (1949) suggest that, between 1630 and 1650, thousands of Africans had lived in, or at least had passed through, St. Kitts" (Deerr 1949, as paraphrased in Cooper 1999: 379). The island thus played a pivotal role and influenced regional varieties of English in the Eastern Caribbean (Huber 1999). Within the island itself, the continuing contact between the two colonial powers led to linguistic contact and mutual influence, too (Parkvall 1999: 68). Even though both the French and the English were evicted from the island by the Spanish in 1629, they soon after returned to St. Kitts. A little over a century of joint rule over the island followed, including constant quarrelling and several small wars between the English and the French. These quarrels also had a major impact on the local economy and its people, with enslaved people repeatedly changing hands between the two colonial powers. In 1782, the French finally left St. Kitts and the island thereafter solely belonged to the British (Parkvall 1999: 64).

In contrast to other Caribbean islands, the prosperity was rather limited in St. Kitts and the demographic increase of the enslaved population relatively slow. According to Parkvall (1995), this can probably be accounted for by the slow shift to sugar cultivation on the island. The downward trends were then further strengthened by several "natural disasters", such as "a devastating hurricane in 1772" (O'Flaherty 1999: 51). Historically, the demographic development can be divided into four main phases (Parkvall 1999: 64):

1. Rapid growth of the population from the colonization until the mid-1600s.
2. Rapid decline from about 20,000 to approximately 3,000 inhabitants due to better sugar cultivation possibilities elsewhere in the Caribbean until the end of the 17th century.
3. Slow and steady growth during the 18th century
4. Steady decrease again until the end of slavery

Overall, it was observed that the enslaved population of St. Kitts passed 50 % of the entire population in the late 17th century, which equals more than half a century. This is rather long when compared to other locations of the region, such as Jamaica with 15 years, or Suriname with 10 years (Parkvall 1999: 71). Nevertheless, as Smith (1999: 168) states, "the formation of a Creole by the 1690s [is] not unreasonable" to have happened in St. Kitts. The definition of a "creole" can here be seen as an English-lexified language that is typologically distant from Standard English, so as to justify its description as a language of its own. As is often the case, documents and archival material written in creole from that period are rather scarce. St. Kitts somewhat forms an exception in this respect, as one source of written material could be preserved, namely a collection of writings by Samuel Augustus Mathews. This material has been used for a detailed analysis of the diachronic development of creoles in St. Kitts and across the region (Baker and Bruyn 1999).

Today, St. Kitts and Nevis enjoys a stably growing economy. The GDP of the island amounts to 0.95 Billion US Dollars (Trading Economics 2019), and St. Kitts finds itself among the five countries with the lowest unemployment rates in the Caribbean with 4.5 % (Times Caribbean 2018). St. Kitts and Nevis both have English as their sole official language and the predominant ethnic groups of the islands, according to the national census of 2011, are Black (90.7 %), white Caucasian (2.7 %), mixed (2.5 %), East Indian (2 %), Hispanic (1.1 %), Chinese (0.3 %), Portuguese (0.1 %), and Syrian/Lebanese (0.1 %) (St. Kitts and Nevis Statistics 2011). A large proportion of the profits stemming from tourism are dominated by traders of Indian descent. After the island gained Independence in 1983, its economy has mainly depended on the citizenship by investment programs set up by the government and the tourist industries with its major cruise ships.

3 Language situation – Kittitian Creole and Kittitian English

St. Kitts has its own unique varieties of English. Due to its history of colonization and slavery, Kittitian English (KE) emerged from the contact between speakers of different varieties of British English with non-native speakers of English, mostly speakers of French or African languages. Moreover, given the highly stratified colonial society in which only a small elite had access to standard-nearer forms of English, also a creole variety evolved alongside KE. Whether this variety is structurally divergent enough to classify as a language of its own, i.e. as a creole in typological terms, is difficult to determine not only due to the lack of data, but also due to the lack of a unanimously accepted feature-based synchronic definition of creoles. While some scholars hold that creolization is not a linguistic, but rather a social process (cf. e.g. Mufwene 2000), others hold that there are certain features that set them apart as a language class of their own (cf. e.g. Bakker 2008; McWhorter 2011; Daval-Markussen and Bakker 2017). One of the most characteristic features is the rather isolating morphological setup of the creole in comparison to its lexifier (McWhorter 2011). For the sake of simplicity, and due to the fact *creole* is a widely used term in the Caribbean linguistic landscape, we will consider the non-standard vernacular spoken in St. Kitts as a creole here and label it *Kittitian Creole* (KC). The features described below and its unintelligibility for speakers of Standard English support such a decision.

Our knowledge of the typological profile of KE and KC is rather scarce. The local studies by Cooper (1979) and Martin (1983), as well as Baker and Pederson's (2013) description provide rather anecdotal data on the typological profile of KE and KC that do not lend themselves to comparative studies. Other than that, KE and KC and their position within the Caribbean have almost exclusively been the subject of diachronic studies (Baker and Bruyn 1999). This historical interest is due to the importance of St. Kitts during colonial times when the island served as a platform from where other islands were explored (Parkvall 2000: 123). In fact, certain linguistic features, or even an "embryonic" basic variety of English (Baker 1999: 347), may have spread from St. Kitts to other islands. A thorough description of its typological inventory will thus contribute valuable data to dialectologists, typologists, and historical linguists alike.

For the illustration of structural differences between the two varieties, we will transcribe KE in English orthography and present KC examples in a more phonetic transcription. The present description is based on recordings of four hours of spoken Kittitian English in seven semi-structured sociolinguistic interviews with four male and 14 female speakers between 17 and 81 years of age. In order to collect data on KC, we carried out different elicitation tasks with adults and secondary school students in which the participants completed translation tasks and retellings of short video clips triggering specific grammatical structures. The data presented here are based on a qualitative analysis and not yet supported by variationist statistics.

The most divergent structures between KE and KC in comparison to Standard English belong to the phonological and lexical inventories. KE is a relatively standard-near variety of English, i.e. its typological structure differs from Standard English to the degree most other dialectal varieties do. Apart from phonology, the most noticeable differences may be found in the verb system, as verbs are often not marked for person or tense by means of suffixes. This pattern is, however, relatively irregular, as missing suffixes may also be the result of word-final consonant cluster reduction, while stem changes may occasionally occur. In (1), for instance, the verb *Mrs. Christopher* **asked** is marked for past tense, whereas *she* **say** is not.

(1) *Remember the question that Mrs. Christopher asked about who […] is responsible for this center? Like, what our role is. And she say 'yeah'.*

As opposed to this rather standard-near variety, the more basilectal vernacular diverges from KE on all levels, particularly on the level of grammar. In the noun phrase, to begin with, nouns are usually marked for number by means of the postnominal plural marker *dem* instead of a suffix, as in English. In some cases, English mass nouns are countable in KC, such as *hee* 'hair' pluralized as *di hee dem* 'the hair' illustrated in ex. (2). This feature is, in fact, also present in many other Caribbean English-lexifier creoles, such as Jamaican Creole (Farquharson 2007: 30). A feature that is similar to other creole varieties in the Eastern Antilles is the marking of possession by means of the juxtaposition of the two elements, the former being the possessor and the latter the possessed as in (3).

(2) a go kat mi **hee dem**
 1SG FUT cut POSS.1SG hair PL
 'I am going to cut my hair'

(3) him boit i bai pan **hi nooz**
 3SG bite DET boy LOC POSS.3SG nose
 'It bites the boy in his nose'

Examples (2)–(3) also illustrate that the verb is used in an unmarked form accompanied by the obligatory pronoun as well as optional preposed TMA markers specifying them for person, tense, mood, and aspect, if required. The preposed item *a*, for instance, marks progressive aspect. The fact that it has the same form as the indefinite determiner as well as the first person singular pronoun shows that multiple meanings of a form may occur due to divergent phonological processes in the history of the variety. This entails that syntactic information is required in order to clarify its meaning, which is a common feature among creole languages (Michaelis et al. 2013). These examples suggest that overall, KC is more isolating than English.

(4) i   bai   **a**   **plee**   wid   di   frag   dem
    DET   boy   PROG   play   with   DET   frog   PL
    'The boy is playing with the frogs'

(5) a   mois   aanda   a   chii   **a**   **sliip**
    DET   mouse   under   DET   tree   PROG   sleep
    'A mouse is sleeping under a tree'

As for lexical aspects, there are a number of English items that have changed their original form due to phonetic restructuring as well as semantic change. A *gladman* 'womanizer' and *kianriid* 'analphabet' (lit. 'can't-read') are now nouns that originate from compounds, and *hepni* 'half-penny' was phonologically reduced and then lexicalized as a chunk. There are, of course, also items that stem from French or Spanish, which were most likely introduced during the colonial rule of these powers, such as *chulet* 'chewing gum' (originally from Nahuatl) that probably came with the Spaniards from Spanish *chicle*. Certain words are likely to stem from African etyma, such as *kuku* 'ugly', and also the use of onomatopoeic items to refer to the local fauna is common, such as *chickchidiwiik*, the name of an endemic bird (Martin 1983).

These lexical features, added to the structural divergence between KE and KC, justify the classification of the latter as a creolized variety that is similar to other Caribbean English-lexifier creoles (cf. Bakker 2008). This structural distance and the recognition of two separate language varieties show that the sociolinguistic situation in St. Kitts is similar to other Caribbean societies, where a creole and a standard variety that are typologically distinct coexist and are assigned to specific domains. The use of KC is common in everyday communication, while official and educational contexts prefer the standard variety. This sociolinguistic situation corresponds to diglossic settings, yet unlike other diglossic societies, such as Switzerland, the two varieties are not accessible to most speakers. Rather, the relation between the high and the low varieties is socially stratified, because the lexifier language was imposed forcefully and restricted to the powerful class, and thus today, the standard variety is only accessible to a certain social stratum. Devonish (2003) holds that most Caribbean societies – be they English- or French-speaking – live in such a (post-)conquest diglossia today in which the limited access to the high variety perpetuates social differences. The following sections analyze the attitudes assigned to the two varieties. The respondents of the questionnaires are all speakers of both varieties, i.e. KE as well as KC, though their individual competence in the two varieties is not taken into consideration.

4 Language attitudes in St. Kitts

So far, research representing the smaller communities and lesser known varieties of the Caribbean is scarce (e.g. Meyerhoff and Walker 2013; Myrick 2014). Thus, the following subsections of Section 4 are a first attempt at grasping the language attitudes present in St. Kitts. For this, semi-structured sociolinguistic interviews were led with 18 participants (age ranging between 17 and 81 years) and a verbal-guise experiment was conducted with 50 speakers with a mean age of 20.6 (ranging from 16 to 49 years of age). About two thirds of these participants attended the local college in Basseterre, or a local school in Cayon (outside of Basseterre), while one third was recruited through the friend-of-a-friend method.

In addition, in a verbal-guise test, the participants were played six sound files of speakers from Jamaica (female and male), St. Kitts (female and male), the US (male), and the UK (male), reading excerpts of the *North Wind and the Sun*. The sound files were then rated on 10 dimensions of a 5-point Likert-scale on dimensions of both the status dimension and the solidarity dimension, namely the perceived level of education, friendliness, trustworthiness, laziness, politeness, pushiness, rurality of the speaker, ease of understanding, ease on the ear, strength of accent, and the likelihood of the speaker to "belong to your group of friends". The sound files were selected according to the speakers' varieties as well as their age in order to make the sound files more comparable. No matched-guise technique was employed, but rather a scripted verbal-guise as we assumed that most participants would not "master more than one dialect" to a proficient degree (Montgomery 2007: 46), especially with a selection of varieties as divergent as the ones used for the present study.

Before looking at the results of the verbal-guise test, however, we turn to the interviews. When taking a closer look at them, five recurrent categories connected to attitudes towards the locally spoken language varieties were mentioned by our participants. These are the geographical distribution of varieties, different language domains, the connection between social class, education, and language, as well as the notion of Standard English. These categories will be defined and described in the following subsections, before turning to the quantitative analysis.

4.1 Geographical distribution

The geographical distribution of language has traditionally been the focus of dialectologists in their search of the documentation of language variation. Just as this horizontal variation has been the focus of scientific research, it is also often the focus of participants in perceptual studies, as geographical space usually is an easily graspable concept. Moreover, perceptual studies often show that the dichotomy between rural and urban spaces are still vivid in speakers' minds, even though population movements such as counter-urbanization or mundane mobility have considerably changed the rural landscape over the last decades and have also affected its linguistic setup (Britain 2006).

Similar patterns could be found in St. Kitts as our participants also frequently mentioned differences in the rural and urban speech of the island. They mentioned that the further away from the city (i.e. the capital of Basseterre) you move, the more of a "real deep dialect" you will hear, i.e. the more creole speech you will hear (6; recording SKM2[1]). This informant also mentioned that even though you tend to move closer to a standard when you are in the city, it is still "nowhere nearer to the Standard" (7; recording SKM2) arguably alluding to the notion of a desired exonormative standard without further elaborating on it.

(6) RES: You get to Conaree [just outside Basseterre], you begin to move away an' the **deeper down you go ((in the)) country area, is the more further away you move to the real deep dialec'**

(7) RES: [...] Ah an' there, **there's a city dialect, there's a town dialect, ((but)) you know, it is, it is, it's ((jus')) closer to the – I, I don' even want to say to the Standard, because the town dialect is nowhere nearer to the Standard**

4.2 Different domains

There is a long tradition of using the creole variety present within a community in differing degrees for different language domains (cf. Fishman 1972). In the

---

[1] In the coding, *SK* represents 'St. Kitts' (as opposed to Nevis), *M* stands for 'male', and the number is assigned to the date.

case of Trinidad, Deuber and Leung (2013: 311) argue that in the postcolonial context, there is a "differentiation in what functions as standard, with a different balance between local and global layers of standardness in different domains". Westphal (2015, 2017) also demonstrates this in his study on attitudes towards news broadcasters in Jamaica. In this domain, Jamaican Creole (JC) is traditionally hardly used at all; however, since the 1960s and 70s, JC has "increasingly infiltrated this domain" (Shields-Brodber 1997: 60–62, as paraphrased in Westphal 2015: 313), which leads to a great level of linguistic diversity within this domain.

A similar picture can be drawn for St. Kitts where different language varieties are expected in different language domains. Quite pronouncedly, the domains of education or the church require a greater degree of Standard English (8, recording SKM2; 9, recording SKM4), while the more social domains (10, recording SKM2) do not.

(8) RES: {BR} Uh, I grew up in **church**, so I heard Standard English all along uh, the preachers preached in Standard English, the **Sunday school teachers were people of ((a)) particular social class**

(9) INT1: But what about the use of, of English and this lingo as you're saying in school?
RES1: Well, **when they're [the children] playing, they use it, the locals' talk, but in school they're suppose', you know, the teacher ask' you a question you have to answer grammatically**
INT1: And that's in English?
RES1: Yes

(10) RES: **Yeah, when I, when I become emotional so, on the Facebook** page, which is how I relax [...] so **occasionally I will use the dialec'** [...]

These findings are in line with the general tendency found in other studies of connecting a form of a locally present standard variety with the status domain and a form of the creole or a non-standard variety of English with the domain of solidarity (cf. Westphal 2015). This tendency can be observed in both multilingual creole communities as well as in more traditional L1 communities, such as the UK, and it is thus arguably a widely present phenomenon.

4.3 Social class

In Excerpt (8) (recording SKM2) above, the interviewee alludes to the connection of a particular variety of speech and different social classes by connecting the Sunday school teachers to a "particular social class" which is arguably a higher social class as said teachers spoke "Standard English all along" (8, recording SKM2). This connection to social classes, as well as the jobs they are associated with, is furthermore stressed in other interviews, as can be seen in the following excerpt (11, recording SKM2):

(11)   RES: ((Yeah, but)) in town you wouldn' fin' that ((so much)) – yeah, that, it's very difficult to fin' that that depth
        INT1:   **It's closer to English here in town**
        RES: Yes it's ((closer)) to English and the **higher the social class is the less of the dialect you'll find**

This connection between language varieties spoken on the island and social class is also reinforced by Cooper's (1979) data. In one of the interviews, a participant told him that "'I only speak creole to those who can't appreciate good English'" (Cooper 1979: 20). In this statement, the connection between social class and language is evident. However, there is also a connection between language and a certain alleged level of education, or a lack thereof, which leads us to the next point.

4.4 Education

The perceptual connection between the usage of a certain language variety, dialect, or accent and the speaker's level of education is frequently found in perceptual research in most English-speaking communities (cf. e.g. Rickford 1985 for Guyana; Coupland and Bishop 2007 for the UK). Generally, the standard variety found in a community will be associated with a higher level of education, which ties in nicely with the connection between the standard and higher social classes, while the locally spoken vernacular or creole will be associated with a lower degree of education. A similar picture emerges in the St. Kitts data, too, where the level of education is strongly linked with the speaker's command of "Standard English". As could be seen in (9) (recording SKM4), when a "teacher ask' you a question you have to answer grammatically", which is in English. Furthermore, the distinction between local dialect and English seems also to be made by the parents when children enter school (12, recording SKM4):

(12) RES2: [LG] then normally, what I would find is that growin' up as a young chil', the **parents would not filter too much** in open speakin' to you they will **speak our own twang**, right, but as the chil' grows a little older where they now **start to pencil an' star' to do grammar** now, right,
      RES1: Yes, yes, that's the point
      RES2: then the mother now will start **to take them a little closer** an' tell 'em: "No, **do not talk that way**, this is how you pronounce this word", an' so on

This is taken a step further in the following Excerpt (13, recording SKM2) in which it is clearly stated that an educated person, in this case the speaker's aunt, would not speak in the local dialect:

(13) RES: Erm, an' I think and she, er, her sister, my aunt, was an **educated person** she lives in the Virgin Islands, {NS} so, er, my mother would not have been **the ((raw)) type of dialec' type** of thing

In (14) (recording SKM2), social class, profession, and education are again mixed within one statement. The informant says that he is a teacher and therefore only uses a certain level of dialect in his job – mainly when he becomes emotional. However, he still wants to maintain a certain social façade, so to speak:

(14) RES: [...] well I might say "all you", but is, is, it's, it's not really the deep dialec', I don't write the deep dialec', I, I don't want to go there, righ', **because I'm a teacher an' [...] I want to be understood**

KC also seems to be linked with "heaviness" (15, recording SKM4) or "laziness" to speak English, which can arguably also be brought into the context of education. A speaker's tongue is "heavy", so allegedly he/she is either lazy, does not know in which contexts he/she is supposed to employ English, or does not want to employ the standard in a certain situation, because the speaker does not care about the implications of his/her language use too much:

(15) RES2: This is when your tongue is heavy

The abovementioned interview sections show that a strong link between the language variety used, the proficiency therein, and the perceived level of education is present. Even though a Standard English was often alluded to, it was never defined clearly, which will be looked at in further detail in the next section.

4.5 The perceived Standard of English

The last recurring notion mentioned by our participants, which can again be brought into connection with the notion of formal education, is the fact that Standard English is considered to be the desirable form of English. This is best illustrated in the following examples from recording SKM2, in which Standard English is directly connected with being "polished" as an individual (16), with pride despite a lack of formal education (17), and a loss of respect if the standard is not adhered to (18):

(16) RES: In my home – my mother was a Nevisian, she was from Nevis, uh, bu' – I would, looking back on, on her now, I think she was one of the **polished** ones

(17) RES: My father [...] was a very **proud** Kittitian, you know [...] I'd I never heard my father speak what we call bad English, right he would always speak – an' he was not an very **educated man, but he was proud**

(18) RES: Right, and I'm – and the, the people who are on my page, I think ((they'll)), they, they can tolerate dialect at a certain depth [...] but if I begin to go below what they expect, er, **they lose respect for me**

The question of what the participants identified as this desirable variety of English, or the standard variety, was not asked in the interviews, but will be subject to further research. The question of the perception of the standard is an often-asked question in both attitudinal research within the Caribbean, as well as in traditional language settings, such as in the UK (cf. Coupland and Bishop 2007). This is also the point where the current data situation in St. Kitts diverges from other research results, since in St. Kitts the perception of the standard seems to be still strongly exonormatively oriented, to the extent of often connecting negative associations with KC. However, in other creole communities, such as Trinidad or Jamaica, the perception of the standard variety, or rather the question of which variety should be regarded as the local standard variety, is currently being renegotiated in favor of a more endonormative standard or higher levels of multinormativity (see e.g. Belgrave 2008; Deuber and Leung 2013; Hackert 2016; Westphal 2017; Meer and Deuber 2020). Furthermore, the renegotiation of perceptions towards standard varieties is arguably also a slight renegotiation of the standard ideology in general (cf. Milroy 2001), which is a more widespread phenomenon taking place in several English-speaking communities around the globe.

In Caribbean speech communities, this renegotiation process is especially complex, as there is not only one influence or one standard variety present, but several possible sources to draw from. On the one hand, there are the two exonormative standards provided by the US and UK, which are favored to a differing degree depending on the location and political and economic ties. On the other hand, and arguably more interestingly, local norms and standards are currently evolving, too, with a shift away from mostly stigmatizing views on creole varieties to overall slightly more equal or neutral attitudes. However, the process of change within attitudes and perceptions is slow, as not only explicit but also implicit attitudes are changing. As Hackert summarizes, "[w]hile Caribbean English-lexifier creoles are no longer overtly stigmatized, standardness in the Caribbean context is still mostly defined negatively, that is, in terms of distance from the creole" (Hackert 2016: 85). These developments hint at a change in attitudes towards a higher appreciation of local varieties, both of creole varieties, as well as local varieties of English. However, Hackert (2016) can only draw from data of better researched varieties within the Caribbean, such as the Bahamas, Trinidad and Tobago, or Jamaica, but not of smaller locations such as St. Kitts. Thus, further research into smaller locations in the Caribbean is needed in order to grasp the bigger picture of potential attitudinal change within the region.

4.6 Quantitative data analysis

To grasp the attitudinal situation in St. Kitts in connection to various exonormative and endonormative varieties, the general perceptual tasks have been analyzed before looking at individual language domains in the future. In Figure 1, the mean values of the results stemming from the rating of the six different sound files on 5-point Likert scales are presented. For the present paper, five different dimensions are analyzed, namely the perceived ease of understanding of the sound file in question and the perceived levels of education, friendliness, trustworthiness, and laziness of the speaker (Figure 1).

A general trend for an overall positive evaluation of the US male, the UK male as well as the Jamaican female speaker can be seen. This general picture can also be confirmed after statistical analysis of the relationships. To analyze if there are significant differences between the ratings of the different sound files, an ANOVA test was conducted.

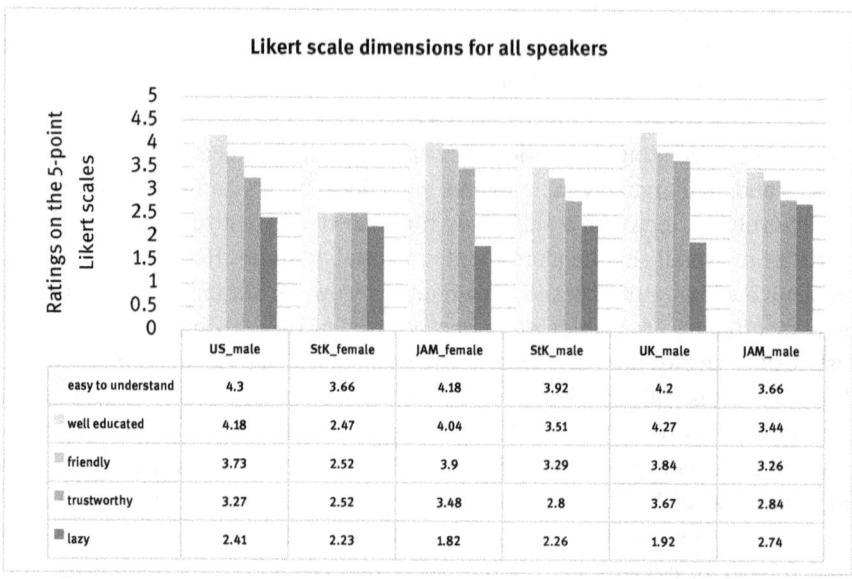

Figure 1: Mean values for 5-point Likert-scale ratings (n=50).

There it could be seen that both the US and the UK male were considered to be significantly more well-educated than the male speaker from Jamaica (US: $T=3.97$, $p=<0.01$; UK: $T=6.21$, $p=<0.01$) as well as the female Kittitian speaker (US: $T=9.07$, $p=<0.001$; UK: $T=9.51$, $p=<0.01$) and the male Kittitian speaker (US: $T=3.56$, $p=<0.05$; UK: $T=3.99$, $p=<0.01$). The female Jamaican speaker was also rated generally more positively for her level of education in comparison to other Caribbean speakers and as significantly more well-educated than the Kittitian female speaker ($T=8.36$, $p=<0.01$). Moreover, within the dimension of friendliness, the US and UK speakers were given rather positive ratings; however, they were only perceived to be significantly more friendly than the female Kittitian speaker (US: $T=5.66$, $p=0.001$; UK: $T=6.19$, $p=0.001$). Apart from the low ratings for the Kittitian speaker, however, all other speakers were considered to be similarly friendly.

Three sound files will now be looked at in more detail, as their results are rather striking, namely the female Kittitian speaker, and the female and the male Jamaican speakers. The female Kittitian voice, who exhibits more creole features than the male Kittitian speaker, was generally rated to be the most negative file when it comes to the levels of ease of understanding, education, friendliness, and trustworthiness – also across the Caribbean sound files. Only for laziness – the only negatively worded item in the questionnaire –, the ratings were not statistically significantly more negative compared to the other sound files from the Caribbean. The fact that the Jamaican female speaker is rated positively is in line with Devonish and Thomas (2012) who argue that the linguistic deference towards British English is losing grounds in the Caribbean. Nevertheless, in St. Kitts, strong positive associations with British English as well as the US, often rating the two varieties higher than Caribbean varieties, can still be seen; both in the qualitative as well as in the quantitative part of this paper.

The male Jamaican speaker is also worthy of consideration as he received more negative ratings than the female counterpart from Jamaica on all levels displayed above, i.e. ease of understanding, level of education, trustworthiness, friendliness. Post-hoc testing showed that the difference between their perceived levels of friendliness ($T=4.24$, $p=<0.05$), trustworthiness ($T=4.73$, $p=<0.05$), as well as laziness ($T=5.23$, $p=<0.01$) were statistically significant. The lower ratings for the Jamaican male can potentially be connected to the low level of recognition the male Jamaican speaker had, especially in comparison to the female Jamaican speaker and the two speakers from the UK and the US (see Figure 2).

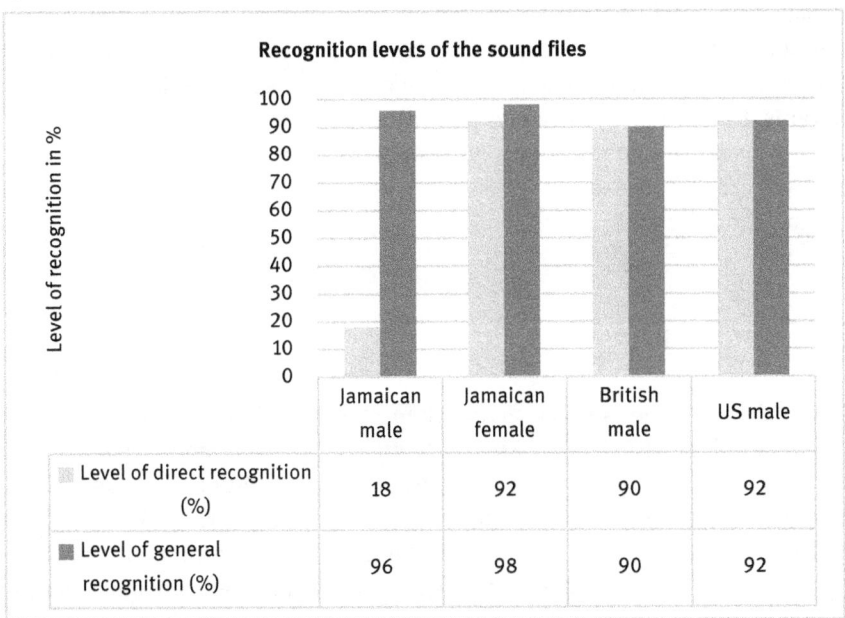

Figure 2: Levels of recognition of the individual sound files in % (n=50).

In Figure 2, the level of general recognition refers to the participants recognizing that the speaker comes from a certain region (i.e. the Caribbean, the UK, North

America), while the direct recognition refers to the participants recognizing the more specific area the speaker is from (i.e. Jamaica, the UK, the US). Following the levels of recognition for these varieties, it seems that if the variety is recognized as being from a certain location, they receive a more positive evaluation, which is the case for the female Jamaican speaker, as well as the US and UK voices. However, the Jamaican male could not be directly associated with any specific variety spoken within the Caribbean, but rather with the Caribbean in general.

To our participants, he did not sound like Jamaicans do, who, according to them, "have a harsh tone" (recording SKF5), "ramble everything" (recording SKF5), and are "hot-headed, they're quick to fight, they're quick to argue, erm, and curse {LG}" (recording SKF4). Our male Jamaican speaker did not match these stereotypes, as he has a calm, pronounced, and controlled way of speaking. The participants' uncertainty can also be seen when looking at the distribution of the ratings, as the male Jamaican speaker shows a much wider spread of answers on the Likert-scale than the Jamaican female, and the British and US males. These results, however, might point to the fact that there is a difference in implicit and explicit perceptions, which in turn points at a change in perceptions (McKenzie and Carrie 2018) with respect to the Jamaican variety. This is a very interesting development, as the perceptions might be changing overall towards a more positive evaluation of local varieties, including the local Kittitian varieties. It might just be a question of time until the assignation of prestige will change on a larger scale. To strengthen those claims, however, more research into this topic is needed.

5 Conclusion

In this first description of our fieldwork in St. Kitts, it has become evident that the linguistic situation in St. Kitts is similar to other Caribbean islands. Two closely related contact varieties of English, labeled as Kittitian English and Kittitian Creole, coexist, and they are typologically removed from Standard English. KE and KC both comprise features that set them apart from Standard English as well as other varieties in the region. KE is grammatically quite close to Standard British English, the phonology and lexicon being the most evident aspects setting it apart from the varieties spoken in the UK or the US. KC, by contrast, shows structures that are very divergent from Standard English. The progressive marker *a* preceding a bare verb, for instance, as well as the postnominal plural marker *dem*, express grammatical information differently and are rather similar to other common creole features frequent in this region. KC is certainly a contact variety of English that needs more in-depth descriptions in order to achieve a more complete picture of its structural inventory and complete the picture of Caribbean varieties both historically as well as synchronically. This will then also allow for a more comprehensive comparison of these varieties with other vernaculars in the region and to better understand language evolution in a high-contact environment with considerable speaker mobility.

On the perceptual level, our experiments showed that exonormative and other Caribbean varieties are rated more positively than Kittitian varieties, with the Jamaican female, the UK male, and the US male ranking highest of them all. Statistical testing has shown that the three abovementioned files have been ranked significantly higher in their perceived levels of education and friendliness than most other sound files. In addition to the perceptual experiments conducted, the sociolinguistic interviews showed strong associations of language varieties with social class, different levels of education, and the overall connotation of Standard English being "good English". Interestingly, the stereotypes attached to certain varieties, such as Jamaican creoles, seem strong enough as to influence an individual's perception of a variety as negative if the speaker cannot be clearly identified, as was the case with the Jamaican male speaker.

In conclusion, this exploratory research as a first attempt at grasping the local language varieties and the present perceptions and attitudes confirms that the locals' perceptions may be changing towards an increased appreciation of local and regional varieties as opposed to varieties nearer to Standard English. More research is needed in order to better understand these dynamics in different language domains.

Abbreviations

DET	determiner
FUT	future
LOC	locative
PL	plural
POSS	possessive
PROG	progressive
SG	singular

References

Baker, Philip. 1999. Investigating the origin and diffusion of shared features among the Atlantic English Creoles. In Philip Baker & Adrienne Bruyn (eds.), *St Kitts and the Atlantic Creoles*, 315–364. London: Westminster Press.
Baker, Philip & Adrienne Bruyn (eds.). 1999. *St. Kitts and the Atlantic Creoles: The texts of Samuel Augustus Mathews in perspective*. London: University of Westminster Press.
Baker, Philip & Lee Pederson. 2013. *Talk of St Kitts and Nevis*. London: Battlebridge.
Bakker, Peter. 2008. Pidgins versus creoles versus Pidgincreoles. In Silvia Kouwenberg & John Victor Singler (eds.), *The handbook of Pidgin and Creole studies*, 130–157. Oxford: Blackwell.
Belgrave, Korah. 2008. Speaking the Queen's English: Attitudes of Barbadians to British, American and Barbadian accents. *La Torre: Revista General de la Universidad de Puerto Rico* 13(49/50). 429–444.
Britain, David. 2006. Which way to look? Perspectives on 'Urban' and 'Rural' in dialectology. In Emma Moore & Chris Montgomery (eds.), *A sense of place: Studies in language and region*, 171–188. Cambridge: Cambridge University Press.
Cooper, Vincent O. 1979. *Basilectal creole, decreolization, and autonomous language change in St. Kitts-Nevis*. Princeton University PhD thesis.
Cooper, Vincent O. 1999. St. Kitts: The launching pad for Leeward Islands Creoles. In Philip Baker & Adrienne Bruyn (eds.), *St. Kitts and the Atlantic Creoles: The texts of Samuel Augustus Mathews in perspective*, 379–386. London: University of Westminster Press.
Coupland, Nicolas & Hywel Bishop. 2007. Ideologised values for British accents. *Journal of Sociolinguistics* 11(1). 74–93.
Daval-Markussen, Aymeric & Peter Bakker. 2017. Typology of creole languages. In Alexandra Y. Aikhenvald & R. M.W. Dixon (eds.), *The Cambridge handbook of linguistic typology*, 254–286. Cambridge: Cambridge University Press.
Deerr, Noel. 1949. *Sugar and slaves: The rise of the planter class in the English West Indies, 1624–1713*. Chapel Hill: University of North Carolina.
Deuber, Dagmar. 2009. Standard English in the secondary school in Trinidad. In Thomas Hoffmann & Lucia Siebers (eds.), *World Englishes – Problems, properties and prospects*, 83–104. Amsterdam & Philadelphia: John Benjamins.
Deuber, Dagmar & Glenda-Alicia Leung. 2013. Investigating attitudes towards an emerging standard of English: Evaluations of newscasters' accents in Trinidad. *Multilingua* 32(3). 289–319.
Devonish, Hubert. 2003. Caribbean Creoles. In Ana Deumert & W. Vandenbussche (eds.), *Germanic standardisations: Past to present*, 41–67. Amsterdam & Philadelphia: John Benjamins.
Devonish, Hubert & Ewart A. C. Thomas. 2012. Standards of English in the Caribbean. In Raymond Hickey (ed.), *Standard English: Codified varieties around the world*, 179–197. Cambridge: Cambridge University Press.
Farquharson, Joseph. 2007. Creole morphology revisited. In Umberto Ansaldo, Stephen Matthews, & Lisa Lim (eds.), *Deconstructing Creole*, 21–37. Amsterdam & Philadelphia: John Benjamins.
Fishman, Joshua A. 1972. Domains and the relationship between micro- and macrosociolinguistics. In John J. Gumperz & Dell Hymes (eds.), *Directions in sociolinguistics: The ethnography of communication*, 435–453. New York: Holt, Rinehart and Winston.

Hackert, Stephanie. 2016. Standards of English in the Caribbean: History, attitudes, functions, features. In Elena Seoane & Cristina Suárez-Gómez (eds.), World Englishes: New theoretical and methodological considerations, 85–112. Amsterdam & Philadelphia: John Benjamins.

Huber, Magnus. 1999. Atlantic English Creoles and the Lower Guinea Coast: A case against Afrogenesis. In Magnus Huber & Mikael Parkvall (eds.), *Spreading the word. The issue of diffusion among the Atlantic creoles*, 81–110. London: Westminster.

Martin, Julie. 1983. *A description of the dialect spoken in St Kitts*. University of the West Indies unpublished BA thesis.

McKenzie, Robert & Erin Carrie. 2018. Implicit–explicit attitudinal discrepancy and the investigation of language attitude change in progress. *Journal of Multilingual and Multicultural Development*. 1–15.

McWhorter, John. 2011. *Linguistic simplicity and complexity. Why do languages undress?* Berlin & Boston: De Gruyter Mouton.

Meer, Philipp & Dagmar Deuber. 2020. Standard English in Trinidad: Multinormativity, translocality, and implications for the Dynamic Model and the EIF Model. In Sarah Buschfeld & Alexander Kautsch (eds.), *Modelling World Englishes: A joint approach towards postcolonial and non-postcolonial varieties*. Edinburgh: Edinburgh University Press.

Meyerhoff, Miriam & James Walker. 2013. *Bequia talk (St. Vincent and the Grenadines)*. London: Battlebridge.

Michaelis, Susanne, Philippe Maurer, Martin Haspelmath & Magnus Huber (eds.). 2013. *Atlas of Pidgin and Creole language structures online*. Leipzig: Max Planck Institute for Evolutionary Anthropology.

Milroy, James. 2001. Language ideologies and the consequences of standardization. *Journal of Sociolinguistics* 5(4). 530–555.

Montgomery, Chris. 2007. *Northern English dialects: A perceptual approach*. National Centre for English Cultural Tradition, University of Sheffield PhD Dissertation.

Mufwene, Salikoko. 2000. Creolization is a social, not a structural, process. In Ingrid Neumann-Holzschuh & Edgar Schneider (eds.), *Degrees of restructuring in Creole languages*, 65–84. Amsterdam & Philadelphia: Benjamins.

Myrick, Caroline. 2014. Putting Saban English on the map. A descriptive analysis of English language variation on Saba. *English World-wide* 35(2), 161–192.

O'Flaherty, Victoria Borg. 1999. Samuel Augustus Mathews: His life and times. In Philip Baker & Adrienne Bruyn (eds.), *St. Kitts and the Atlantic Creoles: The texts of Samuel Augustus Mathews in perspective*, 49–58. London: University of Westminster Press.

Parkvall, Mikael. 1995. On the role of St Kitts in a new scenario of French Creole genesis. In Philip Baker (ed.), *From contact to Creole and beyond*, 41–62. London: University of Westminster Press.

Parkvall, Mikael. 1999. A note on the peopling of English St Kitts. In Philip Baker & Adrienne Bruyn (eds.), *St. Kitts and the Atlantic Creoles: The texts of Samuel Augustus Mathews in perspective*, 63–74. London: University of Westminster Press.

Parkvall, Mikael. 2000. *Out of Africa. African influences in Atlantic Creoles*. London: Battlebridge Publications.

Rickford, John R. 1985. Standard and non-standard language attitudes in a creole continuum. In N. Wolfson & J. Manes (eds.), *Language of inequality*, 145–160. Berlin & New York: De Gruyter.

Ryan, Ellen B., Howard Giles & Richard J. Sebastian. 1982. An integrative perspective for the study of attitudes towards language variation. In Ellen B. Ryan & Howard Giles (eds.), *Attitudes towards language variation: Social and applied contexts*, 1–19. London: Edward Arnold.

Shields-Brodber, Kathryn. 1997. Requiem for English in an 'English-speaking' community: The case of Jamaica. In Edgar W. Schneider (ed.), *Englishes around the world*, 57–67. Amsterdam & Philadelphia: John Benjamins.

Smith, Norval. 1999. The vowel system of 18th-century St Kitts Creole: Evidence for the history of the English Creoles? In Philip Baker & Adrienne Bruyn (eds.), *St. Kitts and the Atlantic Creoles: The texts of Samuel Augustus Mathews in perspective*, 379–386. London: University of Westminster Press.

St. Kitts and Nevis Statistics Department. 2011. St. Kitts and Nevis Statistics Population and Housing Census.

Times Caribbean. 2018. St.Kitts-Nevis listed as having the lowest unemployment rate in the OECS and among the 5 lowest in the Caribbean. http://timescaribbeanonline.com/st-kitts-nevis-listed-as-having-the-lowest-unemployment-rate-in-the-oecs-and-among-the-5-lowest-in-the-caribbean/. (checked 28/02/19)

Trading Economics. 2019. St Kitts and Nevis GDP. https://tradingeconomics.com/st-kitts-and-nevis/gdp. (checked 28/02/19).

Westphal, Michael. 2015. Attitudes toward accents of Standard English in Jamaican Radio Newscasting. *Journal of English Linguistics* 43(4). 311–333.

Westphal, Michael. 2017. *Language variation on Jamaican Radio*. Amsterdam & Philadelphia: John Benjamins.

Winford, Donald. 1976. Teacher attitudes toward language variation in a Creole community. *International Journal of the Sociology of Language* 8. 45–75.

Britta Schneider
The contested role of colonial language ideologies in multilingual Belize

Abstract: In this article, I introduce data collected in an ethnographic field study in Belize. Despite very complex multilingual practices and non-nationality-based language ideologies, the idea that language and national/ethnic groups straightforwardly relate to each other is part of language activism in this postcolonial setting. Language activists conceive of Belizean Kriol as a distinct language and as an index for nationhood (consider e.g. the website of the *National Kriol Council* of Belize). However, because of the locally contested and complex roles of Kriol, Spanish, and English, this enterprise has not been entirely successful. Activists' appropriation of colonial language ideology, aiming at the construction of a 'real' Kriol language with a dictionary and a grammar book, reconstructs colonial language ideologies that assume a one-to-one relationship between ethnicity/nationality and one coherent form of language, and thus disregards multilingual complexities. Despite the problems attached to this, the appropriation of Western language ideologies is an important means to create both a 'voice' and a legitimate identity where colonial hierarchies continue to play a strong role. Overall, this shows that colonial language ideologies of fixed normative languages, tied to ethnic/national groups, exist in multiplex networks of interacting language ideologies and can paradoxically link to liberation and suppression at the same time.

Keywords: multilingualism, attitudes, language ideologies, ethnic identity, discourse, postcolonialism

1 Colonial language ideologies in postcolonial settings

The hypothesis that languages are an effect of particular social discourses, rather than their precondition, has become more and more popular in contemporary sociolinguistics (see e.g. Hymes 1968 for an early discussion, and Errington

---

Britta Schneider, European University Viadrina Frankfurt (Oder), Junior-Professor for Language Use and Migration, Logenstr. 2, 15230 Frankfurt (Oder), Germany, E-mail: bschneider@europa-uni.de

https://doi.org/10.1515/9783110723977-010

2008, Pennycook 1998, see also the related debates on languages as constructs in translanguaging research, e.g. in García and Wei 2014). In these debates, languages have been discussed as part of colonial discourses that construct the world as ordered along cultural groups, residing in particular territories – a conceptualization that is mirrored in national discourses (Billig 1995, Wimmer and Schiller 2002, see also Said 1978 on the relationship between colonialism and nationalism).

The present study attends to the social discourses that frame and construct language in a postcolonial context and is based on ethnographic and interview data collected Belize, a former British colony characterized by strong forms of cultural and linguistic diversity and mixing. I use the nation of Belize as a point of reference in framing the cultural setting in order to explain some of the observed discourses and practices. This is grounded in the assumption that, despite a general increase of transnational interaction, the national and governmental levels remain highly influential in the realm of language policy, education, and framing public discourses related to belonging. Yet, as we will see in later sections, national discourses are embedded in local and oftentimes diverse language ecologies in complex ways. The aim of the article is to introduce such complex language ecologies as found in a Belizean village and relate these to the concepts of language activists. This provides an example of how postcolonial activism may reproduce colonial knowledge about languages, which constructs languages as entities that are unambiguously tied to an ethnic/national group. Thus, while it is analytically inappropriate to assume languages to be a priori categories (as the ethnographic and interview data introduced in Section 4 show), this does not mean that this knowledge is irrelevant. Rather, my observations show that conceptualizations of languages as indexing ethnic or national groups remain socially relevant and are therefore empirically observable phenomena that have to be considered in order to understand postcolonial practices.

The ethnographic analysis reveals the contested and paradoxical status of colonial language ideologies in contemporary postcolonial cultures, which remain marked by national concepts. The example of the paradoxes and complexities of language ideologies in Belize, in a village as well as in the public language activists' discourse, empirically highlights some aspects of postcolonial theoretical debates on the difficulty (or maybe impossibility?) of overcoming a colonial epistemology without using the colonizer's tools (see e.g. Bauman 1998).

In the following, I first introduce the theoretical foundations of the study of language ideologies and of languages as part of colonial knowledge. Secondly, I give insights into the language ideological situation of the country and, thirdly, to the methods used in this study. In the fourth section, I provide a more in-depth analysis of the language ideologies of residents of a Belizean village toward the most prominent languages spoken and of language activist discourse. In my concluding remarks, I discuss the results of the study as well as their theoretical consequences.

2 Languages as colonial language ideologies

The linguistic anthropological tradition of language ideology research (Kroskrity 2000, Woolard 1998) is interested in the relation between the social and the linguistic, defining language ideologies as a "cultural system of ideas about social and linguistic relationships, together with their loading of moral and political interests" (Irvine 1989: 255). According to this strand of research, language use is never free from its social and political embedding, as "acts of speaking are ideologically mediated, since those acts necessarily involve the speaker's understanding of salient social groups, activities, and practices, including forms of talk" (Irvine 2001: 24). The study of language ideologies has demonstrated that languages as separable entities are constructed by people in interpreting and actively shaping their social and linguistic circumstances. At the same time, however, they influence and shape people's behavior.

In sociolinguistics and linguistic anthropology, the concept of languages as separable entities has been discussed as part of colonial and national discourses (Billig 1995, Errington 2008, Pennycook 1998), framed in an overall idea of the world being divided into separable cultural groups that reside in separable territories (see also Wimmer and Schiller 2002). The ordering of peoples into different groups with distinct languages was part of exercising colonial power and domination. While many parts of the world were, and still are, characterized by the parallel use of linguistic resources from different languages (Irvine 1989, Irvine and Gal 2000),[1] colonial language ideologies held that verbal structures and elements should be ordered unambiguously along cultural and territorial lines. Places where this was not the case were regarded as "underdeveloped" or morally questionable (Errington 2008, Gal and Irvine 1995, Makoni and Pennycook 2005). To give one example of the colonial construction of a language, it is documented that in the Andean region, indigenous populations

---

[1] I use the term here as a Western but often useful concept to refer to and classify ways of speaking, the existence of which may impact on speakers' speech behavior.

used a variety of related verbal forms that were referred to as *Quechua* by missionaries. The language *Quechua* was a means to convert the indigenous population (Mannheim 1984), but the practices subsumed under this name remain diverse and contain different practices (referred to as, for example, *Cajamarca–Cañaris, Lambayeque, Wanka* and many more). The colonial interest of converting the population and the practical interest of translating the Bible into one and not into many forms, together with the epistemological framing of people belonging to one culture that uses one language, thus contributed to the formation of Quechua as it exists today (which is in this sense a colonial invention; see Makoni and Pennycook 2005). The fact that these colonial inventions nevertheless may play an important role in today's emancipatory language discourses and policies has also been discussed by Saraceni and Jacob (2019).

Colonists, of course, also brought along their own ways of speaking, which impact on language ideologies in Caribbean postcolonial settings, such as Belize. Due to continuing transnational economic, cultural, and political relationships, the languages of the colonizers have retained a high social status in many postcolonial nations. Research on languages, language attitudes, and language ideologies in Caribbean settings has shown that the colonizers' languages indeed continue to enjoy formal prestige. However, there seems to be a general increase of the prestige of creoles, the languages developed in situations of contact between Africans and Europeans, in many Caribbean contexts (Carrington 2001, Hackert 2016, cf. Perez and Schmalz, this volume). An increase in the use of creole features in written forms has been noted in the context of computer-mediated communication (Hinrichs 2006) but not, for example, in more traditional cultural domains, such as choral singing, where traditional standards of English still hold prestige (Wilson 2017). The sociolinguistic and linguistic anthropological debates on the discursive construction of language are also applicable in contexts where creole languages are spoken. Mühleisen (2002), for example, regards the construction of the entire category of *creole* languages as the result of particular language ideological discourses. In the following, I provide some background to understanding the specific language ideologies of Belize.

2.1 Language ideological discourse in Belize

For the Belizean context, there has been little research on the discursive construction of language or on language ideologies. While the most prominent publications on Belize focus on syntactic aspects and usage patterns of Kriol (Escure 2004; Hellinger 1973), recent work discusses positive language attitudes toward it (Osmer 2013) that may also affect the endangerment of other languages, such as Garifuna (Ravindranath 2009; see also Ravindranath Abtahian 2017; Salmon 2015 for further insight into language attitudes in Belize).

Belize is a small country with about 360,000 inhabitants, located south of Mexico and east of Guatemala, its eastern border being limited by the Caribbean Sea. British colonial rule ended as late as 1981[2] and brought about English as an official language, which is currently used in official settings, including written communication, education, and formal broadcasting. Due to the influence of colonial, monolingual ideologies, this diverse country has been considered an "English-speaking nation". However, it has been assumed that English is nobody's native language in Belize (Escure 1997), since Kriol, Spanish, Mopan, Q'eqchi', Yucatec, Garifuna, Hindi, German, Lebanese, and different Chinese languages are also spoken in the country (Statistical Institute of Belize 2011). Mayan languages, Garifuna, Hindi, German, Chinese, and Lebanese are more directly understood as indexing ethnic belonging; however, in most families, ethnic mixing is common, and most Belizeans grow up speaking at least three languages (Escure 1997: 37). It is therefore a challenging task to map language use to ethnic belonging, as these colonial language ideological links were never enregistered in an absolute way.

Although English is only rarely used in everyday communication in Belize (Escure 1997: 28), it has the highest formal status (already documented by Hellinger 1986 and still is the case today) and overt prestige. Television and music in Belize are often not produced locally; there is strong transnational influence from the US regarding televised media and music, and Jamaican music is also influential. The prestige attributed to English is strongly entwined with these particular postcolonial transnational relationships. It is nevertheless problematic to assume that there is a clear-cut dichotomy of overt vs. covert prestige in this complex setting, as Kriol also holds prestige (already observed in Le Page and Tabouret-Keller 1985, for similar observations in creole-speaking contexts in general, see Lacoste and Mair 2012).

Spanish, due to immigration since the 19th century, is what the largest share of the population indicates to use as home language (Bulmer-Thomas 2012, see also Statistical Institute of Belize). Spanish is not, however, understood as indexing Belizean identity, and in this sense, is a stigmatized language in Belize. Rather, it is Kriol that functions as the Belizean lingua franca and index for belonging. Its historical development into a symbol of "Belizeanness" was described by Le Page and Tabouret-Keller (1985) based on research con-

---

2 For more historical information on Belize, see Shoman (2011).

ducted between the 1950s and 1970s when the country was still a British colony (for more recent work, particularly on attitudes, see Osmer 2013; Salmon 2015: 607; Salmon and Menjívar 2014). Today, despite the lack of official recognition of Kriol and the fact that only about about 30 % of the population considers Kriol to be their home language (Statistical Institute of Belize 2011), it is the language that most Belizeans regard as indexing Belizean identity. This can be explained by the socio-historical discourses of this multilingual nation.

First, positive attitudes toward Kriol are based on Belize's colonial history, and many speakers consider Kriol to be a form of English. Practices regarded as 'English' still enjoy considerable prestige, and many Belizeans remain proud of their British heritage.[3] The history of Belize furthermore resulted in some Creoles[4] rising to the political and social elite before the end of colonial rule (1995). Today, they are still – despite simultaneously existing racist attitudes towards them – often regarded as the 'true' and legitimate Belizeans. This ideology can be inferred from some public discourses, such as those often found in the country's largest newspaper, *Amandala*, which was founded by a former Black Power activist.

Another central explanatory factor in the prestige of Kriol is Belize's hostile relationship with Spanish-speaking Guatemala. In 1862, British settlers threatened by Guatemalan claims, "ask[ed] Britain to lay formal claim on Belize as a colony" (Twigg 2006: 119). The most important national holiday in Belize commemorates a military battle on one of the small reef islands where British settlers and their slaves, purportedly united in a common cause, fought against Spanish invaders. This national belief in Belizean cross-racial unity has had an impact on contemporary discourses regarding Spanish speakers in the country, who are often regarded as foreigners. Spanish is instead typically associated with the neighboring Hispanic countries. In addition, Belize has faced a relatively large influx of Hispanic labor migrants since the 1980s (Statistical Institute of Belize 2010), and Spanish is therefore also associated with lower class immigrants.

Creoles are a cultural and linguistic minority in the overall region of Central America and thus, enforced by their historical national discourses, feel a strong need to differentiate themselves from their Spanish-speaking surroundings. The border between Belize and Guatemala remains a contested territory, and even

---

[3] For example, see the exhibitions in the *Museum of Belize* in Belize City at http://www.nich-belize.org/exhibits/permanent-exhibits.html.
[4] In Belize, 'Creole' refers to the ethnic group of people of Euro-African descent. The spelling with Kriol with a <K> has been introduced by language activists and refers to the language only.

today, the bilateral relationships between Belize and Guatemala remain difficult. Belizeans fear annexation by Guatemala, which has not officially recognized Belize's national status.[5] Kriol has important boundary-marking functions in this context of marking difference from Guatemala (Ravindranath 2009: 129). Additionally, tourism makes up a substantial portion of the Belizean gross national product, and the Belize Tourism Board actively promotes Belize as 'English-speaking' to attract tourists from North America and Europe. Probably due to the strong cultural ties to Jamaica and its worldwide popular music culture, Kriol is also promoted on the tourism market as an authentic expression of Belizeaness. References to Kriol, reggae, and a 'relaxed' lifestyle are also frequently found not only in the tourism marketing discourse but also in local practices.

Overall, the language ideological makeup of Belize is highly diverse and the result of complex cultural-linguistic processes that mirror socio-political and economic histories that include more than a colonizer–colonized dichotomy.

3 Ethnographic language ideological research

This study is interested in language ideological discourse; this means that it is crucial to access local, emic understandings of concepts. Such emic understandings have to be documented qualitatively and in the study presented here, they were collected via ethnographic methods of participant observation and interviewing (Gobo 2008). Ethnographic fieldwork was undertaken in a village in Belize in spring 2015. The project's overall aim was to document the language ideologies of this one village to study how languages are discursively constructed in a very diverse local setting (see Schneider, in preparation). The study is comprised of field notes from three months of participant observation in public spaces, a school, and a kindergarten, as well as photographs and a collection of printed materials. In addition, I conducted 19 qualitative interviews ranging from 30 minutes to 2.5 hours. I also recorded two group discussions with pupils on the role of language in Belize for one hour each, and I recorded 20 hours of school interaction inside and outside of class. On-site data collection has also been supplemented by observation of online interaction, media (radio, newspaper, television), and the study of Belizean history and literature. In the overall

---

[5] See, e.g., http://amandala.com.bz/news/guat-passport-offensive/. For the Guatemalan perspective, see http://www.minex.gob.gt/ADMINPORTAL/Data/DOC/20100929165035248Sintesis delDiferendojunio2010.pdf, 2010.

project, I became also acquainted with language activism and some language activists whose perspective I include to illustrate the role of colonial language ideology in postcolonial language activism.

In ethnographic approaches to data, the social position of the researcher must be taken into consideration. My status as a young, white European woman had a crucial impact on the fieldwork process and how interviewees responded to me. For example, in instances where I observed linguistic insecurity, I regarded my gender (female) and age (in my thirties at the time) as a possible advantage, as it meant I might be perceived as a less threatening interviewer than, for example, a European elderly male professor. During the school observations, I could also more or less blend in with the teachers, who were of a similar age, mostly female, and ethnically mixed (Creole, US American, Garifuna, Mestizo, Maya). In addition, the fact that I had brought along my four and seven-year old children helped to develop closer and more non-hierarchical relationships with female villagers. On the other hand, I was often perceived of as a tourist, which most certainly limited my ability to access local practices. Villagers, not least by their use of Kriol, express a desire to mark a strict boundary between themselves and the white tourist and expat community. All in all, my skin complexion, educational status, and variety of English marked me as a white, affluent, and privileged outsider.

In addition to qualitative data, I collected quantitative material on language attitudes in the form of 155 two to five minute street interviews in which I asked permanent residents of the village about their language use across domains (family, friends, and work). The method of asking people about their language use should not be understood as a documentation of actual language use but rather as a reflection of the language attitudes of the informants. Particularly where language and social belonging is contested, informants tend to say what they think they use, what they think they should use, or what they think the researcher thinks they should use. In the context of this village, many people clearly downplayed their knowledge of Spanish. Furthermore, some language practices may not fit well into such categorizations, which some informants also commented upon; interestingly, these were often informants who did not have access to formal education (e.g. elderly men working in the fishing industries). The fact that respondents challenged the idea of separable languages indicates that the concept of a *language* is indeed perceived by some as a foreign/colonial concept.

The village I focused on has about 1,500 inhabitants. It has a highly diverse linguistic makeup, which illustrates the complexity that Belizean communities face, as can be inferred from Figure 1, which is based on quantitative data on language use across domains, here only showing answers about language use at home of people who permanently live in the village:

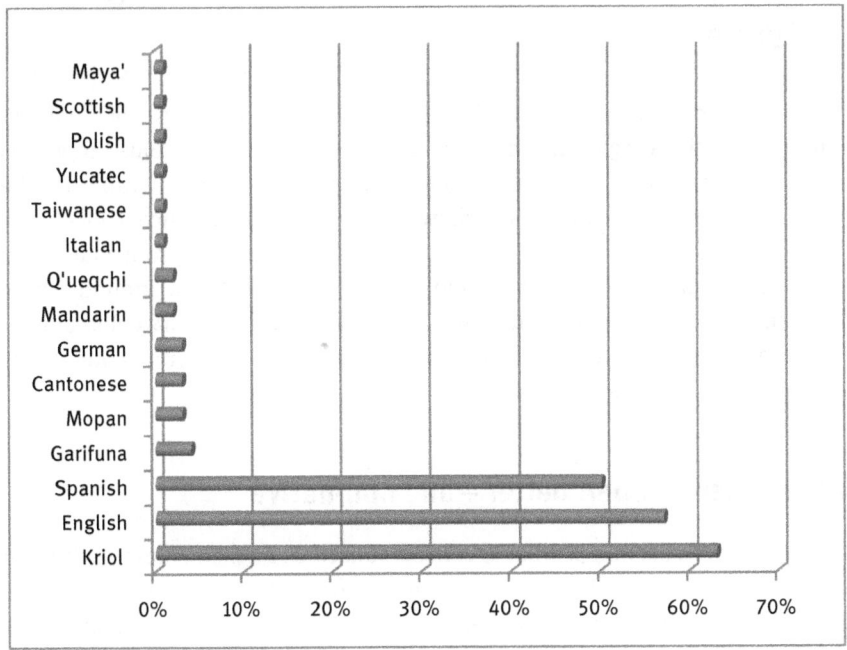

Figure 1: Reported home language use, several answers possible (n=155).

As Figure 1 shows, Kriol is indicated to be the most frequently used home language, alongside many others. I would also like to emphasize that, according to my observation, the boundary between English and Kriol, as well as the boundary between English and Spanish, is often blurred in practice. It is all the more interesting that discursive categories of language remain vital concepts in ordering the world for the informants. However, the colonial discursive construction of a link between ethnicity, territory, and language gains new functions when postcolonial voices campaign for legitimacy. These voices continue to struggle with a history of colonial hierarchy that is reproduced in today's transnational economic relationships. At the same time, they re-enact marginalization that has roots in colonial times.

4 Colonial ideologies and postcolonial reworkings of English, Kriol, and Spanish in multilingual Belize

In this section, I introduce data that exemplifies in more depth the common conceptualizations regarding the three most often mentioned home languages of the permanent island residents – English, Spanish and Kriol (Table 1). The ethnographic and interview data shows that the colonial concept of clearly defined languages, spoken by clearly definable peoples, is problematic and contrasts the complex language ideologies and practices on the ground. These data are supplemented by documents that demonstrate the more colonial constructions of language as in material from the National Kriol Council but also in governmental language policy data.

4.1 English: proper, better – and non-native

As mentioned in Section 3, what is conceptualized as English enjoys traditional overt prestige in Belize. The written version of English in Belize is very similar to globally prestigious forms of Standard English. When it comes to speaking practice, it is rather complex to define the concept of 'English' in Belize. While written language is mostly what also outsiders would understand as 'Standard English' (see, for example, online newspapers such as *amandala.com.bz*), this is different in spoken forms of the language.

Being myself an outsider, it was difficult for me in the beginning of my field stay to differentiate between Kriol and English. During my first days of observations in a high school, some teachers (but not all) used a variety of English that I thought rather resembled Kriol. The concept of the "creole continuum" (see e.g. Bickerton 1975, Hellinger 1998, Sebba 1997) served as a helpful model in approaching this situation where more 'standard' and less 'standard' forms of English were being used.[6] However, I noticed after a while that the use of features that to me appear more Kriol than English (e.g. zero copula, subject-verb agreement marked differently, unmarked plural nouns, pronunciation of <th> as a stop, and monophthongization of [eɪ] and [əʊ]) are not regarded as 'non-standard' and can appear as legitimate forms in teacher talk, on public govern-

---

[6] For a critical approach to the creole continuum model, see Patrick (1999), and see Deuber (2014) for a more recent, style-oriented approach to variation in the Caribbean.

mental signage, and also in national radio and television broadcasting. Speakers classify these formal uses not as Kriol but as English, and they use the notion of "proper English" to refer to language use in these formal domains. The notion of 'standard,' where this is constructed as language use in formal and written domains, seems to be a more fluid category (Hänsel 2015) than what I am acquainted with as a European observer, socialized in a discourse with strong monolingual ideologies of standardization and correctness.[7] Several different forms of 'standard usage' seem to exist side-by-side. The uses of more local (as observed in written and spoken practice in my data) or of more exogamous features (non-local standards of US and British English that also figure in the Belizean school leaving examinations designed by the Caribbean Examination Council and in the speech of some of the informants) intersect with individual upbringing, lifestyle, and also political ideologies – whether or not and how much one aligns with Kriol as an expression of Belizeaness – but not necessarily with ethnic descent or class.

When it comes to meta-linguistic discourse, the traditional colonial hierarchy of (exogamous) English as 'better' is strong in most informants' language ideologies. The idea that English is a more elevated and correct form of language appears frequently in my interviews and is for some interviewees related to feelings of uneasiness as well as insecurity regarding the use of 'correct' forms. For example, in the second week of my field stay, I asked a local high school teacher about the school's conceptual model of Standard English. The question was intended to elicit whether British or US features were seen as more prestigious. The teacher reacted with irritation, and it became obvious that my question aroused feelings of insecurity in her as it seemed to question the legitimacy of local standards of speech. She then said, "What do you mean? We speak proper English." I did not further inquire about this as it felt inappropriate and appeared to me to be as a defensive strategy where post-colonial power relations impacted the individual interaction between us. Even though I am not of British heritage, my appearance and use of English for most local informants indexed belonging to the privileged, wealthy class of former colonizers, which today is more or less synonymous with the local notion of 'tourist.'

The reaction of this informant probably indicates her awareness that the local, more fluid concept of standard does not correspond to what people regard as 'Standard English' elsewhere, and that these practices have a lower status

---

7 Additionally, it needs to be noted that I am not a native speaker of English. My perception of 'Standard English' may therefore be even more monolithic than that of a native speaker as I have learned and use the language in almost exclusively institutional contexts.

than internationally prestigious forms of English. The term *proper English*, as it turned out, is frequently used to describe what is locally constructed as the most formal prestige variety. Exogamous models of the US and the UK continue to function as models in the meta-linguistic awareness of many speakers, even though many Belizeans almost never use *proper English* in informal interaction. The rare everyday use of what is constructed as 'correct' leads to children facing difficulties in formal school education, where they are confronted with a certain range of features that are regarded as 'proper' and which are often distinct from what children have learned before entering school. This becomes clear in the following quote from the headmaster of the local primary school:[8]

Transcript 1[9]

1   Again they [the pupils] are a little bit, ahm, shy of speaking the English
2   So drop back on the Kriol.
3   But we really encourage them to really learn the English
4   Because it's very important that they learn to speak English fluently to communicate
5   throughout the world
6   Because then throughout the world that the English is the international language

The interviewee is aware of the fact that the children do not use English as a family language and reports that they are shy to use it. She regards Kriol as the children's primary language (not mentioning Spanish, despite her own Hispanic heritage) and states a reason why the use of English is important for them: English is here constructed as a medium of communication across national borders and the children need it "to communicate fluently throughout the world" as "English is the international language." The statement confirms that 'English' is conceptualized as an exogamous norm.

There is a very small and very wealthy economic elite in Belize (who is, given their material wealth, rather 'upper' than 'middle class') that speaks what I perceive to be US English, and many of this group have studied in the US. They interact closely with European and US American expatriates in Belize City and appear to be part of a transnational educated, English-speaking class, a group among which a distinction along national lines is not pertinent for belonging, while their language and clothing style reminded me strongly of US American styles. These Belize City residents told me that they were unable to speak Kriol,

---

[8] I refrain from giving further information on my consultants due to ethical considerations.
[9] See Transcription Conventions at the end of the text.

and that they found the use of Kriol among their children either negative or funny. Globally available transnational hierarchies have an impact here on the local and national social hierarchies, as the local elite seems strongly influenced by norms that are available to many upper middle classes worldwide. I therefore hesitate to call them 'US American', even though these norms may have their roots in the US.

The transnational hierarchies of language prestige are part of the knowledge also of non-elite Belizeans. This is visible in the following quote from an interview with a local high school teacher:

Transcript 2
1   And so there's a sense, there's a sense of,
2   If I'm able to speak English,
3   Or if (.)
4   Perhaps, you know, even that
5   If English is the official language of this country it elevates us over our Central American counterparts.

The relationship between English and Spanish, to which the interviewee refers, is described according to transnational value strata where a perception of English being "elevated" is projected onto the relationship of Belize with its Hispanic neighbors. The contested ties to Guatemala may influence this desire to differentiate from these "Central American counterparts."

To briefly summarize the observations of language ideologies regarding English, we can say that English has traditional overt prestige (cf. Labov 1972) in Belize and that we find colonial hierarchies in the relationship of English and Kriol. English is "proper", but Kriol is not; we also see that the historical colonial political struggles between English and Spanish still impact constructions in which today's transnational discourses (e.g. "English is the international language") are embedded. In practice, however, English is not the language of everyday speech. It is regarded as foreign (except by a very small elite), and there is a sense of insecurity as to what constitutes 'proper English,' as the category seems to encompass various forms, which leads to some informants feeling uncomfortable with a question on the 'correct' model of English. Thus, we find the colonial construction of a language, as a monolithic system indexically related to an ethnic group, being questioned in actual practice and on several levels, while the colonial hierarchy of English as a more prestigious language remains in place. As we will see in the following section, the role of English is at the same time challenged by the status of Kriol.

4.2 Kriol – our language!

Kriol, as a mostly oral code, and intertwined with histories of slavery, is by some local consultants associated with the lower end of the social hierarchy. At the same time, it enjoys considerable prestige as the language of Belize (compare to the Jamaican case described by Wassink 1999). Constructions of Kriol as 'broken English' or 'slang' appear in the data set, where some perceive Kriol as an index for lower class and a lack of education, as opposed to 'proper English.' Various local informants thus conceptualize Kriol as a 'dialect' of English and not as a language in its own right. This contrasts with the aims of the National Kriol Council, who emphatically argue that Kriol is a language, as it has a grammar and a dictionary (found in various interviews I held) and is the language of Belize, which is a local reproduction of a colonial ideology of language. The idea that Kriol is an index of being Belizean exists along with the idea that Kriol is a lower class dialect, and the former has become more dominant since the time when the emergence of this relationship was first documented by Le Page and Tabouret-Keller (1985). In the following quote from the headmaster of the high school, whose first family language is Spanish, we detect an indication of the positive attitudes towards Kriol:

Transcript 3
1 Interviewer: And [what do you use] with your friends? / Also Kriol?
2 Person 1: / Ah, Kriol.
3 Interviewer: (4) Ahm, and is there a language you prefer?
4 Person 1: (5) Prefer? Ahm /
5 Interviewer: / For any reason or /
6 Person 1: / Kriol, yeah.

Due to the often-reproduced conceptualization of Kriol as 'non-standard,' I found it curious to learn that this rather strict and authoritative informant very clearly sided with Kriol – consider the pause of four seconds, expressing my surprise. The above quote reveals the rather prestigious status of Kriol that was described to me in several interviews, where several informants also argued that, since the 1970s, Kriol has been used more frequently in public contexts, including, for example, in parliamentary discussion. In line with postcolonial independence and nation-building, the speech forms that index Belizean identity have become more prestigious and partly seem to merge with exogamous norms of English, which also explains the rather fluid conceptualization of 'Standard English.'

In private contexts, it is also appropriate for the educated middle class to use Kriol (except for the above-mentioned very small elite that seems more oriented towards exogamous norms), and the school's headmaster is clear on stating that Kriol is her preferred language (also consider her interrupting me, matter-of-factly, in line 6). For her, Kriol does not express stigmatized lower class belonging; rather, she shows pride in her local and national belonging (which, as will be discussed in more detail below, apparently cannot be expressed by Spanish). The dichotomy of English as having overt prestige and Kriol covert prestige is not clear-cut when educational and social authorities openly identify with and use this 'non-standard' code in semi-public environments (e.g. teachers usually speak Kriol[10] amongst each other and to children unless they act in their role as teacher or by bringing order into school life). The positive attitudes towards Kriol are in part related to the fact that Kriol is constructed as the country's lingua franca in the face of a highly diverse population:

Transcript 4
1   So, everyone who comes to Belize (.)
2   Learns Kriol (.)
3   Because it is spoken everywhere.
4   So, it doesn't matter if you're Chinese, Haitian, Arab, Indian, Mestizo.
5   Kriol is the common language.

In this quote from an interview with an English teacher and Kriol activist whose first language is Kriol, but whose family members also use Spanish and Garifuna, the role of Kriol as a language for inter-ethnic communication within Belize becomes clear. The high number of immigrants from different places in the world is referred to here, and my observations and other interview data confirm that people of very different backgrounds learn and use Kriol for everyday interpersonal communication but also, for example, in sales interactions. It is also interesting that newcomers to Belize who learn Kriol are encouraged to do so and that Kriol is not seen as only legitimate if used by 'real' Creoles, which was noticeably also demonstrated in Transcript 3, as the headmaster is not of Creole descent.

The status of Kriol as the language of Belizeans, with its integrative appeal to non-ethnic Creoles and its positive prestige also in public and sometimes even formal domains, makes Kriol a highly popular code. In the school where I

---

10 The question what constitutes the boundary between Kriol and English, linked to my argument that teachers use Kriol in personal communication, is not easy to answer; yet, the use of certain grammatical features (as depicted above in the description of English), intonation, speed and certain lexical features can be tentatively interpreted as symbolizing 'Kriol' rather than 'proper English'.

conducted research, 77 % of the pupils indicate Kriol as the means of communicating with friends. The dominance of Kriol is very obvious, though the majority of the pupils do not identify with Creole ethnicity, and only 39% say that they use Kriol at home (other home languages: Spanish, English, Garifuna, Mopan, Q'eqchi'). Also in group discussion, pupils express highly positive attitudes towards Kriol, saying that they all learn it is because it is "easy" and because "you can do what you want with Kriol." Thus, Kriol constructs a link between a territory and the people who reside there – Kriol is *the language of Belize* – but, at the same time, one reason for Kriol's popularity is its lack of conforming to colonial ideals regarding normative and regular uses of linguistic features. This is in a state of tension with the activities of the National Kriol Council, whose main aim is to render Kriol a 'real' language. They have, among other things, created a bilingual English-Kriol dictionary (Herrera et al. 2009), and they have published several literary publications (e.g., Gentle 2005, Glock 2005, Sutherland 2004) as well as a spelling guide (informal publication).

The Council has been very active in the last two decades and successful in bringing the idea that Kriol is a legitimate language to the public. These activities, on the one hand, struggle with the remaining formal exogamous prestige of English. On the other hand, as the positive attitudes towards Kriol are partly based on the fact that Kriol is not a code associated with ideologies of formality, standardization, and correctness and is not tied to ethnically essentialist positions, the creation of a dictionary and of spelling norms are not in a completely trouble-free relationship with the postcolonial discourses of Belize. In a way, they re-introduce what above has been defined as colonial language ideologies. Nevertheless, considering the colonial hierarchies with 'proper English' at the top, these strategies may be interpreted as a postcolonial struggle to make the Belizean language Kriol a legitimate expression of national culture. While some consultants find the activities of the Council problematic, others strongly support it:

Transcript 5
1   Interviewer: But do you mean also use [Kriol] in school for example?
2   Person 1: I would definitely support it cause that's, you can't give up our mother tongue, that's our native language.
3   Kriol is a language and you just don't want to lose it. [...]
4   So Kriol should be your first language you learn at home.
5   Then you have English, then you have Spanish.
6   So everybody here should speak three different languages.

This village citizen, originally from Belize City, who indicates Kriol as his first language (although his first and family names are Spanish), strongly supports the position that Kriol should become the official language of Belize. He reconstructs the discourse of Kriol as a genuinely Belizean language by using the essentialist terms "mother tongue" and "native language," in relation to the personal pronoun "our" as to express a natural link between Kriol and the national community of Belizeans. There is also the expression of fear of Kriol being used less: "you just don't want to lose it." The argument that "Kriol should be your first language you learn at home" is reminiscent of conservative nationalist discourses on language and immigration in some Western countries, and from the context, it is likely that this statement is directed particularly towards Spanish-speakers (even though Spanish is also one of his family languages). It is also noticeable that he constructs Kriol as a formal and legitimate language by arguing in favor of its use in schools and by creating a relationship of parallelism between English, Spanish and Kriol: "So everybody here should speak three different languages."

The meta-linguistic discourse on Kriol as a 'real' language that partly reproduces colonial ideologies of languages is well-known among certain members of the population. However, despite the continuing ties of Kriol to informality, its role as expressing Belizean belonging – at least in the local context observed – is strong and probably based on grounds of the discourse that has been actively pushed by the Kriol Council. Some informants thus justify the non-Kriol language practices in their repertoire:

Transcript 6
1   Respondent 1: It's funny cuz,
2   And I'm going to sound very weird, strange
3   But please don't judge me too harshly.
4   But, I, Kriol is what comes naturally out of my mouth
5   But you know for me, you know (.)
6   You know that running narrative that you have in your head when you're talking to yourself or having thoughts?
7   Interviewer: Yes
8   Respondent 1: That is pure English.
9   Interviewer: Ah! Interesting
10 Respondent 1: Yeah it's weird.

This young female interviewee, originally from Belize City, whose grandparents were Spanish-speaking, and who lists Kriol as her first language, has received an elite education in the most prestigious Belizean girls' school. She constructs her use of Kriol as an unmarked practice, which can be interpreted from the fact that she describes her thinking in English with the adjectives "funny," "weird," and "strange." She expects the presence of English in her personal linguistic activities to be evaluated negatively by me as her respondent: "Don't judge me too harshly" and all of lines 1 to 5 represent a legitimation of not using only Kriol in everyday life and thought. Thus, the discourse of Kriol as the language of Belizeans has reached a certain degree of normativity, even for people exposed to exogamous norms for prolonged periods of time, such as the nine years of schooling by US American teachers. However, this interviewee's use of English is, in terms of syntax and pronunciation, almost identical to US American English (a native US American student researcher on this research project maintained that this speaker sounds "like a US Latina," meaning a highly proficient speaker of English with Hispanic background in the US).

Overall, we can thus say that Kriol has developed into an 'authentic' index of local belonging as the 'Belizean language' for many people, although language activists' aims of implementing it as a formal and standardized written medium remain contested and so far have had little success. In the following, we will see that the contested status of Kriol is not only related to English remaining the more overtly prestigious code, but that language ideologies on Kriol as 'truely Belizean' clash with the presence of Spanish.

4.3 Spanish: demographically dominant and socially stigmatized

The Spanish language finds itself in a complex situation in Belize. Firstly, as mentioned, it is the demographically dominant language, which has also been recognized officially by governmental sources since the 1990s: "because of an increased immigration from Spanish speaking neighboring countries, Spanish has become the language with the largest number of native speakers in Belize" (Narain 1996). Despite this fact, Spanish is taught as a foreign language in school curricula. Although a lot of pupils (24 % in the case of my study) say they use Spanish at home, the Spanish teacher of the high school reports that the performance in Spanish language classes is below average. This observation corresponds with national statistics (Statistical Institute of Belize 2010), which show that the performance in Spanish language classes is often poor (reported in personal communication with headmaster).

One reason for this may be that informants report that many Belizeans use an internal variety of Spanish that seems to intermingle with Kriol (Osmer 2013) and does not conform to standardized varieties of Spanish. This variety is commonly referred to as *Kitchen Spanish,* expressing its construction as non-formal, its lack of written use, and also gendered attitudes (if we assume the kitchen to be a gendered space) towards this code. Furthermore, many residents maintain in meta-discourse that they do not use Spanish, while they actually do in practice – which may be interpreted as a sign for the negative attitudes towards the local use of Spanish. The Spanish teacher of the local high school reports that pupils prefer English, but nevertheless often use Spanish:

Transcript 7
1   I get it from my students that their mentality is, you know,
2   We rather speak English and not Spanish
3   But yet when,
4   I'm living here for almost two years
5   And I walk around the island
6   And I meet people who speak Spanish
7   And then speak Spanish to them.

The teacher is of Belizean background and has grown up in a region where Spanish is the dominant language. Phonetically, his use of English shows influence from Spanish, but he also declares Kriol to be his main medium of communication with friends and family, except elderly people. He reports on practices that became more familiar to me the longer I stayed on the island. In meta-discourse, many residents of the island say they use English (presumably, the use of the term English in this quote encompasses uses of Kriol) rather than Spanish and have the "mentality" that English is better than Spanish. Yet, as already mentioned, many people who claim to not speak Spanish actually do so in informal conversation amongst villagers. The teacher then reports that he has started to use Spanish with local people, too. Again, I have no data that would clarify whether these local speakers consciously deny their use of Spanish, whether they are unaware of their use of Spanish, or whether they do not classify their verbal practices as Spanish. In any case, the hostile political relationships with neighboring countries, the immigration of high numbers of immigrants from these locations who come to flee highly precarious living conditions and the construction of Kriol as Belizean certainly impact the conceptualization of Spanish as negative. This is described vividly in the following quote:

Transcript 8
1   And even as a kid growing up
2   I thought that Spanish was not cool.
3   You know, because you're with your friends and if you learn Spanish,
4   You Spánish.
5   And that's a derogative term they use for (1)
6   You Spánish.

The speaker, a village citizen who says that Kriol is his first language and who grew up in Belize City, explains here that the term *Spanish* in Belize is derogatory. There are a number of examples in the data set from interviews where informants use the term *Spanish* in this way. It is also frequently used to refer to the group of people who use Spanish, and where the term is more like an ethnic denominator, referring to people who are of Mayan and/or Hispanic origin. The local understanding of the term is thus no longer associated with its original meaning as referring to people and language structures from Spain.

Based on my observations and the contents of the interviews, it is safe to argue that these negative attitudes are linked to a political discourse (in relation to Guatemala), to colonial times with a history of border conflicts, to right-to-land struggles between the British and Spanish (see Section 3), to associations of Spanish with lower class belonging, and to the Creole dominance among the political elite in Belizean history. This is in a paradoxical relationship to the demographic dominance of Spanish, and it is also an unexpected relationship to the fact that the local and land-owning elite is of Hispanic descent and uses Spanish regularly. Spanish has received negative connotations in Belize, and the complex discursive arrangement in which the Spanish language finds itself today emerges from interrelated local, national, and transnational discourses. This also shows that colonial constructions of language remain relevant in postcolonial contexts, which will be discussed in more detail in the following section.

5 Discussion: colonial language ideologies in postcolonial and transnational contexts

Returning to the main research question of this article on the role of colonial language ideology in a postcolonial context, we can clearly say that a colonial language ideology – the construction of languages as distinct categories that correspond to ethnic groups – is deconstructed in everyday practices in Belize. However, the concept of languages as separate entities continues to play a vital role in symbolic realms and seems to also have an impact on language practices. Roughly speaking, the most dominant discourses pertaining to the three most widely used languages of the village are:

- English is formally prestigious but 'foreign'.
- Kriol is the 'Belizean language'.
- Spanish is stigmatized as a threatening, foreign, and lower-class code.

The modernist European language ideologies of colonial times that construct speech forms as appearing in separate systems that are tied to particular, ethnically ordered groups has not been completely dissolved. Due to the complex mixing of ethnic groups, maybe also because ethnic groups never formed stable social categories in Belize, each of these language ideological positions is contested and often in a contradictory relationship to actual language practices.

When it comes to English, we have seen that although the language has overt prestige, the local conceptions of the standard clash with international norms of Standard English, of which many speakers are aware. The language-ethnicity link is deconstructed in relation to English, as it is the official language of Belize, but at the same time, the idea of 'proper English' is mostly framed in exogamous terms – to which a small elite aligns.

The discourses of colonial linguistic knowledge are appropriated in the language activism of the colonized. Kriol language activists strive to make Kriol a formal, written language and have created the materials to support this effort (grammar, dictionary, orthography). This is, on the one hand, contested by ideologies that regard Kriol as free from normative ideologies. Simultaneously, the construction of Kriol as a 'real' language has an effect on constructing Spanish as 'un-Belizean.' While it is understandable that the Creole population feels threatened by a Hispanic demographic majority, we can see here that the construction of Kriol as an authentic expression of Belizean identity reconstructs colonial ideologies that suppress and stigmatize the use of Spanish. The construction of languages, the knowledge brought about by colonizers, interacts complexly with local and transregional conditions.

Spanish is frequently used but stigmatized, a fact that has roots in colonial history and in the more recent anti-immigration discourse. The term *Spanish*, for some informants, functions like a swear word and implies the discursive construction of ethnic essentialisms. This says little about actual language practices, as people with Hispanic roots who use forms that are of Spanish origin do not necessarily describe these practices as being 'Spanish.' This suppression of Spanish and the negative attitudes towards it are caused by a reproduction of local colonial ideologies that regard English as more "elevated" than Spanish and the Kriol discourse that claims Kriol to be the legitimate language of Belizeans.

When we contemplate the future of Kriol on grounds of the present situation, it nevertheless seems unlikely that Kriol will become a fully standardized national language with all functions in public discourse and education in the sense of the language ideologies described as colonial in Section 2. Strong transnational ties in contemporary culture can be seen as a vital aspect in the continuing simultaneous presence of various and partly contradictory ideologies regarding English and Kriol today, as has been claimed for different forms of English:

> [English] is not likely to follow the example of Latin and break up into mutually only partly intelligible daughter languages –at least not as long as it continues to be supported by economically and demographically strong nation-states and important transnational networks of communication. (Mair 2016: 22)

This consideration also shows that the situation of English in postcolonial nations contrasts with times when the majority of the population was illiterate. In a cultural context in which written language is considered prestigious and is accessible to a large number of people, and where writing has been introduced in English – even before the age of transnational electronic communication –, it seems to be difficult to introduce a new standard of writing.

In any case, what we have seen is that colonial language ideologies of fixed normative languages of power continue to work, but live in partly paradoxical multiplex networks of interacting ideologies. The relationship between Kriol and Spanish is particularly interesting in how it shows that, rather than being an effect of demographic numbers or cultural isolation, the emergence of 'a language' as an index for a particular identity is linked to the desire of powerful groups to maintain and reproduce positions of power; to the desire to differentiate from what is constructed as a cultural 'other;' and to creating a position of territorial legitimacy. These should be considered vital aspects in the formation of any language.

6 Conclusion

This article has discussed the role of colonial language ideologies regarding the languages English, Spanish, and Kriol in present-day Belize. The study shows that the discourses regarding the discursive constructs of languages are in a relationship with each other that contains different kinds of paradoxes. These have to do with the interaction of different discourses, expressing different interests, in the culturally complex context of Belize, with its strong transnational ties to surrounding nations, the UK, and the US. Language ideologies that construct languages as simplex systems that are unambiguously tied to particular ethnic groups are inadequate for analyzing this situation; however, it is vital that these categories do not dissolve but rather gain new meanings in postcolonial struggles for voice and legitimacy.

Transcription conventions

(.)	pause of less than a second
(1.5)	pause with indicated length
/	overlapping talk
strést	rise of tone
strèss	fall of tone
underlined	louder
(word?)	word difficult to hear, analyst's guess
line break	after utterance unit or pause

References

Amandala. 23.01.2016. Belize Received 1.3 Million Tourists in 2015. 23.01.2016.
Barry, Tom. 1995. *Inside Belize*. Albuquerque: Resource Center Press.
Bauman, Emily. 1998. Re-dressing colonial discourse: Postcolonial theory and the Humanist Project. *Critical Quaterly* 40. 79–90.
Belize Tourism Board. 2013. *Travel & Tourism Statistics Digest,* https://perma.cc/R7H7-QT4V (checked 12 Sept 2016) Belize City: https://btb.travelbelize.org/media/download/1672.
Bickerton, Derek. 1975. *Dynamics of a Creole system*. Cambridge: Cambridge University Press.
Billig, Michael. 1995. *Banal nationalism*. London: Sage.
Bulmer-Thomas, Victor. 2012. *The economic history of the Caribbean since the Napoleonic Wars*. Cambridge: Cambridge University Press.
Carrington, Lawrence D. 2001. The status of Creole in the Caribbean. In Pauline Christie. (ed.), *Due respect: Papers on English and English-related Creoles in honour of Professor Robert B. Le Page*, 24–36. Mona: UWI Press.
Deuber, Dagmar. 2014. *English in the Caribbean: Variation, style and standards in Jamaica and Trinidad*. Cambridge: Cambridge University Press.
Errington, Joseph. 2008. *Linguistics in a colonial world: A story of language, meaning and power*. Malden, Mass.: Blackwell.
Escure, Geneviève. 1997. *Creole and dialect continua: Standard acquisition processes in Belize and China*. Amsterdam & Philadelphia: John Benjamins.
Escure, Geneviève. 2004. Belize and other Central American varieties: Morphology and syntax. In Bernd Kortmann, Kate Burridge, Rajend Mesthrie, Edgar W. Schneider & Clive Upton (eds.), *A handbook of varieties of English*, 517–545. Berlin & New York: De Gruyter.
Gal, Susan & Judith T. Irvine. 1995. The boundaries of languages and disciplines: How ideologies construct difference. *Social Research* 62. 967–1001.
García, Ofelia & Li Wei. 2014. *Translanguaging. Language, bilingualism and education*. Basingstoke: Palgrave Macmillan.
Gentle, Hilda. 2005. *Di stoari a Hilda: (wahn chroo chroo stoari)*. Belize City: Belize Kriol Project.
Glock, Naomi. 2005. *Sohn stoari fahn Gaylz Paint (Malanti)*. Belize City: Belize Kriol Project.
Gobo, Giampietro. 2008. *Doing ethnography*. London: Sage.

Hackert, Stephanie. 2016. Standards of English in the Caribbean: History, attitudes, functions, features. In Elena Seoane & Cristina Suárez Gómez (eds.), *World Englishes: New theoretical and methodological considerations*, 85–111. Amsterdam & Philadelphia: John Benjamins.

Hänsel, Eva Canan. 2015. Newscaster accents in St Vincent and the Grenadines and their implication for the standard language ideology. Presentation at *GAPS 2015–Ideology in Postcolonial Texts and Contexts*, Münster.

Hellinger, Marlis. 1973. Aspects of Belizean Creole. *Folia Linguistica* 6. 118–135.

Hellinger, Marlis. 1986. On Writing English-related Creoles in the Caribbean. In Manfred Görlach & John A. Holm (eds.), *Focus on the Caribbean*, 53–70. Amsterdam & Philadelphia: John Benjamins.

Hellinger, Marlis. 1998. The Creole continuum of linguistic variation. *The Creole Continuum of Linguistic Variation* 12. 72–84.

Herrera, Yvette, Paul Crosbie, Cynthia Crosbie, Kendall D. Decker, Myrna Manzanares & Silvana Woods. 2009. *Kriol-Inglish dikshineri. English-Kriol dictionary*. Belize City: Belize Kriol Project.

Hinrichs, Lars. 2006. *Codeswitching on the Web. English and Jamaican Creole in e-mail communication*. Amsterdam & Philadelphia: John Benjamins.

Hymes, Dell. 1968. Linguistic problems in defining the concept of 'Tribe '. In June Helm (ed.), *Essays on the problem of the tribe. Proceedings of the 1967 Annual Spring Meeting of the American Ethnological Society*, 23–48. Seattle: University of Washington Press.

Irvine, Judith T. 1989. When talk isn't cheap: Language and political economy. *American Ethnologist* 16. 248–267.

Irvine, Judith T. 2001. Style' as distinctiveness: The culture and ideology of linguistic differentiation. In Penelope Eckert & John R. Rickford (eds.), *Style and sociolinguistic variation*, 21–43. Cambridge: Cambridge University Press.

Irvine, Judith T. & Susan Gal. 2000. Language ideology and linguistic differentiation. In Paul V. Kroskrity (ed.), *Regimes of language. Ideologies, polities and identities*, 35–83. Santa Fe, New Mexico: School of American Research Press.

Kroskrity, Paul V. 2000. Regimenting languages. Language ideological perspectives. In Paul V. Kroskrity (ed.), *Regimes of language. Ideologies, polities, and identities*, 1–34. Santa Fe, New Mexico: School of American Research Press.

Labov, William. 1972. The social stratification of (R) in New York City Department Stores. In William Labov (ed.), *Sociolinguistic patterns*, 43–69. Philadelphia: University of Pennsylvania Press.

Lacoste, Véronique & Christian Mair. 2012. Authenticity in Creole-speaking contexts: An introduction. *Zeitschrift für Anglistik und Amerikanistik* 60(3). 211–215.

Le Page, Robert Brock & Andrée Tabouret-Keller. 1985. *Acts of identity: Creole-based approaches to language and ethnicity*. Cambridge: Cambridge University Press.

Mair, Christian. 2016. Beyond and between the 'Three Circles': World Englishes research in the age of globalisation. In Elena Seoane & Cristina Suárez Gómez (eds.), *World Englishes: New theoretical and methodological considerations*, 17–35. Amsterdam & Philadelphia: John Benjamins.

Makoni, Sinfree & Alastair Pennycook. 2005. Disinventing and (re)constituting languages. *Critical Inquiry in Language Studies* 2. 137–156.

Mannheim, Bruce. 1984. *Una nación acorralada*: Souther Peruvian Quechua Language Planning and Politics in Historical Perspective. *Language in Society* 13. 291–309.

Mühleisen, Susanne. 2002. *Creole discourse: Exploring prestige formation and change across Caribbean English-lexicon Creoles*. Amsterdam & Philadelphia: John Benjamins.
Narain, Goretti. 1996. *A language policy for primary education in Belize*. Informal Publication, shared by the Ministry of Education, Belize.
Osmer, Balam. 2013. Overt language attitudes and linguistic identities among multilingual speakers in Northern Belize. *Studies in Hispanic and Lusophone Linguistics* 6(2). 247–278.
Patrick, Peter L. 1999. *Urban Jamaican Creole: Variation in the mesolect*. Amsterdam & Philadelphia: John Benjamins.
Pennycook, Alastair. 1998. *English and the discourses of colonialism*. London: Routledge.
Perez, Danae Maria & Mirjam Schmalz. this volume. Complex patterns of variety perception in the Eastern Caribbean. New insights from St. Kitts.
Ravindranath, Maya. 2009. *Language shift and the speech community: Sociolinguistic change in a Garifuna community in Belize*. PhD dissertation, University of Pennsylvania.
Ravindranath Abtahian, Maya. 2017. Language shift, endangerment and prestige. Kriol and Garifuna in Hopkins, Belize. *Journal of Pidgin and Creole Languages* 32. 339–364.
Said, Edward. 1978. *Orientalism*. Harmondsworth: Penguin.
Salmon, William. 2015. Language ideology, gender, and varieties of Belizean Kriol. *Journal of Black Studies* 46. 605–625.
Salmon, William & Jennifer Gómez Menjívar. 2014. Whose Kriol is Moa Beta? Prestige and dialects of Kriol in Belize. *Berkeley Linguistics Society* 40. 456–479.
Saraceni, Mario & Camille Jacob. 2019. Revisiting borders: Named languages and de-colonization. *Language Sciences* 76.
Schneider, Britta. in preparation. Liquid languages. Polymorphous acts of identity and the fluidity of language categories in linguistically complex Belize. (submitted habilitation thesis at European University Viadrina).
Sebba, Mark. 1997. *Contact languages: Pidgins and Creoles*. London: Macmillan.
Shoman, Assad. 2011. *A history of Belize in 13 chapters*. Belize City: Angelus Press.
Statistical Institute of Belize. 2010. *Belize: Population and Housing Census: Country Report 2010*. Statistical Institute of Belize: http://www.sib.org.bz/Portals/0/docs/publications/census/2010_Census_Report.pdf.
Statistical Institute of Belize. 2011. *Main Results of 2010 Population and Housing Census*, https://perma.cc/6WVQ-48VH.
Sutherland, Oswald. 2004. *Anansi an di domplin chree*. Belize City: Belize Kriol Project.
Twigg, Alan. 2006. *Understanding Belize: A historical guide*. Madeira Park, BC: Harbour Publishing.
Wassink, Alicia Beckford. 1999. Historic low prestige and seeds of change: Attitudes toward Jamaican Creole. *Language in Society* 28. 57–92.
Wilson, Guyanne. 2017. Conflicting language ideologies in choral singing in Trinidad. *Language & Communication* 52. 19–30.
Wimmer, Andreas & Nina Glick Schiller. 2002. Methodological nationalism and beyond: Nation-state building, migration and the social sciences. *Global Networks* 2(4). 301–334.
Woolard, Kathryn A. 1998. Introduction: Language ideology as field of inquiry. In Bambi B. Schieffelin, Kathryn A. Woolard & Paul V. Kroskrity (eds.). *Language ideologies: Practice and theory*, 3–47. Oxford: Oxford University Press.

Index of Authors

Abbott, Clifford 62
Acton, Sara 95
Adamou, Evangelia 38
Adelaar, Willem F. H. 3, 181, 183ff., 203
Aikhenvald, Alexandra Y. 57ff., 186
Allard, Ida Rose 88, 100, 104ff., 113f., 117
Almeida, Maria Geralda de 207
Alvar, Manuel 189
Álvarez López, Laura 2
Amaral, Amadeu 220
Andrien, Kenneth 187
Angola, Juan 183, 193
Apaza Apaza, Ignacio 186
Aquilina, Joseph 19
Araújo, Gilberto Paulino de 212
Armoskaite, Solveiga 92
Arwel, Rhisiart 246
Awbery, Gwenllian M. 252

Babel, Anna M. 192f., 200, 203
Baiocchi, Mari de Nasaré 212f., 229
Baker, Philip 272ff.
Bakker, Dik 18
Bakker, Peter 9, 81ff., 88ff., 97, 102, 109, 113, 198, 274, 276
Ball, Martin J. 253
Barkwell, Lawrence 83
Barry, Tom 296
Bauman, Emiliy 292
Baxter, Alan 228
Beck, David 65, 67
Belgrave, Korah 282
Berlin, Brent 58, 76
Bertran, Paolo 212
Bickerton, Derek 300
Billig, Michael 292f.
Birt, Paul 7, 246
Bishop, Hywel 280, 282
Bloomfield, Leonard 82, 88f., 91, 93f., 100, 106, 111, 114
Bortoni-Ricardo, Stella Maris 209, 247
Britain, David 247, 278
Bright, William 21
Brito Neto, Joãmar Carvalho de 212

Brittain, Julie 95
Brody, Jill 18, 21f., 25, 34, 36, 38
Brody, Hugh 3
Brooks, Walter Ariel 244f.
Bruyn, Adrienne 273f.
Bulmer-Thomas, Victor 295
Buenrostro, Cristina 30, 47
Bybee, Joan 250
Byrd, Steven 208, 213, 220

Camargo, Maria Thereza L. de Arruda 215
Campbell, Lyle 3
Campos, Ednalvo Apostolo 209, 232
Canger, Una 50
Cárdenas Martínez, Celestino 48
Cardoso, Hugo 2
Carrie, Erin 286
Carrington, Lawrence D. 294
Carter, Diana 238
Casad, Eugene H.
Catalán, Diego 189
Cerrón-Palomino, Rodolfo 183, 185, 187f., 190f.
Chamoreau, Claudine 21, 30, 52
Chang, Charles B. 251, 262
Clements, J. Clancy 182, 187f., 191, 193, 201
Coelho, Izete L. 215, 221
Coelho-Ferreira, Márlia 215
Comrie, Bernard 55f., 67, 74, 76, 88
Cook, Claire 88, 101, 103, 111, 113, 116
Cooper, Vincent O. 272, 274, 280
Coupland, Nikolas 238, 243ff., 280, 282
Creissels, Denis 104
Crespo, Alberto 202
Crevels, Mily 3, 8

Dahlstrom, Amy 115
Dankel, Philipp 192
Daval-Markussen, Aymeric 274
Davies, Gareth Alban 244f.
Day, Christopher 63, 76
Deerr, Noel 272
Dettoni, Rachel do Valle 229
Deuber, Dagmar 270, 279, 282, 300

Devonish, Hubert 271, 276, 285
Dixon, R. M. W. 213
Dryer, Matthew 86

Eakin, Marshall C. 3
Eberhard, David M. 238
Echegoyen, Artemisa 23, 32
Edwards, Mary 89
Embrey, Virginia 31, 53
Errington, Joseph 291, 293
Escalante Hernández, Roberto 48
Escobar, Anna María 182
Escure, Geneviève 294f.
Estrada Fernández, Zarina 27, 29, 51
Evans, Nicholas 186

Farquharson, Joseph 275
Fernández de Miranda, Mría Teresa 21
Figueroa Saavedra, Miguel 65ff.
Fishman, Joshua A. 279
Fleury, Norman 88f., 113
Flores Farfán, José Antonio 22, 36
Frantz, Donald G. 93, 95
Fry, Peter 208

Gal, Susan 293
García, Erica C. 24
García, Ofelia 292
Garrett, Peter 238, 243ff.
Genee, Inge 92
Gentle, Hilda 306
Giannelli, Luciano 69, 71f.
Giles, Howard 6
Gillon, Carrie 82, 86
Glock, Naomi 306
Gobo, Giampietro 297
Goddard, Ives 82, 88, 90ff., 95
Golla, Victor 84
Gómez, Paula 29
Gómez Rendón, Jorge 20f.
Gonçalves, Clézio Roberto 229
Green, Diana 61
Greenberg, Joseph H. 58ff.
Grinevald, Colette 3
Grosjean, François 240, 260f.
Guerrero, Lilián 27
Gutiérrez Maté, Miguel 192f.

Hackert, Stephanie 270f., 282f., 294
Han, ZhaoHong 240, 261
Hannahs, Stephen J. 253
Hänsel, Eva Canan 301
Hardman, Martha J. 185ff.
Harrigan, Atticus 86, 90f., 97, 101
Harrison, K. David 55f.
Haspelmath, Martin 19
Heggarty, Paul 2, 13
Hekking, Ewald 21
Hellinger, Marlis 294, 300
Hernández, Marciano 48
Herrera, Yvette 306
Hidalgo, Margarita G. 6
Hill, Jane H. 22, 24
Hill, Kenneth C. 22, 24
Hinrichs, Lars 294
Holmer, Nils Magnus 69ff.
Holmes, Janet 247
Horvath, Barbara M. 247
Howe, James 69
Hualde, José Ignacio 190
Huber, Magnus 272
Hymes, Dell 291

Irvine, Judith T. 293
Itier, César 183

Jacob, Camille 294
James, E. Wyn 238
Jamieson, Allan 49
Jamieson, Carole Van den Hoeck 23
Johnson, Ian 238, 242f., 245
Jones, Aled 237
Jones, Ann E. 247
Jones, Bill 237
Jones, Glyn E. 250ff.
Jones, Mari C. 247
Jones, R. Tudur 242
Jones, Robert Owen 240f., 243ff., 252, 255, 260, 262
Jourdan, Christine 182, 202f.
Junker, Marie-Odile 92

Kagan, Olga 247
Karttunen, Frances 62
Kaufman, Terrence 7, 59, 63

Kemmer, Suzanne 111
Klee, Carol A. 188
Knudson, L. 54
Kouwenberg, Silvia 202f.
Kroskrity, Paul V. 293

Labov, William 214, 303
Lacoste, Véronique 295
Lapesa, Rafael 189
Laprade, Richard 188
Lastra, Yolanda 32, 38, 48, 50f.
Laverdure, Patline 88, 100, 104ff., 113f., 117
Law, Danny 58
Le Guen, Olivier 20, 32
Le Page, Robert B. 295, 304
Lehmann, Christian 66, 74
Leung, Glenda-Alicia 270, 279, 282
Levey, Stephen 59
Levisen, Carsten 3
Levy, Paulette 57
Lippi-Green, Rosina L. 247
Lipski, John M. 182f., 189, 194, 197, 199, 222
Lorenzino, Gerardo 189
Lublin, Geraldine 245
Lucchesi, Dante 208ff., 213, 219, 221ff., 227, 229
Lucy, John A. 74
Lüpke, Friederike 2
Lyon, Don D. 34

Macaulay, Monica 94
Maher, Terezinha de Jesus Machado 209
Mair, Christian 295, 312
Makoni, Sinfree 293f.
Mannheim, Bruce 294
Marinho, Thais Alves 212f.
Martin, Julie 274, 276
Mathieu, Eric 82
Matras, Yaron 8, 56f., 59, 198, 238f., 260
Mattissen, Johanna 86
Mattos, Ana Paulla Braga 6, 10, 12, 207, 225
Mattoso, Kátia 211
Mayr, Robert 260
Mazzoli, Maria 2, 6, 9ff., 81, 84ff., 92, 94ff., 100ff., 108ff., 112f., 115ff.
McFarland, Teresa A. 58, 65
McKenzie, Robert 286

McWhorter, John 198, 274
Meakins, Felicity 82
Medeiros Costa Neto, Eraldo 215
Meer, Philipp 282
Mello, Heliana Ribeiro de 209f., 213, 226
Mendoza, José G. 183, 188ff.
Menjívar, Jennifer Gómez 296
Mesthrie, Rajend 8
Meyerhoff, Miriam 214, 277
Michaelis, Susanne M. 228, 276
Michelsen, Truman 109
Michnowicz, Jim 73
Milroy, James 263, 282
Milroy, Lesley 247, 263
Mithun, Marianne 61
Monguilhott, Isabel 221
Monte, Alexandre 210, 212, 221
Montgomery, Chris 277
Morris, Jonathan 238
Muehlbauer, Jeff 88, 90f., 101, 103, 111, 113, 116
Mufwene, Salikoko S. 2, 6, 8, 274
Mühleisen, Susanne 294
Müller, Nicole 253
Muysken, Pieter 3, 19f., 183ff.
Myrick, Caroline 277

Nagy, Naomi 263
Narain, Goretti 308
Nascimento, Cristiana A, R. do 224
Neves, Maria Helena de Moura 225

O'Flaherty, Victoria Borg 272
Olarrea, Antxon 188, 191
Oliveira, Márcia Santos Duarte 208f., 213
Ornelas de Avelar, Juanito 2
Ortega, Lourdes 240
Osmer, Balam 295f., 308
Oxford, Will 92, 96

Pagel, Steve 21
Palacin, Luis 211
Papen, Robert A. 88
Parkvall, Mikael 203, 272ff.
Patrick, Peter L. 300
Pearce, Adrian J. 2, 13
Pederson, Lee 274

Penny, Ralph 186, 188
Pennycook, Alastair 292ff.
Pentland, David H. 90, 95
Perez, Danae Maria 2, 4ff., 8ff., 12, 182f., 188, 193f., 198f., 201f., 294
Petter, Margarida Maria Taddoni 208f., 213
Pickett, Velma 31, 53
Pires, Luís Ricardo Rodriges 229
Polinsky, Maria 247
Pöll, Bernhard 189
Pool Balam, Lorena I.
Poplack, Shana 59

Quartararo, Geraldine 183, 186, 188, 193, 200
Quijano, Aníbal 3f.

Ravindranath Abtahian, Maya 295, 297
Rees, Iwan Wyn 5, 10, 12, 246
Rhodes, Richard A. S. 82f., 86, 88, 95
Rickford, John R. 270, 280
Robbers, Maja 10f., 59, 61, 65, 69
Rodrigues, Clênio G. 215
Rosen, Nicole 84, 86, 88f., 107, 113f.
Rúbio, Cássio Florêncio 221
Russell, Kevin 89ff.
Ryan, Ellen B. 270

Said, Edward 292
Sakel, Jeanette 7f., 19f., 198
Salmon, William 295f.
Salmons, Joseph 94
Sammons, Olivia N. 82, 90, 108
Sánchez, Liliana 192
Santiago Francisco, José 58, 60, 65ff.
Santos Sales, Giovana Patricia dos 215
Saraceni, Mario 294
Saxton, Dean 76
Saxton, Lucille 76
Schiller, Nina Glick 292f.
Schmalz, Mirjam 6, 9f., 12, 294
Schmidt-Brücken, Daniel 2
Schneider, Britta 4, 6, 10, 12f., 291, 297
Schreier, Daniel 8, 182, 203
Schwenter, Scott A. 223
Sebba, Mark 300
Selinker, Larry 239, 261
Seoane, Elena 2

Sessarego, Sandro 2
Sherzer, Joel F. 70f.
Shields-Brodber, Kathryn 279
Shoman, Assad 295
Siegel, Jason 5
Silva Junior, Augusto Rodrigues da 215
Silva, Martiniano José da 211
Sippola, Eeva 2f., 8f., 81
Siqueira, Thaís Teixeira 215
Slavin, Tanya 92
Smeets, Ineke 56
Smith, Norval 272f.
Smythe Kung, Susan 67f.
Sousa, Lilian Teixeira de 223
Souter, Heather 88f., 111, 113
Souza, Emerson Santos 229
Souza, Pedro Daniel dos Santos 221
Spencer, Andrew 94
Stairs, Glem A. 32, 48
Stairs, Emily F. de 32, 48
Steinkrüger, Patrick O. 21
Stewart, Jesse 82
Stolz, Christel 18, 21, 73f.
Stolz, Thomas 2, 6, 10f., 18, 20f., 61, 64, 69
Storch, Anne 2
Suárez, Jorge A. 21, 29
Suárez-Gómez, Cristina 2
Sutherland, Oswald 306

Tabouret-Keller, Andrée 295, 304
Tadmor, Uri 19
Tejeda, Ernesto 49
Thiel, Robert A. 21
Thomas, Ann Elizabeth 247
Thomas, Ewart A. C. 285
Thomason, Sarah G. 7, 59, 63, 238f., 250
Tollan, Rebecca 92, 96
Torres Cacoullos, Rena 9
Travis, Catherine 9
Trudgill, Peter 252
Tuten, Donald N. 251ff., 262
Twigg, Alan 296

Valentine, Randolph 82, 86, 95
Veerman-Leichsenring, Annette 37
Velloso, Alessandra D'Aqui 212
Verbeeck, Lieve 21

Veronelli, Gabriela A. 4
Voigtlander, Katherine 23, 32
Vogt, Carlos 208

Walker, James 277
Wall, Albert 198
Wassink, Alicia Beckford 304
Waterhouse, Viola 29, 47
Weber, Brigitte 2
Wei, Li 292
Weinreich, Uriel 59
Westphal, Michael 270, 279, 282
Wichmann, Søren 52
Williams, Glyn 242f., 245
Williams, Jeffrey 8

Williams, R. Bryn 244
Wilson, Guyanne 294
Wimmer, Andreas 292f.
Winford, Donald 199, 270
Wolfart, H. Christoph 82, 88, 90f., 93ff., 103f., 107ff., 113ff., 117
Woolard, Kathryn A. 293

Yakpo, Kofi 182

Zamponi, Raoul 69, 71f.
Zavala Maldonado, Roberto 47
Zimmermann, Klaus 18
Zipp, Lena 194, 198f., 201
Zúñiga, Fernando 93, 117

Index of Languages

Acatec 26f., 33, 46f.
Angloromani 86
Arawak 202
Atacameño 187
Aymara 12, 35, 55, 182f., 185ff.

Berbice Dutch 202
Bikol 35f.
Blackfoot 92f.

Cebuano 20f.
Chatino 26
Chinantec 26
Chinese 273, 295
– Cantonese 299
– Mandarin 299
Chocho 26, 28
Chontal 26f., 29, 31, 33f., 47, 62, 64, 75
Chuj 26f., 30, 33, 47
Cora 22
Cree 82, 84, 86, 88, 92, 97, 107, 111f.
– East ~ 92
– Michif ~ 84
– Oji ~ 92
– Plains ~ 11, 81ff., 86, 88ff., 97, 101, 104, 107f., 110, 115ff.
Creole 270, 298
– Jamaican ~ 275, 279, 287
– Kittitian ~ (KC) 271, 274ff., 281f., 287
Cusco 183, 187, 192

English 1f., 4, 6, 8f., 11f., 19f., 71, 84, 86, 111, 189, 238, 242, 244, 254, 258, 263, 269ff., 273ff., 278ff., 287, 294ff., 298ff., 305f., 309, 311f.
– Belizean Creole ~ 6
– British ~ 270, 274, 285, 287, 301
– Caribbean ~ 275f., 283
– Jamaican ~ 271
– Kittitian ~ (KE) 12, 271, 274ff., 287
– Standard ~ 270f., 273ff., 278ff., 287, 300f., 304

French 1, 4, 11, 19, 35., 82ff., 86, 226, 272, 274, 276
– Canadian ~ 84
– Metis ~ 81, 84
– Michif ~ 84

Garifuna 295, 298, 305f.
German 295, 299
Guarijío 26, 28, 31
Guaraní 20f., 35

Hindi 295
Huastec 35f.
Huave 26f., 31ff., 48
Huichol 26f., 29, 33f.

Italian 19, 299

Jakaltec 63, 76

Kaqchikel 35
Kikongo 182, 193f., 196, 198
Kiliwa 26, 28
Kriol 6, 291, 294ff., 302ff., 315
Kuna 69ff., 75f.

Latin 186, 312
Lebanese 295
Luxembourgish 19

Malay 61
Maltese 19
Mapuche 55f.
Matlatzinca 26f., 33f., 48
Maya 298f.
Mayo 26
Mazahua 26f., 33f., 48
Mazatec 23, 26f., 31ff., 37, 49
Media Lengua 86
Menominee 93f.
Mestizo 298
Mexicano 22, 24
Mexicanero 26f., 33, 50

Michif 6f., 9ff., 81ff., 88ff., 104, 108f., 111f., 115ff.
Mixe 26, 28, 33f.
Mixtec 26, 28
Mopan 21, 295, 299, 306

Nahuatl 21f., 26f., 31ff., 35, 50, 64, 276

Ojibwe 83f., 86
Okrika Igbo-Ijo 85
Oneida 62
Otomí 18, 20f., 23, 26f., 31ff., 51

Palikúr 61
Papiamentu 194
Pima Bajo 26f., 29, 31, 33f., 51
Popoluca/Popoloca 26f., 33, 37, 52
Portuguese 1f., 4, 8, 11f., 193f., 198f., 207ff., 217ff., 229, 273
– Afro-Brazilian ~ (ABP) 12, 209f., 219, 221f., 227, 229, 231
– Brazilian ~ (BP) 207ff., 213, 219, 221, 228, 232
– Brazilian Vernacular ~ (BVP) 209f., 218ff., 228f., 231
– Kalunga ~ 12, 207f., 210, 212, 214f., 217, 219, 231
– Standard Brazilian~ (SBP) 209f., 219ff.
Purépecha 21, 26f., 30f., 33f., 52

Q'eqchi' 295, 299, 306
Quechua 12, 20f., 35, 55, 182f., 185ff., 190ff., 195ff., 200f., 294

Rapanui 20f.

Seri 26
Spanish 1ff., 6, 8f., 11f., 18, 20ff., 27ff., 35f., 56f., 59f., 62, 64ff., 68, 70ff., 76, 181f., 186ff., 199f., 238f., 241f., 244ff., 250ff., 291, 295f., 298ff., 302ff.
– Afro-Yungueño ~ (AYS) 5, 7, 10, 12, 181ff., 193ff., 197ff.
– Andean ~ 187, 191f.
– Argentinean ~ 251
– Bolivian Highland ~ (BHS) 181ff., 187ff., 197ff.
– Caribbean ~ 189
– Cusco ~ 192
– La Paz ~ 188, 191
– Standard ~ 187, 189, 199

Tagalog 35f.
Tepehua 26, 31
– Huehuetla ~ (HAT) 67f., 75
Tlapanec 26f., 29, 33f.
Toba 35
Tohono O'odham 76
Tojolab'al 21
Totonac 26f., 33, 35, 53, 57ff., 64ff.
– Filomeno Mata ~ (FMT) 58f., 61, 64ff., 75
– Papantla ~ 67
Trique 26, 31
Tzeltal 58, 76

Welsh 5, 7, 10ff., 237ff., 243ff., 250ff., 256, 258, 260ff.
– Patagonian ~ 238ff., 246f., 252, 254f., 263f.

Yaqui 26f., 31
Yucatec 20f., 26f., 32ff., 53, 73ff., 295, 299

Zapotec 21, 26f., 31, 33f., 53
Zoque 26f., 31ff., 54

Index of Subjects

adstrate 12, 182, 187ff., 191ff., 202, 204
adversative connector 11, 19, 22, 24, 34
Andes 3, 12, 181ff., 187, 189, 192f., 200, 203, 242
animacy 60f., 86, 91, 93, 95ff., 117f.
approximant 252, 256f.
areal features 12, 181ff., 200
Argentina 1, 12, 237, 242ff., 251, 262

Bahamas 270, 283
Belize 1, 6, 9f., 13, 292ff.
Bible translation 35, 70, 294
bilingualism 6, 9, 12, 59, 63, 69, 182, 193, 201, 239, 244, 260
borrowability 19f.
borrowing 8, 11, 17ff., 24f., 27, 30ff., 34f., 37f., 56ff., 61ff., 66ff., 71, 73, 76, 84, 189, 198
Brazil 1, 4, 12, 193, 207ff., 213, 215, 217, 219, 226, 231, 247

Canada 1, 3, 7, 9, 11, 83ff.
Chicontla 65
code-switching 9, 27, 238
Colombia 69
colonial discourse 292, 306
colonial era 1, 9
colonial languages 1ff., 11, 55, 62
colonialism 3, 9, 292
colonization 3ff., 55, 68, 189, 273f.
contact language 2, 82, 199, 202, 238f.
contact phenomena 18, 56, 61, 246
creoles 2, 4f., 11, 270f., 273ff., 283, 287, 294, 296, 303

derivation 11, 82f., 88, 93ff., 97ff., 109f., 114ff., 198
dialectology 71, 189, 270
dictionary 71, 88, 304, 306, 311
discourse 4, 34, 36, 38, 186f., 200f., 291ff., 296f., 301, 303, 306ff.
discourse marker 22, 25, 34, 37, 186, 200
documentation 1, 5, 11, 18, 38, 85, 278, 298

domain 2, 9, 17, 21, 23, 28, 37, 56f., 61f., 70f., 81, 238, 244f., 270, 276ff., 283, 287, 294, 298f., 301, 305
dominant language 3, 5, 9, 55f., 59f., 247, 308f.
donor language 17, 19f., 22f.

ethnicity 299, 306, 311
ethnic groups 202, 245, 273, 296, 303, 310ff.
evidentiality 12, 186f., 192f., 200ff.

fieldwork 9f., 30, 57, 77, 183, 213, 246, 252, 261f., 286, 297f.
Filomeno Mata 57, 65, 77
fricative 250ff., 257f.
function words 8, 18, 20f., 24, 31, 38, 86
functional domains 2, 5, 9

Goiás 12, 207, 210ff., 217, 220, 230
grammar 8, 12, 17, 22f., 37f., 59, 64, 75, 86, 186, 201f., 244, 275, 304, 311
grammaticalization 9, 57, 60, 186, 191ff., 200f.
Guatemala 24, 295ff., 303, 310
Guyana 270, 280

Hispanism 18, 22f., 36
Hispanization 10f., 17f., 20f., 24, 27f., 32, 34ff., 187

ideology 4, 282, 293, 296, 298, 304, 310
indigenous languages 1, 3f., 18, 20f., 35, 55, 68, 73, 181f., 184, 202

Jamaica 270, 273, 277, 279, 282ff., 297

Kalunga 6, 10, 12, 207f., 210ff.

La Paz 181ff., 188, 191, 193
language attitudes 5f., 10, 208, 217, 271, 277, 294f., 298
language change 1, 5, 7, 9, 12, 182, 187

Index of Subjects

language contact 1, 4, 7, 10, 13, 18f., 21, 24, 36, 55f., 77, 86, 182, 214, 238f., 246, 250, 252, 263, 270
language endangerment 2ff., 6, 8, 56, 76, 295
language shift 3ff., 7, 11, 55, 59, 62f., 72ff., 76, 118, 193, 198, 219, 246, 263, 272, 283
language vitality 2, 5ff., 11, 74, 238
Latin America 3, 35, 251
Lesser Antilles 269, 272
lexicon 2, 11, 17, 74, 84, 188, 194, 202, 286
lingua franca 83, 187, 295, 305
linguistic variation 6, 10f., 27ff., 32, 37, 70, 112, 189, 217, 221, 240, 242, 246, 249f., 253, 255f., 258, 261f., 278, 300
loanwords 10, 19, 71, 188f., 238, 254f., 258f., 263

mensuratives 11, 58, 60, 76
Mesoamerica 3, 6, 10f., 17f., 20ff., 24, 27, 35ff., 55, 57f., 62, 75
Mexico 1, 24, 64, 73, 295
migration 4, 7ff., 11, 217, 219, 237, 242f., 262, 270, 295, 307ff., 311
minority 5, 27, 59, 208, 215f., 239, 246f., 255, 296
mixed languages/language mixing 1f., 8f., 11, 36, 81ff., 92, 292, 311
morphology 11, 57, 62, 69, 74, 81, 118, 186, 198ff.
morphosyntax 189f., 198, 202
mother tongue 59, 64, 85, 307f.
multilingualism 2, 9f., 13, 208, 279, 296

native speaker 4, 30, 36, 38, 89, 238f., 245, 247, 295, 301, 308
negation 208f., 223ff., 231
Nevis 269ff., 278, 282
numeral classifier 10f., 56f., 60, 62f., 65, 67f., 74f.

orthography 194, 252, 274, 311

Patagonia 5, 7, 10, 12, 237ff., 242f, 246, 256
Philippines 18, 20, 35
phonology 2, 84, 194, 201, 239, 275, 286
plosives 197, 251, 253ff., 260
postcolonial context/setting 1f., 270, 279, 292, 294, 310
postcolonial languages/varieties 1, 3, 5ff., 9, 11ff., 189, 201, 208, 298
preposition 188, 199, 209, 228ff.
prestige 2f., 6, 10, 12, 24, 60, 73, 252, 286, 294ff., 300, 302ff., 311

replica language 11, 17ff., 28, 30ff., 35, 37f.
revitalization 7, 10, 85, 238, 262f.
Romancization 18f.

Saskatchewan 84f., 88
schwa vowel 251f., 255, 257
South America 4f., 7f., 18, 20, 35, 193, 242
St. Kitts 1, 9, 12, 269ff., 277ff., 282f., 285f.
standard 5f., 9, 12, 62, 187, 189, 191, 193, 199f., 209, 221ff., 228f., 231, 252, 258, 264, 269ff., 273ff., 294, 300f., 304f., 311f.
standardization 6, 259, 263, 301, 306, 308, 311
substrate language 182, 193, 198, 228
syntax 11, 24, 74, 84, 86, 308

Tobago 270, 283
transitivity 86, 91ff., 96ff., 118
Trinidad 270, 279, 282f.
typological diversity 1ff., 5, 182, 191, 271, 273, 275f.

valency 88ff., 96ff., 101ff., 109, 117f.
variation 6, 10f., 27ff., 32, 37, 70, 76, 112, 189, 201, 217, 221, 240, 242, 246, 249f., 253, 255f., 258, 261f., 275, 278, 300
verb template 11, 82, 86, 88, 117
voice 88f., 96ff., 109, 111, 114f., 117f., 284

word formation 82, 117

www.ingramcontent.com/pod-product-compliance
Lightning Source LLC
Chambersburg PA
CBHW070935180426
43192CB00039B/2209